PORTFOLIO THEORY
AND CAPITAL MARKETS

WILLIAM F. SHARPE
STANCO 25 Professor Emeritus of Finance
Stanford University

PORTFOLIO THEORY
AND CAPITAL MARKETS

WILLIAM F. SHARPE
STANCO 25 Professor Emeritus of Finance
Stanford University

McGraw-Hill

New York San Francisco Washington, D.C. Auckland Bogotá
Caracas Lisbon London Madrid Mexico City Milan
Montreal New Delhi San Juan Singapore
Sydney Tokyo Toronto

McGraw-Hill

A Division of The McGraw-Hill Companies

Copyright © 2000, 1970 by The McGraw-Hill Companies, Inc. All rights reserved. Printed in the United States of America. Except as permitted under the United States Copyright Act of 1976, no part of this publication may be reproduced or distributed in any form or by any means, or stored in a data base or retrieval system, without the prior written permission of the publisher.

1 2 3 4 5 6 7 8 9 0   DOC/DOC   9 0 9 8 7 6 5 4 3 2 1 0 9

ISBN 0-07-135320-8

The sponsoring editor for this book was Catherine Schwent, the editing supervisor was Janice Race, and the production supervisor was Elizabeth J. Strange. The text was designed by Janet Bollow. The drawings were done by Judith McCarty.

Printed and bound by R. R. Donnelley & Sons Company.

McGraw-Hill books are available at special quantity discounts to use as premiums and sales promotions, or for use in corporate training programs. For more information, please write to the Director of Special Sales, McGraw-Hill, 11 West 19th Street, New York, NY 10011. Or contact your local bookstore.

This publication is designed to provide accurate and authoritative information in regard to the subject matter covered. It is sold with the understanding that neither the author nor the publisher is engaged in rendering legal, accounting, or other professional service. If legal advice or other expert assistance is required, the services of a competent professional person should be sought.
—*From a Declaration of Principles jointly adopted by a Committee of the American Bar Association and a Committee of Publishers.*

 This book is printed on recycled, acid-free paper containing a minimum of 50% recycled, de-inked fiber.

to

HARRY MARKOWITZ

who taught me
portfolio theory
and much more

FOREWORD

It was with mixed emotions that I received the news that McGraw-Hill had decided to publish a new edition of *Portfolio Theory and Capital Markets*. It would be good to have this early work back in print. But the thirty years since it was written have seen monumental changes in both investment theory and practice. I wondered—might the contents of this book seem naive or even laughable when viewed from a new millennium? After rereading the book, I have managed to humor myself that much of the material remains useful today, although this is hardly an unbiased opinion. No matter, since the goal of this publication is to make the book available to a modern audience that can and will ultimately make a judgment about the relevance of its contents.

With minor exceptions, the book is unchanged from its original version. A few graphs have been revised and some typographical errors corrected, but otherwise the material is pristine.

It would be tempting to leave well enough alone and simply recommend that the reader treat this edition as an historic document. However, I cannot resist the opportunity to comment on its contents.

AN OVERVIEW When I wrote the book in 1968 and 1969, the fields of finance and economics were beginning to spawn what is now known as financial economics. Harry Markowitz' first paper on portfolio theory had been published in the early 1950's, as had James Tobin's work on portfolio separation and Kenneth Arrow's and Gerard Debreu's papers on state-preference theory, but this research did not have a substantial impact on finance until the 1960's. My paper on the Capital Asset Pricing Model was published in 1964 and was just beginning to have an impact at the time I wrote this book. I like to think that by bringing together much of this material in a relatively straightforward exposition, I helped accelerate the revolution in the teaching and practice of finance that occurred in the ensuing decades.

To be sure, many of the key theoretical contributions to financial economics came after this book was published. There is nothing here about option theory, in particular the key contributions of Fischer Black, Robert Merton and Myron Scholes. Nor is there any treatment of multi-period problems, which have received a great deal of attention in recent years. It is true that Arrow-Debreu state-preference theory can provide the basis for both subjects, so at least the foundation elements are here. And the book's treatment of utility, while simplistic, provides another ingredient needed to move from state-preference formulations to the class of general equilibrium models of the type developed subsequently by Robert Lucas and others.

There is, mercifully, little empirical material in the book. This is fortunate, since much empirical research has a short half-life. Moreover, the econometric techniques used today are far more sophisticated than those employed when this book was written.

Since its first publication, there have been many extensions of the original Capital Asset Pricing Model, which forms a key part of this book. Moreover, competitive theories have been developed, and seemingly countless empirical tests performed in an attempt to disconfirm one theory or another. Some researchers have even dismissed a key conclusion of the Capital Asset Pricing Model with the assertion that "beta is dead," although one would be hard pressed to find evidence of this in current textbooks or much of current investment practice.

It is useful to remember that almost all empirical research deals with *ex post* manifestations of investor's expectations and their predictions of risks and correlations, and that such measures are subject to considerable error. It is perfectly possible that *ex ante* variables may conform perfectly with a capital market theory and yet this conformance may be impossible to detect with high statistical significance in *ex post* data. The problem is exacerbated if the theoretical relationships hold in each period but with changing parameter values from period to period. In such cases, effective sample sizes may be small, limiting the power of statistical tests.

Some have said in jest: If you don't like the results of an empirical study, wait for an analysis using another statistical method or data from another time or country. While this is far too harsh, it seems unwise to reject out of hand sensible conclusions concerning equilibrium in competitive capital markets unless the empirical evidence is robust to errors in measurement and changes in method, time or location. In my opinion, this condition has not been met regarding the key insights to be gained from capital market theories based on the mean-variance and state-preference approaches, both of which are described in this book.

While it might be best to limit my comments to these general observations, it seems desirable to add some observations about the contents of each of the chapters and appendices in the light of subsequent developments. In doing so, I will allude to contributions made by a number of researchers in the last three decades. Rather than attempt to provide a detailed set of references, I invite the reader to investigate the material at my website (www.wsharpe.com), where many of these subjects are treated in detail. Those interested in practical applications of portfolio theory and capital market theory may also wish to visit the site of an online investment advice company that I cofounded (www.financialengines.com).

The following sections cover each of the chapters and appendices. The order is roughly that which would be chosen by one determined to read all the material.

1. CERTAINTY

This chapter deals with standard economic analysis of decision-making under certainty. It emphasizes the notions of present value and rate of return as economic constructs based on sufficiently complete capital markets. Except for this emphasis, which is sometimes lacking in finance texts, the material is quite standard. Perhaps the most glaring deficiency is the absence of a discussion of multi-period valuation under certainty, including the usual textbook argument that present value is a more appropriate decision variable in such a setting than the internal rate of return, despite the continued reliance of many corporate finance officers on the latter. Fortunately, many marketable investments involve one negative cash flow in the present followed by positive (or non-negative) cash flows at future times, so the issue is not central in this context. Nonetheless, the extension of analysis of certainty to a multi-period setting is sufficiently straightforward that it is unfortunate that it is not included here.

2. PORTFOLIOS This chapter provides the basic concepts of Markowitz' one-period mean-variance approach to portfolio analysis and selection. It could easily be taken as a current textbook treatment. Only one definition is misleading. The efficient frontier is defined as the upper border of available combinations of portfolio expected return and risk. A better definition would include only the upper left-hand border, since no risk-averse investor would choose a portfolio if there were another with a higher expected return and lower risk, even if it were the highest expected-return portfolio for its level of risk.

3. SECURITIES One cannot help but be struck with the differences between discussions of mathematical computations before and after spreadsheet programs became widely available.

This is very evident in this chapter. For example, to compute portfolio expected return one can now put the proportions invested in the securities in one column of a spreadsheet and the security expected returns in the adjacent column. In the next column, type the product of the two entries to the left, copy the formula in the other cells in the column, then put a final formula in the sheet to compute the sum of the products in the third column. This will show the portfolio's expected return. Almost every reader will know exactly how to do this and fully understand the procedure.

Fortunately, many of the expositions in this book are stated in terms that can be implemented almost directly in a spreadsheet program. The procedure given for computing the standard deviation of a portfolio is a prime example. It may surprise current readers to know that at the time the book was written, the actual computation of portfolio risk could only be done by writing a program in a language such as Fortran, using subscripted variables and nested loops to compute the requisite products and cumulate them.

Although spreadsheets have democratized mathematical analysis, in some respects they do not provide the best tools for careful analysis. Portfolio and capital market theory cry out for the use of matrix algebra. Moreover, programming languages (such as MATLAB) now exist that make it possible to do computations directly with matrices and vectors, making problem formulation and solution almost the same task. In addition, some spreadsheet programs (such as Microsoft's Excel) include functions that can perform matrix computations, although in rather clumsy ways.

This book was written for the reader with relatively little mathematical training; hence it seemed inappropriate to require a knowledge of fundamental matrix operations or to provide an appendix covering this material. Now that such procedures can be easily implemented, I believe that the benefits of doing so are large enough to justify the cost. However, this appears to be a minority opinion, since most current finance textbooks utilize the type of exposition found throughout this book.

This appendix includes a rather tedious description of a method for solving simultaneous equations. Present-day readers will justifiably find this curious. After all, if we wish to find a vector x that satisfies A *x=b, all that is required is to compute x = inv(A)*b. The latter can be given as a MATLAB command. Alternatively, the Excel functions MMULT (for matrix multiplication) and MINVERSE (for matrix inversion) can be utilized.

APPENDIX A. ESSENTIAL INGREDIENTS

The appendix also provides a primer on differential calculus and a discussion of the maximization of a function subject to linear equality constraints. A reader familiar with matrix algebra is likely to become impatient with the use of blocks of cells to represent matrix equations. At the very least, a few trees could have been saved if more succinct notation had been utilized.

This being said, neither calculus nor linear algebra has changed in the period since this book was written, so no major corrections are required.

It may be hard for the reader to imagine that at the time this book was written, there were no spreadsheet programs, no simple graphic packages, and no laser or inkjet printers. Graphs were most commonly produced either by hand or with complex programs designed to move pens around on flat-bed plotters. Not surprisingly, most of the graphs in this book were produced more or less free hand, and can be considered (at best) artist's renderings. In most cases this approach was harmless, but in some cases the results were either misleading or wrong.

4. EFFICIENT PORTFOLIOS

An example of a potentially misleading relationship is the distance between the lowest and highest expected return for a given level of risk in the feasible risk-return region, as shown in figure 4-18 (and many others). While this may be representative when the objects of choice are individual securities, it is less likely when the portfolio ingredients are themselves portfolios of securities from different asset classes. In practice, optimization methods are often used (and frequently misused) for this type of "asset allocation" exercise. Examination of the actual feasible regions for such problems frequently reveals that the difference between the expected return of the best and the worst combinations for a given level of risk is relatively small (for example, closer to 1 percent per year than to 10 percent per year).

A graphical relationship that is simply wrong was shown in the original versions of figures 4-19, 4-20, 5-1 and 6-1. For cases in which there are no inequality constraints, the feasible region in mean-variance space is a parabola; in mean-standard deviation space it is a hyperbola. In the original versions of these figures the region was drawn free hand in mean-standard deviation space but with an appearance similar to that of a parabola. Worse yet, the diagrams were drawn with the riskless rate of interest equal to the expected return of the minimum-variance portfolio of risky securities. Given this erroneous feasible region it was possible to draw a line from the riskless rate that was tangent to the efficient frontier at a point well within the diagram. Had the feasible region been drawn correctly it would have been apparent that this was impossible. In current terms, the portfolio with the highest Sharpe Ratio will have infinite risk (and return) if the riskless rate is equal to (or above) the expected return of the minimum-variance portfolio of risky securities. Robert Merton pointed this out after the publication of the book. His observation has important economic content, since it concerns a characteristic required for equilibrium in capital markets.

To avoid seriously confusing readers of the current edition, the four offending figures have been redrawn. The feasible regions are now correctly rendered, with the riskless rate of interest below the expected return of the minimum-variance portfolio of risky securities. All the other figures in the book remain in their original forms. If nothing else, this can serve as a nostalgic reminder of simpler times. However, one cannot help but contemplate the errors avoided by current day authors, who can painlessly plot desired relationships directly using spreadsheets or other programs with graphic capabilities.

Another curiosity in this chapter deserves mention. To find points on the efficient frontier, a character named (unimaginatively) Mr. A is invoked. He has indifference curves that are described using a parameter (lambda) which is, in fact, his marginal rate of substitutions of variance for expected return, although this economic interpretation is not given explicitly. Moreover, it is assumed that this marginal rate of substitution is constant, regardless of the mean or variance being considered. Today we would call this Mr. A's risk tolerance. In this exposition, Mr. A is not offered as a representative investor, his role is only to help formulate the task of finding an efficient frontier (indeed, he is summarily discarded after serving this purpose). But today we sometimes assume that flesh-and-blood investors have such characteristics. Indeed, John Lintner showed that if an investor's utility (in the sense of Chapter 9) is a negative exponential function of portfolio return and the probability distribution of returns is jointly normal, the investor's expected utility will be given precisely by a linear combination of portfolio expected return and variance.

In current expositions, the slope coefficient (lambda) is called the investor's *risk tolerance*. She is assumed to wish to maximize the "utility" (not in the sense of Chapter 9) of her portfolio, which will equal e-v/t, where e is the portfolio's expected return, v is its variance, and t is her investor's risk tolerance. This is equivalent to minimizing alpha in the formulation in this book. Since lambda and t are the same variable, the procedure given here is designed to minimize [-t*e+v]. This is equivalent to maximizing [t*e-v]. But as long as t is positive, this is equivalent to maximizing [e-v/t]. Hence no changes are required in the algorithms given here if the goal is to find in one step the optimal portfolio for an investor with a given risk tolerance of t (lambda).

This exposition could also be shortened substantially if matrix notation were utilized. Moreover, the economics of fund separation could be made more readily apparent, and generalizations provided to cover cases involving additional arguments in the investor's utility function, hedging demands and the like. I took advantage of such a formulation in my presidential address to the American Finance Association in 1980, subsequently published as "Decentralized Investment Management" in the May 1981 *Journal of Finance* and have since used it fruitfully to examine a number of issues. Nonetheless, the analysis in this Appendix reaches the right conclusions, although in a somewhat plodding manner.

APPENDIX B. SOLVING A BASIC PROBLEM

In retrospect, this version of Markowitz' critical line algorithm seems far too devoid of economic interpretation. In writing it I approached the problem in terms of its mathematics, with heavy reliance on the Kuhn-Tucker conditions associated with the solutions of quadratic programming problems. I also attempted to make the procedure as intuitive as possible. But in subsequent years, I (and others) saw the

APPENDIX C: SOLVING A STANDARD PROBLEM

economic aspects of various calculations far more clearly. Moreover, there has been a shift from finding the entire efficient frontier to trying to determine the optimal portfolio for an investor with a given risk tolerance. Further, most investors already have some portfolio that meets the relevant constraints, so the problem becomes one of *optimal portfolio revision*. Not surprisingly, if one can solve this type of problem, it is possible (though maybe not efficient) to solve the parametric problem for different levels of risk tolerance by simply changing the relevant parameter and re-solving. Here, too, changes in technology have brought changes in emphasis. When this book was written, computers were large, expensive and very slow by today's standards. Almost any approach that could reduce computational steps was worthwhile, even if it required simplifying the representation of reality or concealing the economics of the underlying method. The magnitudes of such trade-offs are now very different. Direct, understandable and easily implemented procedures may be perfectly sufficient. This is especially true for cases involving relatively few variables, such as those that often arise in asset allocation analyses when the "securities" are a relatively few portfolios formed from asset classes.

For these reasons I now find it preferable to concentrate on the problem of finding the optimal portfolio for an investor with a specified risk tolerance, given a current feasible portfolio and upper and lower bounds as well as the full-investment constraint that the proportions invested must sum to 1. The feasibility condition is generally met, but if it is not, a simple change to the current portfolio can be made or, in more complex cases, a linear programming problem can be solved. I have called the algorithm that I subsequently developed to handle such problems the *gradient method* for portfolio optimization.

To solve the portfolio revision problem in an economically natural way, one starts by computing the marginal utility of each holding, where the marginal utility of a security is the derivative of portfolio utility [e-v/t] with respect to the holding of the security. Each security is classified (as in the book) as being either *in* the solution, *up* at its upper bound, or *down* at its lower bound. The next step is to search for the best security to purchase. It will be the one with the highest marginal utility among those that are in or down. Following this, search for the best security to sell. It will be the one with the lowest marginal utility among those that are in or up. For a small change, the best possible swap will involve selling the latter and using the proceeds to buy the former. The next step is to compute the feasible amount of such a swap that will maximize the gain in portfolio utility. Then the process is repeated, starting with the computation of the marginal utilities, given the new holdings. The optimal portfolio is obtained when no swap can be found that will improve portfolio utility by an economically significant amount.

This formulation has the great advantage of showing that for the optimal portfolio, all securities that are in the solution will have the same marginal utility. Those that are up will have greater marginal utilities and those that are down will have smaller marginal utilities. This conforms with intuition. Securities at their upper bounds could improve the portfolio if only more could be purchased. Those at their lower bounds could lead to an improved portfolio if only less could be held, or a short position taken.

Another advantage of this formulation is that it provides a solution for both the "standard problem" and, as a special case, the "basic problem," as defined in the book. Moreover, the procedure makes it both apparent and intuitive that the marginal utility will be the same for all securities in an optimal portfolio formed without any binding inequality constraints. Use of these "first-order conditions" can both simplify the derivation of equilibrium models such as the Capital Asset Pricing Model and greatly enhance understanding of the economics that underlie them.

This is not to minimize the importance of Markowitz' critical line algorithm. It is an elegant and efficient procedure for solving the parametric portfolio problem and can provide an exact solution instead of the approximate solution that the gradient method produces. Moreover, the critical line algorithm can handle additional equality constraints directly while the gradient method requires embedded linear programming steps to do so.

There are several other algorithmic approaches for solving quadratic programming problems, any of which can be used to solve the types of problems covered here. Some have characteristics in common with the critical line method; others are similar in a number of respects to the gradient method. It is also possible to use an algorithm designed for more general non-linear problems to find a mean-variance optimal portfolio. Microsoft's Excel program includes a tool called "Solver" that can handle most portfolio problems. Today the user can concentrate on understanding the economics of portfolio problems and leave the solutions to available software.

5. AGREEMENT

This chapter follows and improves upon the approach taken in my September 1964 *Journal of Finance* paper, "Capital Asset Prices—A Theory of Market Equilibrium Under Conditions of Risk." The resulting theory has since become known as the Capital Asset Pricing Model (CAPM). The derivation here follows the reasoning of the original concerning the properties of equilibrium and the effects of marginal changes in portfolio holdings. A central conclusion is that the market portfolio is on the efficient frontier and that all other points are combinations of the market portfolio plus borrowing or lending. This can be shown simply by pointing out that Tobin's separation theorem shows that there will be one optimal combination of risky securities and then arguing that in equilibrium it must include all risky securities in the proportion given by relative market values. It follows that the market portfolio will have the highest possible ratio of expected excess return to standard deviation (a ratio that I called the *reward-to-variability ratio* but that is now commonly called the Sharpe Ratio).

The theoretical superiority of the market portfolio led directly to the concept of the index fund, which purchases securities in market proportions and minimizes transactions and other costs. In the decades since the CAPM was developed, such funds have proliferated—a dramatic case of theory influencing practice.

The other key conclusion of the CAPM is the relationship between a security's expected return and its sensitivity to market moves. In the world of the original CAPM the latter is summarized in a measure that equals the security's covariance with the market divided by the variance of the market. In the book this is called the security's volatility, but it is now universally termed its beta value.

I now prefer to derive the equilibrium relationship between expected returns and beta values by noting that the efficiency of the market portfolio implies that it is an optimal portfolio for a particular risk tolerance (in fact, for the value-weighted average of the risk tolerances of all investors—a value that I have called the *societal risk tolerance*). It then follows from the first-order conditions for portfolio optimality that the marginal utility of every security must be the same when the societal risk tolerance is used in the calculation of marginal utility. From this it is a simple matter to obtain the Security Market Line relationship between expected return and beta, since the marginal utility of a security equals its expected return minus twice the ratio of covariance with the market portfolio divided by the societal risk tolerance. Such a derivation is both relatively simple and full of economically meaningful relationships, virtually one at every step. But the end point is the same. The key conclusions are still those given here.

While the book suggested that non-index funds might be more competitive with index funds if their costs were lower, in fact we have seen that the opposite is almost always the case.

There is no consideration here of investor's possible concerns with higher moments of the probability distribution, the effects of dif-ferential taxation of sources of return, international aspects related to changes in exchange rates, or the desirability of hedging against future changes in the investment opportunity set. These and other issues were addressed after this book was written. In most cases the resulting theories were built on a mean-variance foundation (sometimes in discrete time, sometimes in continuous time) and can be considered extended Capital Asset Pricing Models. In many of these models the market portfolio remains optimal for an investor with preferences equal to the value-weighted average of the preferences of the investors in the society. There is also typically an equilibrium relationship between expected returns and beta values taken relative to the market portfolio. On the other hand, expected returns are also related to other variables, so the Security Market Line is replaced by a Security Market Plane or Hyperplane.

Even with more aspects of reality included, most of the theoretical work in this tradition concludes that other things being equal, securities that are likely to do badly in bad times (have high betas) will have higher expected returns. Few dispute that this applies to broad classes of assets. Thus stocks are assumed to have higher expected returns than bonds, which are assumed to have higher expected returns than cash. But some empiricists have questioned whether such a relationship holds across securities within an asset class. Of particular interest are empirical regularities found in some periods and countries that are consistent with relationships between security expected returns and factors that did not manifest any signs of higher market-related risk in the period studied.

Some researchers have posited that this suggests that investors are not as coldly rational as most economic theories assume them to be. For example, if investors tend to overextrapolate trends in company earnings, stocks of companies with growing earnings could become overpriced and eventually earn lower returns than stocks in companies with stagnant or falling earnings. This implies that so-called growth stocks could have lower expected returns than "value stocks" after adjusting for any differences in their beta values.

The empirical evidence on this score is somewhat mixed. And in cases in which value stocks appear to have outperformed growth stocks, the statistical significance of the difference may be limited.

Moreover, empiricists who believe that value stocks have provided better performance are divided concerning the possible cause. Some hold to the economist's view, contending that the value stocks were exposed to a systematic risk that did not appear in the period studied (for example, the risk of doing very badly in the case of a severe depression). Others take the behavioral road, arguing that value stocks really do offer a superior investment for those astute enough to avoid making cognitive errors.

There is another possibility. The behaviorists may well have been correct that capital markets were inefficient up to the time of the publication of their results. But market participants (or their advisors) read academic and professional journals. Their attempts to profit from market inefficiencies can set in motion powerful forces that serve to reduce or eliminate those inefficiencies. The key conclusions in this book could thus be more relevant for the twenty-first century than they were for the latter portion of the twentieth.

6. DISAGREEMENT

One goal of this chapter is to see what remains of the theory of Chapter 5 if investors are assumed to have different predictions of expected returns, risks and correlations. The answer is not much. It is thus not surprising that most of the capital market equilibrium models built on mean-variance foundations continue to assume agreement among investors concerning the probability distributions of future outcomes. This does not mean that progress has not been made on this front. There is now a rich set of models in which costly information is included explicitly and implications derived concerning differences in predictions and actions. Models built on state-preference foundations can also produce useful implications without requiring agreement among participants on the probabilities of various outcomes. But the work that has followed along the lines of the CAPM has typically assumed agreement.

This chapter also covers the effects of differential borrowing and lending rates, following the work of Fischer Black. At least one of the implications is overstated. It is at least possible that the market portfolio can be efficient in this setting. If so, the Security Market Line relationship will hold, since it follows directly from the efficiency of the market portfolio. On the other hand, combinations of the market portfolio plus lending will still be inefficient, as will combinations of the market portfolio plus borrowing. On a more fundamental level, one should ask why the borrowing and lending rates should differ. To the extent that borrowing is risky, the cost should depend on the portfolio being purchased with the proceeds of the loan. Mean-variance models are not complete enough to deal with such matters endogenously, calling into question not only the cases discussed in this chapter, but also some of the more extreme levered positions associated with the results in the prior chapter.

This is a tortuous and only partially successful attempt to derive CAPM equilibrium relationships from a more fundamental starting point. Investors are assumed to have beliefs about the probability distributions of security end-of-period payoffs. Investors come together in a marketplace and haggle until a set of security prices and a riskless rate of interest are set so that all markets clear (that is, the quantity of every security demanded equals the quantity supplied). This exposition could have been shortened by a judicious use of matrix algebra, but the conclusions would be the same.

APPENDIX D: SECURITY PRICES

While this is a step towards a more general equilibrium, it falls short. There is no productive sector: the securities representing productive processes already exist and are in fixed supply. A more general framework would take into account the fact that present consumption can be deferred to produce outcomes with different probability distributions, that there are different goods, and so on. There are now mean-variance models with endogenous decisions about production, but models based on the state-preference approach are better suited to this purpose. Indeed, the original Arrow-Debreu model started from individual preferences and endowments as well as productive opportunities, then derived equilibrium consumption patterns, investment decisions and, implicitly, security prices. In recent years models of this type have been used to focus on investment decisions, often with important results.

This chapter covers models of the sources of covariance among securities. At the time it was written these were called index models, but they are now known almost universally as *factor models*, a term derived from the literature on the estimation of underlying factors from data. This is unfortunate, for the use of a factor model does not require any specific estimation procedure, in particular, one of the types of factor analysis that relies only on variations in security returns. Indeed, several security factor models employed in the investment industry utilize not only security returns but also additional data, such as that included in corporate accounting statements.

7. INDEX MODELS

When this book was written, factor models were appealing in part because their use could reduce the time required to analyze and/or optimize a portfolio. But computers are much faster and far cheaper now, so this is of less importance. This does not mean that full covariance matrices should be estimated directly, unless the number of assets is small. The reason is simple. If there are N securities, $(N^2-N)/2$ different covariances must be estimated. With returns for T periods, there will be $N*T$ data points. Unless the number of data points is considerably greater than the number of estimates required, the amount of noise in the covariance matrix is likely to be unacceptably large, especially for optimization exercises. By reducing the dimensionality with a factor model, estimation error may be reduced to acceptable levels.

Nothing is said here about Stephen Ross' Arbitrage Pricing Theory (APT), which came into prominence after the book's publication. The APT assumes that returns are generated by a factor model. It then argues that attempts by investors to create zero-investment strategies which provide positive cash flows in at least some states of the world and negative cash flows in none will cause prices to adjust until a specific relationship approximately obtains between expected returns and factor exposures. More precisely, the expected excess return on a security will be approximately equal to a linear combination of its exposures to the factors. The theory does not specify the magnitudes nor the signs of the coefficients for the factor exposures (nor that they will all be non-zero). This is not surprising, since the APT makes minimal assumptions about investor preferences. If the assumptions of the CAPM are added to the assumption that returns are generated by a factor model, the results of both theories are obtained. In such a model, the coefficient for each factor exposure in the APT is determined by the beta of that factor relative to the market portfolio. In this sense the APT and CAPM can be complementary, not competitive.

It is unfortunate that the analysis associated with Figure 7-3 was included in the original edition, but it remains here in the spirit of full disclosure. It shows the effect on portfolio risk of increasing the number of securities under very special assumptions. Returns are assumed to be generated by a single factor model and the portfolio has equal dollar amounts of each security. The text concludes that "a little diversification can go a long way." But the conditions under which this is correct are unrealistic. Modern investment practice uses models with multiple factors—in some applications, dozens. Few portfolios are diversified across all such factors. Hence factor risk remains in a portfolio as well as residual risk, even when many securities are included. Moreover, portfolio security proportions are seldom equal, and even if they are in one period, this will change over time. Finally, seemingly small reductions in portfolio variance may still be worth achieving if there is little or no accompanying reduction in expected return. I thus appeal to the reader to pass by

Figure 7-3 and ignore the dangerous statement that "a Portfolio containing 15 or 20 securities may be considered well diversified in this respect." There are similar graphs and statements later in the book, and the same request applies. Such are the sins of youth.

The similarity of the "responsiveness" (b) of a security to the single factor in a one-factor model to the beta of the security relative to the market portfolio is great enough to have caused considerable confusion in the literature. It cannot be precisely true that returns are generated by a single-factor model in which the factor is the market portfolio and the responsiveness coefficients equal security betas. This can be seen by taking the value-weighted average of the return equation. It implies that the market portfolio has residual variance relative to itself, since security residual returns (the c values) are assumed to be uncorrelated with each other and with the factor. But this cannot be true. At the very least, security residual returns in such a model would have to have an average negative correlation, although the amount would be small in magnitude. This being said, it is tempting to assume that the "market factor" is the only one of importance and use the structure of a one-factor model to emphasize the results of the CAPM. This leads one to focus on "systematic" (market-related) and "unsystematic" (residual, idiosyncratic or non-factor related) risk. It also conforms with concepts emphasized in the APT. However, this can be dangerous, and it seems preferable to keep the concepts carefully delineated, as this chapter does.

An inordinate amount of space in this chapter is devoted to a case in which diversification is required via tight upper bounds on holdings and the exposure of a security to a single factor is used as the sole measure of its contribution to portfolio risk. The algorithm designed to solve such an optimization problem is simple and easily implemented. However, there is no need to impose such drastic simplifications, given today's computer power. The reader should either skip the corresponding sections or regard them as signs of simpler and more naïve times.

This appendix is divided into two main sections. The second provides a flow diagram for the algorithm in Chapter 7 in which responsiveness is used as the sole measure of risk. Since such a formulation is neither needed nor desirable today, this should be considered only an historic artifact. The initial and main part of the appendix shows one way to utilize the special structure of a factor model directly in an optimization algorithm, without computing the full covariance matrix at any point. This can reduce both required computer memory and computation time. For problems with a large number of assets (for example,

**APPENDIX E.
PORTFOLIO
ANALYSIS WITH
SIMPLIFIED MODELS**

several thousand) and a small number of factors (for example, under 100), the advantages can be substantial, even with today's computers. There are other ways to exploit a factor structure when finding optimal portfolios that may be more efficient in some cases. The key point is that the reader interested in actually implementing an optimization procedure for large problems in which covariances are determined by a factor model should seriously consider taking advantage of the structure of the underlying factor structure.

8. THE RECORD This chapter deals with empirical investigations of the implications of capital market theory and the somewhat different but closely related subject of mutual fund performance. With regard to the former, it is useful to repeat the earlier statement that empirical data can tell us only so much. Moreover, old empirical data may tell us less about the future than more recent data. The results shown in this book were based on at most 40 years of history, from 1926 through 1965. We now have 73 years for such series and the additional 33 years have differed considerably from the first 40. Moreover, we no longer need accept indices in which returns are weighted equally as proxies for the market portfolio. Almost all major stock market indices are now value-weighted, as the theory suggests they should be. Best to read hurriedly over these empirical results, heeding as you go the admonitions given in the early paragraphs of the chapter.

The bulk of the chapter deals with measures of mutual fund performance. Three are given and the relevance of each described.

The first measure, which I called the reward-to-variability ratio at the time is, as indicated earlier, now called the Sharpe Ratio. It is widely used.

The second measure, called here the reward-to-volatility ratio has been called the Treynor Ratio. It is used relatively infrequently.

The third measure, called here the differential return, is more generally known as Jensen's alpha. While this version is frequently used, a more general one—the difference between a fund's average return and that of a comparable benchmark portfolio, often called the fund's alpha—is of increasing importance in practice.

Some analysts employ a measure calculated by taking the ratio of (1) the average difference between a fund's return and that of a suitable benchmark to (2) the standard deviation of that difference. Such a measure, which is a generalization of the reward-to-variability ratio described here, has been called the fund's information ratio or Selection Sharpe Ratio.

Current discussions of the relevance of these alternative measures are more complete and more precise than the treatment in this book, which does not deal with the subject of appropriate benchmarks and measures of performance relative thereto. Here again, the book reflects its time. Those who held mutual funds tended to hold one or two, hence the emphasis on a measure that assumed that only one fund was held. Today many more people hold mutual funds, and multi-fund portfolios are the norm. Such portfolios require more complex performance measures.

Numerous studies of mutual fund performance have now been performed with much larger data sets, longer time periods, more attention to survivor bias, better statistical techniques, and more sophisticated performance measures. However, the major conclusions of the earlier studies remain broadly consistent with the subsequent data. The average high-cost manager does not add enough value to offset added expenses, and past fund risk and factor exposures contain useful information for predicting future values of such measures. The average actively managed mutual fund does not beat a comparable passive strategy before costs, and falls below it after costs. While this is perfectly consistent with capital market theory, similar results can be derived from simple arithmetic, as I have written elsewhere. Simply put, the average cannot beat the average.

There is a brief discussion in the chapter of stable Paretian distributions, which have infinite variance. This possibility caused a stir in the late 1960's but the empirical observations that led researchers to entertain such a possibility have since been attributed to time-varying distributions, each of which has a finite variance. It is not unusual for a current model to assume that capital markets are in equilibrium in each period but that the magnitudes of underlying variables such as the market portfolio's risk and expected excess return change from period to period.

It should be noted that studies done in earlier times were less sensitive to practical aspects. For many purposes, measures of performance should involve comparisons with variables that could have been determined before the fact. For this reason, it may not be appropriate to compare a fund with an alternative that had the same beta value over a period as the fund exhibited over that period, since this beta value could not have been known in advance. Current studies labor to provide comparisons that are as "out of sample" as possible, and for good reasons.

The chapter contains the statement that "the overall view is one of a remarkably efficient market—one in which few securities are likely to be seriously underpriced or overpriced for long." This may or may not be true, but our empirical tools are still not strong enough to reach such a conclusion. On the other hand, those who believe that capital markets offer easy ways to fabulous riches by simply buying underpriced securities and selling (or shorting) overpriced securities have frequently been severely disappointed.

9. UTILITY This chapter provides an introduction to utility analysis, which is now a major component of many general equilibrium models used in financial economics. The early sections belabor the justification for assuming that individuals seek to maximize expected utility, but it is still useful to emphasize that this rather abstract notion is very sensible. The notion of risk aversion is also presented in its most fundamental form.

The remainder of the chapter attempts to justify the assumption that investors care about portfolio risk and return on the grounds that their utility is a quadratic function of wealth. This may be useful, but it falls far short by today's standards. We know that investors with such utility functions would exhibit unusual behavior. In particular, they would invest less in stocks as they became wealthier, both as a proportion of their assets and in absolute value. Such *decreasing absolute risk aversion* is inconsistent with both introspection and observation. If mean-variance theories could only be justified in this manner, they would have long since disappeared.

A far better justification, widely used today, is the assumption that returns are jointly normally distributed so that portfolio mean and variance are *sufficient statistics*. In other words, given the mean and variance of a portfolio, one knows the entire distribution. Given a portfolio's return distribution, it is straightforward to determine the portfolio's expected utility. Under mild restrictions on the utility function, an investor will then prefer a portfolio lying somewhere on the efficient frontier.

Today much attention is given to investor utility functions. Classes of such functions have been demarcated based on the investor's change in holdings as wealth changes. Some functions exhibit decreasing absolute risk aversion, some constant, and others increasing. Some exhibit decreasing relative risk aversion, others constant, and others increasing. By combining assumptions about investor utility functions with assumptions about the return-generating process, one can determine whether investors will care about only the mean and variance of the distribution of portfolio returns or additional moments as well. As indicated earlier, in an important contribution, John Lintner showed that a combination of a negative exponential utility function and jointly normal returns leads to preferences which are linear in mean-variance space.

There is now a large and growing literature on dynamic strategies, which involve changing investment portfolios over time based on prior realizations. Such models depend critically on utility theory. Finally, general equilibrium models based on state-preference theory increasingly assume that investors seek to maximize expected utility.

This chapter provides an introduction to a subject of great importance in portfolio and capital market theory, but much more would be included today.

When this book was written, mean-variance analysis was beginning to seep into the teaching and practice of finance, but Arrow and Debreu's state-preference approach was being used by relatively few in the field. This was unfortunate, for the Arrow-Debreu theory provides a profound and complete view of the determination of prices in general equilibrium under uncertainty. My goals in writing the chapter were two. The first was to provide an accessible primer on the approach. The second was to try to translate the results of the CAPM to this more general setting.

10. STATE PREFERENCE THEORY

The chapter starts with the assumption that individuals' preferences over contingent claims are described by indifference curves that are convex to the origin in figures such as 10-1. It forsakes the generality of multiple commodities, using only future wealth as the source of consumption. While the results can be extended simply to multiple periods, the chapter follows the rest of the book in considering only one. The important point is the derivation of what are called here the prices of pure securities and the fact that any uncertain claim can be valued using those prices. Now we call these Arrow-Debreu prices, or state prices, and know that they are related to forward contingent prices, which are frequently termed risk-neutral probabilities.

Modern theories following this type of approach go behind an investor's indifference curves in contingent claim space. The investor is assumed to have preferences over consumption goods, to have a utility function that exhibits risk aversion, to assign probabilities to the various states, and to be indifferent among alternative combinations of contingent claims with the same expected utility. This can be a highly fruitful approach if sufficient restrictions are placed on investor preferences and probability assessments. Many important issues in financial economics have been addressed using such a framework.

Had such an approach been available at the time this book was written, this chapter would have been radically different, but the greatest changes would have affected the latter half. There are counterparts to the key CAPM results in a state-preference world. This is not the place to attempt derivations or to summarize the conditions required to obtain such results. Suffice it to say that under reasonably plausible assumptions it will be the case that prices adjust until the expected return of a "pure security" is lower, the smaller the total amount of goods and services in its associated state. Why? Because investors adjust their holdings until the expected marginal utility of consumption per dollar of investment is the same in each state. Consider two states with different amounts of aggregate consumption and equal probabilities of occurrence. The marginal utility of the representative (market) investor will be higher in the state with less consumption, since risk aversion implies that her marginal utility will decrease with consumption. Thus the expected return for that state must be lower so that the expected marginal utilities in the two states will be the same. Now consider a security that "does badly in bad times." It will have a high expected return since more of its payoffs come in states of high aggregate consumption. Thus there will be a relationship between expected return and the extent to which a security "does badly in bad times." While the measure of doing badly in bad times need not equal the beta value of the CAPM, the qualitative result remains.

This is a far better way to approach the question addressed in the latter part of this chapter. For this reason, the measure of market similarity proposed in the final section is not needed.

LAST THOUGHTS   This book contains important elements of the core of the field now known as financial economics. Without question, the impact of financial economics on the practice of finance has been profound. The importance of the contributions described in this book to the intellectual capital of the world is widely acknowledged, as indicated by the number of those mentioned in this foreword who have been awarded the Nobel Prize in Economic Sciences—the highest award an economist can attain.

Financial economics is an exciting, productive, and evolving field. This book describes its status in its youth. There is much more now, and more to come. Progress did not stop in 1970 and will not stop now. But it is sometimes useful to look back, and it is in this spirit that this edition has been prepared. I hope that you find it helpful.

PREFACE

A skilled economic historian can usually prove that the essential components of a so-called "modern" theory were specified quite nicely by some hitherto-obscure member of a medieval monastic order. The material in this book can be said to have originated in 1730, when Bernoulli published his "Exposition of a New Theory on the Measurement of Risk." But Bernoulli's work had little effect on the fields of finance and economics. Until the 1950s, risk was either assumed away or treated qualitatively. It was rarely included explicitly in models dealing with portfolio construction or conditions in capital markets.

In 1952, Harry Markowitz suggested a simple, yet powerful approach for dealing with risk. Since then, there has been a veritable revolution in the field of finance, and a somewhat less dramatic, though nonetheless important, set of changes in the field of economics.

This book brings together the major contributions of the past two decades in the related areas of portfolio theory and the theory of capital markets. As the bibliography indicates, there are many key references. Taken as a whole, the original material is voluminous and replete with duplication, inconsistent notation, and arguments over issues now settled. On the other hand, the condensed versions now appearing in standard finance and economics textbooks serve only to whet the appetite of the serious student. A middle ground between these two extremes is clearly needed, and this book is an attempt to provide it.

Part I covers procedures for selecting investments. The traditional approach to choice under certainty is described in Chap. 1. Chapters 2 through 4 develop portfolio theory—a set of rules for the intelligent selection of investments under conditions of risk.

Part II deals with models of capital markets based on the assumption that investors act in accordance with the principles described in Part I. Chapter 5 covers the case in which there is a certain amount of agreement among investors. Chapter 6 covers the case in which there is disagreement. Important constructs derived in Part II include: the capital market line, the security market line, the concept of volatility, and the relationships among security characteristic lines.

Part III extends and applies the material in Parts I and II. The chapters need not be read in sequence. Chapter 7 provides important information for those considering the actual utilization of the portfolio-selection procedures described in Part I. Chapter 8 provides relevant empirical data; procedures for performance measurement are described, and the results of extensive studies of mutual-fund performance summarized. Chapter 9 succinctly introduces modern utility theory and relates it to portfolio theory. Chapter 10 presents the more general approach of state-preference theory and relates it to the capital market theory described in Part II.

No mathematics beyond high school algebra is required to understand the material in Parts I, II and III. Most of the proofs are handled graphically, the few requiring more sophisticated methods are included in footnotes. The Supplement is provided for the reader who wishes to cover the material in considerable detail. It may be read in parallel with the main text. Section A summarizes the mathematical procedures utilized. Sections B and C provide the core of portfolio theory; they should be read in conjunction with Part I. Section D parallels the material in Part II. Section E is intended to accompany Chap. 7. Prior contact with calculus will prove helpful, although it is not essential.

The book can be used in several ways. A course on portfolio construction might be based on Chaps. 1 through 5 and Chap. 7. A course on capital markets might rely on Chaps. 1 through 6 plus Chap. 8. A course on the economics of uncertainty might be based on Chaps. 1 through 6 and Chaps. 9 and 10. A course on investments might use Chaps. 1 through 8.

None of the material in Parts I, II, and III should prove too difficult for use at the undergraduate level. The Supplement may prove useful for some courses at the graduate level.

Portfolio managers and security analysts will find Chaps. 1 through 5 and 7 and 8 especially relevant. Operations researchers and computer programmers will find Secs. A, B, C, and E of the Supplement useful.

Little more need be said here about the book. Something should, however, be said about the people who helped to make it useful.

I first attempted to put the material together for a graduate seminar given at the University of Washington in the spring of 1968. Professor Stephen Archer encouraged me to do so and proved an enthusiastic student as well. A number of other colleagues at Washington provided valuable comments—notably, Professors William Alberts, Hans Daellenbach, Charles D'Ambrosio, Charles Haley, Alan Hess, Robert Higgins, Dudley Johnson, Alfred Page, and Kim Tamura.

The manuscript was completed in the spring of 1969, while I was teaching an undergraduate course on the subject with Professor Sheen Kassouf at the University of California at Irvine. I am especially grateful to Professor Kassouf for his help at this critical stage of the project. I am also indebted to the more than one hundred undergraduates who enrolled in the course, seemed to learn a great deal of the material, and professed (by and large) to enjoy it.

Needless to say, I have learned much from co-workers in the field. Several have commented directly on portions of the manuscript and/or my descriptions of the material. I am particularly appreciative of the help given me over the years by John McCall of the RAND

Corporation, Professors Jack Hirshleifer and Fred Weston of the University of California at Los Angeles, Professors Eugene Fama, Lawrence Fisher and Benjamin King of the University of Chicago, Professors Myron Gordon, Michael Jensen and Walter Oi of the University of Rochester, Professor Kalman Cohen of Carnegie-Mellon University, Professor Marshall Blume of the University of Pennsylvania, Professor Jerry Pogue of the Massachusetts Institute of Technology, Professor Seymour Smidt of Cornell University, Professor Donald Farrar of Columbia University, Professors Richard Bower and Peter Williamson of Dartmouth College, Fischer Black of Associates in Finance, and Jack L. Treynor of the *Financial Analysts' Journal.*

I owe a special debt to Nancy Jacob of the University of Washington. She read every draft of the manuscript and participated in the derivation and selection of the material to be included. I have drawn heavily on her original work, particularly in Chapter 10, but she made major contributions to every chapter.

My longest-standing debt is to Harry Markowitz. I have tried to acknowledge it in the dedication. But it should also be recorded that he painstakingly reviewed the manuscript, providing suggestions for revision that have (I hope) made the book much better than it would otherwise have been.

Lani Levine cheerfully typed the first part of the manuscript and suggested improvements in both style and content. She also exercised gentle but necessary pressure to keep its production well on schedule. Helen Dotta flawlessly typed the seemingly endless equations and tables in the Supplement with equal cheer.

WILLIAM F. SHARPE

CONTENTS

4

PART **II.**

**CAPITAL MARKET
THEORY**

5

6

PART **III.**

**APPLICATIONS
AND EXTENSIONS**

A

B

C

D

INTRODUCTION

This is a book on portfolio theory and capital markets. The title is not intended to be misleading. The book presents a rather abstract but rigorous theory of particular relevance for people choosing investment portfolios (and for people interested in the way in which others choose investment portfolios). But the theory has many additional uses. In fact, a more revealing, though aesthetically unacceptable, title would be: The Theory of Making Decisions Involving Interrelated Uncertain Outcomes. Selection of an investment portfolio provides just one example. But it is an important example, and one in which the issues are clear cut. Hence the name. Portfolio theory is concerned with decisions involving outcomes that cannot be predicted with complete certainty. Examples are:

1

1. Whether or not to get married;
2. Whether to take a job or go into business for oneself;
3. Whether or not to withdraw money from a savings account in order to buy shares in a uranium mining company;
4. Whether or not to continue reading this book.

The theory insists that uncertainty be acknowledged and dealt with explicitly. It also insists that *interrelationships* among outcomes be treated explicitly. For example:

1. One prospective marriage partner might leave if investments turn out badly; another candidate for the position might become more attentive in order to provide (needed) solace.
2. A particularly splendid outcome for an investment in Lockheed stock might be associated with a rather disappointing outcome for Boeing stock if the unusual results are due to unexpectedly large orders from Lockheed relative to orders from Boeing.
3. Investment in General Motors stock might lead to a dismal outcome if times turn bad, but under such conditions, so might investment in General Electric stock.

Not all decisions must involve uncertain outcomes. Nor must all outcomes be interrelated. But the theory is intended for problems involving some uncertainty and some interrelationships.

THEORIZING   To theorize is to abstract. One builds a *model*—a description of a toy world; one simple enough to be thoroughly understood. In such a world all relationships are clear, and the implications of any possible change can be determined precisely. Such an approach may be used in two ways. A *normative* model is a guide to action; it indicates the manner in which decisions should be made. A *positive* model is predictive in nature; it describes the manner in which decisions are made and the relationships among things such as prices, quantities sold, etc.

The appropriate test of a model depends on its intended use. The test of a positive model is its predictive ability. The test of a normative model is its ability to help a decision maker achieve his goals. In either case, the requirement for acceptance is not perfection; the model need only give better results than the next best alternative. Its "realism" is relatively unimportant. Any real problem of interest will be extremely complex; an analysis of all the factors that could conceivably influence the outcome would be hopelessly difficult. Abstraction is required. One must focus on a relatively few factors— hopefully, the most important. The test of the appropriateness of the selection is the model's performance—for a positive theory, its predictive ability; for a normative theory, its value to the decision maker.

Portfolio theory is sometimes cast in normative terms. What sort of predictions should an investor make and how should he use them to determine the best portfolio? The approach has also been incorporated into a positive theory of the capital market. If investors act as portfolio theory suggests they should, what can be said about the market in which they buy and sell? In particular, what can be said about the prices at which assets are bought and sold?

PORTFOLIO THEORY AND CAPITAL MARKET THEORY

The line between positive and normative theory is difficult to maintain. The chapters that follow are no exception. In general the term *portfolio theory* will be used to denote the normative approach and the term *capital market theory* to denote the positive approach. However, the difference is primarily in the use to which the theory is put. There is only one basic model.

The capital market theory presented in this book is by no means the only contender for the title. Some alternative approaches yield implications consistent with those obtained here; others do not. The reader is warned that the term will be used in a special sense, i.e., to mean "the capital market theory based on portfolio theory."

Fortunately no problem arises in connection with the other term. Some have questioned the usefulness of portfolio theory but not its name. The material given here *is* portfolio theory in the generally accepted sense of the term.

The material in this book is remarkably young, considering its rather widespread acceptance. The essential elements of portfolio theory were developed by Markowitz in the early 1950s. In 1958 Tobin made the first attempt to use the theory for a positive capital market model. Since then many have contributed.

HISTORY

The identification of the original contributor of an important idea is of little interest to anyone but the contributor (and other claimants to the title). No attempt will be made here to associate each component of the theory with an individual. The bibliography provides references for some of the major works in the area.

Markowitz' contribution was so monumental that it must be noted explicitly. Others have extended, modified, and tested his original theory, but the core remains unchanged. In fact, many prefer the term *Markowitz theory* to *portfolio theory*. The terms are, for all practical purposes, synonomous.

3

PLAN OF THE BOOK   Part I contains the essential elements of portfolio theory. Part II serves a similar function for capital market theory. The chapters in Part III build on this initial material.

The supplement provides a mathematical treatment of the material. Solution methods alluded to in other chapters are treated explicitly. Both portfolio theory and capital market theory receive somewhat more rigorous attention. The material is more difficult than that in the other parts of the book. Some knowledge of differential calculus will prove helpful, but only an understanding of college algebra is absolutely essential.

Many readers will choose to avoid the supplement entirely. Those who do read it will undoubtedly prefer to do so in conjunction with the related material in Parts I, II, and III. Appropriate guidance is provided by means of messages inserted subtly in relevant chapters.

PART I

PORTFOLIO THEORY

1.

CERTAINTY

Portfolio theory is concerned with uncertainty; it extends the classical economic model of investment under conditions of complete certainty. This chapter briefly describes the traditional model, since the model serves as the point of departure for the material in the remainder of the book.

To concentrate on essential principles, assume that time is divided into two (and only two) periods. Call them *this year* and *next year*. Think of an individual as choosing among combinations of two goods: *this year's consumption* and *next year's consumption*. For convenience let the amount of each good be measured in dollars. The individual's problem is to choose the best consumption pattern available to him.

BORROWING AND LENDING

7

Just as there is a market for trading apples and oranges, there is a market for trading this year's consumption and next year's. The terms of trade depend on forces of supply and demand, as do the terms in the market for apples and oranges. In virtually all times and places people have been willing to sacrifice a greater amount of future consumption to obtain a given amount of present consumption. For example, one might trade $1 of this year's consumption for $1.07 of next year's. Such a trade is usually described as *lending*. Alternatively, one might trade $1.07 of next year's consumption for $1 of this year's. This would be described as *borrowing*.

Transaction costs may lead to differences in the terms for borrowing and lending. For purposes of analysis, such differences are usually best ignored; one speaks simply of *the* terms of trade between this year's consumption and next year's. Common practice is to express the terms as a *rate of interest*. For example, if $1 of this year's consumption can be traded for $1.07 of next year's, the rate is .07 or 7 percent.

$$\frac{1.07 - 1}{1} = .07$$

SELECTING A CONSUMPTION PATTERN Consider the situation faced by Mr. *A*, shown in Fig. 1-1. His income consists of $100 this year and nothing next year. If he were to devote all his income to consumption as it is received, he would

FIGURE 1-1

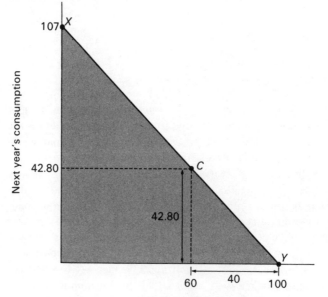

This year's consumption

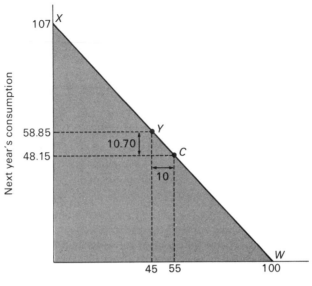

This year's consumption

FIGURE 1-2

obtain the combination shown by point Y. However, this is by no means the only combination available to him. He can trade this year's consumption for next year's by lending some or all of this year's income. If he lends it all, he can consume $107 worth of next year's goods and nothing this year, as shown by point X. If he lends only a portion, he can consume any combination lying on the line XY—the particular point depending on the amount lent. He can, of course, choose to consume less than he might; thus any point lying in the shaded triangle is attainable. But since there is no time except this year and next year, and since consumption is assumed to be desirable, interior points are of no interest.

Which point on the line should Mr. A choose? Obviously, he should choose the one he likes best. The exact point will depend on his preferences, peculiarities, prejudices, etc. It might be point Y. Or point X. In this case it is point C: $60 of this year's goods and $42.80 of next year's. To move from point Y (his income pattern) to point C (his consumption pattern), Mr. A trades $40 of this year's consumption for $42.80 of next year's. Putting it another way, he lends $40 at 7 percent—the market rate of interest.

Next consider Mr. B, whose situation is shown in Fig. 1-2. His income consists of $45 this year and $58.85 next year. If he wishes, he may adopt the identical consumption pattern shown by point Y. But by trading this year's income for next year's (i.e., lending), he

WEALTH

may move to any point along the line segment *XY*. Or by trading next year's income for this year's (i.e., borrowing), he may move to any point along the segment *YW*. His opportunities thus include all the combinations lying within the shaded area and on line *XYW* (its border). In this example Mr. *B* chooses to consume $55 worth of this year's goods and $48.15 of next year's, as shown by point *C*. He does this by trading $10.70 of next year's income for $10 of this year's. Putting it another way, he borrows $10 at the market rate of interest (7 percent).

The consumption patterns available to an individual are those lying on or under a line such as that shown in Fig. 1-2. Such a line can be described by its slope and either intercept (the point at which it cuts an axis). The slope depends entirely on the terms of trade (i.e., the rate of interest). Since this is assumed to be the same for all, any given individual's pattern can be described by an intercept. The convention is to use the horizontal intercept—the amount one could consume this year by foregoing all future consumption (i.e., "eat, drink, and be merry"). This is the *present value* of the individual's income stream. Alternatively, it is his *wealth*. Mr. *B*'s wealth is $100, as is Mr. *A*'s.

SELECTING AN INCOME PATTERN

Consider now the plight of Mr. *C*. He has been offered two jobs. Job *j* pays $45 this year and $58.85 next year; job *k* pays $35 this year and $74.90 next year. Which is better? The answer in no way depends on Mr. *C*'s preferences. Job *j*'s income pattern can be converted into any consumption pattern on or below line $X_j Y_j W_j$ in Fig. 1-3. Job *k*'s income pattern can be converted into any consumption pattern on or below line $X_k Y_k W_k$. Clearly job *k* is better; it allows any consumption pattern attainable with job *j* and more besides. The income pattern of job *k* has a present value of $105; that of job *j* has a present value of only $100. By taking job *k*, Mr. *C* will have a wealth of $105 ($W_k$); if he had taken job *j*, his wealth would have been only $100 ($W_j$).

Mr. *C* should choose job *k*, regardless of his relative preference for this year's consumption vis-à-vis next year's. Having chosen it, he will undoubtedly want to borrow or lend in order to obtain the most desirable consumption pattern. In this example, he borrows to reach point *C**. This latter decision cannot be made without knowledge of Mr. *C*'s preferences, but the choice of jobs can.[1]

ACCEPTING OR REJECTING AN INVESTMENT

Figure 1-4*a* shows the situation faced by Mr. *D*. His income pattern shown by point *Y* ($60 this year and $42.80 next year) can

[1] Assuming, of course, that Mr. *C* has no feelings about the relative desirabilities of the two jobs other than those associated with the money incomes each provides.

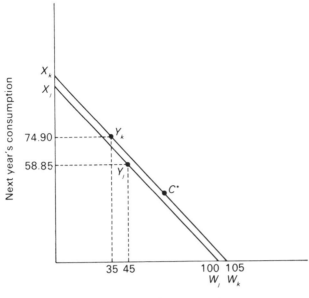

This year's consumption

FIGURE 1-3

be converted into any consumption pattern on or under the line X_1YW_1 by borrowing or lending. His wealth ($100) is shown by point W_1. A friend asserts that by investing $20 this year in an oil-well venture, Mr. D can obtain $32.10 next year. Such a transaction would allow him to trade consumption pattern Y for the combination shown by point Q_a. By borrowing or lending he could then attain any point on or under line $X_aQ_aW_a$. His wealth would increase from $100 ($W_1$) to $110 ($W_a$).

In this simple world, an investment can be characterized by an expenditure this year and a receipt next year. Graphically, the expenditure is shown by a horizontal distance such as YV in Fig. 1-4a, and the receipt is shown by a vertical distance such as VQ_a. The third side of the resulting triangle (line YQ_a in Fig. 1-4a) provides a convenient and complete representation of·the investment.

One measure of the results obtained from an investment is its *rate of return*. In this case it is .605 or 60.5 percent.

$$\frac{32.10 - 20}{20} = .605$$

Another measure is the *net present value*—the increase in wealth obtained by undertaking the investment, given the current terms of trade (i.e., market rate of interest). In this case it is $10.

FIGURE 1-4

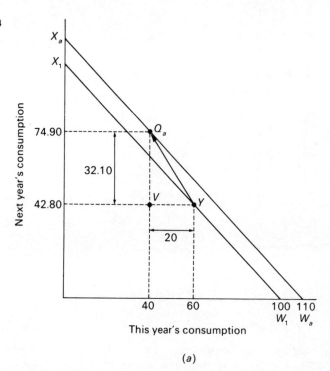

(a)

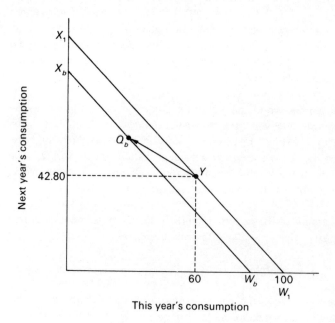

(b)

	Actual amount	Equivalent amount of this year's money (present value)
Expenditure	$20.00	$20.00
Receipt	32.10	30.00
Net present value		$10.00

Decisions of the type faced by Mr. D can be made by following either of two rules:

1. Accept an investment if its rate of return exceeds the market rate of interest.

2. Accept an investment if its net present value is positive.

Figure 1-4b shows a case in which neither condition is met. The investment is represented by line YQ_b. Note that the line is flatter than $X_1 YW_1$; thus the investment's rate of return is less than the market rate of interest. By accepting the investment, Mr. D's opportunities would be reduced to those lying on or under line $X_b Q_b W_b$. His wealth would decrease from W_1 to W_b, since the investment's net present value is negative.

Mr. E must make a more complex decision. He must choose between two alternative (mutually exclusive) investments, indicated by lines YQ_a and YQ_b in Fig. 1-5. Investment b is clearly better, for it allows consumption patterns lying on or under line $X_b Q_b W_b$, while investment a allows only those lying on or under line $X_a Q_a W_a$. Putting it another way, investment b gives Mr. E the maximum possible wealth (W_b). The appropriate decision rule is obviously:

CHOOSING AMONG ALTERNATIVE INVESTMENTS

When choosing among alternative investments, select the one with the largest net present value.[1]

Note that the investments' rates of return may not provide an appropriate guide for choosing among alternatives. In this case, the less desirable investment has the higher rate of return—line YQ_a is steeper than line YQ_b. This situation may occur when investments require different levels of expenditure, as these do. Investment b provides less net present value per dollar, but it also uses more dollars (E_b is larger than E_a). The latter factor more than offsets the former in this case, giving b the larger overall net present value.

Mr. E must choose one of two investments. Moreover, each is an all-or-none proposition. The selection of investment a requires an expenditure of E_a dollars and provides a receipt of R_a. The selection

DIVISIBLE INVESTMENTS

[1] Unless none gives a positive net present value; in this case, choose none.

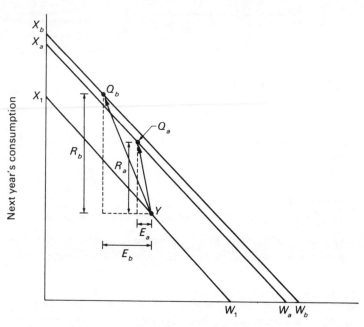

FIGURE 1-5

This year's consumption

of investment b requires an expenditure of E_b dollars and provides a receipt of R_b. No other alternative is available. Each investment is indivisible, and only one can be chosen.

In fact, few investments are completely indivisible. One need not purchase an entire oil well, nor an entire apartment, nor all of General Motors. It is possible to "go in with a friend," or two thousand, or two million. Investment securities (stocks, bonds, etc.) are designed to make such arrangements convenient. Securities markets exist to bring together people interested in dividing up investments.

Portfolio theory assumes that all investments are perfectly divisible. Each individual can thus select as much or as little of an investment as he desires (and is able to afford). Among other things, this assumption restores the usefulness of rate or return as a measure of performance.

Figure 1-6 shows the situation faced by Mr. F; it is very similar to that of Mr. E. In this case, however, the two investments are perfectly divisible. Suppose that Mr. F has decided in advance to invest (expend) the amount E, regardless of the investment selected. This will buy him 35 percent of investment b or 80 percent of a. The former would give him the combination shown by point $Q_{b'}$, the latter the combination shown by point $Q_{a'}$. Since the expenditures

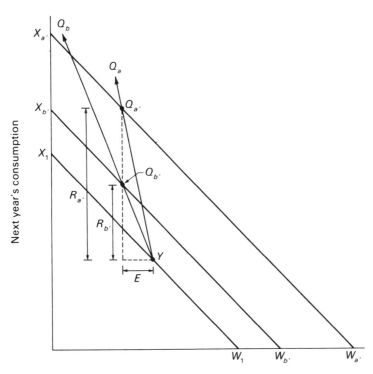

This year's consumption

FIGURE 1-6

are precisely the same, the investment with the greater rate of return (steeper line) must provide the greater receipt and thus the greater net present value. Investment *a* is clearly better; by choosing it and borrowing or lending, Mr. *F* can obtain any combination lying on or under line $X_{a'}Q_{a'}W_{a'}$.

These examples summarize the essential concepts of the traditional economic theory of investment under conditions of certainty. Much has been done to broaden it. One important set of extensions retains the assumption of certainty, expanding the analysis to deal explicitly with more than two time periods. The extensions that form the subject of this book are of a different type. They attempt to come to grips with the problem of uncertainty. To focus on that problem, it is convenient to retain the assumption that time is dichotomous. The two periods may be *this year* and *next year*, or *this year* and *seven years from now*, or simply *now* and *later*. An investment requires an expenditure *now* and provides a receipt *later*. Its performance is expressed as a rate of return:

CERTAINTY VERSUS UNCERTAINTY

$$\text{Rate of return} = \frac{\text{receipt} - \text{expenditure}}{\text{expenditure}}$$

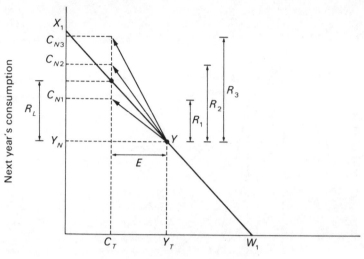

FIGURE 1-7   This year's consumption

If *later* is one year hence, the rate of return is on an annual basis. If not, it can be converted to an annual basis if desired.[1]

In a world of certainty, one knows precisely what next year will bring. The problem is simply to choose a combination of this year's consumption and next year's. In a world of uncertainty, the problem is more difficult. Most choices involve a specific amount of consumption this year and a number of possible amounts next year. Consider Mr. G, whose situation is shown in Fig. 1-7. He has chosen to spend (consume) C_T dollars from this year's income (Y_T). He thus has E dollars to invest. If he is unlucky, the investment will provide a receipt of only R_1 dollars; if he is reasonably lucky, R_2; if he is very lucky, R_3. He may thus have as little as C_{N1} dollars to spend on consumption next year. On the other hand, he may have as much as C_{N3}.

Should Mr. G make this investment and take his chances? Or should he instead lend E dollars, insuring a respectable but unspectacular receipt of R_L dollars next year? Or should he consider some other strategy? Portfolio theory is designed to help answer such questions.

SHORT RUN VERSUS LONG RUN   Thus far, the alternative to *consumption now* has been described as *consumption later*. A more general approach would use *money available for consumption and/or investment later*. Imagine an

---

[1] The annual rate of return is

$$(1 + \text{rate of return})^{\frac{1}{N}} - 1$$

where N = number of years between expenditure and receipt.

investor planning for a ten-year period. He will undoubtedly wish to engage in consumption throughout the period. Assume that he intends to review his investments at the beginning of every year, then sell some and perhaps purchase others, using the net proceeds to finance his consumption in the following year. From one year to the next, the change in the market value of his holdings plus any cash received will clearly be of major importance. The greater the value at year-end, the greater the money available for consumption and/or investment (which will, hopefully, provide additional consumption in future periods).

Many investments are highly liquid (easily and inexpensively marketed). The market value of such an investment can be turned into a receipt if desired, and it can thus be considered equivalent to a receipt for purposes of analysis. In many cases, it is thus reasonable to approach a long-run investment decision as a series of short-run decisions. Only one modification is required: The desirability of money *later* is based on its possible use for consumption at the time and/or for consumption in subsequent periods (via reinvestment).

Short-sighted procedures provide more than expository convenience. They are likely to be reasonable methods for approaching complex long-range problems.

Not all transactions involve uncertainty. The terms *borrowing* and *lending* will be used here to refer to trades of present for future money in which there is complete assurance of full and prompt payment. The expression *pure rate of interest* will be used to refer to the terms of trade under such conditions.

TERMINOLOGY

In popular usage, the terms *borrowing*, *lending*, and *rate of interest* are given broad meanings. Many loans involve considerable risk of nonpayment, partial payment, or late payment. The rate of interest charged for a loan attempts to take such risks into account. Thus nominal interest rates often exceed the pure rate. Capital market theory provides important insights concerning the differences among such rates. To fix ideas, however, terms such as *investment*, *security*, and *asset* will generally be employed, reserving *lending* and *borrowing* to refer to special cases in which the actual outcome is known with complete certainty.

2.

PORTFOLIOS

THE PROBLEM   In theory an individual can consume all his wealth immediately, fore-going all future consumption. In practice he will not. Recall the definition of Chap. 1: An individual's *wealth* is the maximum amount of present money he can obtain. He chooses to consume less than this in order to (hopefully) obtain future consumption. The difference is *saving*. It may be invested in risky assets, lent, or held as cash. From the viewpoint of portfolio theory, all these alternatives are considered *investment*.

Figure 2-1 illustrates the situation faced by Mr. *T*, a typical individual. His wealth is *W*. He has chosen a job, a house or apartment, an insurance policy, and perhaps one or more shares of stock. The result of all these decisions is shown in the figure. He will consume

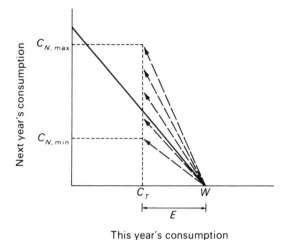

This year's consumption

FIGURE 2-1

C_T of this year's goods. He may be able to consume only $C_{N, min}$ next year; on the other hand, he may be able to consume as much as $C_{N, max}$. The actual amount will depend on a multitude of factors, none of which is completely predictable.

Formally, Mr. *T*'s situation is equivalent to that of a typical investor. He has *invested*, or expended, *E* dollars in foregone present consumption. His receipt will be the amount of future consumption actually obtained. As usual, the rate of return will be

$$\frac{\text{Receipt} - \text{expenditure}}{\text{Expenditure}}$$

The totality of decisions determining an individual's future prospects is called a *portfolio*. Figure 2-1 shows Mr. *T*'s prospects, given a particular set of decisions—in other words, his chosen portfolio.

In the broadest sense, the selection of a portfolio involves the choice of a job, an insurance policy, a wife, etc. However, portfolio theorists usually concern themselves with a more mundane type of decision— the selection of an appropriate set of liquid investments. Thus a portfolio is said to be composed of *securities*. In general, a security is a decision affecting the future. The totality of such decisions constitutes a portfolio.

After the fact, the performance of a portfolio is measured by its actual rate of return—the receipt (future consumption) relative to the expenditure (foregone present consumption).

Individuals are, above all, interested in consumption. Investment is merely a means to the end of future consumption. However, the act is so closely related to portfolio selection, that it is traditional to use the term *investor* rather than *consumer*. The problem is thus to determine the manner in which an *investor* should select one of a possibly large number of alternative *portfolios*.

Imagine an investment adviser faced with the following request:

I am considering the purchase of a portfolio composed of 100 shares of General Motors stock, 50 shares of Control Data, and 50 shares of Polaroid. I plan to hold the portfolio for a year and then sell. How will I do?

Some preliminary discussion about terms would be required. Is performance to be measured before or after taxes? What is the investor's tax bracket? And so on. In any event, the relevant measure is rate of return, treating dividends and capital gains appropriately. The customer simply wants to know what the portfolio's rate of return will actually be.

The adviser will undoubtedly respond, "It will depend." It will depend on conditions in the automobile industry, on the reliability of Control Data's latest computer, on the success of Polaroid's research laboratory, on the course of the United States' involvement in Southeast Asia, on the health of the President of France, etc.

Agreed. But the customer wants a prediction. After some persuasion the adviser may provide one: for example, 10 percent. What does this mean? Probably that he expects the return to be below, above, or equal to 10 percent. The figure does not represent the largest value he thinks possible, nor the smallest. It is, in a sense, a "middling" estimate. Neither overly optimistic nor overly pessimistic, it is a "best guess."

Under pressure, an investment adviser may provide a single number to describe his feelings about a portfolio's prospects. But both he and his client may feel uncomfortable about relying on a single value. The actual rate of return will probably differ from the predicted value. But by how much? Perhaps the adviser is very confident about his prediction of 10 percent, feeling that the actual return is very likely to be between 9 and 11 percent. On the other hand, he may suspect that the actual amount could easily turn out to be anything from 5 to 15 percent.

Some estimate of the "fuzziness" or uncertainty associated with a prediction is needed. One approach is to indicate the extent to which the actual rate of return is likely to diverge from the predicted value.

If the adviser is almost certain that his prediction is correct, he might rate the "fuzziness" at 1 percent; i.e., the actual value is likely to lie between 10 − 1 (= 9) and 10 + 1 (= 11) percent. If he is rather uncertain, he might rate it at 5 percent, implying a likely outcome between 10 − 5 (= 5) and 10 + 5 (= 15) percent.

To conclude this rather fanciful scenario, a portfolio's performance may be forecast using two summary measures:

1. A predicted rate of return: a "best guess" or "middling" estimate;
2. A measure of uncertainty: the extent to which the actual return is likely to diverge from the predicted value.

Some investment advisers prefer to state their predictions very precisely. So do some investors who act as their own advisers. For example,

Rate of return, %	Likelihood
6%	1 chance out of 20
7	2 chances out of 20
8	4 chances out of 20
9	5 chances out of 20
10	3 chances out of 20
11	2 chances out of 20
12	1 chance out of 20
13	1 chance out of 20
14	1 chance out of 20

Figure 2-2 shows this set of predictions graphically.

The likelihood of an outcome is usually stated as a fraction: "2 chances out of 20" is replaced by .10. Such a figure is called a *probability*. A graph such as Fig. 2-2 is called a *probability distribu-*

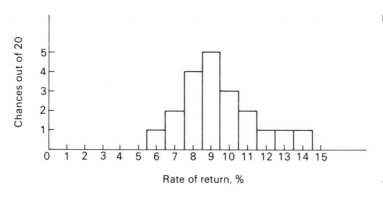

FIGURE 2-2

tion. Unless some possible outcome has been omitted, the probabilities should sum to 1, since it is certain that one of the outcomes will occur.

The notion of a probability distribution can be generalized. Let the number of different possible outcomes be M. The first outcome is O_1; the second is O_2, etc. The probability that the actual outcome will be O_1 is P_1; the probability that it will be O_2 is P_2, etc. In this case,

$M = 9$	
$O_1 = 6\%$	$P_1 = .05$
$O_2 = 7$	$P_2 = .10$
$O_3 = 8$	$P_3 = .20$
$O_4 = 9$	$P_4 = .25$
$O_5 = 10$	$P_5 = .15$
$O_6 = 11$	$P_6 = .10$
$O_7 = 12$	$P_7 = .05$
$O_8 = 13$	$P_8 = .05$
$O_9 = 14$	$P_9 = .05$
	$\overline{1.00}$

It is often desirable to succinctly express the notion of *the sum of the first, second, . . . terms.* A capital Greek sigma is used for the purpose. For example,

$$\sum_{i=1}^{m} P_i \quad \text{means } P_1 + P_2 + P_3 + \cdots + P_M$$

The requirement that probabilities sum to 1 can thus be stated as

$$\sum_{i=1}^{m} P_i = 1$$

A probability distribution involving relatively few possible outcomes will look like the bar chart in Fig. 2-2. The larger the number of outcomes, the smoother the distribution is likely to appear. Figure 2-3 illustrates a case involving a great many outcomes. The number of different alternatives to be considered is a matter of choice. In this example, the outcome *6 percent* is taken to mean $5\frac{1}{2}$ to $6\frac{1}{2}$ *percent*. An alternative approach would define a return between $5\frac{1}{2}$ and 6 percent as one outcome and a return between 6 and $6\frac{1}{2}$ percent as another, assigning specific probabilities to each.

Be it gross or fine, a probability distribution provides a rather detailed prediction. But how can an investor choose the best distribution (portfolio)? Were there but two, five, or twenty alternative distributions (portfolios), he might consider each one explicitly. But typically

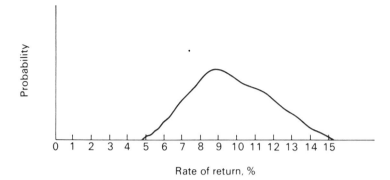

Probability

0 1 2 3 4 5 6 7 8 9 10 11 12 13 14 15

Rate of return, %

FIGURE 2-3

there are millions. If comparisons are to be made, only the essential characteristics of each distribution can be considered.

How many numbers should be used to summarize information such as that in Fig. 2-3? At least two are required if both the location and the "spread" of the distribution are to be described. Two are thus better than one. By the same argument, three are better than two, four better than three, etc. The problem is to determine the point at which the added benefit becomes less than the added cost of comparison and computation. It is a difficult problem. Suffice it to say that at least two numbers are required if uncertainty is to be taken into account adequately.[1] Moreover, computational procedures, formidable enough with two measures, become almost hopelessly complex with more.

Portfolio theory uses two numbers to characterize the probability distribution of a portfolio's rate of return. The particular pair selected can be recommended on the basis of computational convenience as well as familiarity.

The center, "central tendency," or middle of the distribution is measured by its *expected value*. This is simply the weighted average of the possible outcomes, with each outcome weighted by its likelihood:

$$E = \sum_{i=1}^{m} P_i O_i$$

The "spread" of the distribution is measured by its *variance* or the square root of variance, the *standard deviation*. The expected value lies at the center of the distribution. Most possible outcomes are

[1] Consider the implications of an analysis using only a measure of estimated return. Everyone would be advised to invest in one security. This is clearly unacceptable as a decision rule and wildly inconsistent with observed behavior (i.e., diversification).

either above or below it. The deviation of an outcome from the expected value is the difference:

$$O_i - E$$

For purposes of computing the variance, this deviation is squared. The variance is the weighted average of the squared deviations, with each weighted by its likelihood:

$$V = \sum_{i=1}^{m} P_i[(O_i - E)^2]$$

The standard deviation, denoted by a lowercase sigma, is the square root of variance:

$$\sigma = \sqrt{V}$$
$$V = \sigma^2$$

For the example under consideration, the expected value is 9.4 percent, the variance is approximately 4 percent, and the standard deviation is approximately 2 percent.

The manner in which the standard deviation measures the "spread" of a probability distribution is particularly clear if the distribution is *normal*, i.e., follows the familiar bell-shaped curve. In such a case:

The chances are roughly 2 out of 3 that the actual outcome will be between $(E - \sigma)$ and $(E + \sigma)$.

The chances are roughly 95 out of 100 that the actual outcome will be between $(E - 2\sigma)$ and $(E + 2\sigma)$.

These relationships do not hold in general, and there is no reason to expect the distribution of a portfolio's rate of return to be normal. However, the function of the standard deviation is the same in every case—to measure the *likely* divergence of the actual outcome from the expected value.

THE EQUALITY OF THE TWO APPROACHES Two methods for stating predictions have been described. One provides two numbers for each portfolio directly. The other obtains them by performing certain computations using the numbers comprising a probability distribution. The meaning attached to the measures is the same in each case. The *predicted* or *expected* rate of return is a "middling" estimate, a "best guess," or "central tendency." The *uncertainty* or *standard deviation* measures the likely divergence of the actual from the predicted (expected) outcome.

Portfolio theory assumes that an investor is willing to choose among portfolios solely on the basis of these two measures. Formally, it assumes that each pair summarizes a particular probability distribution. In practice such distributions need not be stated explicitly. The theory may be just as useful if predictions are provided directly and intuitively as if they are stated "scientifically."

To make clear the formal meanings, when referring to a portfolio, the two measures will be denoted:

E_p = expected (predicted) rate of return for a portfolio

σ_p = standard deviation (uncertainty) of rate of return for a portfolio

Nothing has been said here about the manner in which predictions are obtained, only the manner in which they are stated.

Precisely what does it mean to assume that the predictions about a portfolio's rate of return can be stated in terms of a probability distribution? Consider the earlier example. Assume that a perfectly balanced roulette wheel with 20 positions is available. Now, paint the number 6 in one position, the number 7 in two positions, the number 8 in four positions, etc. Offer an investor two alternatives: (1) to hold the original portfolio or (2) to spin the wheel, letting the position in which the ball lands determine the outcome. If the investor is indifferent about the choice, he is willing to act as if the distribution summarizes the portfolio's prospects.

Some consider such alternatives qualitatively different. They assert that the behavior of a roulette wheel can be predicted *objectively*, while that of a portfolio can be predicted only on the basis of *subjective* considerations. For the purposes of portfolio theory, such a distinction is not particularly relevant. All predictions are subjective in the sense that an investor is willing to base his decisions on them. A distribution may, of course, be derived entirely from the frequency of past occurrence of each possible outcome. If so, its acceptance requires the (perhaps implicit) assumption that the future will not differ from the past in certain respects. In such a case the investor may be said to have adopted an *objectively derived subjective* distribution. But it is subjective nonetheless.

SUBJECTIVITY AND OBJECTIVITY

The terms *risk* and *uncertainty* are sometimes given different meanings. A situation of *risk* is said to exist if an individual is willing to base his actions on probability distributions.[1] Otherwise there is either *certainty* or *uncertainty*.

RISK AND UNCERTAINTY

[1] Some restrict the term even further, so that it refers only to situations in which the probability distributions are objectively derived.

Portfolio theory involves decision making under conditions of risk. However, the term *uncertainty* is too convenient to abandon. It is used here in its popular sense, to refer to a situation in which the future cannot be predicted with certainty. More to the point, it is used as a synonym for risk.

Portfolio theory cannot directly help those for whom probability distributions are fuzzy. The extent of such "fuzziness" has been termed the *degree of ignorance*. A decision maker has two alternatives. He can act as if some distribution is relevant; portfolio theory can then be utilized directly. Or, he can refuse to do so; the theory is then of no use.

To summarize, portfolio theory assumes that investors are uncertain, but not ignorant.

INVESTORS' PREFERENCES The desirability of a portfolio is expressed by the values of E_p and σ_p. Two portfolios with quite different probability distributions might nonetheless have the same E_p and the same σ_p. The theory assumes that any investor would consider such portfolios equivalent—he would just as soon have one as the other. This may not be strictly true in every instance. As always, abstraction may lead to error. But the chance of error may be small; and the error, if made, may not be serious.

Any portfolio can be represented by a point on a graph such as that shown in Fig. 2-4. Standard deviation of rate of return is plotted on the horizontal axis, and expected rate of return is plotted on the vertical axis.[1]

How does an investor choose among alternative portfolios? The following rules are assumed to apply for any investor:

1. If two portfolios have the same standard deviation of return and different expected returns, the one with the larger expected return is preferred.

2. If two portfolios have the same expected return and different standard deviations of return, the one with the smaller standard deviation is preferred.

3. If one portfolio has a smaller standard deviation of return and a larger expected return than another, it is preferred.

[1] Some reverse the arrangement, plotting σ_p on the vertical axis and E_p on the horizontal. Others use the fourth quadrant, with E_p on the horizontal axis and σ_p measured downward on the vertical axis. The latter procedure gives indifference curves a familiar appearance, i.e., they are similar to the curves of economic theory in which "goods" are plotted on both axes.

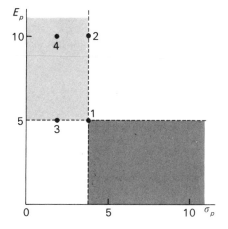

FIGURE 2-4

The rules may be summarized succinctly:

4. E_p is *good*: other things equal, more is preferred to less.
5. σ_p is *bad*: other things equal, less is preferred to more.

Assumption 5 is often termed *risk aversion*. A large body of evidence indicates that almost everyone is a risk averter when making important decisions. Clear counterexamples are rarely found. A day at the horse races provides something besides risk and probable loss, and even the ardent fan seldom takes his entire earnings to the track.

Figure 2-5 shows the distributions of rate of return for four portfolios; their E_p and σ_p values are plotted in Fig. 2-4. Among other things, the assumptions about investor preferences imply that:

Portfolio 2 is preferred to portfolio 1 (rules 1, 4).
Portfolio 3 is preferred to portfolio 1 (rules 2, 5).
Portfolio 4 is preferred to portfolio 1 (rules 3, 4, and 5).

Graphically, the rules assert that for any investor:

Portfolios represented by points lying to the northwest of the point representing a portfolio are better (i.e., preferred).

Portfolios represented by points lying to the southeast of the point representing a portfolio are worse (i.e., the original portfolio is preferred).

Portfolios represented by points lying in the lightly shaded area in Fig. 2-4 are preferred to portfolio 1, but portfolio 1 is preferred to all those represented by points lying in the darkly shaded area.

The major results of portfolio theory follow directly from the assumption that investors like E_p and dislike σ_p. Of course, more can be said about the preferences of any *given* investor. How strong is his dislike for σ_p vis-à-vis E_p? How much uncertainty is he willing to accept to enhance his prospects for a likely rate of return?

The feelings of a particular investor can usefully be represented by a family of *indifference curves.* Consider Fig. 2-6. The lightly shaded

FIGURE 2-5

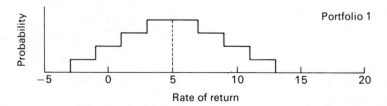

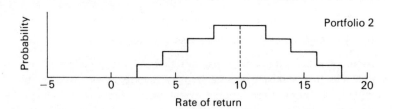

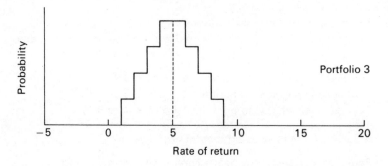

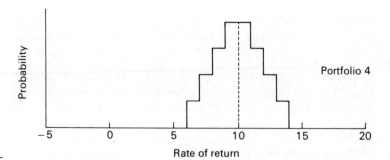

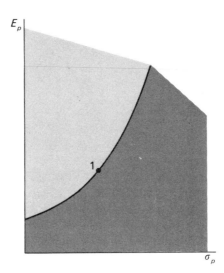

E_p

σ_p **FIGURE 2-6**

area contains all the points representing portfolios that Mr. T prefers to portfolio 1. The darkly shaded area contains all the points representing portfolios that he considers inferior to portfolio 1. The curve that divides the region contains all the points representing portfolios that he considers equivalent to portfolio 1; he has no preferences among them—he is *indifferent* about the choice.

As long as E_p is desired and σ_p is not, every indifference curve will be upward-sloping. Generally, each curve will become steeper as E_p and σ_p increase.

The indifference curve in Fig. 2-6 captures some of Mr. T's feelings. But to represent the manner in which he would make choices in a great variety of circumstances, many more curves are required. Figure 2-7 repeats the curve of Fig. 2-6 as I_1. In addition it shows another curve derived by starting with portfolio 2. Since portfolio 2 is preferred to portfolio 1, every point on I_2 must be preferred to every point on I_1. This follows from the concept of indifference and minimal requirements for rational choice.[1] Indifference curves may not cross.

The number of indifference curves is almost limitless. Only a selected few are shown in graphical examples. It is conventional to label those shown in order of preference. Thus points on I_2 are preferred to those on I_1; points on I_3 are preferred to those on I_2, etc.

A set of indifference curves summarizes the preferences of a given

---

[1] I.e., transitivity of preferences.

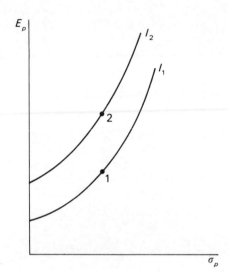

FIGURE 2-7

individual. Figure 2-8 shows two extreme cases. Mr. Fearless is oblivious to risk; Mr. Chicken is oblivious to everything except risk. Figure 2-9 shows more common cases. Mr. Birch is relatively conservative, requiring substantial increases in E_p to induce him to accept greater uncertainty (σ_p). Mr. Flynn is more adventuresome. Neither likes uncertainty, but Mr. Birch dislikes it more (relative to his preference for E_p).

CHOOSING A PORTFOLIO   Consider Mr. Z. His preferences are shown by the indifference curves in Fig. 2-10. Many portfolios are available to him. Their E_p and σ_p values may be shown by a group of points in the figure. Such points will entirely fill the shaded area. Which will Mr. Z prefer? Obviously the one shown by point B.

FIGURE 2-8

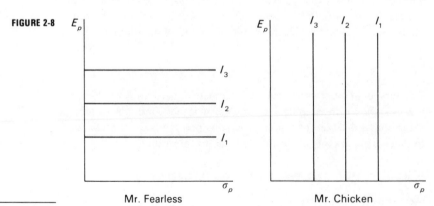

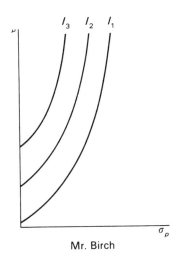

Mr. Birch

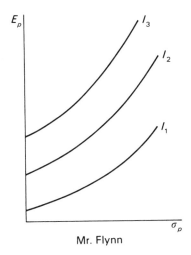

Mr. Flynn

FIGURE 2-9

The decision illustrated in Fig. 2-10 can be broken into three separate phases: security analysis, portfolio analysis, and portfolio selection.

THE THREE PHASES

Security analysis is an art. It requires predictions about the future prospects of securities (stocks, bonds, jobs, wives, etc.). These predictions must take into account both uncertainty and interrelationships. In particular, they must be suitable for use in the next phase.

Portfolio analysis produces predictions about portfolios. The predictions, in the form of E_p and σ_p estimates, are derived entirely from the predictions about securities produced in the first phase. No artistry is required, just computation.

FIGURE 2-10

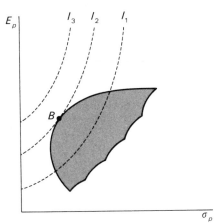

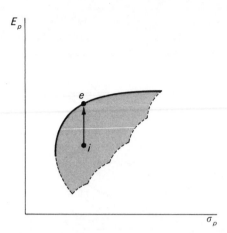

FIGURE 2-11

Portfolio selection is the final phase. Given the available E_p, σ_p combinations, the investor, or someone knowing his preferences,[1] selects the best.

PORTFOLIO ANALYSIS The first phase requires the skills of a seer. The last requires knowledge of a specific investor's preferences. Portfolio analysis requires only technical skills. One person (e.g., the investor) can, of course, do the entire job. But comparative advantage may dictate a division of labor.

Portfolio theory is concerned primarily with the task of portfolio analysis. Given predictions about securities, what E_p, σ_p combinations can be obtained by the proper choice of a portfolio? The answer to such a question will be a large number of points (e.g., several million) entirely filling an area such as the shaded region of Fig. 2-10.

[1] Latané advocates the adoption of a single set of indifference curves to summarize the preferences of all investors. Each curve has the form

$$E_p = \sqrt{k + \sigma_p{}^2}$$

where k is a constant. The investor is assumed to wish to maximize long-run wealth and to regard the selected portfolio as one of a series of consecutive investments. The approach is described in Henry A. Latané and Donald L. Tuttle, Criteria for Portfolio Building, *Journal of Finance*, September, 1967, pp. 359–373.

Markowitz has derived a somewhat more accurate criterion. The preferences of an investor wishing to maximize long-run wealth can better be described by a family of indifference curves of the form

$$k = \ln\left(1 + E_p\right) - \frac{1}{2}\left[\frac{\sigma_p{}^2}{(1 + E_p)^2}\right]$$

where k is a constant and $\ln(1 + E_p)$ denotes the natural logarithm of $1 + E_p$. The general approach is described in Harry Markowitz, "Portfolio Selection: Efficient Diversification of Investments," John Wiley & Sons, Inc., New York, 1959, pp. 116–125.

PORTFOLIO THEORY

The portfolio analyst cannot normally choose the single best portfolio for a given investor. But he can reject certain possibilities. In particular, he can reject any portfolio not represented by a point on the upper border of the region. This is illustrated in Fig. 2-11. Portfolio *e dominates* portfolio *i*; it has a larger E_p and the same σ_p. Portfolio *e* is said to be an *efficient portfolio*; portfolio *i* is inefficient.

The upper border of the region of available E_p, σ_p combinations is called the *efficient frontier*. The portfolios whose E_p, σ_p values are plotted on the frontier comprise the set of efficient portfolios.

The task of portfolio analysis is to find the set of efficient portfolios and the associated efficient frontier.

3.

SECURITIES

A great many different securities can be included in a portfolio, especially if the term *security* is given its broadest meaning. In practice only a subset of all possibilities is considered. The proper selection of a group of potential candidates is not a simple task. If information and computation were free, all possibilities should be considered. Since they are not, benefits must be balanced with costs.

The investor is assumed to select a portfolio including one or more of N securities. The number considered may be small (for example, $N = 10$) or large (for example, $N = 10,000$), depending on the advantages and disadvantages of a limited versus a more complete selection.

Securities are assumed to be perfectly divisible. Within specified limits, any desired amount may be invested in each. The actual rate of return is assumed to be unaffected by the amount invested.

A portfolio can be described by the proportion invested in each security. For example:

Security	Proportion invested
1	.10
2	.50
3	.00
4	.30
5	.00
6	.10
	1.00

The proportion invested in security 1 is denoted X_1; the proportion invested in security 2 is X_2, etc. Since the whole equals the sum of its parts, the proportions must sum to 1:

$$\sum_{i=1}^{N} X_i = 1$$

If $X_i = 0$, the portfolio includes none of security i. A negative value denotes the issuance of a security instead of its ownership;[1] this may or may not be possible, depending on the investor's situation. A value greater than 1 denotes holdings requiring more than the funds the investor has provided; this is possible only if he can obtain the additional money by issuing one or more securities. Often each X_i is restricted to the range from 0 to 1, inclusive.

A portfolio *is* a set of X_i values summing to 1. To be feasible, it must typically meet other restrictions (e.g., all $X_i \geq 0$).

The actual rate of return on a portfolio is the weighted average of the rates of return of its component securities, using the proportions invested as weights. Let R_p denote the actual rate of return on the portfolio and R_i the actual rate of return on security i. Then

$$R_p = \sum_{i=1}^{N} X_i R_i$$

Table 3-1a provides computations for the portfolio described earlier. Its actual rate of return is 18 percent. Note that the formula "works"

[1] If Mr. *A* has promised to pay someone else half his earnings, he has issued a (risky) security.

for all securities. If a security is not included in the portfolio, X_i equals zero; thus $X_i R_i$ equals zero as well, and the total is not affected.

Table 3-1*b* shows the dollar amounts of expenditures and receipts, assuming a total expenditure of $100. Needless to say, the overall return is 18 percent.

TABLE 3-1*a*	Security	Proportion invested	Actual rate of return	
Rates of return	(*i*)	(*X_i*)	(*R_i*)	*X_i R_i*
	1	.10	.10	.010
	2	.50	.20	.100
	3	.00	.05	.000
	4	.30	.15	.045
	5	.00	.07	.000
	6	.10	.25	.025
		1.00		.180

TABLE 3-1*b*	Security	Expenditure	Receipt
Expenditures	(*i*)		
and receipts	1	$ 10.00	$ 11.00
	2	50.00	60.00
	3	0.00	0.00
	4	30.00	34.50
	5	0.00	0.00
	6	10.00	12.50
		$100.00	$118.00

STATING PREDICTIONS ABOUT INDIVIDUAL SECURITIES

If the actual rate of return on each security could be predicted accurately, one could predict the actual rate of return on every possible portfolio. But neither a portfolio's rate of return nor that of every one of its component securities can be predicted with certainty. The problem is to state predictions about securities that can be used to produce predictions about portfolios—in particular, the E_p and σ_p of each possible portfolio.

An estimate of the *predicted* or *expected* rate of return on each security is required. Such an estimate may be provided directly, as a "best guess" or "middling" estimate. Or it may be obtained as the expected value of a (subjective) probability distribution of the security's rate of return.

In addition to the predicted rate of return, some measure of uncertainty—the likely divergence of actual from predicted outcome—is required. This, too, may be provided directly or derived from a probability distribution. Formally, it is considered to be the standard deviation of such a distribution.

To summarize, two measures are used to state the prospects for each of the N securities:

E_i = expected (predicted) rate of return on security i
σ_i = standard deviation (uncertainty) of rate of return on security i

However obtained, such numbers are assumed to summarize a subjective probability distribution for the security's rate of return.

One of the major attributes of portfolio theory is its insistence that interrelationships be taken into account. The relationships among securities' rates of return may be stated in terms of *correlation coefficients, coefficients of determination,* or *covariances.* **INTERRELATIONSHIPS**

The problem is to estimate the extent to which each security's rate of return is related to that of every other. How *related* are the rates of return on securities 1 and 2? 1 and 3? 2 and 3? In practice such estimates are often derived from some relatively simple model of the relationships among securities. But the theory provides for a separate value for each pair.

How related are the returns on securities 1 and 2? Putting it another way, how likely are various pairs of actual values? **CORRELATION**

Figure 3-1a shows an extreme case. Only pairs plotting along the straight line are considered possible. The returns are *perfectly* correlated.

Figure 3-1b shows a more likely case. Any pair plotting within the shaded area is considered possible. Large values of R_1 are likely to be associated with large values of R_2, but the association is not exact. The returns are *correlated*, but not perfectly.

Figure 3-1c shows a case in which the returns are *uncorrelated.*

In Fig. 3-1a and b the correlation is *positive*; a high return on one security is likely to be associated with a high return on the other. Figure 3-1d and e shows situations in which a high return on one is likely to be associated with a low return on the other. The securities in Fig. 3-1d are *negatively correlated.* Those in Fig. 3-1e are *perfectly negatively correlated.*

The relationship between two securities' rates of return can be

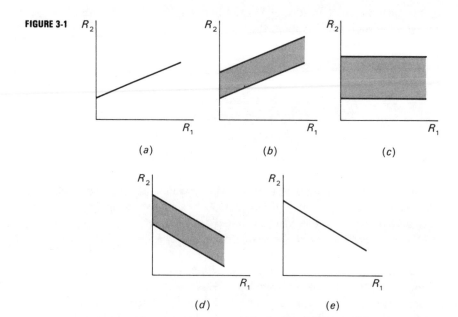

FIGURE 3-1

(a)   (b)   (c)

(d)   (e)

expressed by means of a *correlation coefficient.* A value of +1 indicates perfect positive correlation (Fig. 3-1*a*). A value of 0 indicates no correlation (Fig. 3-1*c*). A value of −1 indicates perfect negative correlation (Fig. 3-1*e*). In a case such as that shown in Fig. 3-1*b*, the value is between 0 and +1; in a case such as that shown in Fig. 3-1*d*, it is between 0 and −1.

The correlation coefficient is represented by the lowercase Greek letter rho (ρ). Subscripts are used to indicate the securities: $\rho_{1,2}$ is the correlation coefficient for R_1 and R_2, and ρ_{jk} is the coefficient for R_j and R_k (the returns on securities j and k).

The numeric value of the correlation coefficient depends on the likelihood of each possible pair of outcomes. A set of predictions of such likelihoods is called a *joint probability distribution.* Table 3-2 provides an illustration. It asserts, for example, that there is a probability of .07 that the return on security j will be between 3 and 4 percent, *and* that the return on security k will be between 2 and 3 percent. The entries must, of course, sum to 1.

Joint probability distributions may be stated in very gross terms or in great detail. Ranges may be wide (3 to 4 percent), or narrow (3.1 to 3.2 percent). Whatever the range, its midpoint is utilized for purposes of computation.

The joint probability distribution contains all the information required to compute the expected value and standard deviation of each security's rate of return. The column sums, shown at the bottom of Table 3-2, provide the probability distribution for R_j. The row sums, shown to the left, provide the probability distribution for R_k.

The divergence of a security's actual return from its expected value can be expressed in standard-deviation units. For security j,

$$d_j = \frac{R_j - E_j}{\sigma_j}$$

If R_j is two standard deviations above the expected value, $d_j = +2$; if it is two standard deviations below, $d_j = -2$; if it equals the expected value, $d_j = 0$.

Consider a possible pair of values for R_j and R_k. Each can be expressed as a normalized deviation from its expected value. The product provides a measure of the overall deviation:

$$d_j d_k = \left(\frac{R_j - E_j}{\sigma_j}\right)\left(\frac{R_k - E_k}{\sigma_k}\right)$$

The correlation coefficient is simply the weighted average of all such products, with the likelihood of each used as its weight:

$$\rho_{jk} = \sum Pr(d_j, d_k)(d_j d_k)$$

TABLE 3-2

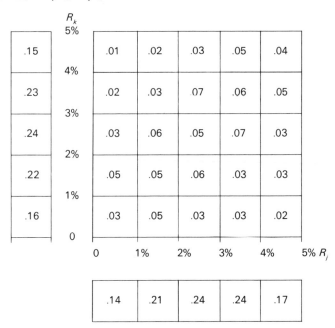

R_k		R_j				
5%						
.15		.01	.02	.03	.05	.04
4%						
.23		.02	.03	.07	.06	.05
3%						
.24		.03	.06	.05	.07	.03
2%						
.22		.05	.05	.06	.03	.03
1%						
.16		.03	.05	.03	.03	.02
0						
		0	1%	2%	3%	4%	5% R_j

.14	.21	.24	.24	.17

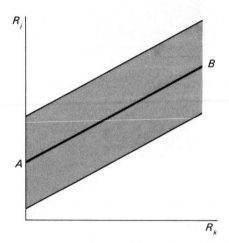

FIGURE 3-2

where $Pr(d_j, d_k)$ = probability of the pair d_j, d_k. Alternatively

$$\rho_{jk} = \sum Pr(R_j, R_k)\left(\frac{R_j - E_j}{\sigma_j}\right)\left(\frac{R_k - E_k}{\sigma_k}\right)$$

where $Pr(R_j, R_k)$ = probability of the pair R_j, R_k.

Correlation does not necessarily imply causation. As the name suggests, it only indicates the extent to which the two outcomes move together (i.e., are *co*related).

It is, of course, possible to derive a correlation coefficient from a joint probability distribution. However, in many cases it may be preferable to directly estimate the "relatedness" of two securities' rates of return without specifying such a distribution. If such an estimate is to be obtained, the correlation coefficient must be given a meaning with some sort of intuitive appeal.

In a case of perfect correlation, there is an exact linear relationship between the returns on two securities. If correlation is less than perfect, no such relationship holds exactly. But it is possible to construct a *best possible* linear relationship. Assume that the line *AB* in Fig. 3-2 best relates R_j to R_k. The uncertainty about the actual value of R_j is measured by σ_j. Some is due to the possibility of an outcome not on line *AB*. But if only values along *AB* were possible, there would still be some uncertainty about R_j, since a number of points along the line are likely. If, however, R_k were known in advance, such uncertainty would be removed. In a sense it can be said to be attributable to the uncertainty about R_k and to the relationship between R_j and R_k. This part of the uncertainty about R_j is denoted $\sigma_{j \leftarrow k}$.

The value of the correlation coefficient indicates the ratio of (1) the uncertainty attributable to the relationship between two securities to (2) the total uncertainty associated with one of them. In this case,

$$\frac{\sigma_{j \leftarrow k}}{\sigma_j}$$

The *coefficient of determination* is the square of the correlation coefficient:

$$D_{jk} = \rho_{jk}^2$$

$$\rho_{jk} = \sqrt{D_{jk}}$$

It indicates the percent of the total *variance* attributable to the relationship between the securities:

$$D_{jk} = \rho_{jk}^2 = \left(\frac{\sigma_{j \leftarrow k}}{\sigma_j}\right)^2 = \frac{\sigma_{j \leftarrow k}^2}{\sigma_j^2}$$

Assume that a security analyst feels that roughly 60 percent of the variation in the return on General Motors stock is attributable to its relationship with General Electric stock (and 40 percent is not).[1]

Then

$$\rho_{jk}^2 = .60$$

$$\rho_{jk} = \sqrt{.60} = \pm .77$$

If the returns are positively correlated, $\rho_{jk} = +.77$; if they are negatively correlated, $\rho_{jk} = -.77$.

The correlation coefficient measures the relationship *between* two securities' rates of return. The order in which they are indicated is irrelevant:

$$\rho_{jk} = \rho_{kj} \quad \text{and} \quad \rho_{jk}^2 = \rho_{kj}^2$$

If 60 percent of the variance associated with the return on GM stock is attributable to its relationship with that on GE stock, then 60 percent of the variance associated with GE stock must be attributable to its relationship with GM stock.[2]

The covariance between two securities' rates of return is the weighted average of the product of the unnormalized deviations: **COVARIANCE**

$$C_{jk} = \sum Pr(R_j, R_k) \ [(R_j - E_j)(R_k - E_k)]$$

---

[1] The proportion of the variance attributable to the relationship plus that not attributable to it will equal 1. Letting $\sigma_{j \dotplus k}$ represent the latter, $\sigma_{j \leftarrow k}^2 + \sigma_{j \dotplus k}^2 = 1$. Note that $\sigma_{j \leftarrow k}$ and $\sigma_{j \dotplus k}$ need *not* sum to 1.

[2] This is true even though the *best* linear relationship will typically depend on the return being "explained." The best line relating R_j to R_k is the one maximizing $\sigma_{j \leftarrow k}$. The best line relating R_k to R_j is the one maximizing $\sigma_{k \leftarrow j}$.

More important for the analysis that follows, the covariance equals the product of the correlation coefficient and the standard deviations of the securities' rates of return:

$$C_{jk} = \rho_{jk}\sigma_j\sigma_k$$

EXPECTED RETURN A portfolio's expected return is the weighted average of the expected returns of its component securities, using the proportions invested as weights:

$$E_p = \sum_{i=1}^{N} X_i E_i$$

Note that all securities (X's) may be included, since $X_i = 0$ if security i is not included in the portfolio.

The actual return on a portfolio is the weighted average of the actual returns on its component securities, using the proportions invested as weights. The formula for E_p indicates that a comparable relationship holds for expected (predicted) returns.

STANDARD DEVIATION OF RETURN The standard deviation of a portfolio's rate of return depends on the standard deviations of return for its component securities, their correlation coefficients, and the proportions invested:

$$\sigma_p^2 = \sum_{i=1}^{N} \sum_{j=1}^{N} X_i X_j \rho_{ij} \sigma_i \sigma_j$$

The formula "works" for all securities since $X_i = 0$ if security i is not included in the portfolio.

This forbidding relationship is not as complicated as it may appear. The double summation indicates that N^2 numbers are to be added together. Each of the numbers is obtained by substituting one of the possible pairs of values for i and j into the expression. For $N = 2$,

$$\sigma_p^2 = X_1 X_1 \rho_{1,1} \sigma_1 \sigma_1 + X_1 X_2 \rho_{1,2} \sigma_1 \sigma_2$$
$$+ X_2 X_1 \rho_{2,1} \sigma_2 \sigma_1 + X_2 X_2 \rho_{2,2} \sigma_2 \sigma_2$$

The first and last terms can be simplified. Clearly, the return on a security is perfectly (positively) correlated with itself. Thus $\rho_{1,1} = 1$, as does $\rho_{2,2}$. The second and fourth terms can be combined, since $\rho_{2,1} = \rho_{1,2}$. The result is

$$\sigma_p^2 = X_1^2 \sigma_1^2 + X_2^2 \sigma_2^2 + 2X_1 X_2 \rho_{1,2} \sigma_1 \sigma_2$$

The product $(\rho_{ij}\sigma_i\sigma_j)$ is C_{ij}—the covariance between i and j. The general formula can thus be written

$$\sigma_p^2 = \sum_{i=1}^{N} \sum_{j=1}^{N} X_i X_j C_{ij}$$

Table 3-3 shows the computations for an example involving three securities. In each part the numeric values are shown on the right and the variables on the left.

Table 3-3a shows the correlation coefficients and standard deviations for the securities. Note that there are 1s along the diagonal in the table of correlation coefficients. Note also that each entry in the bottom-left triangle equals the corresponding entry in the upper-right triangle. This must, of course, be true for any table of correlation coefficients.

Table 3-3b shows the covariances. Each entry in the table is the product of (1) the correlation coefficient in the corresponding position in the previous table, (2) the standard deviation beside its row, and (3) the standard deviation above its column.

Table 3-3b also shows the proportion invested in each of the three securities. Fifty percent of the portfolio is invested in security 1, 30 percent in security 2, and 20 percent in security 3.

Table 3-3c shows the results of a second set of computations. Each entry in the table is the product of (1) the covariance in the corresponding position in the previous table, (2) the X value beside its

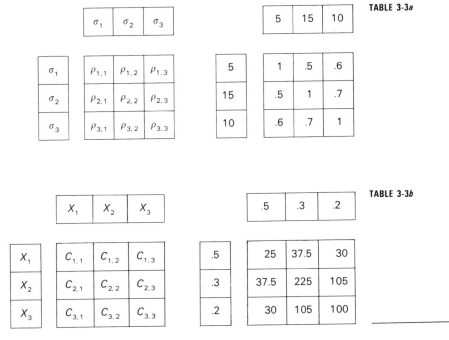

TABLE 3-3a

	σ_1	σ_2	σ_3
	5	15	10

	σ_1	σ_2	σ_3				
σ_1	$\rho_{1,1}$	$\rho_{1,2}$	$\rho_{1,3}$	5	1	.5	.6
σ_2	$\rho_{2,1}$	$\rho_{2,2}$	$\rho_{2,3}$	15	.5	1	.7
σ_3	$\rho_{3,1}$	$\rho_{3,2}$	$\rho_{3,3}$	10	.6	.7	1

TABLE 3-3b

	X_1	X_2	X_3
	.5	.3	.2

	X_1	X_2	X_3				
X_1	$C_{1,1}$	$C_{1,2}$	$C_{1,3}$	.5	25	37.5	30
X_2	$C_{2,1}$	$C_{2,2}$	$C_{2,3}$	.3	37.5	225	105
X_3	$C_{3,1}$	$C_{3,2}$	$C_{3,3}$	.2	30	105	100

TABLE 3-3c

$X_1X_1C_{1.1}$	$X_1X_2C_{1.2}$	$X_1X_3C_{1.3}$	6.25	5.625	3.0
$X_2X_1C_{2.1}$	$X_2X_2C_{2.2}$	$X_2X_3C_{2.3}$	5.625	20.25	6.3
$X_3X_1C_{3.1}$	$X_3X_2C_{3.2}$	$X_3X_3C_{3.3}$	3.0	6.3	4.0

row, and (3) the X value above its column. The sum of the numbers in Table 3-3c is 60.35. Thus

$$\sigma_p^2 = 60.35 \quad \text{and} \quad \sigma_p = \sqrt{60.35} = 7.76$$

As this simple example suggests, it is not a trivial matter to compute the standard deviation of return for a portfolio, especially one containing many securities. To find the set of efficient portfolios by a process of enumeration and elimination would require computing the standard deviations of return (and expected returns) for a vast number of portfolios. This is obviously impossible. Some procedure must be invoked to find the set of efficient portfolios directly.

4.

EFFICIENT PORTFOLIOS

Portfolios are composed of securities. To understand portfolios, one must understand the effects of combining securities.

Consider the choice of a portfolio involving at most two securities, neither of which provides a certain return. For concreteness, assume that security 1 has a lower expected return and standard deviation of return than security 2.

$$N = 2 \qquad E_1 < E_2 \qquad 0 < \sigma_1 < \sigma_2$$

A portfolio is characterized by the proportions invested in the two securities. The values must, of course, sum to 1 :

$$X_1 + X_2 = 1$$

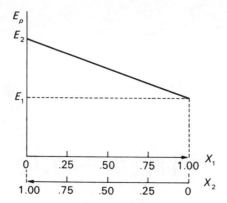

FIGURE 4-1

The expected return depends on the proportions invested in various securities. In this case,

$$E_p = X_1 E_1 + X_2 E_2$$

Figure 4-1 shows the relationship between E_p (plotted on the vertical axis) and X_1 or X_2 (plotted on the horizontal axis). The choice of a portfolio can be considered the selection of a value for X_1, since $X_2 = 1 - X_1$. Alternatively, it can be considered the selection of a value for X_2, since $X_1 = 1 - X_2$. Only positive or zero values are considered in this case; the investor is assumed to be unable to issue securities.

Expected return is *linearly* related to X_1 (or X_2). This must be the case whatever the predictions about the securities' expected returns.

Standard deviation of return is also related to the portfolio's composition. In this case,

$$\sigma_p^2 = X_1^2 \sigma_1^2 + X_2^2 \sigma_2^2 + 2X_1 X_2 \rho_{1,2} \sigma_1 \sigma_2$$

Obviously

$$\sigma_p = \sigma_1 \qquad \text{if } X_1 = 1 \text{ and } X_2 = 0$$
$$\sigma_p = \sigma_2 \qquad \text{if } X_1 = 0 \text{ and } X_2 = 1$$

In these special cases in which the portfolio is composed entirely of one security, correlation is of no relevance. In general, however, σ_p will depend on the extent to which the two securities' rates of return are correlated.

Consider the situation in which the rates of return are perfectly correlated. Since $\rho_{1,2}$ equals $+1$,

$$\sigma_p^2 = X_1^2 \sigma_1^2 + X_2^2 \sigma_2^2 + 2X_1 X_2 \sigma_1 \sigma_2$$

Factoring the right-hand expression,

$$\sigma_p^2 = (X_1\sigma_1 + X_2\sigma_2)^2$$

Thus

$$\sigma_p = X_1\sigma_1 + X_2\sigma_2$$

Line AB in Fig. 4-2a shows the relationship between σ_p (plotted on the vertical axis) and X_1 or X_2 (plotted on the horizontal axis) when $\rho_{1,2} = +1$. In this case, but *only* in this case, σ_p is linearly related to X_1 (or X_2).

What about cases in which the returns are not perfectly correlated? Rewriting the general formula slightly,

$$\sigma_p^2 = X_1^2\sigma_1^2 + X_2^2\sigma_2^2 + (2X_1X_2\sigma_1\sigma_2)\rho_{1,2}$$

The parenthesized expression will be positive if:

1. Some of each security is held ($X_1 > 0$ and $X_2 > 0$).
2. Neither security promises a certain return ($\sigma_1 > 0$ and $\sigma_2 > 0$).

FIGURE 4-2

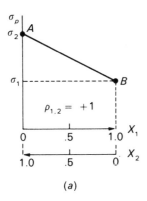

(a)

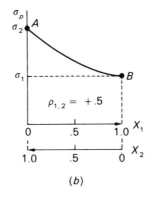

(b)

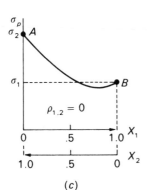

(c)

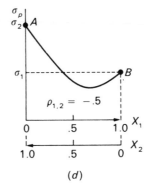

(d)

EFFICIENT PORTFOLIOS

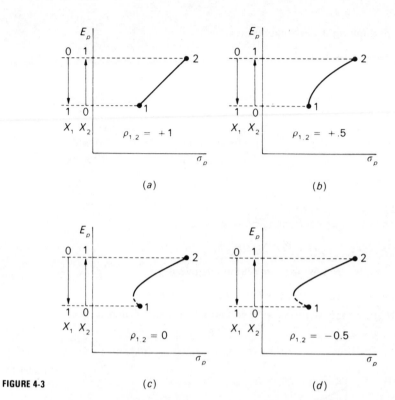

FIGURE 4-3

(a)   (b)   (c)   (d)

Under these conditions, for a given portfolio, the smaller $\rho_{1,2}$, the smaller will be σ_p^2, and thus the smaller $\rho_{1,2}$, the smaller will be σ_p.

Figure 4-2b to d shows the relationship between σ_p and X_1 or X_2 for cases in which $\rho_{1,2} = +.5$, 0, and $-.5$. As Fig. 4-2c and d illustrates, if the securities' rates of return are not too highly correlated,[1] some combinations (portfolios) will provide a smaller standard deviation of return than either security taken alone. In such situations, diversification is particularly useful. However, it is likely to be beneficial in any case. And the smaller the correlation, the greater the potential benefit.

Figure 4-3a to d summarizes the relationships shown in Figs. 4-1 and 4-2 for the four cases in which $\rho_{1,2} = +1$, $+.5$, 0, and $-.5$. The curve in each diagram shows the E_p, σ_p values associated with possible combinations of the two securities. In Fig. 4-3a and b, all combinations are efficient. In Fig. 4-3c and d, only those with

[1] The correlation coefficient must be less than the ratio of the smaller standard deviation to the larger. In this case,

$$\rho_{1,2} < \frac{\sigma_1}{\sigma_2} = .5$$

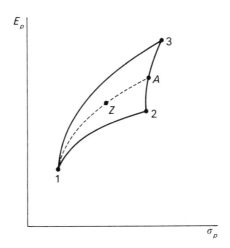

FIGURE 4-4

E_p, σ_p values plotting on the solid portion of the curve are efficient. The composition of the portfolio corresponding to each point can be determined from its expected return. Axes indicating the values of X_1 and X_2 associated with each value of E_p have been included in the diagrams to illustrate the relationship.

Figure 4-4 extends the analysis to a case involving three securities. Portfolios composed entirely of securities 1 and 2 provide E_p, σ_p combinations lying on curve 1, 2. Portfolios composed entirely of securities 2 and 3 provide combinations lying on curve 2, 3. Those composed entirely of securities 1 and 3 provide combinations lying on curve 1, 3.

Consider the portfolio made up of equal parts of securities 2 and 3, represented by point A in Fig. 4-4. Now assume that some entrepreneur sets up a mutual fund, selling shares and investing the money equally in securities 2 and 3. Future returns will be distributed to the fund's shareholders (with no deduction for management fees). Obviously a share in the fund is equivalent to holding equal amounts of securities 2 and 3. Equally obvious, the investor can act as his own mutual fund.[1] Point A can thus be considered a security for purposes of the analysis.

It is, of course, possible to combine "security" A with any other. For example, consider a portfolio composed of equal parts of A and security 1 :

$$X_A = .5$$
$$X_1 = .5$$

[1] Although transaction costs may make it inadvisable. At this stage, such costs are not included in the analysis.

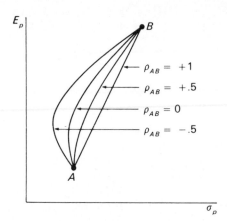

$\rho_{AB} = +1$

$\rho_{AB} = +.5$

$\rho_{AB} = 0$

$\rho_{AB} = -.5$

FIGURE 4-5

Or in terms of the original securities,

$$X_1 = .5$$
$$X_2 = .25$$
$$X_3 = .25$$

What E_p, σ_p combination will such a portfolio provide? The answer depends on the correlation between the return on A and that on security 1. If the returns are perfectly correlated, the combination will lie along a straight line connecting points A and 1. If not, it will lie above and to the left of such a line (for example, on the dashed curve in Fig. 4-4).

Any portfolio may be treated as a security. Assume that points A and B in Fig. 4-5 represent the E_p, σ_p values associated with two portfolios. The E_p, σ_p values for combinations of A and B will lie along some curve connecting the two points. If the returns on the two portfolios are perfectly correlated, the curve will be a straight line. Otherwise it will lie above and to the left of the straight line connecting the points. Everything said earlier about combining two securities is applicable.

What does it mean to say that a portfolio is a combination of two others? Assume that C is such a portfolio, described by

X_A—the proportion invested in portfolio A
X_B—the proportion invested in portfolio B

with $X_A + X_B = 1$.

Let X_i^A be the proportion of portfolio A invested in security i, X_i^B the proportion of portfolio B invested in security i, and X_i^C the proportion of portfolio C invested in security i. Needless to say,

$$\sum_{i=1}^{N} X_i^A = 1$$

$$\sum_{i=1}^{N} X_i^B = 1$$

$$\sum_{i=1}^{N} X_i^C = 1$$

The proportion of portfolio C invested in any security will be a weighted average of the proportions of portfolios A and B invested in the security:

$$X_i^C = X_A X_i^A + X_B X_i^B$$

Table 4-1 provides an example in which $N = 4$, $X_A = .2$, and $X_B = .8$; Fig. 4-6 shows the composition of every combination of the two portfolios. The figure indicates the reason for calling any portfolio obtained in this manner a *linear* combination of two other portfolios.

TABLE 4.1a

Security (i)	Proportion of portfolio A (X_i^A)	Proportion of portfolio B (X_i^B)	Proportion of portfolio C† (X_i^C)
1	0	.3	.24
2	.5	.2	.26
3	.2	.4	.36
4	.3	.1	.14
	1.00	1.00	1.00

† $X_A = .2$, $X_B = .8$

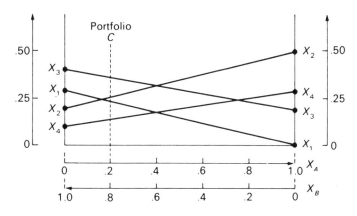

FIGURE 4-6

THE E_p, σ_p REGION   Any security can be described by a point in an E_p, σ_p diagram. So can any portfolio. Depending on the constraints placed on the investor, only certain portfolios will be *feasible* (legal, attainable). In general, any combination of two feasible portfolios will also be feasible. If so, the points representing feasible portfolios will entirely fill some region in the E_p, σ_p diagram. And the region will be convex along its upper (efficient) border.

Figure 4-4 can be used to show why the region will be entirely filled with points. Assume points 1, 2, and 3 represent three feasible portfolios. Curves 1,2, 2,3, and 1,3 indicate E_p, σ_p combinations obtainable by combining portfolios 1 and 2, 2 and 3, and 1 and 3, respectively. Consider an arbitrary point, such as Z, inside the region. Some combination of the three portfolios will have the desired values of E_p and σ_p. In this case it may be viewed as a combination of portfolios 1 and A, the latter being itself a combination of portfolios 2 and 3.

The E_p, σ_p region will be convex along its efficient border. What does this mean? Rather vaguely, the region may bulge out, but it will never cave in along this border. More formally,

Let V and W be any two points on the efficient E_p, σ_p border. All points on the border between V and W will lie on or above a straight line connecting the two points.

Figure 4-7*a* and *b* shows possible cases. Figure 4-7*c* shows an impossible case.

Why is a situation such as that shown in Fig. 4-7*c* impossible? Because a portfolio made by combining portfolios V and W will have values of E_p and σ_p plotting either along line VW (in the case of perfect correlation) or above it. In any event, such a point will dominate one or more of those along the supposedly efficient border bulging downward from line VW. Thus it cannot possibly be the *true* efficient border.

The appearance of the feasible region will depend on the constraints placed upon the investor. Figure 4-8*a* to *d* shows four major cases.[1] The efficient border in each diagram is the dark portion of the boundary.

[1] Figure 4-8*a* and *b* represents cases in which no security promises a certain return; Fig. 4-8*c* and *d* includes such a security. In the cases shown in Fig. 4-8*b* and *c*, the investor may not issue securities; in the other two (Fig. 4-8*a* and *d*), he may.

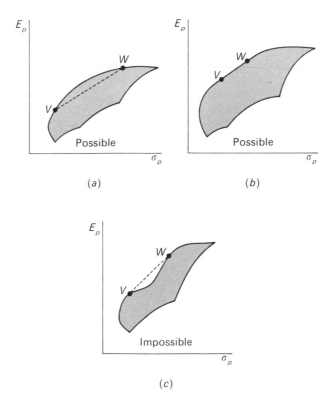

(a)

(b)

(c)

FIGURE 4-7

As Fig. 4-8c and d shows, the efficient E_p, σ_p border may be linear. Note, however, that:

If two portfolios plot along a linear segment of the efficient E_p, σ_p border, their returns must be perfectly correlated.

Why? Because otherwise, combinations of the two portfolios would give E_p, σ_p values lying above the line connecting their points. But that line is supposed to be the efficient border. Thus the two portfolios' returns must be perfectly correlated.

For purposes of decision making, uncertainty is expressed in terms of the standard deviation of return. For purposes of computation, the square of the standard deviation, the variance of return, is often more convenient.

THE E_p, V_p REGION

The characteristics of a portfolio may be shown by a point in an E_p, σ_p diagram. Points representing all feasible portfolios will fill a region such as that shown in Fig. 4-9a. Portfolios plotting on the upper border are efficient; all others are inefficient.

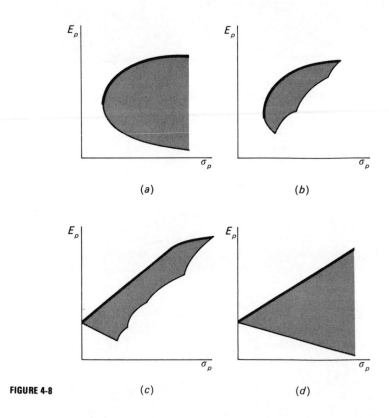

FIGURE 4-8   (c)   (d)

An alternative representation is shown in Fig. 4-9b. Each portfolio is represented by a point indicating its expected return (E_p) and *variance* of return ($V_p = \sigma_p^2$). The portfolios plot as a series of points filling a feasible E_p, V_p region. Those plotting on its upper border are efficient; all others are inefficient.

Portfolios plotting on the efficient E_p, V_p border plot also on the efficient E_p, σ_p border, and vice versa. Consider all portfolios with the same standard deviation of return (say σ_p^*). To be efficient in an E_p, σ_p analysis, a member of this group must have the largest value of E_p. Now consider all portfolios with a variance of $(\sigma_p^*)^2$. To be efficient in an E_p, V_p analysis, a member of this group must have the largest value of E_p. But the two groups are the same. Therefore the efficient portfolio (or portfolios, in case of ties), will be the same.

Putting it another way, in a group of portfolios with the same value of E_p, efficiency dictates the selection of a portfolio with the smallest possible value of σ_p. But such a portfolio will also have the smallest possible value of $\sigma_p^2(V_p)$. Either criterion may be used; the result will be the same.

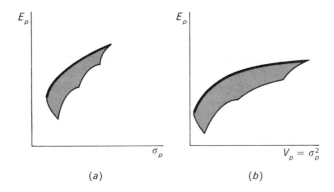

(a) (b) FIGURE 4-9

The goal is to obtain the set of efficient portfolios. It is usually easier to do this by finding the efficient border of the E_p, V_p region. It is a simple matter to convert the efficient E_p, V_p border to the efficient E_p, σ_p border, or vice versa.

The E_p, V_p border will have more curvature since $V_p = \sigma_p^2$. Figure 4-9a and b provides one example, Fig. 4-10a and b another. As the latter figure indicates, even if the E_p, σ_p border is linear, the E_p, V_p border will increase at a decreasing rate:

Let Y and Z be any two points on the efficient E_p, V_p border. All points on the border between Y and Z will lie above a straight line connecting the two points.

The techniques of portfolio analysis are designed to find the efficient border of the E_p, V_p region and the portfolios that plot along it.

Portfolio analysis requires the solution of an *optimization* problem. **THE OBJECTIVE** Such a problem usually includes:

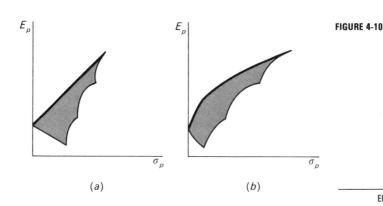

FIGURE 4-10

(a) (b)

1. One or more *decision variables*;
2. One or more *constraints*;
3. An *objective* to be maximized or minimized.

The decision variables are the proportions invested in the various securities. A value must be assigned to X_1 another to X_2, . . . , etc. There are N securities, thus there are N different decision variables.

Various constraints may be placed on the assignment of values to the X's. The values must always sum to 1. In some cases, negative values may not be allowed. In others, there may be an upper limit on the amount invested in a given security or group of securities. The appropriate set of constraints depends on the investor's situation.

The objective for any given investor is to select the best portfolio. In other words, to find the feasible portfolio lying on the most desirable indifference curve.

Figure 4-11*a* and *b* shows the preferences of Mr. *A*. He is artificial; no real person is likely to have his tastes. But although he may not exist, it is extremely convenient to have invented him.

Mr. *A*'s most important attribute is shown in Fig. 4-11*a*. His indifference curves drawn in an E_p, V_p diagram are parallel to one another and linear. As usual, the higher a curve (line), the more desirable the situations lying along it.

Mr. *A*'s problem is to find the feasible E_p, V_p combination lying on the best attainable indifference curve (line). In Fig. 4-12*a*, it is point *B*. The solution will have two important characteristics:

FIGURE 4-11

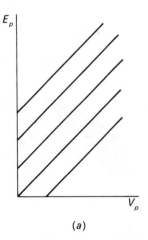

(*a*)

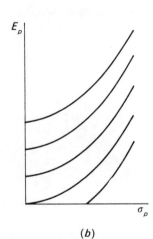

(*b*)

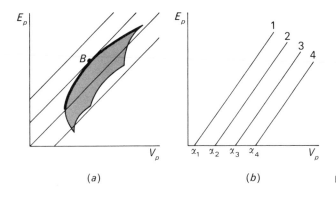

(a) (b) **FIGURE 4-12**

1. The selected portfolio will be efficient.
2. At the selected point, the border will be tangent to the indifference curve (line). In other words, the indifference curve (line) will touch the region but not enter it.

The equation of any one of Mr. A's indifference curves (lines) can be written

$$V_p = \alpha + \lambda E_p$$

Figure 4-12b shows four selected indifference curves (lines). Their equations are:

Curve 4 : $V_p = \alpha_4 + \lambda E_p$
Curve 3 : $V_p = \alpha_3 + \lambda E_p$
Curve 2 : $V_p = \alpha_2 + \lambda E_p$
Curve 1 : $V_p = \alpha_1 + \lambda E_p$

The value of λ (lambda) indicates the steepness of the line; it is the same for every curve (line). The value of α (alpha) indicates the horizontal intercept; it differs from line to line.

Which indifference curve (line) in Fig. 4-12b is the best? The highest; or in other words, the farthest to the left (the one with the smallest horizontal intercept). Mr. A's objective is to minimize α. Rewriting the equation, for any indifference curve (line)

$$\alpha = -\lambda E_p + V_p$$

The objective is thus to

minimize $-\lambda E_p + V_p$

where $E_p = \sum_{i=1}^{N} X_i E_i$

and $V_p = \sum_{i=1}^{N} \sum_{j=1}^{N} X_i X_j C_{ij}$

Mr. A's problem in its entirety is thus:

(decision variables)   Select $X_1, X_2, \ldots, X_N$

(objective)   to minimize $- \lambda \sum_{i=1}^{N} X_i E_i + \sum_{i=1}^{N} \sum_{j=1}^{N} X_i X_j C_{ij}$

(constraints)   subject to $\sum_{i=1}^{N} X_i = 1$

and any other relevant constraints.

FINDING THE SET OF EFFICIENT PORTFOLIOS Mr. A's attitude regarding expected return vis-à-vis variance of return is described by the value of λ. The larger the value, the greater his interest in E_p relative to V_p. Figure 4-13a to d illustrates this relationship. In Fig. 4-13a, λ is sufficiently large to make V_p unimportant. Mr. A wishes simply to maximize E_p, that is, minimize $-E_p$. Figure 4-13d illustrates the other extreme: $\lambda = 0$; the investor

FIGURE 4-13

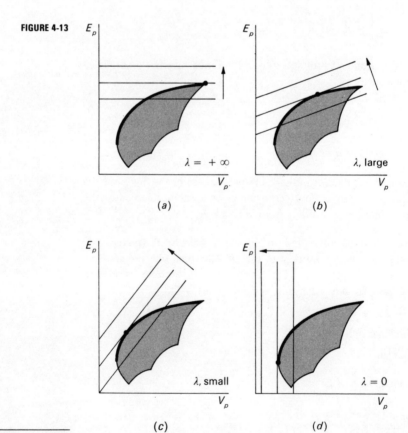

(a) $\lambda = +\infty$

(b) λ, large

(c) λ, small

(d) $\lambda = 0$

wishes only to minimize V_p. The value of λ indicates the importance to be accorded E_p relative to V_p.

For any given value of λ, the solution to Mr. A's problem will provide an efficient portfolio. And at the selected point, one of his indifference curves (lines) will be tangent to the E_p, V_p region. Two characteristics of the efficient border of the region are particularly relevant:

1. Its slope differs at every point.
2. It is vertical at the bottom, becoming progressively flatter until the top is reached.

Both follow from the convexity of the efficient E_p, σ_p border and the relationship between V_p and σ_p.

Now assume that Mr. A's problem has been solved over and over again for every relevant value of λ. Obviously, every efficient portfolio will be obtained.[1] To find the entire set of efficient portfolios,

minimize $-\lambda E_p + V_p$

for all possible values of $\lambda \geqq 0$.

This is the portfolio-analysis problem. Mr. A has served his purpose and may now be discarded.

From a computational standpoint, portfolio-analysis problems differ primarily in their constraints. Only one is essential: the proportions invested must sum to 1. A problem involving no further constraints may be termed a *basic* problem:

THE BASIC PROBLEM

$$\text{minimize } -\lambda \left(\sum_{i=1}^{N} X_i E_i \right) + \left(\sum_{i=1}^{N} \sum_{j=1}^{N} X_i X_j C_{ij} \right)$$

for all possible values of $\lambda \geq 0$,

$$\text{subject to } \sum_{i=1}^{N} X_i = 1$$

Such a problem can be solved relatively easily. One approach would assign a particular numeric value to λ, then solve the problem, obtaining a specific set of numeric values for the X_i's. However, this would provide only one efficient portfolio; the entire procedure would have to be repeated over and over. To avoid this, λ should be

---

[1] The border may have *kinks*. Thus the same point (and thus efficient portfolio) may be obtained for several values of λ. This causes no complications. At least one positive value of λ will lead to the selection of each efficient portfolio.

included explicitly in the calculations. The solution will then be a series of equations of the form

$$X_1 = K_1 + k_1\lambda$$
$$X_2 = K_2 + k_2\lambda$$
$$\vdots$$
$$X_N = K_N + k_N\lambda$$

where $K_1, \ldots, K_N$ and $k_1, \ldots, k_N$ are constants.

Any particular efficient portfolio can be found by substituting the appropriate value of λ into each equation. For $\lambda = 10$,

$$X_1 = K_1 + 10k_1$$
$$X_2 = K_2 + 10k_2$$
$$\vdots$$
$$X_N = K_N + 10k_N$$

For $\lambda = 0$,

$$X_1 = K_1$$
$$X_2 = K_2$$
$$\vdots$$
$$X_N = K_N$$

The K_i's thus indicate the composition of the minimum-variance portfolio.[1]

The result for a case involving three securities is shown in Fig. 4-14. The efficient portfolio corresponding to any given value of λ is indicated by the heights of the lines representing the various securities.

In the absence of additional constraints, every value of λ will give a different efficient portfolio. Consider portfolios C and R, obtained when $\lambda = 0$ and $\lambda = \lambda^*$ (some very large value). As Fig. 4-14 shows, any efficient portfolio corresponding to an intermediate value of λ can be regarded as a combination of portfolios C and R since each X_i is linearly related to λ.

The relationship between the expected return of an efficient portfolio and the value of λ which generates the portfolio will also be

[1] The sum of the K_i's must thus be 1. Since the X_i's must sum to 1 for any value of λ, the sum of the k_i's must be 0.

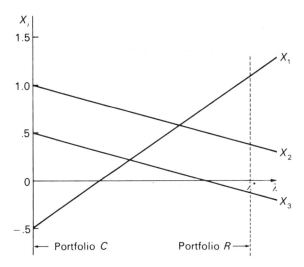

FIGURE 4-14

Portfolio C ◄—   Portfolio R —►

linear. It can be found by substituting the equations obtained from the solution:

$$E_p = \sum_{i=1}^{N} X_i E_i$$

$$= \sum_{i=1}^{N} (K_i + k_i \lambda) E_i$$

$$= \left(\sum_{i=1}^{N} K_i E_i \right) + \left(\sum_{i=1}^{N} k_i E_i \right) \lambda$$

Each of the parenthesized sums is simply a number. The first is the expected return of the minimum-variance portfolio. The second indicates the additional expected return per unit of λ.

If at least two securities have different expected returns, the value of E_p will continue to increase as λ increases. There will be no limit to the potential expected return. Why? Because the investor is allowed to issue one type of security without limit, using the proceeds to purchase a security with a greater expected return. For example:

Investor's capital: $100

Issue $1,000 worth of securities with an expected return of 5 percent.

Purchase $1,100 worth of securities with an expected return of 6 percent.

Expected receipts: 106% of $1,100 = $1,166
Expected outlays : 105% of $1,000 = 1,050
                                   $ 116

$$\text{Expected rate of return on capital}: \frac{\$116 - 100}{100} = 16\%$$

By issuing \$2,000 worth of securities, an expected return of 26 percent could be obtained. The greater the amount issued, the greater the expected return and the greater the risk. In the real world, one can rarely obtain pleasure without incurring pain.

The relationship between the variance of return on an efficient portfolio and the value of λ which generates the portfolio will be quadratic.[1] It can also be found by substituting the equations obtained from the solution:

$$V_p = \sum_{i=1}^{N} \sum_{j=1}^{N} X_i X_j C_{ij}$$

$$= \sum_{i=1}^{N} \sum_{j=1}^{N} (K_i + k_i \lambda)(K_j + k_j \lambda) C_{ij}$$

$$= \left(\sum_{i=1}^{N} \sum_{j=1}^{N} K_i K_j C_{ij} \right) + \left(\sum_{i=1}^{N} \sum_{j=1}^{N} K_i k_j C_{ij} + k_i K_j C_{ij} \right) \lambda$$

$$+ \left(\sum_{i=1}^{N} \sum_{j=1}^{N} k_i k_j C_{ij} \right) \lambda^2$$

Each of the parenthesized sums will simply be a number. The first is the variance of the minimum-variance portfolio. The others indicate the manner in which V_p increases with λ.

The equation of the efficient border will show V_p to be a quadratic function of E_p. It can be obtained by combining the formulas for E_p and V_p, eliminating λ.

It is not overly difficult to find the K_i and k_i values for a particular problem. However, an electronic computer is useful if very many securities are involved.

Section B of the Supplement describes the method used to solve such a problem and shows why it works. Section A provides the necessary background.

CONSTRAINTS Most portfolio-analysis problems are too complicated to fit the specifications of the *basic* problem. The values that may be assigned to the decision variables are typically constrained in various ways. Such constraints may take the form of equalities or inequalities. Traditionally, all terms involving decision variables are placed on the left-hand side, leaving only a constant on the right-hand side. Standard solution techniques require that the expression on the left-

---
[1] I.e., it will include a λ^2 term.

hand side be a linear function of the decision variables. The following functions would thus be allowed:

$$X_5 \quad \text{and} \quad .03X_5 + .92X_8 - .10X_{12}$$

The following would not:

$$X_5^2 \quad \text{and} \quad 3X_1X_2 - X_7$$

Equality constraints state that the left-hand side must equal the right-hand side. The required constraint is of this type:

$$X_1 + X_2 + \cdots + X_N = 1$$

An investor determined to place exactly 10 percent of his funds in security 12 would add

$$X_{12} = .10$$

One wishing to hold twice as much of security 11 as security 3 would add

$$2X_3 - X_{11} = 0$$

A *strict inequality* constraint requires either (1) that the left-hand side be strictly greater than the right-hand side or (2) that it be strictly less than the right-hand side. For example,

$$X_5 + X_7 > .12$$
$$X_6 + X_8 < .08$$

A *weak inequality* allows either of two possibilities. For example,

$$X_5 \leq .12$$

means that X_5 must be either less than .12 or equal to .12. Strict inequality constraints are never used in portfolio analysis. Weak ones often are. From a computational standpoint, the difference is substantial. The meaning of a strict inequality is uncertain while that of a weak inequality is precise. For example, instead of

$$X_5 + X_7 > .12$$

say (precisely) $X_5 + X_7 \geq .1200001$

Adding equality constraints to the basic problem does not significantly affect the nature of the solution. Each X_i will be a linear function of λ, and V_p will be a quadratic function of E_p along the efficient border. Usually, the more constrained the problem, the smaller the feasible region and the lower its efficient border. Adding equality constraints requires more computation and changes the problem's solution. But no qualitative changes result.

This is not the case if inequality constraints are added. A different method must be employed to solve the problem, and the solution will have different characteristics.

THE STANDARD PROBLEM   The inclusion of one or more inequality constraints makes portfolio analysis a *mathematical programming problem*. A common example arises when the investor is not able to issue securities. Formally, this involves the addition of N inequality constraints:

$$X_1 \geq 0$$
$$X_2 \geq 0$$
$$\vdots$$
$$X_N \geq 0$$

This is a special case of a more general formulation, termed the *standard problem*. It has the form:

$$\text{Minimize } -\lambda \left(\sum_{i=1}^{N} X_i E_i \right) + \left(\sum_{i=1}^{N} \sum_{j=1}^{N} X_i X_j C_{ij} \right)$$

for all possible values of $\lambda \geq 0$,

$$\text{subject to } \sum_{i=1}^{N} X_i = 1$$

plus any other linear *equality* constraints,

$$\text{plus } L_1 \leq X_1 \leq U_1$$
$$L_2 \leq X_2 \leq U_2$$
$$\vdots$$
$$L_N \leq X_N \leq U_N$$

U_i is the *upper bound* for the proportion invested in security i; L_i is the *lower bound*. For example, if any amount of security 5 may be held, but none may be issued,

$$L_5 = 0$$
$$U_5 = +\infty \qquad \text{(or some suitably large number)}$$

If from 5 to 10 percent must be invested in security 8,

$$L_8 = .05$$
$$U_8 = .10$$

If exactly 12 percent must be invested in security 23,

$$L_{23} = .12$$
$$U_{23} = .12$$

By employing "phoney" securities, a great many cases may be stated as standard problems.

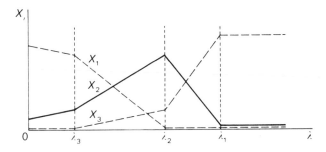

FIGURE 4-15

Section C of the Supplement describes a method for solving a standard problem.

Figure 4-15 shows the results for a case involving three securities.[1] It differs from comparable figures obtained when analyzing a basic problem. First, there may be ranges of values of λ over which the composition is unchanged. In Fig. 4-15, point λ_1, or any point to its right, shows the composition of the portfolio with the greatest possible expected return. Second, and even more important, the values of the X_i's do not vary linearly with λ throughout the entire range of values. The relationships are linear over certain ranges. But there are *corners*.

Consider the manner in which X_2 varies as λ is reduced. For values greater than λ_1, $X_2 = 0$. At λ_1, there is a corner. As λ is reduced below λ_1, X_2 increases linearly until $\lambda = \lambda_2$. Further reductions in λ lead to decreases in X_2. These proceed at a constant and rather rapid rate until $\lambda = \lambda_3$. Thereafter, X_2 decreases at a slower rate as λ is reduced.

At points λ_1, λ_2, and λ_3, one or more of the relationships has a corner. The portfolios represented by such points are called *corner portfolios*. For completeness, the portfolio obtained when $\lambda = 0$ is also considered a corner portfolio. Figure 4-16 shows the E_p, V_p region for this example and the location of each of the four corner portfolios. As the figure shows, the border of the region need not have a corner (kink) at the point representing a corner portfolio. In general it will be relatively smooth throughout.[2]

Constraints of any type tend to reduce the size of the region of feasible E_p, V_p values. Upper and lower bounds on holdings are likely to lead to upper and lower bounds on the attainable levels of E_p and V_p. The region in Fig. 4-16 is typical of cases in which negative holdings are precluded and no security provides a certain return.

[1] All lower bounds were zero. Upper bounds were sufficiently large to have no effect.
[2] Although a kink is possible. If there is one, the X_i lines in a diagram such as Fig. 4-15 will all be horizontal over an associated range of λ.

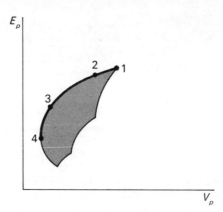

FIGURE 4-16

Standard portfolio-analysis problems are rather difficult to solve. But computers can usually do the job for little cost. The answers are generally limited to the composition of each corner portfolio, its expected return, variance of return, and standard deviation of return. The associated value of λ is also indicated. This is enough. Why? Because the relationships *are* linear between any two adjacent corner portfolios. Thus:

Every efficient portfolio is a combination of two *adjacent* corner portfolios.

Moreover, between any two adjacent portfolios, the efficient border will have the usual characteristics:

1. The relationship between E_p and λ will be linear.
2. The relationship between V_p and λ will be quadratic.
3. The relationship between V_p and E_p will be quadratic.

A standard portfolio-analysis problem is solved when the set of (efficient) corner portfolios is obtained. Other information can easily be computed when needed.

BORROWING AND LENDING Thus far nothing has been said explicitly about borrowing or lending. Lending is best viewed as investment in a particular security, one with no risk—a "sure thing." By definition, its expected return equals the pure interest rate. Since the outcome is certain, the standard deviation of return is zero.

Borrowing may be viewed in a number of ways. For present purposes borrowing will be considered the issuance of a riskless security. In other words, a negative value will be assigned to the relevant X_i.

Let security 1 be riskless:

 if $X_1 > 0$, the investor lends
 if $X_1 < 0$, he borrows

if $X_1 = 0$, he neither borrows nor lends

The security's characteristics are:

$E_1 = p$ (pure interest rate)
$\sigma_1 = 0$
$C_{1,1}(= \sigma_1^2) = 0$
$C_{1,2}(= C_{2,1}) = 0$
$\vdots$
$C_{1N}(= C_{N1}) = 0$

The covariances are zero because the outcome for security 1 is certain.[1]

$C_{1j} = \rho_{1j}\sigma_1\sigma_j$
but $\sigma_1 = 0$
therefore $C_{1j} = 0$

Consider the effect of combining two securities, one of which is riskless. As always,

$E_p = X_1E_1 + X_2E_2$
$\sigma_p^2 = X_1^2\sigma_1^2 + X_2^2\sigma_2^2 + 2X_1X_2\rho_{1,2}\sigma_1\sigma_2$

If security 1 is riskless, the latter formula becomes

$\sigma_p^2 = X_2^2\sigma_2^2$
thus $\sigma_p = X_2\sigma_2$

Figure 4-17 shows the result. Combining a riskless security with a risky security gives E_p, σ_p values lying along a straight line through the points representing the two securities. Combinations between the points are obtained by lending and investing in the risky security. Combinations above the point representing the risky security are obtained by borrowing money and investing the proceeds of the loan (along with the investor's own funds) in the risky security.

The risky security in this example could in fact be a portfolio of many risky securities. Combining it with a riskless security would give the same results.

The inclusion of a riskless security makes part or all of the efficient border of the E_p, σ_p region (*not* the E_p, V_p region) linear.[2]

[1] Strictly speaking, ρ_{1j} is undefined. It is a weighted average of the products of the normalized deviations. But all possible outcomes involve the same value for R_1. The deviation in each case is zero. The normalized deviation is this value divided by the standard deviation, or in other words, zero divided by zero. Thus the correlation coefficient is undefined. But the covariance is defined, and it is zero.

[2] This holds only if additional constraints do not make it infeasible to place all the investor's funds in the riskless security; the point is discussed more fully in Sec. B of the Supplement.

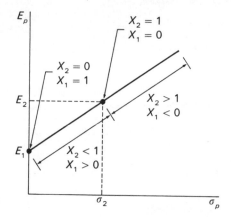

FIGURE 4-17

Figure 4-18 shows a case in which no negative holdings are allowed. The darkly shaded area is the feasible E_p, σ_p region in the absence of the riskless security. The entire shaded area is the region when such a security is available. The portfolio represented by point R^* is particularly important since any point on the efficient (linear) border between points p and R^* can be obtained by a combination of lending (point p) and investment in portfolio R^*.

Figure 4-19 shows a case in which negative holdings are allowed. As before, the darkly shaded area represents the feasible E_p, σ_p region in the absence of the riskless security, and the entire shaded area represents the region when such a security is available. The portfolio represented by point R^* is even more important in this case. *Any* point on the efficient (linear) border can be obtained by an appropriate combination of the riskless security and portfolio R^*. For point p, the investor lends all his funds. For points between

FIGURE 4-18

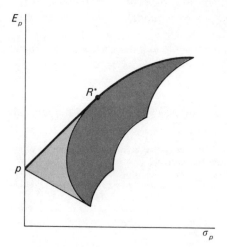

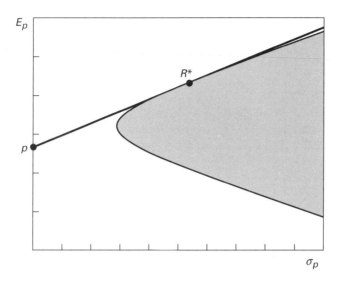

E_p

R^*

p

σ_p

FIGURE 4-19

p and R^*, he invests some in portfolio R^* and lends the rest. For point R^*, he puts all his funds in portfolio R^*. For points above R^*, he borrows, investing everything in portfolio R^*.

Portfolio R^* is sufficiently important to deserve a name. It is called the *optimal combination of risky securities*. The name is clearly appropriate for the case shown in Fig. 4-19. Whatever the appearance of the investor's indifference curves, as long as he likes E_p and dislikes σ_p, some combination of (1) portfolio R^* and (2) borrowing or lending will be optimal. In the case shown in Fig. 4-18, the name is appropriate only for an investor whose preferences lead to the selection of a point between p and R^* (inclusive). Figure 4-20a to c shows three cases in which negative holdings are allowed. Figure 4-21a to c shows three cases in which they are not. Only in the situation shown in Fig. 4-21c is R^* not the optimal combination of risky securities.

THE OPTIMAL COMBINATION OF RISKY SECURITIES

How can the optimal combination be found? Computational procedures are described in Secs. B and C of the Supplement. For present purposes, a graphical method will suffice. Let point p in Figure 4-22 represent the riskless security (i.e., the pure interest rate), and let curve AB represent a section of the efficient border of the feasible E_p, σ_p region in the absence of the riskless security. Combinations of p and portfolio 1 give results along line $p1$, combinations of p and portfolio 2 are along line $p2$, etc. Obviously portfolio 3 is the optimal combination of risky securities. It can be found by swinging a ray from point p until it becomes tangent to the efficient border of the E_p, σ_p region.

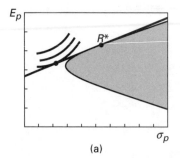

(a)

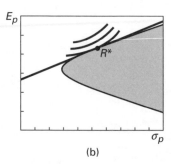

(b)

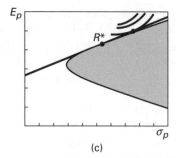

(c)

FIGURE 4-20

The existence of an optimal combination of risky securities greatly simplifies the task of portfolio selection. The investor need only decide how much to borrow or lend. There is but one appropriate combination of risky securities in which to invest the remainder of his funds. The consideration of alternative combinations of risky securities can thus be separated from the consideration of the investor's attitude towards uncertainty (risk) relative to expected return. This result has been accorded a dignified title. It is called the *separation theorem.*

The relationship is most obvious when one of the securities in a *basic problem* is riskless. Recall the form of the solution to such a problem:

$$X_1 = K_1 + k_1\lambda$$
$$X_2 = K_2 + k_2\lambda$$
$$X_3 = K_3 + k_3\lambda$$
$$\vdots$$
$$X_N = K_N + k_N\lambda$$

The efficient portfolio with the smallest possible variance is obtained when $\lambda = 0$. In this case it will consist entirely of security 1—the riskless security. Thus $K_1 = 1$ and K_2 to K_N must equal 0:

$$X_1 = 1 + k_1\lambda$$
$$X_2 = k_2\lambda$$
$$X_3 = k_3\lambda$$
$$\vdots$$
$$X_N = k_N\lambda$$

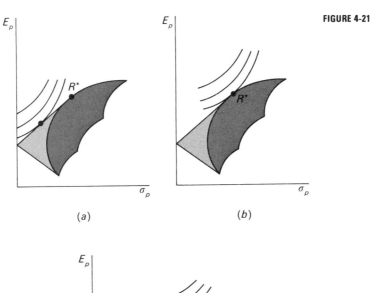

(a)   (b)

FIGURE 4-21

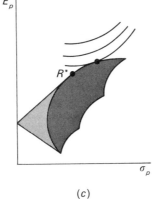

(c)

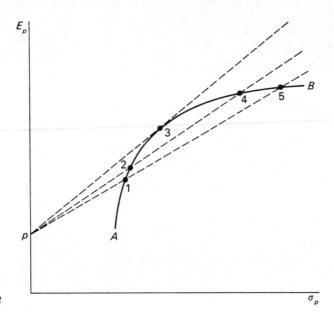

FIGURE 4-22

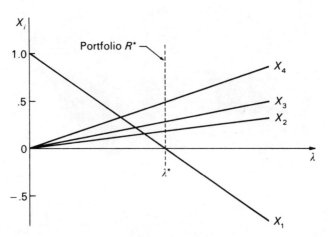

FIGURE 4-23

Figure 4-23 shows the composition of all efficient portfolios for a case involving three risky securities and one riskless security. Portfolio R^* is optimal at λ^*. Values of λ below λ^* lead to combinations of R^* and lending, values above λ^* lead to combinations of R^* and borrowing. As λ changes, the amount invested in any given risky security remains a constant porportion of the amount invested in all *risky* securities.[1]

[1] For security i, the proportion will be

$$\frac{X_i}{\sum_{j=2}^{N} X_j} = \frac{k_i \lambda}{\sum_{j=2}^{N} k_j \lambda} = \frac{k_i}{\sum_{j=2}^{N} k_j}$$

which is independent of λ.

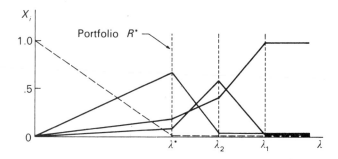

FIGURE 4-24

When one of the securities in a *standard problem* is riskless, the result will be similar to that shown in Fig. 4-24. To the left of point λ^* (representing portfolio R^*), the diagram has the characteristics of Fig. 4-23; to the right, it is similar to a diagram for a standard problem without a riskless security. The portfolios representing only lending ($\lambda = 0$) and portfolio R^* are adjacent corner portfolios. In this example there are two additional corner portfolios at λ_1 and λ_2.

This concludes the essential core of portfolio theory. Part II is concerned with a positive theory of capital markets built on this foundation. Computational aspects, extensions to the theory (both normative and positive), and empirical results are discussed in Part III.

PART II.

CAPITAL MARKET THEORY

5.

AGREEMENT

Capital market theory is an exercise in positive economics. Assuming **BASIC ASSUMPTIONS** that people act in certain ways, what is implied about prices, quantities held, etc.? As indicated earlier, the realism of the assumptions matters little. If the implications are reasonably consistent with observed phenomena, the theory can be said to "explain" reality. More important, it may provide useful predictions. A discussion of the acceptability of the theory must await the derivation of its implications. The theory assumes that:

1. Each investor acts on the basis of predictions about the future performance of securities—predictions stated in terms of expected returns, standard deviations of return, and correlation coefficients of rates of return.

2. Each investor selects a portfolio as indicated in Part I.

77

In short, investors behave as portfolio theory suggests they should behave. The normative theory of Part I is thus cast in a positive role.

Capital market theory also assumes that:

3. Each investor can borrow or lend as much or as little as he wishes at the pure rate of interest. The rate is the same whether the investor wishes to borrow or lend. Moreover, it is the same for every investor.

All investors may use the same set of predictions, i.e., expected returns, standard deviations of return, and correlation coefficients of rates of return. On the other hand, different investors may use different predictions. This chapter deals with the former case—a world in which there is complete agreement about future prospects. The next chapter considers the case in which there is disagreement.

Capital market theory is concerned with *equilibrium conditions*. An equilibrium situation, once attained, will be maintained. In *disequilibrium*, there are pressures for change; in equilibrium, there are none.

Change in the capital market takes the form of alterations in the holdings of securities and in their prices. In equilibrium there are no pressures for further change. *Equilibrium prices* (and holdings) are consistent with people's wealth, preferences, and predictions. In a broader sense, equilibrium prices are *determined* by people's wealth, preferences, and predictions.

Capital market theory seeks to predict the relationships among important variables in equilibrium. Two questions are of particular interest:

1. What will be the relationship between expected return and risk for portfolios?
2. What will be the relationship between expected return and risk for securities?

Implicit in these questions are two others:

1a. What is the appropriate measure of risk for a portfolio?
2a. What is the appropriate measure of risk for a security?

FINANCIAL SECURITIES AND CAPITAL ASSETS The decision variables of portfolio theory are called *securities*, but they may represent almost anything—jobs, apartments, shares of common stock, etc. Capital market theory is concerned with a more narrow domain. Only financial securities and capital assets are of interest.

A *capital asset* is a contract between an investor and the "outside world." A *financial security* is a contract between investors. The two types may or may not be related. If Mr. *A* plants a tree, he owns an asset. His future receipts will depend on the productivity of the tree as well as the future demand for its product. Mr. *A* may also contract to pay Mr. *B* some amount in the future. The evidence of such a promise is a financial security. The amount paid may depend on the productivity of Mr. *A*'s tree; Mr. *A* might even contract to pay Mr. *B* the entire receipts from the tree. For all practical purposes, Mr. *B* would then own the tree; Mr. *A* would simply act as a middle-man. This is a common, although not universal, situation. Consider Mr. *Y*, who contracts to pay Mr. *Z* whatever Mr. *A* pays Mr. *B*. The evidence of Mr. *Y*'s promise is also a financial security. But it does not represent ownership of a capital asset by Mr. *Y* (or Mr. *Z*); it is simply evidence of a financial transaction between two investors.

Why do people issue financial securities? Often to take advantage of economies of scale. It may be more efficient to plant and manage thousands of trees, but no single individual may want to own them all. Mr. *A*, acting as an entrepreneur, may plant the trees and then issue hundreds or even thousands of securities, each representing a promise to pay a proportionate share of the eventual receipts. Mr. *B* might buy one of the securities, Mr. *C* several, etc. Mr. *A* might choose to hold a number of them himself. In any event, the asset (1,000 trees) can be divided easily and cheaply. The corporate form of ownership is, in essence, a legal arrangement designed to facilitate such divisions. If there were no efficient (i.e., low-cost) method for sharing ownership, the assumption of perfect divisibility would represent an extreme oversimplification. For the analysis of modern capital markets, however, it is quite acceptable.

In the real world, entrepreneurs expect to receive some compensation for their efforts, but their earnings are not the major concern of this theory. To focus on other aspects, all transaction costs are assumed to be zero.

Clearly, there is a role for financial securities representing pro-portionate shares of ownership in capital assets. But are there other roles for such securities? There are at least two: the first derives from differences in preferences, the second from differences in predictions.

Two investors may have different preferences. If so, both may gain by engaging in a trade of present for future money. This can be accomplished by the issuance of a (riskless) financial security. The borrower *issues* a security promising to pay the lender a given sum in the future; the lender *purchases* the security.

Two investors may disagree about future prospects. If so, one may be willing to issue a (risky) financial security and sell it to the other at a price below the maximum the latter is willing to pay. Even if their preferences are identical, the values they attach to a given promise may differ if they disagree about the likelihood of various future outcomes.

This chapter deals with a world in which there is complete agreement about future prospects. In such a world, financial securities would be issued only to facilitate the division of ownership in capital assets and to accommodate differences in preferences.

For the purposes of the theory, no distinction need be made between financial securities and capital assets. A *security* simply represents a prospect for a future receipt. Given its present price, any security can be characterized by an expected return, standard deviation of return, and a set of correlation coefficients relating its outcome to that of each of the other securities. The source of the receipt may be another investor or the "outside world." In the former case, the security is a financial security; in the latter, it is a capital asset (or a portion of one). In the former case, some investors will "hold" negative amounts of the security; i.e., they will issue it. In the latter case, none need "hold" a negative amount.

Security 1—the riskless security—is (by definition) a financial security. Some investors will hold positive amounts; they will lend. Others will hold negative amounts; they will borrow. In equilibrium, the total amount borrowers wish to borrow will equal the total amount that lenders wish to lend. Putting it another way, the total value of riskless securities issued will equal the total value purchased. If an issue is represented by a negative number and a purchase by a positive number, the sum will be zero.

Risky securities may be either capital assets or financial securities. The owner of a firm may "hold" all its assets. He may also issue securities with similar characteristics (e.g., common stock) and/or securities with other characteristics (e.g., bonds). If an issue is represented by a negative number and a purchase by a positive number, the sum will be zero or positive—zero for a financial security, positive for a capital asset. The process of adding up positive and negative numbers "washes out" contracts between investors, leaving the entire investment community's net holdings of capital assets (i.e., contracts with the "outside world").

Consider an investor (any investor). Given predictions about risky securities, given the pure interest rate, and given the ability to borrow or lend at that rate, he will face a situation similar to that shown in Fig. 5-1. All efficient portfolios plot along a straight line such as pR^*Z. Every point along the line can be obtained by (1) borrowing or lending (or neither) and by (2) placing all funds *at risk* in portfolio R^*, composed entirely of risky securities. Portfolio R^* is, as before, the optimal combination of risky securities.

The situation an investor faces (or thinks he faces) will depend on his predictions and on his opportunities to borrow and lend. In this chapter each investor is assumed to make the same predictions and to be able to borrow or lend at the same rate of interest. Thus every investor will face the same situation (i.e., draw the same diagram). In particular:

All investors will agree concerning the optimal combination of risky securities.

This does not imply that all investors will choose the same portfolio. Some will lend; others will borrow; some will do neither. But each *will* distribute the amount of his funds *at risk* in the same way. The composition of R^* indicates the proportion of such funds invested in each of the risky securities.

In equilibrium, the amount borrowed must equal the amount lent. The net amount invested in security 1 (the riskless security) must be zero.

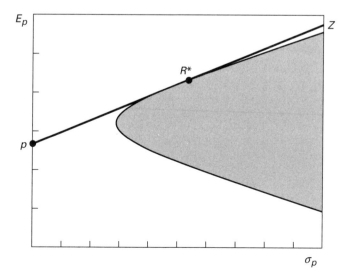

FIGURE 5-1

What will be the composition of portfolio R^*? The answer is almost (but not quite) obvious:

In equilibrium, the optimal combination of risky securities must include *all* securities; moreover, the proportion of each security must equal its proportionate value in the market as a whole.

To see why this must be the case, consider some counterexamples. What if R^* included a negative amount of some security, say number 5? This would mean that the investor should *issue* security 5. But all investors feel the same about the prospects for securities. Thus all who choose to place funds at risk will want to issue security 5. Obviously all cannot do so (to whom would they sell?). A negative value for the proportion of R^* invested in any risky security is thus inconsistent with equilibrium.

What about a positive value differing from the security's proportionate value in the market as a whole? Assume that security 8 constitutes 2 percent of the total market value of all risky securities, but that in R^*, $X_8 = .015$. This means that each investor placing funds at risk will invest 1.5 percent of such funds in security 8. Thus 1.5 percent of the *total* funds at risk will be invested in security 8. But security 8 constitutes 2 percent of the total value of risky securities. How can it comprise 2 percent and 1.5 percent of the same total? Obviously it cannot. The proportions must be the same.

The conclusion is inescapable. Under the assumed conditions, the optimal combination of risky securities is that existing in the market. Portfolio R^* is the *market portfolio.*

Let P_i represent the price per share of security i, and let Q_i be the number of shares outstanding. The definition of a *share* is arbitrary. If security 23 is General Motors, a natural unit is a share of common stock. The choice is a matter of convenience; of course, both price and quantity must be expressed in the same units.

The market portfolio is denoted portfolio M. Let X_i^M represent the proportion invested in security i. Then

$$X_i^M = \frac{P_i Q_i}{\sum\limits_{j=2}^{N} P_j Q_j} \qquad \text{for } i = 2, 3, \ldots, N$$

Note that security 1—the riskless security—is excluded. The market portfolio (by definition) includes only risky securities. Note also that the sum will equal 1, as required:

$$X_2^M + X_3^M + \cdots + X_M = 1$$

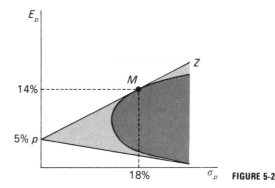

FIGURE 5-2

The usual relationships between the characteristics of securities and the characteristics of a portfolio apply, of course. The actual return on the portfolio, denoted R_M, will be the weighted average of the actual returns on the component securities:

$$R_M = \sum_{i=2}^{N} X_i^M R_i$$

The expected return, denoted E_M, will be the weighted average of the expected returns of the component securities:

$$E_M = \sum_{i=2}^{M} X_i^M E_i$$

The standard deviation of return, denoted σ_M, will be related in the usual way to the characteristics of the component securities and the proportions invested:

$$\sigma_M^2 = \sum_{i=2}^{N} \sum_{j=2}^{N} X_i^M X_j^M \rho_{ij} \sigma_i \sigma_j$$

In equilibrium, everyone will choose some point along a line such as *pMZ* in Fig. 5-2. The more conservative investors will lend some of their money, placing the rest in the market portfolio. The less conservative will borrow in order to place more than their initial funds in the market portfolio. But all will end up at some point along line *pMZ*. It is called the *capital market line*.

THE CAPITAL MARKET LINE

Two of the four questions posed earlier have now been answered for the case of perfect agreement. The appropriate measure of risk for a portfolio is (by assumption) standard deviation of return. In equilibrium, there will be a linear relationship between risk (so measured) and expected return *for efficient portfolios*.

Note that only efficient portfolios will plot along the capital market line. Others will plot below it (in Fig. 5-2, somewhere in the shaded region). Individual securities, each of which may be regarded as a decidedly inefficient portfolio, will plot at scattered points within the feasible E_p, σ_p region. There will be no simple relationship between expected return and standard deviation of return for inefficient portfolios nor, *a fortiori*, for individual securities. The remaining questions are, as yet, unanswered.

Two characteristics of the capital market line provide a complete description.

The vertical intercept is the pure interest rate. It is the price of immediate consumption; one must give up, say, 5 percent to consume now instead of later. Alternatively, it is the reward for waiting; one may consume, say, 5 percent more by waiting until later. The pure interest rate is often (but somewhat inaccurately) termed the *price of time*.

The slope of the capital market line indicates the trade-off between expected return and risk (uncertainty). To increase expected return, one must take on more risk. The slope thus indicates the expected return that can be obtained if additional risk is accepted. Alternatively, it indicates the expected return that must be given up to reduce risk. The slope can thus be viewed as the price (in decreased expected return) of risk reduction. This is often (but somewhat inaccurately) called the *price of risk*.

In the capital market illustrated by Fig. 5-2 the pure rate of interest is 5 percent (the period between *now* and *later* is one year). The market portfolio's expected return is 14 percent; its standard deviation of return is 18 percent. The market portfolio thus provides a reward of 9 percent in expected return (14 minus 5 percent) for bearing a risk (uncertainty) of 18 percent. The ratio is .5 (9 percent divided by 18 percent). Each unit of additional risk undertaken is rewarded with an additional half-unit of expected return. Putting it another way, the price of risk reduction is .5 percent in decreased expected return per unit (percent standard deviation of return) of risk avoided.

To summarize, in equilibrium the capital market can be characterized by a line showing the relationship between expected return and risk for efficient portfolios, with the standard deviation of return used to measure risk. The relationship can be described by two values: (1) the price of immediate consumption (i.e., the pure interest rate), and (2) the price of risk reduction.

The equation of the capital market line will be written in slope-intercept form:

$$E_p = p + r_e \sigma_p$$

where p = pure interest rate

r_e = price of risk reduction for efficient portfolios

All efficient portfolios must plot on the capital market line. The market portfolio must be efficient. Thus

$$E_M = p + r_e \sigma_M$$

Given the characteristics of the market portfolio and the pure interest rate, the price of risk reduction for efficient portfolios is easily determined:

$$r_e = \frac{E_M - p}{\sigma_M}$$

The numerator indicates the reward in excess expected return (over and above the pure interest rate) for bearing risk (uncertainty). The denominator indicates the risk (uncertainty) borne.

In empirical work, the actual results over a number of periods are often used to obtain estimates for E_M, σ_M, and p. A ratio based on such estimates is termed (more properly) a *reward-to-variability ratio.* It provides an estimate of the price of risk—an estimate that may or may not properly reflect the actual situation during any given period.

There is no reason to expect that the capital market line necessarily remains fixed over time. The line indicates the relationship between expected return and risk foreseen for a particular period of time. Both the price of immediate consumption and the price of risk reduction will be determined by the forces of demand and supply (as will other prices). If demand and supply conditions change over time, prices are also likely to change.

Capital market theory concerns people's perceptions concerning opportunities. Actual results may (and usually will) diverge from predictions. The values of capital market theory are ex ante (before-the-fact) estimates. Observed values are ex post (after-the-fact) results. The portfolios that do, in fact, turn out to be efficient will lie along some line, but not necessarily the ex ante capital market line. In fact, the market portfolio invariably proves to be inefficient ex post. If the future could be predicted with certainty, investors would shun diversification—the optimal portfolio would contain only the security with the best (actual) performance.

But the future cannot be predicted with certainty, and estimates must be made. The lack of certainty provides the motivation for both portfolio theory and capital market theory.

THE SECURITY MARKET LINE

By assumption, the risk (uncertainty) of a portfolio is measured by the standard deviation of its rate of return. In equilibrium there is a simple relationship between expected return and risk for efficient portfolios. But the relationship does not hold for inefficient portfolios nor for individual securities. Some other measure of risk must be found.

To determine the desired relationship a little mathematics is required. Fortunately the results prove to be "reasonable"—a comforting prospect for those with little enthusiasm for such arguments.

Figure 5-3 shows a typical equilibrium situation. Line pMZ is the capital market line. Point M represents the market portfolio. Point i, representing a particular security, lies somewhere below the capital market line, reflecting the fact that investment in only one security is inefficient. Security i can be any risky security. The results obtained when its characteristics are analyzed will thus apply to every risky security.

Consider the effect of dividing funds between (1) the portfolio consisting entirely of security i and (2) the market portfolio. Let X_i be the proportion invested in portfolio i and X_M the proportion invested in the market portfolio. The two must, of course, sum to 1:

$$X_i + X_M = 1$$

Let the resulting portfolio be portfolio Z. Then

$$E_Z = X_i E_i + X_M E_M \qquad \sigma_Z^2 = X_i^2 \sigma_i^2 + X_M^2 \sigma_M^2 + 2X_i X_M \rho_{iM} \sigma_i \sigma_M$$

where E_i = expected return of security i

$\quad E_M$ = expected return of the market portfolio

$\quad \sigma_i$ = standard deviation of return of security i

$\quad \sigma_M$ = standard deviation of return of the market portfolio

$\quad \rho_{iM}$ = correlation coefficient between R_i (return on security i)

$\qquad$ and R_M (return on the market portfolio)

Depending on the proportions invested in i and M, portfolio Z will plot at some point along a curve connecting points i and M; it will be termed *curve iM*. The shape of the curve will depend, of course, on ρ_{iM}—the correlation between R_i and R_M. The slope of the curve at point M is of particular interest. The footnote[1] proves that at point M the slope will be

$$s_M = \frac{(E_i - E_M)\sigma_M}{C_{iM} - \sigma_M^2}$$

where s_M = slope of curve iM at point M

$\quad C_{iM}$ = covariance between R_i and R_M = $\rho_{iM}\sigma_i\sigma_M$

Why is this important? Because at point M, curve iM must be tangent to the capital market line. To see why, consider the cases shown in Fig. 5-4a to c.

---

[1] The proof requires a little calculus.

Substituting $(1 - X_i)$ for X_M and C_{iM} for $(\rho_{iM}\sigma_i\sigma_M)$,

$$\sigma_z = [X_i^2\sigma_i^2 + (1 - X_i)^2\,\sigma_M^2 + 2X_i(1 - X_i)\,C_{iM}]^{\frac{1}{2}}$$

Differentiating with respect to X_i,

$$\frac{\partial\sigma_z}{\partial X_i} = \frac{X_i(\sigma_i^2 + \sigma_M^2 - 2C_{iM}) + C_{iM} - \sigma_M^2}{\sigma_z}$$

Substituting $(1 - X_i)$ for X_M,

$$E_z = X_i E_i + (1 - X_i)\,E_M$$

Differentiating with respect to X_i,

$$\frac{\partial E_z}{\partial X_i} = E_i - E_M$$

The desired value is the slope $\partial E_z/\partial\sigma_z$:

$$\frac{\partial E_z}{\partial\sigma_z} = \frac{\partial E_z/\partial X_i}{\partial\sigma_z/\partial X_i} = \frac{E_i - E_M}{\left[X_i(\sigma_i^2 + \sigma_M^2 - 2C_{iM}) + C_{iM} - \sigma_M^2\right]/\sigma_z}$$

At point M, $X_i = 0$ and $\sigma_z = \sigma_M$. Substituting,

$$\frac{\partial E_z}{\partial\sigma_z}\bigg|_{x_i=0} = \frac{E_i - E_M}{(C_{iM} - \sigma_M^2)/\sigma_M} = \frac{(E_i - E_M)\sigma_M}{C_{iM} - \sigma_M^2}$$

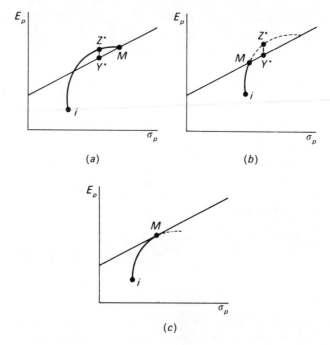

FIGURE 5-4

(a)

(b)

(c)

In Fig. 5-4*a*, curve *iM* is flatter than the capital market line at point *M*. This implies that at least one combination of *i* and *M* (for example, Z^*) is better than at least one portfolio on the capital market line (for example, Y^*). But all efficient portfolios are supposed to plot on the capital market line. The case shown in Fig. 5-4*a* is thus inconsistent with equilibrium.

In Fig. 5-4*b*, curve *iM* is steeper than the capital market line at point *M*. The problem here concerns the extension of the curve beyond point *M*. The formulas for E_Z and σ_Z imply a smooth curve. At point *M*, $X_i = 0$ and $X_M = 1$. If X_i is allowed to become negative and X_M to exceed 1, points along the dashed segment in Fig. 5-4*b* will be obtained. Again, at least one combination of *i* and *M* (for example, Z^*) will be better than at least one portfolio on the capital market line (for example, Y^*), a result inconsistent with equilibrium.

If investors are allowed to issue securities, points along the extension of curve *iM* in Fig. 5-4*b* are clearly legal. But even if investors are not allowed to issue securities, some points on the extension near *M* will be legal. Recall the composition of portfolio *M* —it includes *all* securities, including security *i*. Thus a portfolio with X_i negative and X_M greater than 1 need not involve net negative holdings of any security. For example:

Security	Portfolio i	Portfolio M	Portfolio Z ($X_i = -.01$ $X_M = 1.01$)
1	0	.	.
2	0	.	.
:	:	:	:
i	1	.02	.0102
:	:	.	.
.	.	.	.
N	0	.	.

Clearly, the greater X_M and the more negative X_i, the more likely the possibility that portfolio Z will require the issuance of security i. But at least some points on the extension of curve iM near point M will be feasible. Thus the situation in Fig. 5-4b is inconsistent with equilibrium whether investors are allowed to issue securities or not.

Only the situation shown in Fig. 5-4c can obtain in equilibrium. Curve iM must be tangent to the capital market line at point M; the slopes must be equal. The trade-off between expected return and risk for small changes in the amount of security i included in the (market) portfolio must equal the trade-off in the capital market as a whole. In formal terms,

$$s_M = r_e$$

Substituting the formulas for each,

$$\frac{(E_i - E_M)\sigma_M}{C_{iM} - \sigma_M^2} = \frac{E_M - p}{\sigma_M}$$

Simplifying and rearranging terms,

$$E_i - p = \left(\frac{E_M - p}{\sigma_M^2}\right)C_{iM}$$

This is the desired relationship. The term on the left is the reward for bearing risk—the excess of the security's expected return over and above the pure interest rate. The formula shows that it will equal some constant times the covariance between the security's rate of return and that of the market as a whole. In equilibrium, all securities will plot along a straight line—the *security market line*. Figure 5-5 provides an example.

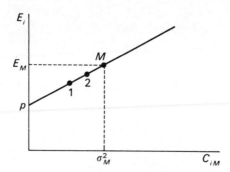

FIGURE 5-5

The equation of the security market line can be written:

$$E_i = p + r_s C_{iM}$$

where r_s = price of risk reduction for securities.

The value of r_s indicates the expected return that must be sacrificed per unit of risk reduction, where risk is measured by the covariance between the security's rate of return and that of the market. Note the difference between r_s and r_e:

$$r_s = \frac{E_M - p}{\sigma_M^2} \qquad r_e = \frac{E_M - p}{\sigma_M}$$

The two measures are closely related, but they are not identical.

The relationship shown in Fig. 5-5 holds for individual securities— each will plot at a point along the line. But it also holds for any combination of securities (i.e., portfolio)—efficient or inefficient. Consider securities 1 and 2, whose characteristics are shown in Fig. 5-5. Let portfolio Z be made up of these securities. Its expected return will be

$$E_Z = X_1 E_1 + X_2 E_2$$

As shown in the footnote,[1] the covariance between the rate of return

---

[1] Recall the definition of *covariance*. It is the weighted average of the products of the unnormalized deviations, using probabilities as weights. Let the superscript o represent an outcome (i.e., set of values for R_i, R_j, and R_M) and P_o the probability of outcome o. Then:

$$C_{iM} = \sum_o P_o (R_i^o - E_i)(R_M^o - E_M) \qquad C_{jM} = \sum_o P_o (R_j^o - E_j)(R_M^o - E_M)$$

Let portfolio Z be composed of securities i and j:

$$R_Z = X_i R_i + X_j R_j$$

Then,

$$C_{ZM} = \sum_o P_o (R_Z^o - E_Z)(R_M^o - E_M) = \sum_o P_o [(X_i R_i^o + X_j R_j^o) - (X_i E_i + X_j E_j)](R_M^o - E_M)$$

$$= \left[X_i \sum_o P_o (R_i^o - E_i)(R_M^o - E_M) \right] + \left[X_j \sum_o P_o (R_j^o - E_j)(R_M^o - E_M) \right] = X_i C_{iM} + X_j C_{jM}$$

on portfolio Z and that of the market will be

$$C_{ZM} = X_1 C_{1M} + X_2 C_{2M}$$

Depending on the proportions invested in the two securities, portfolio Z's expected return and covariance with the market will plot at some point along a line connecting points 1 and 2. It will thus lie on the security market line.

The argument can be extended. In equilibrium, *every* portfolio and security will plot along the security market line.

The market portfolio is no exception. Of course, its covariance with the market (itself) can be written more succinctly:

$$C_{MM} = \rho_{MM} \sigma_M \sigma_M = 1 \sigma_M \sigma_M = \sigma_M^2$$

In Fig. 5-5, point M represents the market portfolio. The relationship between its characteristics and the slope of the security market line is now even clearer:

$$r_s = \frac{E_M - p}{\sigma_M^2}$$

The four questions posed at the beginning of the chapter have now been answered. For efficient portfolios, an appropriate measure of risk is σ_p, and all such portfolios will plot along a security market line relating E_p to σ_p. For securities, an appropriate measure of risk is C_{iM}, and all will plot along a security market line relating E_i to C_{iM}. Unfortunately the notion of *covariance with the market* lacks intuitive appeal. An alternative is available: the volatility of a security's rate of return relative to changes in market performance.

As suggested in connection with the concept of correlation, it is often desirable to approximate the relationship between two variables with a straight line. The relationship between R_i and R_M is no exception.

The goal is to construct a "proper" line of the type shown in Fig. 5-6. It will be termed the security's *characteristic line*.

To properly summarize the relationship between R_i and R_M, such a line should indicate that when R_M equals its expected value, R_i is most likely to equal its expected value. In other words:

Security i's characteristic line should pass through the point at which

$$R_M = E_M \text{ and } R_i = E_i.$$

VOLATILITY

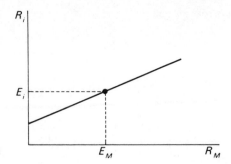

FIGURE 5-6

This fixes one point on the line. All that is needed to complete its specification is a requirement that will fix the slope.

Security i's characteristic line is designed to summarize the relationship between R_i and R_M. If it does so properly, one should be able to determine C_{iM} from the position of the line and the probabilities of various values of R_M.

If only values lying on the line were possible, with the probability of each equal to that of the associated value of R_M, the covariance would be

$$C_{iM}^* = \sum Pr(R_M)(R_i^* - E_i)(R_M - E_M)$$

where R_i^* is equal to the value of R indicated (predicted) by the characteristic line for each value of R_M.

If the line properly portrays the relationship between R_i and R_M, this value should equal the true covariance. The characteristic line should be drawn so that

$$C_{iM}^* = C_{iM}$$

Fortunately, this is simply done.

The equation of security i's line can be written

$$R_i^* = a_i + b_i R_M$$

Since it is required to go through the point E_M, E_i:

$$E_i = a_i + b_i E_M$$

Substituting these relationships in the equation for C_{iM}^*:

$$C_{iM}^* = \sum Pr(R_M)[(a_i + b_i R_M) - (a_i + b_i E_M)](R_M - E_M)$$
$$= b_i \sum Pr(R_M)(R_M - E_M)(R_M - E_M)$$
$$= b_i \sum Pr(R_M)(R_M - E_M)^2$$

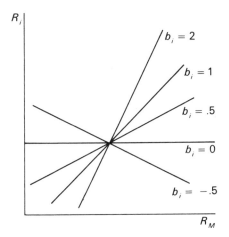

FIGURE 5-7

But the latter sum is simply the variance of R_M. Thus

$$C^*_{iM} = b_i \sigma^2_M$$

C^*_{iM} is required to equal C_{iM}; this can be accomplished by simply selecting the appropriate value of b_i. The second requirement is thus:

$$b_i = \frac{C_{iM}}{\sigma^2_M}$$

The value of b_i indicates the slope of security i's characteristic line. It measures the volatility of the security's rate of return relative to changes in the market rate of return. Figure 5-7 shows several possibilities.

A security with a value of b_i below 1 is said to be *defensive*. A 1 percent increase in the market rate of return is likely to be accompanied by a less than 1 percent increase in the security's rate of return. On the other hand, a 1 percent decrease in the market rate of return is likely to be accompanied by a less than 1 percent decrease in the security's rate of return. The investor is thus "defended" to some extent against the occurrence of a major disaster. The smaller the value of b_i, the greater his defense.

A security with a value of b_i above 1 is said to be *aggressive*. A 1 percent decrease in the market rate of return is likely to be accompanied by an even greater decrease in the security's rate of return. On the other hand, in the event of a rise in the market rate of return, the security's rate of return is likely to rise by an even larger amount. The larger the value of b_i, the more *aggressive* the security.

As shown earlier, the covariance between a portfolio's rate of return and that of the market will be a weighted average of the comparable

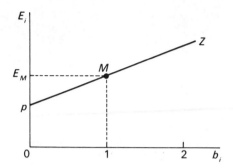

FIGURE 5-8

values for its component securities. In the case of a two-security portfolio,

$$C_{zM} = X_1 C_{1M} + X_2 C_{2M}$$

In terms of volatility,

$$b_z \sigma_M^2 = X_1 b_1 \sigma_M^2 + X_2 b_2 \sigma_M^2$$

Dividing through by σ_M^2,

$$b_z = X_1 b_1 + X_2 b_2$$

The volatility of a portfolio is thus the weighted average of the corresponding values for its component securities, using the proportions invested as weights. In general,

$$b_p = \sum_{i=1}^{N} X_i b_i$$

Figure 5-8 shows the security market line in terms of b_i. The conversion from C_{iM} is straightforward. If a security's rate of return is completely uncorrelated with the market, b_i and C_{iM} equal zero. This fixes one point. The market portfolio's rate of return equals itself; thus $b_{iM} = 1$. This fixes another. The equation of the security market line in terms of volatility is thus especially simple:

$$E_i = p + (E_M - p)b_i \quad \text{or} \quad E_i - p = (E_M - p)b_i$$

The latter form shows that any security's *risk premium* or *excess expected return* $(E_i - p)$ will be proportional to its risk, measured by volatility.[1]

---

[1] The security market line can be used directly as a criterion for the acceptance or rejection of investment projects by a firm. The key is to consider such a project as a potential security to be held by the firm's owners. Thus, if a project plots above the security market line, it should be accepted; if it plots below the line, it should be rejected. In more traditional terms, the *cost of capital* for a project is the expected rate of return shown by the security market line for projects of equal volatility. The expected dollar cash flow should be discounted at this rate of interest; if the present value is positive, the project should be undertaken; if not, it should be rejected.

The security market line indicates the relationship between expected return and volatility. It thus indicates the manner in which characteristic lines are related.

This is easily shown. Security i's characteristic line can be described in terms of E_i and b_i:

$$R_i = E_i + b_i(R_M - E_M) \quad \text{where } b_i = \frac{C_{iM}}{\sigma_M^2}$$

This meets the two requirements stated earlier: $R_i = E_i$ when $R_M = E_M$ and b_i has been chosen properly.

The security market line specifies a relationship between the expected return and volatility:

$$E_i = p + (E_M - p)b_i$$

Substituting the right-hand side of this equation for E_i in the equation for security i's characteristic line gives

$$R_i = p + (E_M - p)b_i + b_i(R_M - E_M)$$

Simplifying,

$$R_i = p + b_i(R_M - p)$$

As the latter form shows, when the return on the market equals the pure interest rate, so does the return on security i. And this is true for any security (or, for that matter, any portfolio).

Figure 5-9 shows the relationship. Every security (and every portfolio) can be described by a characteristic line of the type shown. It will pass through the point corresponding to the pure interest rate on both axes. The greater the volatility, the steeper the line. And of course, the greater the volatility, the greater the expected return.

Security Z in Fig. 5-9 warrants a brief comment. It represents the ultimate in defensiveness—the value of b is actually negative. As the characteristic line indicates, such a security will have an expected return below the pure interest rate. But it is risky; why would anyone hold it? The answer is simple. No one will hold it alone. But by adding a small amount of such a security to a portfolio with a small positive beta one can reduce overall portfolio beta and portfolio risk. The expected return on the security with a negative beta must thus be negative so the expected return on the combination will be decreased.

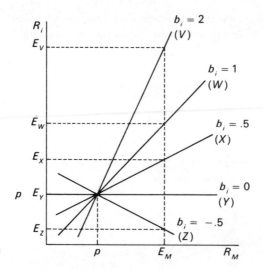

FIGURE 5-9

There are precious few securities with returns negatively correlated with market performance. However, such securities may be expected to return less than the pure interest rate.

SYSTEMATIC RISK
A security's characteristic line is an approximation for the true relationship between R_i and R_M. Points not on the line are usually both possible and probable. There are thus two sources of uncertainty about a security's actual return:

1. The actual value of R_M is uncertain.
2. The extent of the divergence of the actual point from the security's characteristic line is uncertain.

These two sources of uncertainty can be given formal definitions. The first is called *systematic risk*, the second *unsystematic risk*.

Consider the systematic risk. If only points on the characteristic line were possible, it would be the only source of uncertainty. The variance would then be

$$\sum Pr(R_M)\,[(a_i + b_i R_M) - (a_i + b_i E_M)]^2$$
$$= \sum Pr(R_M)\,[b_i(R_M - E_M)]^2$$
$$= b_i^2 \sigma_M^2$$

Security i's systematic risk is thus

$$\sigma_i^s = b_i \sigma_M$$

Unsystematic risk is defined as the difference between total risk and systematic risk, using variances:

$$(\sigma_i^u)^2 = (\sigma_i)^2 - (\sigma_i^s)^2$$

where σ_i = standard deviation of R_i
$\quad \sigma_i^s$ = security i's systematic risk ($= b_i \sigma_M$)
$\quad \sigma_i^u$ = security i's unsystematic risk

These relationships apply to portfolios as well:

$$(\sigma_p^u)^2 = (\sigma_p)^2 - (\sigma_p^s)^2$$

where σ_p = standard deviation of rate of return on portfolio
$\quad \sigma_p^s$ = portfolio's systematic risk
$\quad \sigma_p^u$ = portfolio's unsystematic risk

The relationship between systematic risk and volatility is the same for securities and portfolios. Thus,

$$\sigma_p^s = b_p \sigma_M$$

All efficient portfolios plot along the capital market line. This implies that their rates of return will be perfectly correlated with one another.[1] Since the market portfolio is efficient, all efficient portfolios' rates of return must be perfectly correlated with R_M. But if a portfolio's rate of return is perfectly correlated with R_M, its characteristic line will completely represent its relationship with the market. Thus:

EFFICIENT PORTFOLIOS AND SYSTEMATIC RISK

Systematic risk is the *only* source of uncertainty about the rate of return on an efficient portfolio.

Putting it another way:

Efficient portfolios have no unsystematic risk. The converse also holds:

A portfolio (or security) with unsystematic risk is inefficient.

This makes clearer the relationship shown by the security market line. The relevant measure of risk for a security is its volatility (i.e., its systematic risk). This portion will remain when the security is combined with others to form an efficient portfolio. The unsystematic risk is irrelevant; it will "wash out" when the security is combined with others.

The total risk of a security is not relevant if the security is to be part of a diversified portfolio (as it should be). Only the systematic portion of the risk need be considered; the rest can be diversified away.

[1] With one exception: the return from lending is not correlated with the return from *any* risky portfolio.

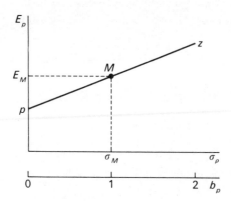

FIGURE 5-10

Figure 5-10 shows the capital market line with a scale added to indicate the values of b_p for the efficient portfolios that lie along the line. Inefficient portfolios will have smaller values of b_p than indicated by the scale, since their total risk (σ_p) exceeds their systematic risk (which is related directly to b_p).

ADJUSTMENT   The capital market line and the security market line depict equilibrium relationships. If these relationships do not hold, there will be pressures for change. But will the pressures lead towards equilibrium or away from it? Is there an equilibrium at all? Or are there several?

Economists often require the proponent of a model of this type to show (1) that an equilibrium exists, (2) that it is unique, and (3) that it is stable (i.e., departures from equilibrium will create pressures leading back to equilibrium). Fortunately, the theory described in this chapter meets all three requirements. Section D of the Supplement shows that an equilibrium exists and that it is unique. This present discussion briefly describes the process through which it can be attained.

To do this, prices must be brought into the analysis explicitly. As indicated earlier, the quantity of each security is measured in terms of shares. The price of a share of security i is P_i.

Investors' perceptions of the future can be cast in terms of predicted receipts. Let $A_i^\$$ be the dollar amount actually received from a share of security i. Then,

$$R_i = \frac{A_i^\$}{P_i} - 1$$

Given a set of prices (P_i's), investors predictions can be stated in terms of the expected values, standard deviations, and correlations of the rates of return (R_i's). More fundamental predictive measures concern the dollar amounts ($A_i^\$$'s):

let $E_i^\$$ = expected dollar amount paid per share of security i (i.e., expected value of $A_i^\$$)

$\sigma_i^\$$ = standard deviation of the dollar amount paid per share of security i (i.e., standard deviation of the probability distribution of $A_i^\$$)

$\rho_{ij}^\$$ = correlation coefficient between $A_i^\$$ and $A_j^\$$

The footnote[1] shows that

$$E_i = \frac{E_i^\$}{P_i} - 1$$

$$\sigma_i = \frac{\sigma_i^\$}{P_i}$$

$$\rho_{ij} = \rho_{ij}^\$$$

Given a set of predictions about the $E_i^\$$'s, $\sigma_i^\$$'s, and $\rho_{ij}^\$$'s, and given a set of prices (P_i's), predictions about rates of return can be derived.

[1] Let o stand for an outcome and P_o for its probability. Then,

$$E_i = \sum_o P_o R_i^o = \sum_o P_o \left(\frac{A_i^{\$o}}{P_i} - 1\right)$$

$$= \frac{\sum_o P_o A_i^{\$o}}{P_i} - 1 = \frac{E_i^\$}{P_i} - 1$$

And $\sigma_i^2 = \sum_o P_o (R_i^o - E_i)^2 = \sum_o P_o \left[\left(\frac{A_i^{\$o}}{P_i} - 1\right) - \left(\frac{E_i^\$}{P_i} - 1\right)\right]^2$

$$= \sum_o P_o \left(\frac{A_i^{\$o} - E_i^\$}{P_i}\right)^2 = \frac{\sum_o P_o (A_i^{\$o} - E_i^\$)^2}{P_i^2} = \frac{(\sigma_i^\$)^2}{P_i^2}$$

Thus,

$$\sigma_i = \frac{\sigma_i^\$}{P_i}$$

Finally,

$$\rho_{ij} = \sum_o P_o \left(\frac{R_i^o - E_i}{\sigma_i}\right)\left(\frac{R_j^o - E_j}{\sigma_j}\right)$$

$$= \sum_o P_o \frac{\left(\frac{A_i^{\$o}}{P_i} - 1\right) - \left(\frac{E_i^\$}{P_i} - 1\right)}{\frac{\sigma_i^\$}{P_i}} \frac{\left(\frac{A_j^{\$o}}{P_j} - 1\right) - \left(\frac{E_j^\$}{P_j} - 1\right)}{\frac{\sigma_j^\$}{P_j}}$$

$$= \sum_o P_o \left(\frac{A_i^{\$o} - E_i^\$}{\sigma_i^\$}\right)\left(\frac{A_j^{\$o} - E_j^\$}{\sigma_j^\$}\right) = \rho_{ij}^\$$$

Note that predictions about the future dollar payoffs ($A_i^\$$'s) have been assumed to be unaffected by present prices (P_i's). This rules out, for example, cases in which people base their predictions about future price in whole or in part on the level of present price.

Given predictions about rates of return plus the value of the pure interest rate, the optimal combination of risky securities can be determined. Each set of security prices thus implies a particular optimal combination of risky securities. Equilibrium exists if the prices are such that this combination is the market portfolio.

Assume that the capital market is in equilibrium, as shown by Fig. 5-11. Portfolio M, on the capital market line, is the market portfolio. Now let a new security be created. Given its initial price, it will plot at some point. Assume it is i_1. At such a price, people will not want to hold the security. What will happen? Obviously the price will fall, raising both the security's expected return and standard deviation of return. It will then plot at some other point. However, the point must lie along a ray such as AB in Fig. 5-11. Recall that

$$E_i = \frac{E_i^\$}{P_i} - 1 \qquad \text{and} \qquad \sigma_i = \frac{\sigma_i^\$}{P_i}$$

Thus

$$\frac{E_i + 1}{\sigma_i} = \frac{\left(\dfrac{E_i^\$}{P_i} - 1\right) + 1}{\dfrac{\sigma_i^\$}{P_i}} = \frac{E_i^\$}{\sigma_i^\$}$$

and $\quad E_i = \left(\dfrac{E_i^\$}{\sigma_i^\$}\right)\sigma_i - 1$

FIGURE 5-11

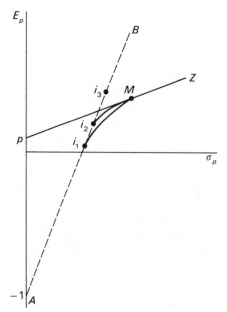

Whatever its price, security i will plot at a point along a ray that (1) originates at the point ($E = -1, \sigma = 0$) and (2) has a slope of $E_i^\$ / \sigma_i^\$$.

The lower a security's price, the farther out it will plot along its ray. As the price falls, the security will eventually become an attractive candidate for inclusion in the market portfolio. In Fig. 5-11 this occurs at point i_2 (the curve showing the effect of combining security i with the market is tangent to the capital market line at point M when security i plots at point i_2).

Any price below that associated with point i_2 would lead to an excessive demand for security i. An extreme case is shown by point i_3. Here, security i by itself constitutes a better portfolio than all other securities combined. There will be a rush to purchase it, with the security becoming less and less attractive as its price is bid up (and the point moves down the ray).

The actual dynamic process through which disequilibrium is turned into equilibrium is likely to be very complex. Prices of other securities (and hence the location of the capital market line) are likely to change. The process may be smooth and rapid or slow and jerky. For present purposes, it suffices to assume that the forces of demand and supply will act on security prices in such a way that equilibrium will eventually be reached.

IMPLICATIONS

The formal description of capital market theory under conditions of complete agreement is now complete. It is time to assess the implications.

Consider first the capital market line. It provides a formal construct for the widely held notions of a *price of risk* and a *price of immediate consumption* (i.e., pure interest rate). It also provides a simple measure of efficiency. A portfolio is efficient if (and only if) its expected return equals the pure interest rate plus the product obtained by multiplying the risk involved times the price of risk.

The security market line provides a formal construct for the relationship between expected return and risk for securities (and portfolios, for that matter). Moreover, it is based on a measure of risk that takes into account the existence and desirability of diversification. The. concept of volatility gives a formal and quantifiable meaning to widely used but somewhat fuzzy notions such as *defensiveness* and *aggressiveness*. And the related concept of systematic risk gives precision to the notion of *uncertainty that cannot be diversified away.*

Characteristic lines succinctly relate the rates of return of securities or portfolios to that of the market portfolio. The concept of efficiency can be related to such lines in a relatively natural way. A portfolio is efficient if (and only if) its characteristic line summarizes *all* the uncertainty regarding its rate of return. The line is an exact representation for an efficient portfolio; it is only an approximation for an inefficient one.

Not all the implications are as easy to accept. A particularly distasteful one concerns people's holdings of risky securities. According to the theory, in equilibrium every investor will distribute funds *at risk* in the same manner. Moreover, everyone will hold either (1) no risky securities at all or (2) some amount of every risky security. The only efficient portfolios will be combinations of the market portfolio and borrowing or lending.

This is clearly inconsistent with observed behavior. How can the divergence be explained? Putting it another way, what assumption(s) should be modified?

One possibility is to drop the assumption of complete agreement. This is done in the next chapter. A less drastic modification will be examined here.

In equilibrium, all efficient portfolios lie on the capital market line, and all are based on the market portfolio. Each portfolio includes thousands of different securities. Portfolios with, say, 100 different securities will be inefficient; they will plot below the capital market line.

How far below? Not far, if at least some attempt is made to benefit from diversification when selecting securities. This assertion rests primarily on empirical results described in later chapters, but it should not seem unreasonable. A principle akin to the law of diminishing returns applies to diversification. The added gain is smaller, the greater the number of securities already included. A portfolio with 100 reasonably selected securities will usually be almost completely diversified; almost all its risk will be systematic.

So what? A point below the line is dominated by points on the line, even if the difference is slight. Why would anyone choose an inefficient portfolio?

According to the theory presented thus far, no one would. One of the reasons is the assumed absence of any transactions or portfolio-management costs. In the real world, of course, such costs do exist.

In particular, it costs more to acquire and manage thousands of different securities than to acquire and manage 100. If the rewards differ little, a portfolio with fewer securities will be preferred. Putting it another way, the market portfolio will be inefficient if the expected return *net* of transaction and management costs is considered instead of expected return per se.

Acknowledging the existence of transaction and management costs leads to a more palatable conclusion regarding security holdings, even under the assumption of complete agreement. Unfortunately, the explicit inclusion of such costs would complicate the model tremendously. No attempt will be made to formally treat such a case. Suffice it to say that the presence of transaction and management costs provides a convenient explanation for the seeming disparity between observed behavior and some of the theory's implications.

Before concluding this chapter, a comment on the precise meaning of equilibrium is in order. Both the capital market line and the security market line are loci of equilibrium values. Given investors' preferences, wealth, and predictions, all portfolios actually held will plot along the capital market line, and all securities will plot along the security market line. Strictly speaking, it is incorrect to think of the capital market line as a set of alternatives open to an investor. Similarly, it is incorrect to think of a security as overpriced if it plots below the security market line (or underpriced if it plots above it). Formally, the relationships apply only to an equilibrium situation in which every investor has selected a point on the capital market line and every security is priced so as to plot at a particular point on the security market line.

In practice, one specifies formal models and derives implications from them, with appropriate attention to the rules of logic. Then rigorous concepts (such as the standard deviation of a subjective probability distribution) are replaced with somewhat vague notions (such as the *degree of uncertainty*). And relationships that strictly apply only after equilibrium has been reached are assumed to face the person who has yet to make a decision. Moreover, the possibility of a disequilibrium departing from equilibrium in only a limited manner is acknowledged, accepted, and perhaps even asserted to be likely.

In sum, there comes a time when the model builder is thanked for providing insights into the real world. The practical man then takes over, using those insights to help solve practical problems. The change is usually worthwhile, but it is often painful, especially when one person must play both roles.

6.

DISAGREEMENT

The assumptions considered in Chap. 5 lead to implications that are more or less consistent with observed behavior. One of the less satisfactory implications concerns people's holdings of risky securities. Even if transaction costs are acknowledged, the assumptions imply that portfolios will differ primarily with respect to the number of securities included. By assumption, there is complete agreement about future prospects.

Even the most casual empiricism suggests that this is not the case. People often hold passionately to beliefs that are far from universal. The seller of a share of IBM stock may be convinced that it is worth considerably less than the sales price. The buyer may be convinced that it is worth considerably more.

In a world of complete agreement, there is no incentive for anyone to sell a security "short." Short sales are equivalent to the creation of risky securities. But both buyer and seller must expect a positive return to engage in a transaction involving risk. Short sales are thus inconsistent with the model of Chap. 5. To explain such activity (and much else), one must allow for differences of opinion as well as differences in preference.

This chapter may be viewed as an exercise in assumption dropping. The previous chapter developed in great detail the implications of a convenient set of assumptions about investors' behavior. Many of the implications proved to be consistent with reality. It would be comforting to find that they could be derived even if some of the assumptions were dropped. If this were the case, the results could be said to be *robust*. In the best of all possible worlds, as simplifying assumptions are dropped, only the unsatisfactory implications fall away, leaving those that are strong, satisfying, and consistent with observed behavior.

Allowing disagreement serves one useful purpose—it implies that people may hold different portfolios and feel very strongly about such differences. But the effect on the other implications is not immediately apparent.

Most of this chapter is concerned with a world in which:

1. Each investor acts on the basis of *his own* predictions about the future performance of securities—predictions stated in terms of expected returns, standard deviations of return, and correlation coefficients of rates of return.
2. Each investor selects a portfolio in the manner described in Part I.
3. Each investor can borrow or lend as much or as little as he wishes at the pure rate of interest. The rate is the same whether the investor wishes to borrow or lend. Moreover, it is the same for every investor.

Modifications of the third assumption are discussed briefly at the end of the chapter. Until then, the world is assumed to differ from that of Chap. 5 in only one respect—people are allowed to disagree about the future.

Anyone applying portfolio-analysis techniques will view his alternatives in terms of the expected return and standard deviation of return of an entire portfolio. Given the ability to borrow or lend at a common pure rate of interest, all efficient combinations will lie

CAPITAL MARKET LINES

FIGURE 6-1

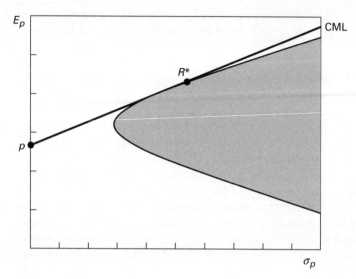

along a straight line. Every individual will thus face a situation such as that shown in Fig. 6-1. Point p represents the pure interest rate and point R^* the optimal combination of risky securities. The straight line is the capital market line (CML) for the individual in question.

It is important to note that two people will not necessarily face the same (supposed) prospects. An optimist might predict higher expected returns and/or lower standard deviations of return for most securities than would a pessimist. One person might estimate more rosy prospects for General Electric stock than for General Motors; another might estimate just the reverse. People may also differ in their assessment of correlations among rates of return.

In short, the locations of the points representing individual securities may differ, as may the set of efficient combinations of E_p and σ_p.

By assumption, everyone faces the same pure interest rate. It is a known quantity, agreed upon by all. But the optimal combination of risky securities will depend on subjective predictions. One person's optimal combination may be another's inefficient portfolio.

The market portfolio will seem inefficient to some, and perhaps to all investors.

Every individual will face a capital market line. Everyone will be able to characterize his choice in terms of (1) the selection of an optimal combination of risky securities and (2) the determination of the appropriate amount to be borrowed or lent (or neither).

Future prospects are uncertain. Risk is thus a subjective attribute. In a world of complete agreement, it is possible to discuss *the* price of risk (i.e., the slope of *the* capital market line). In a world of disagreement, there is individual *A*'s price of risk (i.e., the slope of *his* capital market line), individual *B*'s price of risk (i.e., the slope of *his* capital market line), etc.

Given his feelings about the future, the prices of risky securities, and the pure interest rate, each individual will face a set of alternatives similar to that shown in Fig. 6-1. Depending on his preferences, he will select some point along his capital market line. Every investor will perform a similar analysis and select his own preferred portfolio. The results will typically differ, since both preferences and predictions differ among investors.

In any event, there is a straightforward and direct relationship among the pure interest rate, the prices of risky securities, and the portfolios preferred by investors.

A pure interest rate and set of security prices will lead to equilibrium if:

1. The amount people wish to borrow equals the amount others wish to lend.
2. The difference between (*a*) the amount of each risky security people wish to hold and (*b*) the amount others wish to provide (create) equals the amount of the comparable capital asset in existence.

Intuitively, the existence of an equilibrium should seem plausible. As long as predictions are not altered by changes in current prices, an increase in the price of a security should make it less attractive to every investor. A decrease should have the opposite effect. An increase in the pure interest rate should encourage lending and discourage borrowing, while a decrease should have the opposite effect. Thus an imbalance between the quantity of a security demanded and the quantity supplied should lead to a change in its price (and possibly to changes in the prices of other securities). Such changes should eventually lead to a restoration of the appropriate balance.

Before continuing, some attention must be given to the notion of a *security* in a world of disagreement. If everyone agrees about future prospects, a security may be defined in terms of its expected return, standard deviation of return, and correlation with other securities. If two financial instruments are identical with respect to every one of these attributes, for all practical and theoretical purposes, they are the same security.

In a world of disagreement, things are not so simple. Given one person's predictions, two promises may be considered identical. Given another's predictions, they may be considered quite different. Formally, every financial instrument and capital asset must be regarded as a unique security unless every investor considers its prospects equal to those of some other. A security can thus be defined as a future prospect that differs in at least one respect from every other future prospect in the eyes of at least one investor. This definition covers both a world of agreement and one of disagreement.

Note that no distinction has been made between capital assets and financial securities. A security is simply a future prospect. The holder is an investor. If the issuer is another investor, it is a financial security. If the issuer is "nature," it is a capital asset.

These notions allow a more formal statement of the requirements for equilibrium. Let Q_{ij} represent the quantity (number of shares) of security i held by individual j. A negative value indicates that the individual is an issuer (creator) of shares; a positive value indicates that he holds shares. Let Q_i^A represent the amount of the capital asset of type i available to be held (i.e., the number of shares of security i issued by "nature"). The equilibrium conditions require that

$$\sum_{j=1}^{M} Q_{ij} = Q_i^A$$

for every security (i) from 1 to N where M is equal to the number of investors in the society.

In Chap. 5 it was assumed that nature made no sure bets: Q_1^A equalled zero. The only riskless securities were financial securities. This assumption is not essential. Neither the analysis of a world of complete agreement nor that of a world of disagreement is affected if Q_1^A is allowed to be positive.

There is no difference between the equilibrium condition specified here and that utilized in the previous chapter. The notation has simply been altered to accommodate differences in holdings due to disagreement about future prospects.

Each investor looks into the future, checks the prices of securities and the pure interest rate, and then comes up with a picture such as that shown in Fig. 6-1. His optimal combination of risky securities is R^*. It may include positive holdings of some securities, negative holdings of others, and zero holdings of the rest. In any event, the investor will combine such a portfolio with borrowing, lending, or neither, to reach the preferred position on his capital market line.

In a world of complete agreement everyone reaches the same conclusion regarding the optimal combination of risky securities. Every investor's R^* must be the market portfolio. For this reason, the symbol M was substituted for R^* before deriving relationships concerning individual securities in the previous chapter. But the derivation did not require the assumption that every investor's optimal combination of risky securities would be the market portfolio.

Let R_j^* represent investor j's optimal combination of risky securities. The conclusions of Chap. 5 regarding individual securities can be applied to a world of disagreement by substituting R_j^* for M.

The relevant measure of risk is the covariance between a security's (or portfolio's) rate of return and that of portfolio R_j^*:

$$\text{Risk} = C_{iR_j^*}$$

Alternatively, risk may be expressed in terms of volatility:

$$b_{ij} = \frac{C_{iR_j^*}}{\sigma_{R_j^*}^2}$$

where b_{ij} – volatility of security i as seen by investor j

$C_{iR_j^*}$ = covariance between return on security i and on portfolio R_j^* as seen by investor j

$\sigma_{R_j^*}$ = standard deviation of rate of return on portfolio R_j^* as seen by investor j

R_j^* = optimal combination of risky securities as seen by investor j

Now let E_{ij} = expected return on security i as seen by investor j.

Any given investor might adjust his holdings until every security plots along his (own) security market line, as shown in Fig. 6-2. Point R_j^* indicates the volatility and expected return of investor j's optimal combination of risky securities.

This may seem to involve some legerdemain. In Chap. 5 every

FIGURE 6-2

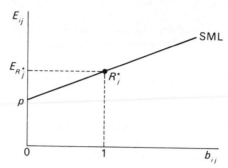

security was included in the optimal combination of risky securities (the market portfolio). Thus a situation of the type shown in Fig. 5-4*b* could not arise, even if the investor were precluded from issuing risky securities. This fact, along with the impossibility of a situation of the type shown in Fig. 5-4*a*, directly implies the required tangency condition shown in Fig. 5-4*c*. And the latter implies that every security will plot along the relevant security market line.

With disagreement, the situation may be more complicated. If the investor can issue risky securities, the results are the same—all securities will plot along his security market line. On the other hand, if he is unable to issue such securities, a situation of the type shown in Fig. 5-4*b* could arise (with R^* substituted for M) if security i is not included in R^*. Securities that the investor would like to issue, but cannot, will plot below his security market line. All others will plot along the line.

As long as every investor is able to purchase or issue securities without limit, each will face his (own) capital market line and his (own) security market line. All efficient portfolios will plot along the former; all securities and portfolios will plot along the latter.

By assumption, everyone faces the same pure interest rate. But investors may differ in every other respect—in particular, with regard to the assessment of risk, the appropriate way to measure it, and the expected return that must be sacrificed to reduce it by any given amount.

LIMITATIONS ON PORTFOLIOS Thus far it has been assumed that every investor is able to hold as much or as little of every attractive security and to issue as much or as little of every unattractive security as he wishes, subject only to the constraint that he not exceed his overall budget. Among other things, this assumes that a security's prospects are affected by neither the

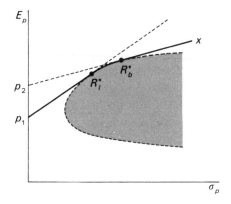

FIGURE 6-3

amount held nor the amount issued. The former may be a reasonably acceptable assumption. The latter may not be.

In the real world, a buyer's assessment of a financial security depends on the issuer's assets and liabilities. The price obtained for a given promise will typically be greater, the fewer such promises issued. But the price received for a security affects its prospects stated in terms of rate of return. Thus prospects will depend, to a greater or lesser extent, on the amount issued.

The consequences of accommodating such aspects of reality are likely to be disastrous in terms of the usefulness of the resulting theory. This is most easily seen in connection with the issuance of riskless securities (i.e., borrowing).

The very notion of a capital market line depends on the assumption that the investor can borrow or lend without limit at a common pure rate of interest. In the real world, of course, one must usually pay more, the greater the amount borrowed. Figure 6-3 shows a simple case in which the investor can lend at one rate (p_1), but must borrow at a greater rate (p_2). The efficient combinations of E_p and σ_p lie along the curve $p_1 R_l^* R_b^* x$. Portfolio R_l^* is the optimal combination of risky securities if the investor's preferences lead him to lend (i.e., choose a point along the line $p_1 R_l^*$). Portfolio R_b^* is the optimal combination if his preferences lead him to borrow (i.e., choose a point along the line $R_b^* x$). Neither is optimal if he chooses to neither borrow nor lend (i.e., selects a point along the curve $R_l^* R_b^*$).

Even more realism could be incorporated by limiting the amount that could be borrowed at p_2—requiring further borrowing to take place at an even greater rate of interest. But the damage is done as soon as the assumption of equal borrowing and lending rates is dropped.

The capital market line no longer exists. Instead there is a capital market curve—linear over some ranges, perhaps, but becoming flatter as σ_p increases over other ranges. Moreover, there is no single optimal combination of risky securities; the preferred combination depends on the investors' preferences. In short, the separation theorem no longer holds.

The demise of the capital market line is followed immediately by that of the security market line. The theory is in a shambles.

THE REMAINS It is time to survey the results of this exercise. They are not atypical. The more realistic a model, the more general its implications. But the more it explains, the less its value. The power of a model lies in the possible occurrences it precludes. The theory of Chap. 5 is quite powerful. Unfortunately, some of its implications are less than perfectly· consistent with reality. The theory considered in the preceding section of this chapter is not powerful at all. Its implications are sufficiently general to be consistent with almost any observation. By explaining everything, it explains nothing.

The conclusion is obvious: The assumption of equal borrowing and lending rates is essential if a model of much value is to be obtained. The assumption may not be perfectly realistic, but this is not important in itself. More relevant, the implications are not wildly inconsistent with observed behavior.

Two viable alternatives remain. Both include the assumption of a common borrowing and lending rate. One model assumes complete agreement, the other does not. Each implies that the investor selects first an optimal combination of risky securities and then the preferred amount to borrow or lend (or perhaps neither). In other words, each investor views his alternatives in terms of a capital market line. Associated with the capital market line is the investor's security market line, relating expected return to its risk, suitably defined in terms of volatility.

The models differ with respect to the uniformity of views. Under the assumption of complete agreement, every investor faces the same capital market line and the same security market line. There is a common measure of risk and a common price of risk. The market portfolio is the optimal combination of risky securities for all, and volatility is uniformly defined in terms of the market portfolio.

If disagreement is allowed, the pure interest rate is the only common denominator. Everything else is subjective and individual.

People do disagree about the future. Short sales reflect this. But many people invest indirectly via pension funds, mutual funds, and trust funds—institutions that choose highly diversified portfolios with returns highly correlated with that of the market as a whole. The activities of many investors are thus consistent with the implications of the model based on the assumption of complete agreement.

The model of Chap. 5 explains much of the behavior in the real world. Moreover, it yields implications sufficiently strong to be tested empirically. It is the essential theory for positive applications.

The alternative—a model based on disagreement—has little value in a positive role. But it provides the motivation for normative applications of more complicated portfolio-analysis techniques. Unless an investor can make superior predictions about the future, there is very little to be gained from the use of complicated mathematical procedures. Instead, very simple approaches can be employed.

To describe the behavior of the capital market as a whole and to determine sensible portfolio-selection procedures for the investor lacking superior information, the model of Chap. 5 is preferable. The investor who believes that he has exceptional predictive abilities (and/or "inside" information) will assert that the model does not apply to him, although it may apply to others. In a sense he will be right, since he really does disagree with other investors about the future. In another sense he may be wrong. His predictions may not, in fact, be superior. He may thus engage in wasted effort analyzing such predictions in great detail. Even worse, he may select an inferior portfolio, investing too much of his wealth in a single security that is, in fact, no better than any other. An investor unable to detect seriously mispriced securities should diversify rather extensively. Only an especially underpriced security should be allowed to constitute a large portion of one's portfolio.

In sum, the economist interested in the behavior of the capital market may prefer the model based on an assumption of complete agreement. The investor hoping to profit from superior predictive ability may reject the model.

APPLICATIONS AND EXTENSIONS

7.

INDEX MODELS

Simplified models of the relationships among securities' rates of return can provide substantial reductions in the effort required to prepare and process the data for a portfolio analysis. This chapter describes several such models and shows how to take advantage of their properties when performing portfolio analyses.

Suppose that you wished to select efficient portfolios from a set of **THE PROBLEM** N different securities. What information would be required? At the very least, an estimate of each security's expected return and risk (standard deviation of return) would be required. It would not be unreasonable to ask a security analyst to provide such information— $2N$ different numbers in all.

But more is needed. A great many estimates are required if the relationships among securities' rates of return are to be stated explicitly. Consider the table of correlation coefficients:

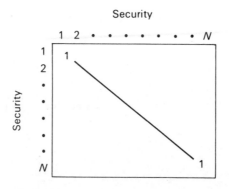

There are $N \times N (= N^2)$ entries. Each of the N entries along the diagonal equals 1, leaving $(N^2 - N)$ to be estimated. But every value below the diagonal equals a corresponding value above it (since $\rho_{ij} = \rho_{ji}$). Thus the number of different correlation coefficients is

$$\frac{N^2 - N}{2}$$

To fully describe the relationships among 100 securities requires 4,950 different estimates. To fully describe the relationships among 500 securities requires 124,750 estimates. Few security analysts would be willing (or able) to estimate so many different values. But few portfolio managers would be willing to consider only 50 or 60 securities.

Some simple method for representing the relationships among securities is obviously needed. Such an approach may also prove beneficial when the portfolio analysis is performed; by taking advantage of the special properties of the underlying model, the computations can usually be greatly simplified.

Ease of processing is desirable. But ease of estimation is likely to be absolutely essential. The simplified models described in this chapter satisfy both goals.

A SINGLE-INDEX MODEL   All the models described in this chapter rely on *indexes*. The return on each security is assumed to be related, to a greater or lesser extent, to the level of one or more of the indexes. Relationships among securities derive from common relationships with the indexes.

A particularly simple but practical model uses only one index. For example:

1. The gross national product
2. Per-capita income
3. The Dow-Jones Index of the prices of 30 industrial stocks
4. Standard and Poor's Index of the prices of 500 stocks
5. The rate of return on a portfolio composed of all securities listed by the New York Stock Exchange

The actual level of the index (denoted I) is assumed to be uncertain. For purposes of prediction, two estimates are used:

E_I—the expected value of the index
σ_I—the risk associated with the index, i.e., the standard deviation of the probability distribution of I

Each security's rate of return is assumed to be related to the level of the index. For security i,

$$R_i = a_i + b_i I + c_i$$

where R_i = actual return on security i
a_i = constant
b_i = constant
I = actual level of index
c_i = uncertain variable

Neither I nor c_i can be predicted with certainty. An expected value and standard deviation serve to describe predictions concerning the value of the index. The expected value of c_i is assumed to be zero, leaving only its risk to be predicted:

σ_{c_i} = standard deviation of probability distribution of c_i

The overall approach can be described in two ways. First, c_i can be considered to be a prediction error:

$$c_i = R_i - (a_i + b_i I)$$

The parenthesized expression provides an unbiased prediction for R_i, given the level of the index. The actual value of c_i is thus the difference between the actual rate of return and the best estimate of its value, given the actual level of the index. Figure 7-1 provides an illustration.

The other interpretation is shown in Fig. 7-2. The linear relationship $(R_i = a_i + b_i I)$ provides the best single estimate of R_i, given I. The

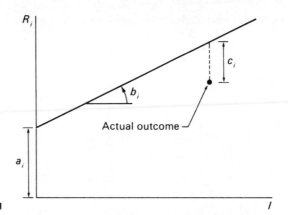

FIGURE 7-1

value of σ_{c_i} indicates the risk associated with the security itself, over and above that due to the unpredictability of the level of the index.

The expected rate of return on a security is the value predicted by the linear relationship when the index equals its expected value:

$$E_i = a_i + b_i E_I$$

Obviously, E_i can be determined if a_i, b_i, and E_I are known. Alternatively, a_i can be determined if E_i, b_i, and E_I are known. It is usually more important to know the value of E_i than that of a_i. A useful and complete description of a security's prospects would thus include:

1. E_i —its expected return (based on the assumption that the index attains its expected value)

2. b_i —its responsiveness to changes in the level of the index

3. σ_{c_i}—the risk attributable to its particular characteristics (over and above the risk due to its relationship with the index)

No additional values must be estimated, since all other relationships are assumed to be insignificant. In particular, it is assumed that the actual value of the index will not affect the actual value of c_i, and vice versa. More precisely:

The correlation between I and c_i is assumed to be zero for every security (i).

In addition, the rates of return on any two securities are assumed to be related only through their common relationship with the index. More precisely:

The correlation between c_i and c_j is assumed to be zero for every pair of (different) securities (i and j).

FIGURE 7-2

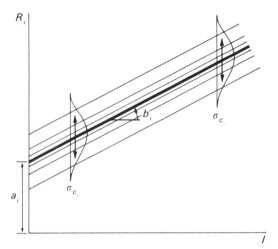

As usual, the expected return of a portfolio equals the weighted average of the expected returns of its component securities:

$$E_p = \sum_{i=1}^{N} X_i E_i$$

The actual rate of return will, of course, be equal to the weighted average of the actual returns of the component securities:

$$R_p = \sum_{i=1}^{N} X_i R_i$$

Substituting the assumed relationship:

$$R_p = \sum_{i=1}^{N} X_i (a_i + b_i I + c_i)$$

The overall return is thus the sum of $3N$ terms:

$$R_p = X_1 a_1 + X_2 a_2 + \cdots + X_N a_N$$
$$+ X_1 b_1 I + X_2 b_2 I + \cdots + X_N b_N I$$
$$+ X_1 c_1 + X_2 c_2 + \cdots + X_N c_N$$

To determine the standard deviation of R_p, only terms involving uncertain elements need be considered. The c_i's and I are such elements. Thus the relevant terms are those in the second and third rows. Rearranging,

$$R_p = X_1 a_1 + X_2 a_2 + \cdots + X_N a_N$$
$$+ (X_1 b_1 + X_2 b_2 + \cdots + X_N b_N) I$$
$$+ X_1 c_1 + X_2 c_2 + \cdots + X_N c_N$$

The parenthesized expression is determined once a portfolio (set of X_i's) is selected. It indicates the response of R_p to changes in I.

(It is simply the weighted average of the b_i values of the component securities.) Define

$$b_p = \sum_{i=1}^{N} X_i b_i$$

In the formula for R_p, only $N + 1$ terms involve uncertain elements:

$b_p I$
$X_1 c_1$
$X_2 c_2$
$\vdots$
$X_N c_N$

To find the variance of R_p, one would normally sum the variances of every one of these terms plus twice their covariances. But the simplified model assumes that every variable is uncorrelated with every other. Thus all the covariances equal zero and can be disregarded. As intended, the result is quite simple:

$$\sigma_p^2 = b_p^2 \sigma_I^2 + X_1^2 \sigma_{c_1}^2 + X_2^2 \sigma_{c_2}^2 + \cdots + X_N^2 \sigma_{c_N}^2$$

This is easily interpreted. The latter N terms indicate the risk associated with the particular characteristics of the individual securities. The first term indicates the risk due to the relationships of the securities with the index.

This approach can greatly simplify the task of finding efficient portfolios. One decision variable (b_p) is added, along with one constraint:

$$b_p = \sum_{1=1}^{N} X_i b_i$$

The benefit gained more than outweighs the cost. The variance involves only $N + 1$ terms. If the solution technique is modified to take advantage of this characteristic, the process can be completed with relatively few computations.

MULTI-INDEX MODELS In many cases a security analyst may be unwilling to assume that relationships among securities are due entirely to common relationships with a single index. On the other hand, explicit estimation of every correlation coefficient is likely to be out of the question. A compromise is needed. Indexes provide an answer, but more than one index must be allowed.

This discussion deals with index models in a general manner. The single-index model of the previous section is a special case of the wider class to be described here.

Assume that there are M indexes. Their actual levels can be denoted $I_1, I_2, \ldots, I_M$. In general,

I_j = actual level of index j

The actual rate of return on security i is assumed to be linearly related to the actual levels of the indexes:

$$R_i = a_i + b_{i1}I_1 + b_{i2}I_2 + \cdots + b_{iM}I_M + c_i$$

The actual value of c_i can be considered the difference between the actual return and the predicted return, given the actual levels of the indexes. The expected value of c_i is assumed to be zero. Its standard deviation, σ_{c_i} must be estimated. The value of σ_{c_i} provides a measure of the risk associated with security i over and above that attributable to its relationships with the indexes.

The expected value of R_i is related to the expected values of the indexes:

$$E_i = a_i + b_{i1}E_{I_1} + b_{i2}E_{I_2} + \cdots + b_{iM}E_{I_M}$$
where $\quad E_{I_j}$ = expected value of I_j

If E_i is estimated directly, the expected values of the indexes need not be used explicitly when performing a portfolio analysis. However, the risk associated with each index is required.

The minimal set of values needed to perform a portfolio analysis based on a model involving M indexes includes:

1. For each of the M indexes (j):

    σ_{I_j}—the risk associated with index j, i.e., the standard deviation of the probability distribution of I_j

2. For each of the N securities (i):

    E_i —the expected return on security i (based on the assumption that each index attains its expected value)

    b_{i1}
    $\vdots$ —the responsiveness of R_i to changes in the levels of each of the M indexes
    b_{iM}

    σ_{c_i} —the risk attributable to security i's particular characteristics (over and above its relationships with the indexes)

The rate of return on a portfolio will, as always, equal the weighted average of the returns on its component securities:

$$R_p = \sum_{i=1}^{N} X_i R_i$$

Substituting,

$$R_p = \sum_{i=1}^{N} X_i(a_i + b_{i1}I_1 + b_{i2}I_2 + \cdots + b_{iM}I_M + c_i)$$

Rearranging the terms,

$$
\begin{aligned}
R_p = X_1 a_1 \quad &+ X_2 a_2 \quad + \cdots + X_N a_N \\
X_1 b_{11} I_1 \quad &+ X_2 b_{21} I_1 \quad + \cdots + X_N b_{N1} I_1 \\
\vdots \qquad & \qquad \vdots \qquad\qquad \vdots \\
+ X_1 b_{1M} I_M \quad &+ X_2 b_{2M} I_M + \cdots + X_N b_{NM} I_M \\
+ X_1 c_1 \qquad &+ X_2 c_2 \qquad + \cdots + X_N c_N
\end{aligned}
$$

The responsiveness of R_p to changes in each of the indexes will simply be a weighted average of the corresponding values for the component securities. Denote

$$b_{p1} = \sum_{i=1}^{N} X_i b_{i1}$$

$$b_{p2} = \sum_{i=1}^{N} X_i b_{i2}$$

$$\vdots$$

$$b_{pM} = \sum_{i=1}^{N} X_i b_{iM}$$

Substituting,

$$
\begin{aligned}
R_p = X_1 a_1 \quad &+ X_2 a_2 + \cdots + X_N a_N \\
&+ b_{p1} I_1 \\
&\quad \vdots \\
&+ b_{pM} I_M \\
&+ X_1 c_1 \quad + X_2 c_2 + \cdots + X_N c_N
\end{aligned}
$$

The terms in the first row are all certain. For purposes of determining the standard deviation of R_p, they may be ignored.

An especially simple case arises when it is assumed that none of these variables is correlated with another. In other words:

1. The correlation between c_i and c_j is assumed to be zero for every pair of (different) securities (i and j).

2. The correlation between I_j and c_i is assumed to be zero for every index (j) and security (i).

3. The correlation between I_j and I_k is assumed to be zero for every pair of (different) indexes (j and K).

Under these conditions,

$$\sigma_p^2 = b_{p1}^2 \sigma_{I_1}^2 \quad + b_{p2}^2 \sigma_{I_2}^2 + \cdots + b_{pM}^2 \sigma_{I_M}^2$$
$$+ X_1^2 \sigma_{c_1}^2 + X_2^2 \sigma_{c_2}^2 + \cdots + X_N^2 \sigma_{c_N}^2$$

This relationship is easily interpreted. The latter N terms indicate the risk associated with the particular characteristics of the individual securities. The first M terms indicate the risk due to the securities' relationships with the indexes.

A multi-index model can be accommodated directly by adding M variables (b_{p1} to b_{pM}) and M constraints to the portfolio-analysis problem. The constraints have the form

$$b_{p1} = \sum_{i=1}^{N} X_i b_{i1}$$
$$\vdots$$
$$b_{pM} = \sum_{i=1}^{N} X_i b_{iM}$$

The larger the number of indexes (M), the larger the problem (in terms of the number of variables and constraints). The advantage of a multi-index model over a full analysis of all relationships lies in the simplified formula for portfolio variance. Under the assumed conditions (no correlation among indexes and c_i values), the variance involves only ($N + M$) terms. If a solution technique designed to take advantage of this characteristic is used, a multi-index formulation can provide substantial computational advantages, in addition to ease of estimation.

The assumption that the c_i values are uncorrelated is usually considered acceptable. So is the assumption that the indexes are not correlated with the c_i values. But it may seem unreasonable to assume that no two indexes are correlated. Consider a common example. Assume that one index represents the overall level of the economy, while each of the others measures the level of activity in a particular industry. Presumably the health of each industry is related (to some extent) to that of the economy as a whole. The levels of some of the indexes are thus correlated.

In a case of this sort, an additional assumption may take care of the problem. To illustrate, consider a situation involving two indexes—the first (I_1) representing the level of activity in a particular industry and the second (I_2) the overall level of the economy. Each security's return can be represented as

$$R_i = a_i + b_{i1}I_1 + b_{i2}I_2 + c_i$$

Now make the (fairly reasonable) assumption that I_1 is linearly related to I_2 as follows:

$$I_1 = \alpha + \beta I_2 + \gamma$$

where α(alpha) = constant
β(beta) = constant
γ (gamma) = uncertain variable with expected value of zero and standard deviation of σ_γ

Substituting,

$$R_i = a_i + b_{i1}(\alpha + \beta I_2 + \gamma) + b_{i2}I_2 + c_i$$

Rearranging,

$$R_i = (a_i + b_{i1}\alpha) + (b_{i1}\beta + b_{i2})I_2 + b_{i1}\gamma + c_i$$

The first parenthesized expression is a constant. The second $(b_{i1}\beta + b_{i2})$ indicates the impact of a change in I_2 on R_i; both the direct effect (b_{i2}) and the indirect effect via I_1 $(b_{i1}\beta)$ are included. The next term $(b_{i1}\gamma)$ indicates the effect of a deviation of I_1 from its predicted relationship with I_2. The final term measures the risk due to the particular characteristics of security i.

Making the usual substitutions to find the return on a portfolio,

$$R_p = \sum_{i=1}^{N} X_i(a_i + b_{i1}\alpha)$$

$$+ \sum_{i=1}^{N} X_i(b_{i1}\beta + b_{i2})I_2$$

$$+ \sum_{i=1}^{N} X_i b_{i1}\gamma$$

$$+ \sum_{i=1}^{N} X_i c_i$$

Adopting the standard notation,

$$b_{p1} = \sum_{i=1}^{N} X_i b_{i1}$$

$$b_{p2} = \sum_{i=1}^{N} X_i b_{i2}$$

Substituting and simplifying,

$$R_p = \sum_{i=1}^{N} X_i(a_i + b_{i1}\alpha)$$

$$+ (b_{p1}\beta + b_{p2})I_2$$

$$+ b_{p1}\gamma$$

$$+ \sum_{i=1}^{N} X_i c_i$$

The first sum may be regarded as a constant. Only I_2, γ, and the c_i's are uncertain. Moreover, they may reasonably be assumed to be uncorrelated. Thus

$$\sigma_p^2 = (b_{p1}\beta + b_{p2})^2\sigma_{I_2}^2 + b_{p1}^2\sigma_\gamma^2 + X_1^2\sigma_{c_1}^2 + X_2^2\sigma_{c_2}^2 + \cdots + X_N^2\sigma_{c_N}^2$$

In essence, the original model has been replaced with another, derived from it. The relevant coefficient for the term involving the risk of I_2 includes both the direct and indirect effects of a change in I_2. The entire risk of I_1 is no longer relevant, since the part attributable to its relationship with I_2 is included in the first term. Only the risk due to the particular characteristics of I_1 (the portion measured by γ) should be accounted for separately.

In the original formulation of this problem, I_1 was defined as the level of activity in an industry; thus its relationship with I_2 had to be taken into account Had the index been defined differently, this might not have been necessary. For example, consider the following model:

$$R_i = a_i^* + b_{i1}I_1^* + b_{i2}^*I_2 + c_i$$

where a_i^*, b_{i1}, and $b_{i2}^* =$ constants
  $I_1^* =$ index of difference between level of activity in particular industry and that expected, given level of economy
  $I_2 =$ level of economy
  $c_i =$ uncertain variable with expected value of zero

Clearly, I_1^* and I_2 may be assumed to be uncorrelated.

This formulation is, in essence, the model derived from the one used as the original example. Only the notation differs:

$$I_1^* = \gamma$$
$$b_{i2}^* = b_{i1}\beta + b_{i2}$$
$$a_i^* = a_i + b_{i1}\alpha$$

More complicated examples could be given, but the point should be clear enough. Correlations among indexes may often be avoided by defining (or redefining) indexes as *deviations* from typical relationships. If security analysts find it difficult to think in these terms, a little algebraic manipulation may serve to transform their predictions into the desired form.

Section E of the Supplement includes a discussion of methods for adapting portfolio-analysis techniques to take advantage of the special characteristics of index models of the type discussed thus far. Suffice it to say here that the use of such methods can often significantly reduce the cost of portfolio analysis.

RESPONSIVENESS AS A MEASURE OF RISK Recall the single-index model treated earlier. The underlying assumption relates the return on each security to the level of one especially important index:

$$R_i = a_i + b_i I + c_i$$

where R_i = actual return on security i
a_i = constant
b_i = constant
I = actual level of index
c_i = uncertain variable

Given the assumption that the c_i's are uncorrelated with one another and with the level of the index, portfolio risk is a relatively simple function of predicted values:

$$\sigma_p^2 = b_p^2 \sigma_I^2 + X_1^2 \sigma_{c_1}^2 + X_2^2 \sigma_{c_2}^2 + \cdots + X_N^2 \sigma_{c_N}^2$$

Now consider a well-diversified portfolio. For concreteness, assume that n securities are to be included, each in the same dollar amount. In other words,

$$X_i = \frac{1}{n} \qquad \text{for every security included in the portfolio}$$

$$X_i = 0 \qquad \text{for every other security}$$

To simplify the exposition, assume that the securities have been renumbered, with those included in the portfolio first. In other words:

$$X_i = \frac{1}{n} \qquad \text{for } i = 1, 2, \ldots, n$$

$$X_i = 0 \qquad \text{for } i = n + 1, \ldots, N$$

Given this convention, securities $(n + 1)$ to N can be disregarded, since they are not included in the portfolio. Thus

$$\sigma_p^2 = b_p^2 \sigma_I^2 + X_1^2 \sigma_{c_1}^2 + X_2^2 \sigma_{c_2}^2 + \cdots + X_n^2 \sigma_{c_n}^2$$

where $\quad b_p = X_1 b_1 + X_2 b_2 + \cdots + X_n b_n$

Now consider the risk due to the unique characteristics of the securities:

$$X_1^2 \sigma_{c_1}^2 + X_2^2 \sigma_{c_2}^2 + \cdots + X_n^2 \sigma_{c_n}^2$$

Since the portfolios under consideration involve equal dollar holdings of securities 1 to n, each of the corresponding X_i's equals $(1/n)$. The risk due to unique characteristics of securities is thus

$$\left(\frac{1}{n}\right)^2 \sigma_{c_1}^2 + \left(\frac{1}{n}\right)^2 \sigma_{c_2}^2 + \cdots + \left(\frac{1}{n}\right)^2 \sigma_{c_n}^2$$

Summing and rearranging terms gives

$$\frac{1}{n}\left(\frac{\sigma_{c_1}^2 + \sigma_{c_2}^2 + \cdots + \sigma_{c_n}^2}{n}\right)$$

The expression in parentheses represents the average value of $\sigma_{c_i}^2$ for the n securities included in the portfolio. But for the portfolio as a whole, the total risk due to such factors is only one-nth the average value for the component securities.

This is an important result. If 20 securities are held in equal dollar amounts (i.e., $n = 20$), the portfolio risk due to unique attributes of the component securities will be only 5 percent of that associated with the average security. The principle is not new: Diversification can greatly reduce risk due to uncorrelated but uncertain events.

The converse also holds. Diversification per se provides little advantage when events are highly correlated. This applies directly to the other component of portfolio risk:

$$b_p^2 \sigma_I^2$$

Recall the definition of b_p: it is the average of the b_i values of the component securities. Thus the portfolio risk due to uncertainty about the level of the index is no smaller than that associated with the average security.

The greater a portfolio's diversification, the smaller the risk due to the c_i values, both in absolute terms and relative to the risk due to uncertainty about the level of the index. For purposes of analysis, it may be perfectly reasonable to completely ignore such risk: For well-diversified portfolios

$$\sigma_p^2 \approx b_p^2 \sigma_I^2 \qquad \text{and} \qquad \sigma_p \approx b_p \sigma_I$$

where "$\approx$" means "is approximately equal to."

Figure 7-3 illustrates the accuracy of the approximation if half the typical security's variance is attributable to its relationship with the

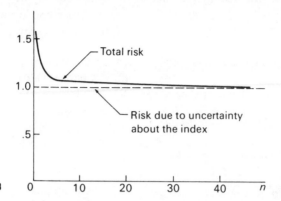

FIGURE 7-3

index (an assumption consistent with the results of some of the empirical studies described in Chap. 8). More precisely, the figure is based on the assumption that the two components of risk are approximately equal (on the average); that is,

$$b_p^2 \sigma_I^2 \approx \frac{\sigma_{c_1}^2 + \sigma_{c_2}^2 + \cdots + \sigma_{c_n}^2}{n}$$

The horizontal axis in Fig. 7-3 indicates the number of securities in the portfolio (assuming equal dollar amounts of each). The vertical axis measures risk: standard deviation of return (σ_p). For generality, risk is stated in relative terms, a value of one representing the risk associated with a perfectly diversified portfolio (i.e., a portfolio containing an infinitely large number of securities). The solid curve indicates the total risk of each portfolio; the dashed line indicates the portion due to uncertainty about the level of the index.

As the figure shows, a little diversification can go a long way toward reducing risk. A portfolio containing 15 or 20 securities may be considered well diversified in this respect.

Some investors are required by law to diversify. For example, many mutual funds are precluded from investing more than 5 percent of their capital in any single security. Moreover, they may not sell securities short. In selecting portfolios, the manager of such a fund must thus satisfy the following set of constraints:

$$0 \leq X_1 \leq .05$$
$$0 \leq X_2 \leq .05$$
$$\vdots$$
$$0 \leq X_N \leq .05$$

Needless to say, any investor may impose upper- and lower-bound constraints on a portfolio analysis to force some degree of diversification. Such a procedure guards against overinvestment in seemingly (but not actually) underpriced securities. Forced diversification thus offers protection against excessively optimistic predictions. It may also make it possible to entirely avoid the explicit consideration of the unique risk associated with each of the securities (i.e., the values of the σ_{c_i}'s). If upper and lower bounds are sufficiently constraining, b_p may reasonably be used to measure risk, since total risk (σ_p) will be approximately equal to b_p times a constant (σ_I).

To summarize, if a single-index model appears to be appropriate, and if relatively stringent upper and lower bounds on holdings are either required or appear to be desirable, then b_p (the *responsiveness* of a portfolio's rate of return to changes in the level of the index) may be used to measure risk.

The discussion of the previous section suggests that in some (but not all) circumstances, it is useful to substitute responsiveness for standard deviation (the traditional measure of risk). The associated portfolio analysis problem is surprisingly easy to solve. This section shows how it is done.

PORTFOLIO ANALYSIS USING RESPONSIVENESS AS A MEASURE OF RISK

Few estimates are required for the analysis. Two predictions are needed for each security:

E_i—expected return on security i
b_i—responsiveness of the return on security i to a one-unit change in the (single most important) index

No estimates concerning the performance of the index need be made explicitly. Of course some notion about the expected level of the index is required to form the set of E_i values. And after the analysis is complete, some estimate of the possible variability of the level of the index will be required in order to meaningfully evaluate the desirability of alternative values of b_p. But only the E_i and b_i values are needed to actually find the set of efficient portfolios.

Figure 7-4 shows the typical shape of the region of feasible combinations of E_p and b_p. Efficient combinations lie along the upper left-hand border; they provide the maximum attainable value of E_p for each value of b_p. The goal is to find the set of efficient portfolios—those plotting along the efficient border.

As usual, it is convenient to invoke a function that includes both the

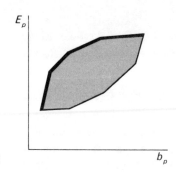

E_p

b_p

FIGURE 7-4

measure of risk and the expected return. For this problem, a useful objective is to

maximize $\quad Z = (1 - \lambda)E_p - \lambda b_p$

Consider the case in which λ equals zero: Z equals E_p, and maximizing Z is equivalent to maximizing E_p. Figure 7-5a shows a set of equal-Z lines for this case. Combinations of E_p and b_p lying along any given line have the same value of Z. Higher lines represent larger values of Z. When λ equals zero, the portfolio with the largest attainable value of Z is the one lying at the upper right-hand end of the efficient border.

Figure 7-5b shows a case in which $\lambda = .5$. E_p and b_p are given equal weight; the equal Z lines slope upward at a 45-degree angle. The higher (and farther left) a line, the greater the value of Z it represents. As before, the portfolio with the largest attainable value of Z plots on the efficient border.

Figure 7-5c illustrates a case in which λ equals 1. Only b_p is important; maximizing Z is equivalent to minimizing b_p. The portfolio with the largest attainable value of Z plots at the lower left-hand end of the efficient border.

The meaning of λ should be clear: it indicates the relative importance of risk vis-à-vis expected return. To find the complete set of efficient portfolios,

maximize $Z = (1 - \lambda)E_p - \lambda b_p$

for all values of λ between 0 and 1 (inclusive).

Since all constraints are linear and the objective function is also linear (due to the selection of b_p as a measure of risk), the efficient border is simply a series of linear segments. This means that several values of λ may lead to the choice of the same portfolio, while other values may lead to the choice of several alternative portfolios. This is illustrated in Fig. 7-6a to e. When λ equals λ_1, portfolio a gives the largest attainable value of Z. When λ rises to λ_2, portfolio a is still optimal. But when it rises further, to λ_3, portfolio a, portfolio b, and any portfolio made up by combining them, all have the same value of Z. When λ rises further yet, to λ_4, only portfolio b is optimal. And it remains so as λ rises even more, to λ_5.

These characteristics cause no harm. In fact, they make the solution procedure especially simple.

Recall the objective function:

$$Z = (1 - \lambda)E_p - \lambda b_p$$

Substituting the definitions of E_p and b_p,

$$Z = (1 - \lambda)(X_1 E_1 + X_2 E_2 + \cdots + X_N E_N) \\ - \lambda(X_1 b_1 + X_2 b_2 + \cdots + X_N b_N)$$

FIGURE 7-5

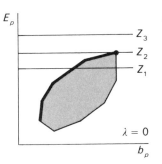

(a)

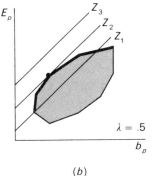

(b)

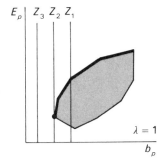

(c)

FIGURE 7-6

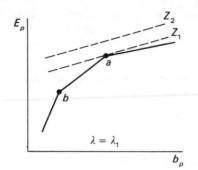

(a)

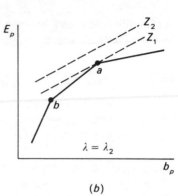

(b)

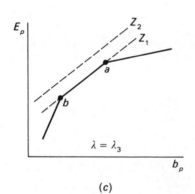

(c)

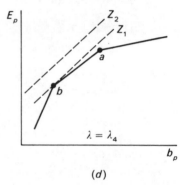

(d)

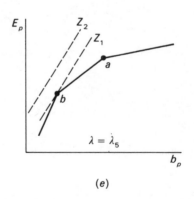

(e)

Regrouping,

$$Z = X_1[(1 - \lambda)E_1 - \lambda b_1]$$
$$+ X_2[(1 - \lambda)E_2 - \lambda b_2]$$
$$+$$
$$\cdot$$
$$\cdot$$
$$\cdot$$
$$+ X_N[(1 - \lambda)E_N - \lambda b_N]$$

To simplify the notation, let

$$z_i = (1 - \lambda)E_i - \lambda b_i$$
$$\text{then} \quad Z = X_1 z_1 + X_2 z_2 + \cdots + X_N z_N$$

For any given value of λ, a figure of merit (z_i) can be computed for each security. The higher z_i, the more desirable the security. In the absence of upper bounds on holdings, the optimal portfolio would simply consist of the security with the largest value of z_i. Given upper bounds, the solution involves the maximum allowable holding of the most attractive security, plus the maximum allowable holding of the next most attractive, etc., until all funds have been invested.

The simplest case arises when the proportion invested in each security can be no more than $1/n$, where n is an integer. For example, assume that n equals 20. Then

$$X_1 \leqq .05$$
$$X_2 \leqq .05$$
$$\vdots$$
$$X_N \leqq .05$$

For any given value of λ, the solution to such a problem would be to hold the 20 most attractive securities — each one at its upper bound.

In general, to maximize Z for any given value of λ when holdings are constrained so that:

$$X_i \leqq \frac{1}{n} \qquad \text{for every security } i \text{ (where } n \text{ is an integer)}$$

1. Compute $z_i = (1 - \lambda)E_i - \lambda b_i$ for every security.
2. Select the n securities with the largest values of z_i.

Problems of modest size can be solved graphically. Each security is represented by a line relating the value of z_i to that of λ. Figure 7-7 provides an example. When $\lambda = 0$, $z_i = E_i$. The vertical axis on the left can thus be regarded as plotting the expected return of each security. When $\lambda = 1$, $z_i = -b_i$. The vertical axis on the right can thus be regarded as plotting the negative of the responsiveness of each security. To draw the line associated with a security, plot and connect the points representing its expected return and responsiveness. In the example shown in Fig. 7-7, $E_i = 2$ and $b_i = 1$.

Figure 7-8 illustrates a case involving five securities with the constraint that at least two be held. In terms of the notation used earlier,

$$N = 5 \qquad n = 2$$

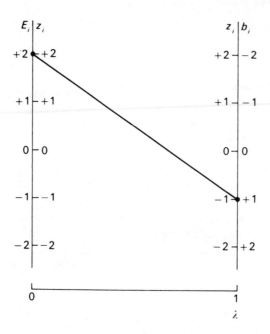

FIGURE 7-7

For any given value of λ, the optimal portfolio can be determined by simple inspection. It consists of the securities associated with the top n lines (each one constituting one-nth of the portfolio).

It is convenient to denote the nth line from the top as the *border line*. Formally:

The line associated with security j is the border line for a given value of λ if there are $(n-1)$ securities for which $z_i > z_j$ for the given value of λ.

The security associated with the border line is *in* the optimal portfolio for the specified value of λ, as are all securities associated with lines above the border. All others are *out* of the portfolio.

For certain values of λ there will be ties; in Fig. 7-8, λ_y is such a value. Either the line associated with security 1 or that associated with security 3 could be considered the border. Any of the following portfolios would be optimal:

1. A portfolio with
    $X_1 = .5$
    $X_2 = .5$
2. A portfolio with
    $X_2 = .5$
    $X_3 = .5$

3. Any combination of these portfolios (in other words
   $X_2 = .5$
   and values of X_1 and X_3 that sum to .5)

This is a case of the type shown earlier in Fig. 7-6c. Portfolios 1 and 2 above, like those in Fig. 7-6c, lie at *corners* along the efficient E_p, b_p boundary. Portfolios meeting the requirements of portfolio 3 above lie along the linear section of the E_p, b_p boundary joining the points representing portfolios 1 and 2.

In general, values of λ for which the border line is unique give portfolios lying at corners along the efficient E_p, b_p boundary. All other efficient portfolios are simply combinations of adjacent corner portfolios.

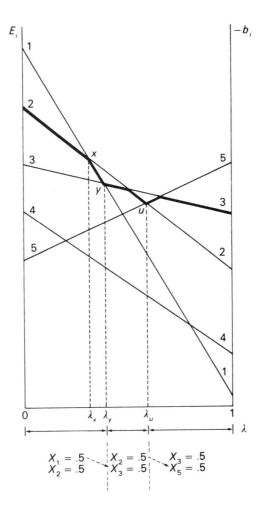

FIGURE 7-8

To find the full set of efficient portfolios requires the determination of the border line corresponding to every value of λ in a diagram such as that shown in Fig. 7-8. This is easily done. To begin, let $\lambda = 0$. The border line is the nth from the top at the left-hand side of the diagram. It corresponds to the security with the nth-highest expected return. The first corner portfolio is the one with the greatest attainable expected return. In Fig. 7-8 it consists of securities 1 and 2, as indicated at the bottom of the figure. Line 2 is the initial border line (throughout the diagram, the border line is shaded for emphasis).

Now consider larger values of λ. As λ increases, line 2 remains the border line for a while. Obviously it will remain so until another line crosses it. This occurs at point x, when $\lambda = \lambda_x$. As λ increases to values above λ_x, line 1 becomes the border line. Note, however, that the composition of the efficient portfolio has not changed—only the border line. In general:

If a border line is intersected by a steeper line (i.e., from above) moving from left to right, only the border line changes; the composition of the efficient portfolio is unaffected.

As λ increases further, no change takes place until the new border line (line 1) is intersected. This occurs at point y, when $\lambda = \lambda_y$. As λ increases to values above λ_y, line 3 becomes the border line. The efficient portfolio now includes securities 2 and 3, as indicated at the bottom of the figure. Security 1 (associated with the previous border line) has been replaced by security 3 (associated with the new border line). In general:

If a border line is intersected by a line that is less steep (i.e., from below) moving from left to right, both the border line and the composition of the efficient portfolio change.

In the case shown in Fig. 7-8 there are three *corner portfolios*. The first, obtained when λ lies between zero and λ_y, includes securities 1 and 2. The second, obtained when λ lies between λ_y and λ_u, includes securities 2 and 3. The third, obtained when λ lies between λ_u and 1, includes securities 3 and 5. The final portfolio is, of course, the minimum-risk (b_p) portfolio consistent with the stated diversification constraints.

Graphical solution of a large problem would be tedious at best. Fortunately the procedure can easily be automated. Section E of the Supplement provides the details.

The procedure may be modified to handle more complex problems. Variations in upper and lower bounds can be accommodated. For any given value of λ, every security is initially included in the minimum amount required. Then securities are set at their upper bounds, one at a time, proceeding in order of decreasing z_i until the sum of the X_i's exceeds 1. The amount of the last security considered is then reduced to make the sum equal precisely 1.

Another modification can accommodate further restrictions on holdings. There is always a danger that the standard procedure may select too many securities from a single industry. To guard against this, it may be desirable to place an upper bound on the number of securities selected from any (industry) group. For example, assume that 200 securities are to be analyzed and that 25 of them are associated with the electronics industry. The analyst might require that at least 20 securities be included in any portfolio selected, with no more than 5 from the electronics industry. Of course in every case, the most attractive securities (those with the highest values of z_i) should be given priority in the selection process.

To accomplish this, a preanalysis of the securities in each industry is required. In this example, the lines associated with the 25 electronics securities would be drawn in the usual way. Then an analysis would be performed as if portfolios consisting of five securities were to be selected. A series of border lines would be constructed — each the fifth from the top for the given value of λ. Next, the lines (and portions of lines) lying below this border would be deleted. Only the border lines and those line segments lying above them would be used for the final analysis. This would insure that only the five best electronics securities are considered for every value of λ.

To summarize, the procedure is initially applied to each subgroup of securities (e.g., those in a given industry) to determine the line segments to be used in the final analysis. The selected line segments are then used to determine the overall set of efficient portfolios consistent with the full set of requirements for diversification.

The procedures described in this chapter are normative in nature. They are intended for use with predictions (however derived). No assumptions are made about the manner in which the predictions are obtained nor about their overall merit.

INDEX MODELS AND CAPITAL MARKET THEORY

Superficially, index models bear a close resemblance to the results obtained when markets are assumed to be perfect, investors are assumed to completely agree with one another, and borrowing and lending are assumed to be available on identical terms. Under such conditions all efficient portfolios are perfectly correlated with one another, and the appropriate measure of risk is *volatility* — a concept closely related to the responsiveness of rate of return to changes in the level of a single (all-important) index. To obtain an efficient portfolio in such a world, one need only invest in a cross section of the market, borrowing or lending to the extent required to obtain an appropriate combination of risk and expected return.

How do the implications of capital market theory differ from the assumptions behind the models described here—particularly the single-index model and the model based on responsiveness? In a world of complete agreement and perfect markets, these models would not prove particularly useful. Capital market theory implies that prices will adjust until each security's expected return is neither too low nor too high, given its risk (appropriately measured). If this were the case, there would be no reason to explicitly consider both expected return and risk when selecting a portfolio (although the exercise might prove harmless). Portfolio analysis as a normative technique is based on the assumption that some securities may be overpriced or underpriced. Both expected return and risk are considered for the express purpose of finding cases in which one does not bear the appropriate relationship to the other (according to the predictions under consideration).

Portfolio analysis is designed for the investor who believes his predictions to be superior to those implicit in the current prices of securities. Index models simply make it easy to state and analyze such predictions.

8.

THE RECORD

Theory enables one to cope with reality. This is primarily a book about theory, both normative and positive. However, some elements of reality need to be examined. This is the task of the present chapter.

Both portfolio theory and capital market theory deal with predictions about the future. But empirical work must deal with the past. How can the two be related?

The past may provide evidence about earlier predictions. If people predicted the future properly ten years ago, the record of the last ten years might be used to measure their previous predictions. Capital market theory may be tested in this manner. But such a test does not concern capital market theory per se; instead, it deals with a combination—capital market theory plus the assumption that the record reflects earlier predictions.

What of the predictions of today? Perhaps people assume that the future will be like the past. If they don't, perhaps they should. Predictions based on past relationships may be as useful as those obtained with more traditional methods (e.g., security analysis). Normative procedures employing such methods may be tested. Again, a combination is considered—portfolio theory plus the assumption that the future will be like the past.

These issues will be considered in greater detail in later sections. At this point, it suffices to raise them.

STATISTICS AND PREDICTIONS

Simple measures are needed to adequately summarize the past. It is not difficult to redefine the concepts introduced in Parts I and II for this purpose. To predict the future, possible outcomes are assigned weights on the basis of their *probabilities* of occurrence. To summarize the past, outcomes are assigned weights on the basis of their *relative frequencies* of occurrence.

The *expected* rate of return is found by multiplying every possible rate of return by its probability of occurrence. A counterpart, the *average* rate of return, is found by multiplying every observed rate of return by its relative frequency of occurrence.

The *risk* of a portfolio is measured by the standard deviation of rate of return, based on the probabilities that various deviations from the expected value will occur. The *variability* of a portfolio's rate of return is also measured by the standard deviation of rate of return, based instead on the relative frequencies of various deviations from the average rate of return.

In some cases the same name is used for a measure, whether relative frequencies or probabilities are employed. The relationship between two variables in the past may be summarized with an (actual) correlation coefficient; the (actual) volatility of a security or portfolio may be computed. The nature of the measure should be clear from the context in which it is discussed.

Summary measures may be used to *describe* a set of data. For such purposes, the formulas given in Parts I and II suffice (with relative frequencies substituted for probabilities). But there may be another reason for obtaining such measures. The data may be considered simply a small set of results generated by some underlying process; the goal is to *infer* from the data something about the more general process. For such purposes the formulas may be modified slightly[1] and various statistical procedures invoked to test the *significance* of the results as indicators of the characteristics of the underlying process.

The techniques of statistical inference lie outside the domain of this book. The reader is simply cautioned to regard with skepticism any presumption that summary measures obtained from past data will accurately predict the values of corresponding measures in the future.

A key element in the theory presented in Part II is the *market portfolio*, composed of proportionate holdings of all securities. Theoretically, it includes many kinds of capital assets. But it would be impractical to actually measure the performance of such a portfolio. For empirical work, some sort of surrogate is required.

THE MARKET PORTFOLIO

Several indexes of security prices are available; two of the more popular are Dow-Jones' Index of 30 Industrial Stocks and Standard and Poor's Composite Index. Neither includes dividends. However, it is possible to estimate the dividends received by the owner of such a group of securities and then compute the overall rate of return.

A number of investigators have taken a different approach. First, the rate of return for each of a number of securities in each time period of interest is determined. The rate of return on the market portfolio is assumed to equal the average of the values for the individual securities:

$$R_{Mt} = \frac{1}{N} \sum_{i=1}^{N} R_{it}$$

where R_{Mt} = rate of return on the market portfolio in time period t
R_{it} = rate of return on security i in time period t
N = number of securities

The value of R_{Mt} is equivalent to the return obtained by investing an equal dollar amount in every security.

Figures 8-1 to 8-3 summarize the results obtained by Fisher and

---

[1] For example, to account for the paucity of data, the variance is multiplied by $n/(n-1)$, where n is the number of observations. This will have little effect on the result (as intended) if n is reasonably large.

Lorie,[1] applying this procedure to all the securities listed on the New York Stock Exchange for the forty years from 1926 to 1965. Figure 8-1 shows the annual rate of return; both dividends and price appreciation (or depreciation) are included, but no allowance has been made for taxes or brokerage commissions.[2]

As Fig. 8-1 indicates, return has fluctuated more or less randomly around a value of about 16.5 percent per year. However, the fluctuations were more violent prior to World War II than afterwards. The change has been attributed to factors such as improved securities regulation, increased governmental control over the business cycle, greater investor sophistication, and changes in attitudes toward risk. Whatever the causes, it is widely believed that there has been a permanent change in the behavior of securities listed on the New York Stock Exchange.

[1] The data are based on figures given in Lawrence Fisher and James H. Lorie, Rates of Return on Investments in Common Stock: The Year-by-Year Record, 1926–1965, *Journal of Business*, July, 1968, pp. 291–316.

[2] Fisher and Lorie provide results for a number of cases that differ with respect to tax rates, commisions paid and dividends reinvested. The values given here were derived in the following manner:

1. The elements along the main diagonal in Fisher and Lorie's table 3a were assumed to represent

$$100\left[\frac{V_{t+1}}{V_t(1 + c_t)} - 1\right]$$

where V_{t+1} = value of portfolio in year $t + 1$
V_t = value of portfolio in year t
c_t = commission rate in year t

2. The elements along the main diagonal in Fisher and Lorie's table 3b were assumed to represent

$$100\left[\frac{V_{t+1}(1 - c_{t+1})}{V_t(1 + c_t)} - 1\right]$$

3. The values from tables 3a and 3b were used to obtain estimates of the commission rate in each year.

4. The elements along the main diagonal in Fisher and Lorie's table 2a were assumed to represent

$$100\left[\frac{V_{t+1} + d_{t,t+1}}{V_t(1 + c_t)} - 1\right]$$

where $d_{t,t+1}$ = dividends paid on portfolio between years t and $t + 1$

5. Then the values from table 2a and the derived commission rates were used to estimate

$$100\left[\frac{V_{t+1} + d_{t,t+1}}{V_t} - 1\right] \qquad \text{for each year}$$

The resulting values are given in Fig. 8-1. The year specified refers to the end point; e.g., the year 1965 ends on December 31, 1965.

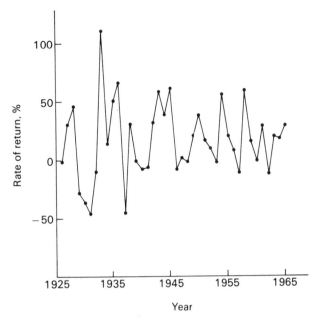

FIGURE 8-1

Rate of return on the market
portfolio, 1926–1965.

Figures 8-2 and 8-3 summarize the data for (*a*) the first twenty years,
(*b*) the second twenty years, and (*c*) the entire period. The diagrams
in Fig. 8-2 are frequency distributions—they indicate the number of
years in which the rate of return fell within various ranges (for
example, 0 to 10 percent). The diagrams in Fig. 8-3 are cumulative
distributions—they indicate the percent of the years in which the rate
of return fell below each possible level. For example, Fig. 8-3*a* shows
that the rate of return was below zero in approximately 45 percent
of the years from 1926 to 1945.

Table 8-1 (page 148) shows the differences between the two periods
numerically. Although the average return fell slightly, the really
dramatic change was in variability; the rate of return fluctuated far
less from year to year during the latter period (though the variation
was still substantial).

As indicated in Part II, the real importance of the market portfolio
lies in its correlation with highly diversified portfolios. Fluctuations
in its rate of return should explain more of the variation in the returns
of individual securities than the fluctuations in any other portfolio's
return. Some investigators have used this attribute to construct an
index directly. Given the rates of return for a number of securities
over time, statistical techniques are employed to derive a series of
values (one for each period) with the desired property.

Clearly there are many ways to construct an index or market-portfolio surrogate. Fortunately, those that have been obtained appear to be highly correlated with one another. Table 8-2 provides some examples. For either testing positive theory or applying normative theory, the choice of a particular index may not be especially crucial; if two indexes are highly correlated, either may be used.

THE EFFECTIVENESS OF DIVERSIFICATION The high degree of correlation among indexes of rate of return is not too surprising. If much of the risk of most securities is systematic (in reaction to market fluctuations), then the rate of return on any

FIGURE 8-2

(a) Distribution of the rate of return on the market portfolio, 1926–1945. (b) Distribution of the rate of return on the market portfolio, 1946–1965. (c) Distribution of the rate of return on the market portfolio, 1926–1965.

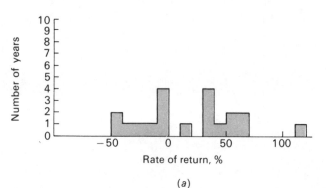

(a)

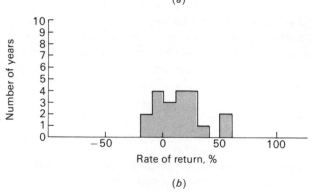

(b)

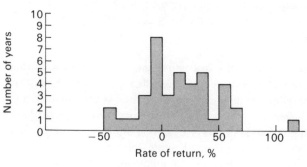

(c)

reasonably well-diversified portfolio will be highly correlated with that of the market as a whole. But how many securities must be included to obtain a *reasonably well-diversified* portfolio? In other words, how effective is diversification in reducing variability?

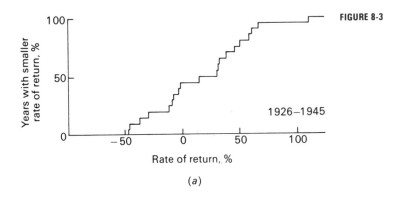

FIGURE 8-3

(a)

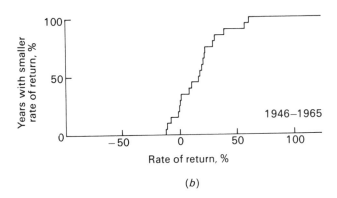

(b)

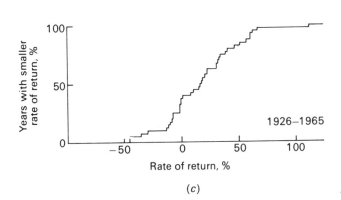

(c)

	TABLE 8-1	Period	Average annual rate of return	Standard deviation of annual rate of return (variability)

TABLE 8-1
Summary data: Rate of
return on the market
portfolio

Period	Average annual rate of return	Standard deviation of annual rate of return (variability)
1926–1945	17.8%	41.2%
1946–1965	15.1	19.8
1926–1965	16.5	32.3

TABLE 8-2
Correlations between indexes

Indexes	Period	Correlation coefficient	Source
1. Fisher's Combination Investment Performance Index (includes dividends) 2. Fisher's Combination Price Index (excludes dividends)	1926–1960	.9997	a
1. Fisher's Combination Price Index 2. Standard and Poor's Composite Index	1926–1960	.9191	a
1. Fisher's Combination Price Index 2. Dow-Jones' Industrial Average	1926–1960	.9852	a
1. Standard and Poor's Composite Index 2. Dow-Jones' Industrial Average	1926–1960	.9754	a
1. King's Derived Market Factor 2. Standard and Poor's Index of 90 Stocks	1927–1960	.9714	b
1. Feeney and Hester's Derived Rate of Return Index 2. Index of Rate of Return on Dow-Jones' 30 Industrial Stocks	1951–1963	.915	c

a. Lawrence Fisher, Some New Stock-Market Indexes, *Journal of Business*, January, 1966, pp. 191–225.
b. Benjamin F. King, Market and Industry Factors in Stock Price Behavior, *Journal of Business*, January, 1966, pp. 139–190.
c. George J. Feeney and Donald D. Hester, Stock-Market Indices: A Principal Components Analysis, in Donald D. Hester and James Tobin, eds., "Risk Aversion and Portfolio Choice," John Wiley & Sons, Inc., New York, 1967, pp. 110–138.

A study by Evans[1] provides an answer. The variability of rate of return over the period 1958 to 1967 was measured for 2,400 portfolios chosen from a set of 470 common stocks.[2] Each of the first 60 portfolios included only one security. Each of the next 60 portfolios included two securities (in equal dollar amounts). Each of the last 60 portfolios included 40 securities (in equal dollar amounts).[3] For each group of 60 portfolios, the average value of the standard deviation of rate of return[4] was computed. This figure provides an estimate of the variability of rate of return for a typical portfolio of comparable diversification. Of particular importance, the systematic component of variability should approximate that of a portfolio with volatility equal to 1.

Figure 8-4 shows Evans' results. Each point indicates the average variability of a group of 60 portfolios of comparable diversification. As diversification is increased, the standard deviation of rate of return falls, approaching a level readily interpreted as the standard deviation of return for the market portfolio. As the figure shows, the data can be approximated very well by a simple formula:

$$\sigma_p = 11.91 + \frac{8.63}{n}$$

where n = number of securities in the portfolio (held in equal dollar amounts).

The greater the diversification (i.e., the larger the value of n), the closer σ_p will be to 11.91. The variability due to systematic risk for a portfolio with volatility equal to 1 can be assumed to be approximately 11.9 percent per six months.

According to the formula, the total variability of a typical 1 security portfolio (with $n = 1$) is approximately 20.5 percent per six months. Assuming that each point in the figure does in fact represent a portfolio with volatility equal to 1, it is a simple matter to estimate the proportion of an average security's total risk due to its relationship

[1] John Leslie Evans, "Diversification and the Reduction of Dispersion: An Empirical Analysis," doctoral dissertation, Graduate School of Business Administration, University of Washington, Seattle, Wash., 1968.
[2] Each of the 470 securities was included in Standard and Poor's 500 Stocks in 1958.
[3] The securities for each portfolio were chosen randomly.
[4] Evans used the natural logarithms of value relatives computed every six months to represent semiannual rates of return. This procedure has been used by several investigators. In essence, it expresses rate of return in terms of an equivalent rate compounded continuously.

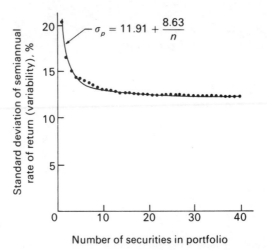

FIGURE 8-4

Variability versus portfolio diversification.

with the market as a whole. Let σ_T and σ_S represent total and systematic risk, respectively. For a typical security,

$$\sigma_T = 20.5 \quad \text{and} \quad \sigma_S = 11.9$$

$$\text{thus} \quad \frac{(\sigma_S)^2}{(\sigma_T)^2} = .34$$

During the period studied, approximately 34 percent of the variance in a typical security's rate of return appeared to be attributable to its relationship with the market as a whole. As Fig. 8-4 indicates, under such conditions diversification can be highly beneficial. A typical portfolio with equal dollar amounts of five securities will have only 14 percent more risk (measured by σ_p) than the most highly diversified portfolio imaginable (i.e., one with n sufficiently large to make the second term in the formula insignificant). A typical portfolio with equal dollar amounts of 10 securities will have only 7 percent more risk than the minimum possible; while a typical portfolio with equal amounts of 20 securities will have only 3 percent more than the minimum.

In sum, a little diversification can go a long way.

MARKET AND INDUSTRY FACTORS

A study by King[1] provides further evidence on the relation between market fluctuations and the variability of a typical security's rate of return. Sixty-three common stocks were analyzed, with rates of return computed on a monthly basis from June, 1927 to December, 1960.[2]

[1] Benjamin F. King, Market and Industry Factors in Stock Price Behavior, *Journal of Business*, January, 1966, pp. 139–190.
[2] King used the natural logarithms of monthly value relatives to represent the rates of return.

For each month, the average value of the 63 rates of return was used to represent the return on the market portfolio.[1] The volatility of each security was estimated, along with the proportion of variance attributable to market fluctuations. To estimate the typical proportion of variance attributable to market factors, King used the average value of the corresponding figures for the 63 securities.

The analysis was performed for four separate time periods and for the overall period. Table 8-3 shows the results. The figure for the most recent subperiod does not differ substantially from Evans' estimate, but the others do. Over the entire period, about one-half the variance in a typical security's rate of return was attributable to market fluctuations. Under such conditions, diversification can reduce risk very rapidly; the hypothetical case described in the previous chapter (shown in Fig. 7-3) provides an illustration.

Period	Average proportion of variance attributable to market fluctuations
June 1927–September 1935	58.4%
October 1935–February 1944	55.7
March 1944–July 1952	41.2
August 1952–December 1960	30.7

TABLE 8-3
Proportion of security risk attributable to market factors

As shown earlier, the rate of return on the market portfolio fluctuated less after World War II than before, causing a corresponding decrease in the amount of variation in a typical security's rate of return attributable to the market (i.e., systematic risk). Evidence obtained by Blume[2] suggests that variability due to other factors (i.e., unsystematic risk) also declined. However, the decline in the *proportion* of variance attributable to market factors indicates that systematic risk decreased more than unsystematic risk. Some have attributed this to greater investor sophistication; each security is presumably valued (and revalued) more on its own merits than formerly. Some have argued that the change may not be permanent, no matter what its (temporary) cause. For investors planning to hold reasonably well-diversified portfolios, the change is not crucially important—only systematic risk will matter; moreover, relatively little diversification will go a long way, even if no more than 30 percent of a typical security's total risk is systematic.

For normative applications it may suffice to take into account risk

[1] Another procedure was also tested.
[2] Marshall E. Blume, II, "The Assessment of Portfolio Performance: An Application of Portfolio Theory," doctoral dissertation, University of Chicago, March, 1968.

due to market fluctuations (i.e., use a single-index model), but additional indexes may prove useful. How should they be chosen? And how useful might they be?

King's detailed analysis of the relationships among securities over the entire period (June, 1927 to December, 1960) provides some relevant evidence. As indicated earlier, market fluctuations accounted for 52 percent of the variance in a typical security's rate of return. A group of industry indexes accounted for another 11 percent. Perhaps most gratifying, a procedure designed to group securities solely on the basis of comovement in their returns during the period produced results conforming almost perfectly to those implied by traditional industrial classifications.

If an index model is to be used for normative purposes, it is clearly imperative that the market as a whole be represented by some sort of index. If additional indexes are to be used, it appears reasonable to let them represent conditions in major industries, using standard classifications.

MEASURING PERFORMANCE Many measures of past performance have been proposed; most of them either ignore risk entirely or treat it inadequately. There are exceptions; at least three measures attempt to account for risk in an acceptable manner. Each is related to the implications of capital market theory. The three measures are defined in this section; their use to assess the performance of mutual funds is discussed in the next.

Recall the definition of the capital market line. Its slope can be considered the price of risk reduction for efficient portfolios:

$$r_e = \frac{E_M - p}{\sigma_M}$$

where r_e = price of risk reduction for efficient portfolios
E_M = expected rate of return on market portfolio
p = pure rate of interest
σ_M = standard deviation of rate of return on market portfolio

All these values deal with predictions. To measure the past performance of the market portfolio, actual values must be employed. An analogous measure would be

$$\frac{A_M - p'}{\sigma'_M}$$

where A_M = average rate of return on market portfolio
p' = actual pure interest rate

σ'_M = variability (standard deviation of actual rate of return) of market portfolio

The past performance of any portfolio can be summarized using such a *reward-to-variability ratio* as:

$$\left(\frac{r}{v}\right)_p = \frac{A_p - p'}{\sigma'_p}$$

where $\left(\dfrac{r}{v}\right)_p$ = reward-to-variability ratio for portfolio

A_p = average rate of return for portfolio

p' = actual pure interest rate

σ'_p = variability (standard deviation of actual rate of return) of portfolio

Figure 8-5 illustrates the usefulness of the construct. Point p' indicates the actual interest rate for riskless commitments; points i and j represent the performance of portfolios i and j. Which portfolio was better? In terms of average return, portfolio i was better; in terms of variability, portfolio j was better. Note however that by combining borrowing or lending with investment in portfolio j, an investor could have attained any point along line $p'jx$. By combining borrowing or lending with investment in portfolio i, he could have attained any point along line $p'iy$. But line $p'jx$ dominates line $p'iy$. Given the ability to borrow or lend at rate p', portfolio j's performance was clearly superior to that of portfolio i. A natural measure of performance is thus the slope of the line associated with the portfolio. But the slope of the line *is* the reward-to-variability ratio, as Fig. 8-5

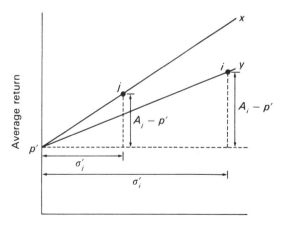

FIGURE 8-5

Variability (standard deviation of rate of return)

indicates. The greater the ratio, the steeper the line and the better the performance of the portfolio.

Now consider a world in which $A_p = E_p$, $\sigma'_p = \sigma_p$, and $p' = p$. Under such conditions all portfolios that appear to be efficient (including the market portfolio) will prove to be efficient after the fact (and vice versa). In a diagram of the type shown in Fig. 8-5, all such portfolios will lie along the same line—the empirical counterpart to the predicted capital market line. Moreover, they will all have the same reward-to-variability ratio. Inadequately diversified portfolios will all have smaller ratios.

Needless to say, such a situation is not very likely. Portfolios that appear to be efficient before the fact may not prove to be so after the fact. And portfolios that appear to be inefficient may prove to be efficient. Even among highly diversified portfolios, reward-to-variability ratios are likely to differ considerably.

Although inaccurate, predictions may be unbiased (i.e., as likely to be optimistic as pessimistic). Under such conditions, the reward-to-variability ratios of highly diversified portfolios (including the market portfolio) will vary more or less randomly around the value associated with the predicted capital market line. The ratios for other portfolios will vary more or less randomly around lower values. Persistent differences among reward-to-variability ratios will arise only in cases involving inadequately diversified portfolios.

The reward-to-variability ratio is designed to measure the performance of a portfolio. The investor is presumed to have placed a substantial portion of his wealth in the portfolio in question. Variability is thus the relevant measure of the amount of risk actually borne.

To evaluate the performance of a single security, or that of a portfolio constituting only part of an investor's holdings, a different measure is needed. Variability will not adequately represent the risk actually borne. A more appropriate choice is volatility.

Recall the definition of the security market line. Its slope can be considered the price of risk reduction for securities. For any security or portfolio plotting along the line,

$$r_s = \frac{E_i - p}{b_i}$$

where r_s = price of risk reduction for securities

E_i = expected rate of return on security (or portfolio) i

p = pure interest rate

b_i = volatility of security (or portfolio) i

The corresponding measure of past performance is the *reward-to-volatility ratio*:

$$\left(\frac{r}{b}\right)_i = \frac{A_i - p'}{b_i'}$$

where $\left(\dfrac{r}{b}\right)_i$ = reward-to-volatility ratio of security (or portfolio) i

A_i = average rate of return on security (or portfolio) i

p' = actual pure interest rate

b_i' = actual volatility of security (or portfolio) i

Figure 8-6 illustrates the usefulness of this construct. Point p' represents the actual pure interest rate, points i and j the performance of two securities or portfolios. By combining security or portfolio i with borrowing or lending, any point along line $p'iy$ can be attained. But such points are clearly dominated by points along line $p'jx$—attainable by borrowing or lending combined with security or portfolio j. The steeper the line associated with a security or portfolio, the better it is. As Fig. 8-6 indicates, the reward-to-volatility ratio *is* the slope of such a line.

In a world in which $A_i = E_i$, $b_i' = b_i$, and $p' = p$, all securities and portfolios would have identical reward-to-volatility ratios. In the real world, this is not likely to be the case. But if predictions are unbiased,

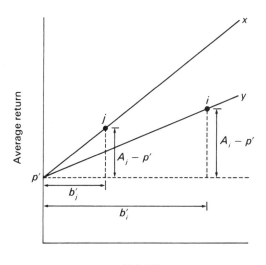

FIGURE 8-6

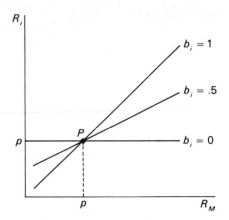

FIGURE 8-7

reward-to-volatility ratios will vary randomly around the value associated with the predicted security market line. There will be no persistent differences.

It is instructive to consider the relationship between a security or portfolio's characteristic line and its reward-to-volatility ratio. Recall the equilibrium condition for characteristic lines based on predictions: Each must pass through the point at which both rates of return equal the pure interest rate. Three lines meeting the requirement are shown in Fig. 8-7.

The actual relationship between the rate of return of a security or portfolio and that of the market portfolio can be represented by an *actual* characteristic line. The procedure differs from that described in Part II in only one respect: Relative frequencies are used instead of probabilities. Thus the line must pass through the point at which both returns equal their average values, and the slope (volatility) is determined by dividing the actual covariance by the actual variance of rate of return on the market portfolio.[1] Figure 8-8 provides an example.

Consider the performance of the market portfolio. It can be described by a characteristic line making a 45-degree angle with the origin, such as line *OPY* in Fig. 8-9. The performance of a riskless security (i.e., lending) can be described by a perfectly horizontal characteristic line, such as *p'PZ* in Fig. 8-9 (as before, *p'* represents the actual pure rate of interest). Any combination of lending plus investment in the market portfolio can be represented by a line between these two—for example, *VPW*. Any combination of borrowing plus

[1] The line obtained in this manner gives the minimum sum of squared deviations of actual values of return on the security or portfolio from the values indicated by the line. The procedure for finding the line is termed *linear regression by the method of least squares.*

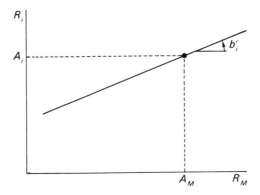

FIGURE 8-8

investment in the market portfolio can be represented by a line such as *TPU*.

Given the ability to borrow or lend at rate p', an investor could have obtained results lying along any desired characteristic line going through point P, at which both rates of return equal p'.

Consider the security or portfolio whose actual performance is represented by characteristic line *YY* in Fig. 8-10. The same volatility could have been obtained by selecting an appropriate combination of borrowing or lending plus investment in the market portfolio. Such an alternative is represented by characteristic line *ZPZ*, constructed to be parallel to line *YY* and to pass through point *P* (at which both rates of return equal the pure interest rate).

FIGURE 8-9

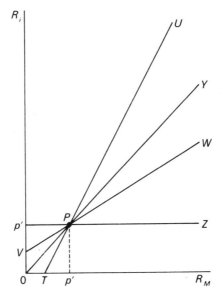

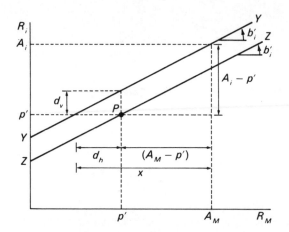

FIGURE 8-10

The slope of a security or portfolio's characteristic line equals its volatility. Thus in Fig. 8-10,

$$b'_i = \frac{A_i - p'}{x}$$

Rearranging,

$$x = \frac{A_i - p'}{b'_i}$$

The expression on the right is the reward-to-volatility ratio. Separating the total distance (x) into two components:

$$\frac{r}{b} = d_h + (A_M - p')$$

The reward-to-volatility ratio can thus be regarded as a constant $(A_M - p')$ plus the horizontal distance from point P to the characteristic line of the security or portfolio in question. If this distance (d_h) is positive, performance was superior to that of a market-based portfolio of comparable volatility; if d_h is negative, it was worse.[1]

An alternative measure is the vertical distance from point P to the characteristic line, indicated in Fig. 8-10 by the distance d_v and denoted the *differential return*. Its meaning should be clear. According to the characteristic line, the security or portfolio in question offered an average differential return of this amount over and above that obtainable from a market-based portfolio of comparable volatility.

A positive differential return indicates that performance was superior to that of a market-based portfolio of comparable volatility; a negative differential return indicates that it was worse.

[1] Assuming positive volatility; if volatility was negative, the converse holds.

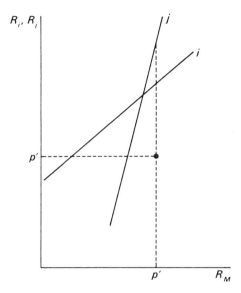

FIGURE 8-11

Obviously, differential return is closely related to the reward-to-volatility ratio. Either may be used to compare the performance of a security or portfolio with that of a market-based portfolio of similar volatility. However, they may give different results when used to make other comparisons. Figure 8-11 provides an example. On the basis of differential returns, the performance of the security or portfolio associated with characteristic line *j* was superior to that of the security or portfolio associated with line *i*. But on the basis of reward-to-volatility ratios, the performance of *i* was superior to that of *j*.

Which one was really better? The answer is security or portfolio *i*. Figure 8-12 shows why. By combining borrowing or lending with investment in *i*, results lying along any desired characteristic line through point *i'* could have been obtained. By combining borrowing or lending with investment in *j*, results lying along any desired characteristic line through point *j'* could have been obtained. Any combination based on *j* could thus have been outperformed by a combination of equal volatility based on *i*.

To summarize, the reward-to-volatility ratio may be used to compare securities or portfolios with one another. Either the reward-to-volatility ratio or the measure of differential return may be used to compare the performance of a security or portfolio with that of the market.[1]

[1] However, differential return offers certain statistical advantages. In particular, if $R_i - p'$ is regressed on $R_M - p'$, the intercept will be the differential return. Its deviation from zero can then be analyzed using standard statistical tests of significance.

FIGURE 8-12

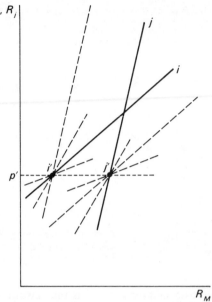

Each of the measures described in the previous section was
developed to assess the performance of mutual funds: the reward-
to-variability ratio by the present author,[1] the reward-to-volatility
ratio by Treynor,[2] and the measure of differential return by Jensen.[3]

An open-end mutual fund is an institution designed to provide both
diversification and professional management at relatively low cost.
The managers stand ready to issue new shares or retire old shares at
virtually any time. The *net asset value per share* is computed by
dividing the current market value of the fund's holdings by the
number of its shares outstanding. Generally, old shares can be
redeemed for the full (current) net asset value. New shares are usually
sold for an amount equal to the (current) net asset value plus a
"load" charge (typically 8 to 10 percent), which goes to the sales
organization. The managers of the fund are paid separately (an
annual fee of $\frac{1}{2}$ of 1 percent of the total net asset value is typical).
When securities are purchased or sold, an additional expense is
incurred for brokers' commissions. Such costs are not reported
explicitly; they are simply added to the purchase price when com-

[1] William F. Sharpe, Mutual Fund Performance, *Journal of Business*, January, 1966,
pp. 119–138.
[2] Jack L. Treynor, How to Rate Management of Investment Funds, *Harvard Business
Review*, January-February, 1965, pp. 63–75. Treynor proposed the term "volatility"
but did not provide a name for his measure of overall performance.
[3] Michael C. Jensen, "Risk, the Pricing of Capital Assets, and the Evaluation .of
Investment Portfolios," doctoral dissertation, University of Chicago, July, 1967.
Jensen did not propose a name for his measure; *differential return* seems suitable.

puting purchase costs and subtracted from the sales price when computing sales receipts.

Mutual funds are important for two reasons. First, their managers invest a great deal of money for a great many people. Second, the performance of a mutual fund is a matter of public record. Much effort (and money) is devoted to their management. The results can reasonably be considered typical of the performance of professional security analysts and investment managers (at least those required to invest large amounts of money).

Most mutual funds hold highly diversified portfolios—over 100 different securities are usually included. This may be due more to the fund's size than to the desire to minimize risk. The very act of investing 1 or 2 percent of the capital of a large fund could conceivably bid up the price of a security sufficiently to rob it of its initial appeal.

Because most mutual-fund portfolios are highly diversified, their performance is highly correlated with that of the market as a whole. Figure 8-13 shows the proportion of variance in the rate of return attributable to market fluctuations for a group of 115 mutual funds studied by Jensen.[1] On the average, approximately 85 percent of the

[1] *Ibid.* All 115 funds were in existence during the period 1955 to 1964. Of the total, 56 were in existence in 1945. The period covered for each fund runs from 1945 or the first year after 1945 for which data were available, to 1964. The securities included in Standard and Poor's Composite Index were used to represent the market portfolio. Jensen used the natural logarithms of value relatives computed every twelve months to express rates of return as continuously compounded annual values.

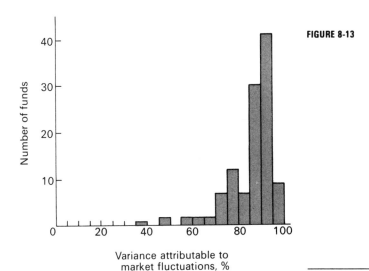

FIGURE 8-13

Variance attributable to
market fluctuations, %

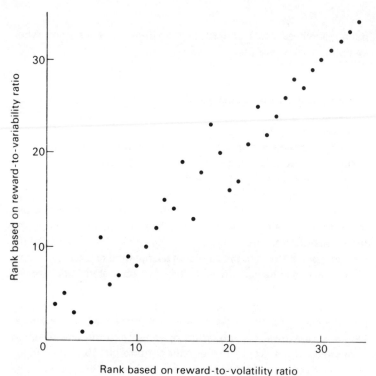

FIGURE 8-14

Rank based on reward-to-volatility ratio

variance could be attributed to market fluctuations. In other words,

$$b_p^2 \sigma_M^2 \approx .85\sigma_p^2$$

Taking the square root of both sides and rewriting,

$$\sigma_p \approx (1.085\sigma_M)b_p$$

Since most funds diversify extensively, volatility (b_p) should provide a good surrogate for variability (σ_p). Figure 8-14 shows that it does.[1] The performance of each of 34 mutual funds during the period 1954 to 1963 was assessed using the reward-to-variability ratio and the funds ranked from best (rank 1) to worst (rank 34). Then the procedure was repeated, using the reward-to-volatility ratio. As Fig. 8-14 shows, the rankings were very similar.

Although funds differ little in terms of correlation with the market, they differ considerably in volatility, as Fig. 8-15 shows.[2] The typical

[1] Based on data given in Sharpe, *loc. cit.*

[2] The figure is based on data given in Jensen, *op. cit.* Jensen used the securities in Standard and Poor's Composite Index to represent the market portfolio. Others have used the 30 securities in Dow-Jones' Industrial Average—a more conservative group of common stocks. This explains the somewhat higher levels of volatility obtained in other studies. For example, Treynor, *op. cit.* reported values ranging from "roughly one-third to about two" for a group of mutual funds.

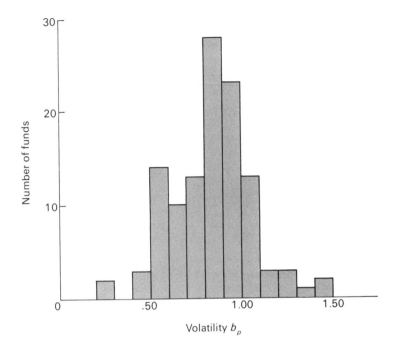

Volatility b_p **FIGURE 8-15**

mutual-fund portfolio appears to be more conservative than one made up of the securities in Standard and Poor's Composite Index (used by Jensen to represent the market); the average value of b_p was approximately .84.

The differences in volatility shown in Fig. 8-15 are not due to chance alone. Table 8-4 provides a breakdown, using the classifications assigned by a major reference service, based on the stated objectives of the funds.[1] By and large, mutual funds appear to do what they say they will do.

But do they do well? Figure 8-16 provides some evidence.[2] Each unlabeled point indicates the performance of one of 34 mutual funds during the period 1954 to 1963. Point M shows the results that would have been obtained from a portfolio consisting of the 30 securities used to compute the Dow-Jones' Industrial Average. Point P represents the approximate level of the pure interest rate during the period. Line PM is the empirical counterpart of the capital market line.

More funds plot below the line in Fig. 8-16 than above it. This is reflected in the distribution of reward-to-variability ratios shown in

[1] The material in the table is from Jensen, *op. cit.*, pp. V-29 to V-31. Quotations are from Arthur Wiesenberger, *Investment Companies*, Arthur Wiesenberger Company, 1961, p. 134.

[2] The figure is based on data given in Sharpe, *op. cit.*

TABLE 8-4

Volatility by type of fund

Classification	Number of funds	Average volatility
Growth Funds: Primary objective is the long-term growth of capital . . . "risk of price depreciation in declining periods is normally higher . . . than for many others."	31	.970
Growth-income Funds: Combine an emphasis on long-term growth of capital with a consideration of "income and/or relative stability."	30	.941
Income-growth Funds: Combine an emphasis on current income with the possibility of long-term capital growth.	15	.856
Income Funds: "Primary objective is the most generous possible current income."	9	.674
Balanced Funds: "Place more emphasis on relative stability and continuity of income than do those in the preceding groups."	30	.645

Fig. 8-17. Only 11 funds had ratios exceeding that of the Dow-Jones' portfolio; 23 funds had smaller ratios.

Such results are not especially encouraging for the proponent of mutual funds. Inferior performance might be attributable to insufficient diversification; but the very nature of the portfolios held, as well as the high correlation of fund returns with market fluctuations rules out this explanation. It hardly seems likely that on the average, mutual-fund managers make perverse judgments. More likely, they generate excessively large expenses in the search for desirable investments.

The results shown in Figs. 8-16 and 8-17 are based on *net* returns, obtained by the investor *after* management fees and brokers' commissions have been deducted.[1] Reported figures make it difficult to

[1] Load charges have not been deducted. The comparison with the return on the market portfolio is thus reasonably "fair." Even if he must purchase securities in odd-lot quantities, an investor managing his own portfolio is not likely to pay brokers' fees totaling as much as 8 percent for a "round trip" (purchase and subsequent sale).

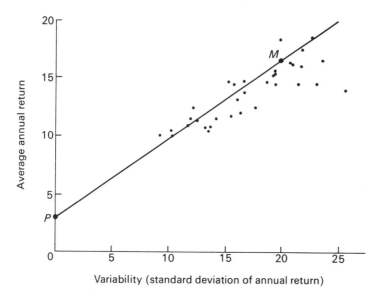

FIGURE 8-16

Average annual return versus variability. Thirty-four open-end mutual funds, 1954–1963 (net returns).

determine the amounts spent for brokerage fees. But other expenses can be found. Adding back such costs gives the *gross* return for each year.

Reward-to-variability ratios based on gross returns scatter more randomly around the value associated with the market portfolio. Of the 34 funds depicted in Figs. 8-16 and 8-17, 19 had ratios based on gross returns larger than that of the Dow-Jones' portfolio; only 15 had smaller ratios.

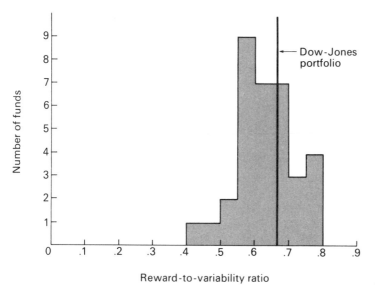

FIGURE 8-17

Reward-to-variability ratios. Thirty-four open-end mutual funds, 1954–1963 (net returns).

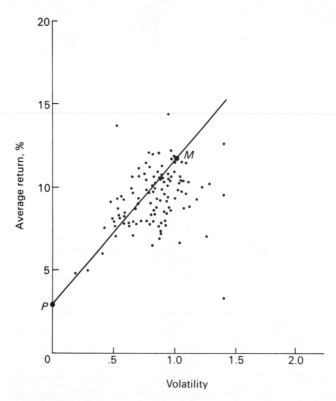

FIGURE 8-18

Average return and volatility,
1955–1964. One hundred
fifteen mutual funds (based
on net returns).

Figure 8-18 shows the average return and volatility during the period 1955 to 1964 for the 115 funds studied by Jensen; all values are based on net returns. Point *M* indicates the performance of a market portfolio composed of the securities in Standard and Poor's Composite Index. Point *P* represents the pure interest rate (based on the return from a ten-year government bond).[1] Line *PM* is the empirical counterpart of the security market line.

Figure 8-19 shows the results obtained using gross returns.

In Fig. 8-18, showing net performance, more funds plot below the security market line than above it. But in Fig. 8-19, showing gross performance, the points scatter more or less randomly around the line. Differences in diversification cannot possibly have caused these results, since risk was measured by volatility, not variability. The most plausible explanation is, again, excessive expenditures for portfolio management.

[1] Although the return of such a bond for an entire ten-year period is certain, the annual return (which depends on the market price of the bond) will undoubtedly vary from year to year. Some have proposed that the returns on one-year bonds be used instead to measure the actual pure interest rate.

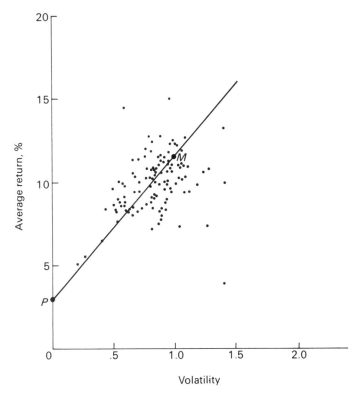

FIGURE 8-19
Average return and volatility, 1955–1964. One hundred fifteen mutual funds (based on gross returns).

Figure 8-20 shows the differential returns for the 115 funds based on net values.[1] The average was −1.1 percent per year. Of the 115 funds, 76 had negative differential returns.

Figure 8-21 shows the differential returns based on gross values. The average value was −0.4 percent per year. Only 55 of the 115 funds had negative differential returns.

Figure 8-22 shows characteristic lines for 20 funds studied by Treynor,[2] using net annual returns from 1953 to 1962. The securities included in the Dow-Jones' Industrial Average were chosen to represent the market. Overall, the funds did no better than comparable market-based portfolios. Taking 4 percent as an approximation of the pure interest rate, 8 of the lines lie to the left of point P

[1]The results reported in Figs. 8-20 and 8-21 are based on data covering the period 1945 to 1964. Although some of the funds were not in existence at the beginning of the period, the measure of differential return should be relatively invariant to the period covered; thus it is reasonable to compare values based on different periods. This is not the case for average return; thus Figs. 8-18 and 8-19 are based on results covering the period 1955 to 1964, when all 115 funds were in existence.
[2]Based on data given in Treynor, *op. cit.*

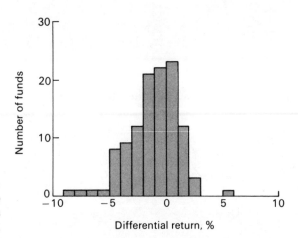

FIGURE 8-20
Differential returns, one
hundred fifteen mutual funds
(based on net returns).

while 12 lie to the right. Taking 3 percent as an approximation, 8 lines lie to the left of point P' while 12 lie to the right.

The procedure used to fit a characteristic line may not fully reveal a possible strength of a fund's management. Consider the two characteristic lines shown in Fig. 8-23. Each is consistent with equilibrium in a perfect capital market. Suppose that the manager of a mutual fund could anticipate the general direction of the market as a whole—i.e., predict whether R_M would be above or below p. Assuming that brokerage commissions would not prove excessive, it would be desirable to alter the fund's portfolio from time to time, holding portfolio A when R_M is expected to fall below p, and portfolio B when R_M is expected to exceed p.

Is there any evidence that mutual-fund managers predict major market swings correctly? No. If they did, actual results could be approximated more accurately by a curve such as cc in Fig. 8-23

FIGURE 8-21
Differential returns, one
hundred fifteen mutual funds
(based on gross returns).

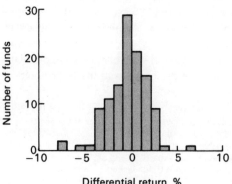

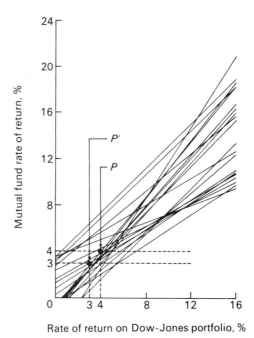

FIGURE 8-22

Actual characteristic lines.
Twenty open-end mutual
funds, 1953–1962.

than by a straight line. Treynor and Mazuy[1] examined the performance of 57 funds over the period 1953 to 1962. In only one case was a curve[2] significantly better than a straight line; and even in that case, the curvature was not particularly impressive.

Mutual funds apparently do no better on the average than market-based portfolios of comparable volatility. But during any given period, some funds do outperform the market. Are their managers superior, or just lucky? And what of the other funds—are their managers inferior, or just unlucky?

Figure 8-24 compares the performance of 34 funds during the period 1944 to 1953 with their performance during the period 1954 to 1963.[3] The horizontal axis plots the rank of each fund based on the reward-to-variability ratios for the earlier period. The vertical axis plots the rank based on the reward-to-variability ratios for the latter period. There appears to be a slight positive relationship.

Figure 8-25 provides further evidence.[4] The horizontal axis plots the

[1]Jack L. Treynor and Kay K. Mazuy, Can Mutual Funds Outguess the Market?, *Harvard Business Review*, July-August, 1966, pp. 131–136.
[2]More precisely, a curve for which R_p is a quadratic function of R_M.
[3]Based on data given in Sharpe, *op. cit.*
[4]Based on data given in Sharpe, *op. cit.*

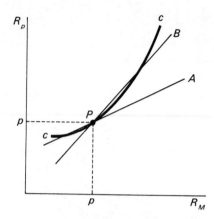

FIGURE 8-23

rank of each of the 34 funds based on the ratios of expense[1] to total assets in 1953. The vertical axis plots the rank based on the reward-to-variability ratios for the period 1954 to 1963. Again, there is a slight positive relationship.

A comparison of Figs. 8-24 and 8-25 suggests that persistent differences in performance based on net returns may be due more to differences in the cost of management than to differences in its effectiveness.

[1] Neither brokers' fees nor load charges are included, only management fees.

FIGURE 8-24

Differences in reward-to-variability ratios (based on net returns).

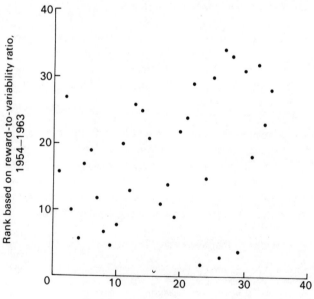

Rank based on reward-to-variability ratio, 1954–1963

Rank based on reward-to-variability ratio, 1944–1953

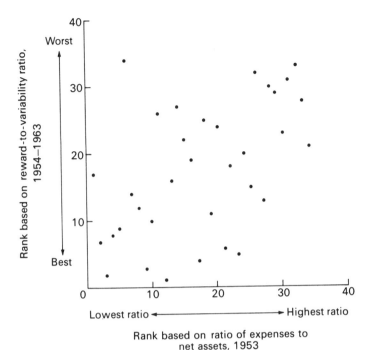

FIGURE 8-25

Reward-to-variability ratios (based on net returns) versus expense ratios.

The recurrence of superior performance based on *gross* returns was examined by Jensen and Black.[1] They analyzed 115 funds, categorizing the performance of each one in every year from 1955 to 1964 as either *superior* or *inferior* to that of a comparable market-based portfolio. Figure 8-26 illustrates the method. Each point plots the rate of return on the fund (R_p) and the rate of return on the market portfolio (R_M) for one year. Line *cc* is the characteristic line for the fund, estimated from the actual results (i.e., "fit" to the points). Line *MM* represents a market-based portfolio of comparable volatility (constructed to be parallel to *cc* and pass through point *P*). For any single year, the differential return is simply the vertical distance from the corresponding point to line *MM*.[2] If the distance is positive (for example, dr_a), the performance was superior to that of a market-based portfolio. If the distance is negative (for example, dr_b), performance was inferior.

In all, 1,150 differential return figures were obtained in this manner (10 for each of the 115 funds). Since gross returns were utilized,

[1] Reported in Jensen, *op. cit.*
[2] The previously described measure of differential return used to categorize performance over the entire period is simply the average of the annual values calculated in this manner.

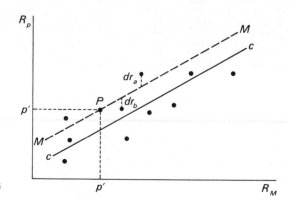

FIGURE 8-26

the results were relatively balanced; 578 of the values (50.2 percent) were positive, and 572 negative.

Funds with truly superior management should enjoy *runs* of successive years of superior performance. The mere fact that a fund had such a run does not necessarily reflect superior management; it may simply reflect luck. But if very many funds have superior management, a disproportionately large number of them will be included in any group of funds with a record of successive years of superior performance. This will be evidenced in the subsequent year; a disproportionately large number of the funds in such a group will enjoy superior performance.

The record does not reveal major differences of this type. For example, there were 41 cases involving runs of five successive superior years. Only 19 (46.4 percent) were followed by another superior year. Values for runs of other lengths were only slightly encouraging:

Length of run (number of successive years of superior performance)	Number of instances	Percent of instances followed by another year of superior performance
1	574	50.4%
2	312	52.0
3	161	53.4
4	79	55.8

The typical fund obtained superior performance 50.2 percent of the time. Funds with one to four successive prior years of superior performance had slightly better success. But the differences were not great.

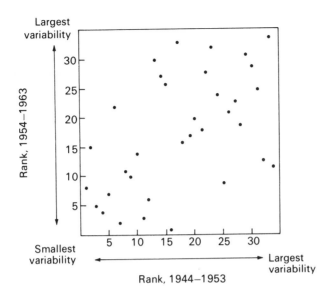

Largest variability

Rank, 1954–1963

Smallest variability

Largest variability

Rank, 1944–1953

FIGURE 8-27

Consistently superior performance may be rare. But what about consistent performance per se? The management of each mutual fund states a set of objectives. In the context of capital market theory, such a statement might be considered to indicate a target level of variability or volatility. If a fund shifts from one efficient portfolio to another (efficient) portfolio with a different risk and expected return, investors will have to alter their holdings to regain preferred positions. It is thus desirable for management to make a policy regarding risk vis-à-vis average return, then hold portfolios consistent with that policy.

Evidence supporting this interpretation has already been presented (in Table 8-4). Figure 8-27 provides more.[1] Each point represents 1 of 34 mutual funds. The horizontal axis plots the rank of each, based on variability of net return during the period 1944 to 1953. The vertical axis plots the rank based on variability during the period 1954 to 1963. There appears to be a positive relationship, although it is far from perfect.

Figure 8-28 provides evidence concerning volatility.[2] Each point represents 1 of 56 funds. The horizontal axis plots the volatility of net return during the period 1945 to 1954; the vertical axis plots volatility during the period 1955 to 1964. The relationship is clearly positive (although still far from perfect).

[1] Based on data given in Sharpe, *op. cit.*
[2] Based on data given in Jensen, *op. cit.*

This has been a lengthy section. The extensive analyses of mutual-fund performance in the two decades following World War II warrant detailed treatment. And the key results deserve restatement. At the risk of oversimplification, the findings may be summarized as follows :

1. Most funds diversified well.
2. Most managers elected a general-risk class and maintained their stated positions reasonably well.
3. On the average, funds did no better, *before expenses*, than market-based portfolios of comparable volatility.
4. On the average, funds did worse, *after expenses*, than market-based portfolios of comparable volatility.
5. Few, if any, funds consistently performed better than market-based portfolios of comparable volatility.
6. Most funds appear to have spent too much searching for mis-priced securities.

In the latter half of the 1960s, a new type of mutual fund became popular—the "performance" or "go-go" fund. The managers of such funds typically select high-volatility portfolios. They should thus achieve greater average returns than their more conservative competitors. In good years, they should do especially well. But in bad years, high volatility may be expected to take its inevitable toll.

Capital market theory suggests that one cannot get something for nothing. Mutual-fund performance appears to be remarkably consistent with the implications of capital market theory.

FIGURE 8-28

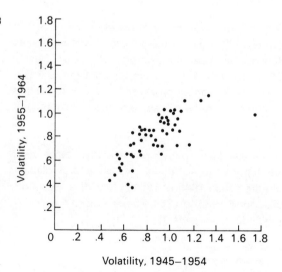

Volatility, 1945–1954

FIGURE 8-29

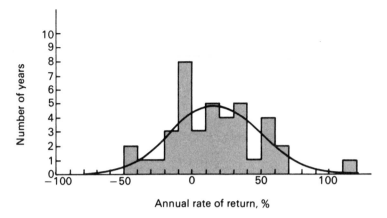

Annual rate of return, %

Figure 8-29 shows the frequency distribution of the rate of return on the market portfolio from 1926 to 1965 (repeated from Fig. 8-2c). The smooth curve represents a normal (bell-shaped) distribution with the same mean (average return) and standard deviation. The curve does not represent the actual results very well. Normal distributions assign little likelihood to the occurrence of really extreme values. But such values occur quite often. (The return of more than 110 percent in Fig. 8-29 provides a good example.)

THE SHAPES OF DISTRIBUTIONS

Why consider only curves that have the familiar bell shape? Why not use a broader class of distributions? Many investigators have. Thus far the greatest attention has been accorded the class of *stable Paretian* or *Pareto-Levy* distributions—a class that includes the normal distribution as a special case.[1]

Two parameters fully specify a normal distribution—the mean and standard deviation. Four parameters fully specify a stable Paretian distribution:[2]

α—the *characteristic exponent*; a measure of the height of the extreme tail areas of the distribution
β—an index of skewness
γ—a scale parameter
δ—a location parameter

The value of beta is usually assumed to be 0 (i.e., the distributions are assumed to be symmetric). The appropriate value of alpha is

[1] This class has desirable (but not essential) properties for portfolio analysis. It is by no means clear that some other class would not prove more desirable for the purpose (in particular, some class which includes only distributions with finite variances).
[2] The notation follows that of Eugene F. Fama, The Behavior of Stock-Market Prices, *Journal of Business*, January, 1965, pp. 34–105.

almost certain to exceed 1; this implies that delta will equal the expected value of the distribution. What is left? A family of symmetric distributions, any member of which can be described by three values: the characteristic exponent indicates the general shape, the expected value its location, and the scale parameter its spread.

A stable Paretian distribution is normal if the characteristic exponent takes on its maximum possible value (2). The scale parameter then has a familiar interpretation: it is half the variance. For a normal distribution:

$\alpha = 2$
$\delta = $ expected value
$\gamma = \sigma^2/2$

Empirical work suggests that actual rates of return are best approximated by distributions with characteristic exponents between 1.7 and 1.9.[1] Formally, the variance of such a distribution is infinite.[2] The scale parameter (γ) still measures spread, but it cannot easily be given an obvious interpretation (it certainly does not equal variance).

The shapes of distributions are of more than passing interest. The fact that alpha appears to be less than 2 may have serious implications for portfolio theory and capital market theory.

Portfolio theory assumes that investors choose among portfolios on the basis of (1) expected rate of return and (2) risk, stated in terms of standard deviation of rate of return. Given any probability distribution for portfolio rate of return that can be somehow drawn on a piece of paper, both values can be calculated. The set of possible outcomes need only be bounded. This is by no means a restrictive requirement. For example, there is no chance that a portfolio now worth $100 will be worth $1 billion next year; and limited liability rules out values below zero. Similar statements can be made about individual securities. As long as predictions are cast in terms of a finite set of possibilities, portfolio-analysis procedures apply without change.

Clearly, probability distributions of future returns cannot really have

[1] Eugene F. Fama, Portfolio Analysis in a Stable Paretian Market, *Management Science*, January, 1965, pp. 404–419.
[2] It is hardly surprising that this procedure results in values implying infinite variances, since the only allowed distribution with finite variance is normal. Putting it another way, only if alpha takes on its maximum possible value will the variance be finite. By restricting attention to stable Paretian distributions, the contest is, in a sense, "stacked" in favor of infinite variance.

infinite variances; nor can frequency distributions of past returns. But it may be best to approximate both with formulas that imply infinite variance. Portfolio-analysis procedures must then be modified to account for the nature of the predictions. The stable-Paretian scale parameter (γ) can be used to measure risk. Unfortunately, no construct analogous to the correlation coefficient is available. This makes the use of some form of index model mandatory.

The single-index model provides a good example. The return on security i is related to the level of index I in the usual manner:

$$R_i = a_i + b_i I + c_i$$

where a_i, b_i = parameters
c_i = uncertain variable with expected value of zero
I = level of index

The probability distribution of I and the distributions of the c_i's may be assumed to be members of the stable Paretian family and independent of one another. Moreover, each may be assumed to be described by the same characteristic exponent (α^*).

Under these conditions, the risk of a portfolio will be related to the risks of the securities and the index in the following manner:[1]

$$\gamma_p = \sum_{i=1}^{N} X_i^{\alpha^*} \gamma_{c_i} + b_p^{\alpha^*} \gamma_I$$

where γ_p = scale parameter of probability distribution of portfolio rate of return (i.e., portfolio risk)
γ_{c_i} = scale parameter of probability distribution of c_i (i.e., risk unique to security i)
b_p = responsiveness of portfolio to changes in I

$$= \sum_{i=1}^{N} X_i b_i$$

γ_I = scale parameter of probability distribution of I (i.e., risk associated with the index)

If distributions are assumed to be normal, portfolio risk can be measured and calculated in the familiar way. Let $\alpha^* = 2$ (normality). Then

$$\gamma_p = \frac{\sigma_p^2}{2}$$

[1] This result is given by Fama, *loc. cit.* This version applies only in the usual case in which all X_i's and b_p are positive (or when $\alpha^* = 2$). In general, the absolute values of the X_i's and of b_p should be used.

$$\gamma_{c_i} = \frac{\sigma_{c_i}^2}{2}$$

$$\gamma_I = \frac{\sigma_I^2}{2}$$

from which it follows that

$$\sigma_p^2 = \sum_{i=1}^{N} X_i^2 \sigma_{c_i}^2 + b_p^2 \sigma_I^2$$

If distributions are not normal, a full portfolio analysis may require complex calculations. But for well-diversified portfolios, b_p may provide a perfectly adequate measure of risk, obviating such procedures. Figure 8-30 shows the relationship between portfolio risk and the number of securities held (in equal amounts) for two values of the characteristic exponent. Half the risk of a typical security is assumed to be due to uncertainty about the value of the index.[1] As the figure shows, even when alpha equals 1.7, modest degrees of diversification reduce portfolio risk virtually to the level attributable to uncertainty about the index—a level that can be measured directly by b_p.

It is perfectly possible to cast predictions in terms of stable Paretian distributions with characteristic exponents between 1.7 and 1.9. This has no effect on the concepts of responsiveness (to changes in an index) and volatility (relative to the market portfolio).[2] For normative applications, the procedure using responsiveness as the sole measure of risk (with upper bounds to force diversification) becomes particularly attractive—no changes are required. Other

[1] These assumptions imply the formula

$$\gamma_p = [(1/n)^{\alpha*}n + 1] b_p^{\alpha*} \gamma_I$$

where n = the number of securities held (in equal amounts).

[2] Except that it may be more desirable to estimate the values by fitting a line to past data that will minimize the sum of the absolute deviations rather than the sum of the squared deviations.

FIGURE 8-30

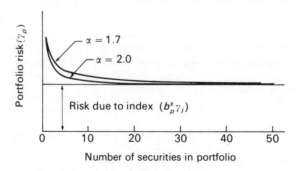

Portfolio risk (γ_p)

$\alpha = 1.7$

$\alpha = 2.0$

Risk due to index ($b_p^{\alpha} \gamma_I$)

0   10   20   30   40   50

Number of securities in portfolio

normative procedures must be modified if predictions implying infinite variances are to be used.

Turning from the somewhat rarified atmosphere of a world in which variances are infinite, what are the practical implications of "fat-tailed" distributions of rate of return? Primarily, they make variance an untrustworthy indicator of risk. Even if the underlying "true" characteristics of a security did not change from period to period, variability (standard deviation of rate of return) could change substantially. Past variability will be at best a poor guide to future variability. Fortunately, similar arguments cannot be levied against volatility.

The shapes of distributions of rate of return do not make portfolio and capital market theory irrelevant. But they do provide additional reasons for using index models in normative applications and for emphasizing the importance of volatility when describing the capital market.

Thus far little has been said about the predictions required to perform a portfolio analysis. To obtain them, one might simply assume that the future will be like the past. Historical values (e.g., average returns, variabilities, actual correlations, actual volatilities) could then be used directly (as expected returns, standard deviations of return, correlations, and volatilities). Needless to say, such procedures rest on heroic assumptions, whether made explicitly or not. The underlying processes (e.g., distributions) must be stable over time, and the historical record must adequately reveal their essential characteristics.

USING THE PAST TO PREDICT THE FUTURE

A number of objections can be made concerning such procedures. To assess the nature of a security or portfolio, a relatively long period must be studied. But the longer the period, the less likely may be the assumption of the stability of the underlying process. The risk associated with a company's present commitments may not be related in a simple way to the behavior of its returns over the past twenty years. But estimating risk using only the record of, say, the past five years may be equally dangerous (especially if the standard deviation of rate of return is used to measure risk, for the reasons given in the previous section). The investigator may be faced with the choice of learning enough about the wrong thing or too little about the right one.

What might cause the future to differ from the past? Chance events (an unusual set of "draws") or changes in management policy. As an example of the latter, consider a corporation that has recently diversified its product line and consciously taken on new projects relatively unaffected by swings in the economy; neither the variability nor the volatility of rate of return in the past is likely to provide a satisfactory guide to future prospects.

A more crucial problem is the very process by which prices are established. In an efficient market, current price is based on all relevant information concerning the future, including information about the past. If the record shows that a security was particularly attractive in the past, its price is likely to have risen so that it will not be particularly attractive in the future. If the record shows that a security was particularly unattractive in the past, its price is likely to have fallen, so that it will not be particularly unattractive in the future.

In a "perfect market," the past has only limited relevance for the future. Some observers claim that the past has *no* relevance at all. One version of this argument assumes (often implicitly) that investors are concerned only with the expected rate of return. Under such conditions, in a market with complete agreement, prices would adjust until every security (and portfolio) offered the same expected return. No alternative would differ from another in any significant way (since by assumption, only expected return is significant). The past would be of no relevance.

Needless to say, this conclusion is not consistent with the view of a capital market derived from portfolio theory. Under conditions of complete agreement, prices will adjust so that securities (and portfolios) fall along a security market line. There will be differences— the greater the volatility, the greater the expected return. No security will be *mispriced*, and efficient portfolios can be obtained by choosing securities randomly—for example, by throwing at least 20 darts (wildly) at a board listing the names of securities from many industries. But to obtain an efficient portfolio that is suitable for a particular investor, some notion of volatility and/or expected return is required. For this, the past record may prove quite useful indeed.

In a "perfect market," any particular security's rate of return will be *random* in a very special sense; it will be randomly distributed along (and around) a characteristic line passing through the point at which the rate of return on both the security and the market portfolio equal the pure rate of interest.

The term *random walk* has been used to describe markets in which all past information has been considered by investors and is thus reflected in current prices. Those who assume that investors consider only expected return assert that no single investor need bother to reanalyze the data. Those who follow the approach described in this book would assert that analysis of past events may be useful, but that consideration of the *order* (sequence) in which they occurred may not. Both groups would disagree with the traditional stock-market "technician" or "chartist," who attaches particular importance to certain sequences of past prices, rates of return, etc. Satisfactory evidence of the success of any chartist technique is currently lacking. Even if some method could be shown to have given outstanding performance in the past, widespread use would destroy its value. Systems designed to "beat the market" contain the seeds of their own destruction.

These comments suggest the danger of performing a portfolio analysis based entirely on historical data—the procedure is far too likely to seize on a few securities with unusually attractive records. In a market with no mispriced securities there is but one inviolate rule: diversify. If prices adequately reflect current information, almost any well-diversified portfolio will be efficient. If the market is perfect, any group of, say 40 securities may be chosen. But if some securities are slightly mispriced, the past record might help to identify a slightly superior group. This suggests a procedure that can do little harm, and may do some good: Perform an analysis using historical data with reasonably stringent upper bounds on security holdings.

Figure 8-31 shows a case in which such an approach proved beneficial; it is based on results obtained by Cohen and Pogue.[1] The vertical axis plots average return from 1958 to 1964; the horizontal axis plots variability (standard deviation) of annual rate of return during the period. Values based on net returns are shown for 78 mutual funds. Values based on gross returns are shown for 60 *random portfolios*, each of which includes 40 securities (in equal amounts), drawn at random from a group of 150 common stocks. The straight line provides an empirical counterpart to the capital market line; it connects the point representing the average values obtained for the 60 random portfolios with that representing the approximate pure interest rate during the period.

[1] Kalman J. Cohen and Jerry A. Pogue, An Empirical Evaluation of Alternative Portfolio-Selection Models, *Journal of Business*, April, 1967, pp. 166–193, and Some Comments Concerning Mutual Fund Versus Random Portfolio Performance, *Journal of Business*, April, 1968, pp. 180–190. As the title of the first paper indicates, Cohen and Pogue's study was intended to compare alternative approaches to portfolio selection. Only with reluctance did the authors discuss the performance of portfolios obtained in this manner vis-à-vis that of randomly selected groups of securities. And they specifically disavowed direct comparisons with the performance of mutual funds.

Cohen and Pogue performed portfolio analyses using the historical record of the group of 150 common stocks over the eleven-year period from 1947 to 1957, with upper bounds of .025 (thus at least 40 securities were included in every portfolio). Several approaches were tried, ranging from a full analysis using all 11,175 correlation coefficients to a simple one-index model based on the market rate of return. All gave similar results; the (purportedly) efficient portfolios performed well in the subsequent seven-year period—every one plotted within the circle shown in Fig. 8-31.

One swallow does not make a summer. But in this instance, at least, portfolio analysis based on historical data was able to more than hold its own against competition from randomly selected portfolios and mutual funds. Another instance might give less satisfying results. But if reasonably stringent upper bounds are included, such a procedure is not likely to lead to disastrous consequences.

Granted, portfolio analysis based on historical data may be useful. But must a full analysis be performed, or will some sort of index model suffice?

Cohen and Pogue found that a simple one-index (market) model adequately summarized the historical record of 150 common stocks. The results obtained using an even simpler model are shown in Table 8-5.[1] The monthly rates of return for 63 securities during the period 1927 to 1960 were analyzed to determine average returns, standard deviations of return, correlation coefficients, and volatilities. The first three sets of values were utilized to perform a full portfolio analysis with upper bounds of .05 (thus at least 20 securities were included in each portfolio). Thirty efficient portfolios were selected, ranging from the one with the minimum variability (portfolio 1) to the one with the maximum average return (portfolio 30). The securities included in each portfolio are indicated by circles in Table 8-5.

A separate analysis was performed using only the first and last sets of values (i.e., average returns and volatilities), with the same upper bounds (.05). Thirty (purportedly) efficient portfolios were selected. Their composition is indicated by slashes in Table 8-5.

As always, generalization may be dangerous. But at least in this instance, average return and volatility appear to have captured enough of the historical record to serve adequately for portfolio analysis subject to reasonably stringent upper bounds.

[1] Based on results in William F. Sharpe, A Linear Programming Algorithm for Mutual Fund Portfolio Selection, *Management Science,* March, 1967, pp. 499–510.

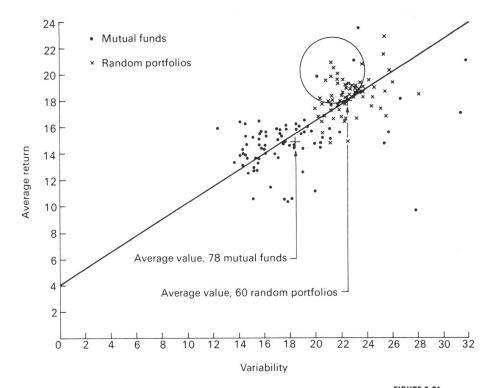

FIGURE 8-31

Average return and
variability : mutual funds,
random portfolios,
and selected portfolios,
1958–1964.

How relevant is past volatility for estimating the risk surrounding the future? More directly, how stable is volatility over time? If a corporation changes its activities and/or mix of financial obligations frequently, past volatility may prove misleading. On the other hand, to reduce the need for investors to alter their holdings periodically, corporation managers may very likely try to avoid drastic changes in the volatility of outstanding securities.

The record suggests that managers do try.[1] Figure 8-32 compares volatilities in two periods for 12 securities and 12 portfolios. The results, obtained by Blume,[2] show that the volatilities of individual securities are reasonably stable over time; the volatilities of portfolios are even more stable. Each of the portfolios in Fig. 8-32 includes 20 securities (in equal amounts). The very act of diversification increases predictability—the volatility of some securities may have declined, but that of others may have increased. The volatility of a

[1] Or that during market swings, the public revalues securities in accord with consistent views regarding relative volatilities.
[2] Marshal E. Blume, II, "The Assessment of Portfolio Performance: An Application of Portfolio Theory," doctoral dissertation, University of Chicago, March, 1968. The portfolios were obtained by ranking 240 securities on the basis of volatility, then taking groups of 20 in order.

		Portfolio		
TABLE 8-5	**Security**	**1**	**10**	**20**	**30**

Portfolios selected using volatility to measure risk (/) versus those selected using full information (0)

Security	Pattern
1	0 0 0 0 0 0 0 0 0 0 0 0 0 0 0 0 0 0 0 0 0 0 0 0 0 0 0 0 0 0 0
2	0 0 0 0 0 0 0 0 0 0 0 0 0 0 0 0 0 0 0 0 0 0 0 0 0 0 0 0 0 0
3	0 0 0 0 0 0 0 0 0 0 0 0 0 0 0 0 0 0 0 0 0 0 0 0 0 0 0 0 0 0
4	0 0 0 0 0 0
5	0 0 0 0 0 0 0 0 0 0 0 0 0 0 0 0 0 0 0 0 0 0 0 0 0 0 0 0 0 0 0
6	0 0 0 0 0 0 0 0 0 0 0 0 0 0 0 0 0 0 0 0 0 0 0
7	0 0 0 0 0 0 0 0 0 0 0 0 0 0 0 0 0 0
8	/ / 0 0 0 0 0 0 0 0 0 0 0 0 0 0 0 0 0 0 0 0 0 0 0 0 0 0 0 0 0
9	0 0 0 0 0 0 0 0 0 0 0 0 0 0 0 0 0 0 0 0 0 0 0 0 0 0 0 0 0 0
10	0 0 0 0 0 0 0 0 0 0 0 0 0 0 0 0 0 0 0 0 0 0 0 0 0 0 0 0 0 0
11	0 0 0 0 0 0 0 0 0 0 0 0 0 0 0 0 0 0 0 0 0 0 0 0 0 0 0 0 0
12	0
13	0 0 0 0 0 0 0 0 0 0 0 0 0 0 0 0 0 0 0 0 0 0 0 0 0 0 0 0 0 0
14	0 0 0 0 0 0 0 0 0 0 0 0 0 0 0 0 0 0 0 0 0 0 0 0 0 0 0 0 0 0
15	0 0 0 0 0 0 0 0 0 0 0 0 0 0 0 0 0 0 0 0 0 0 0 0 0 0
17	0 0 0 0 0 0 0 0
18	0 0 0 0
20	0 0 0 0 0 0 0 0 0 0 0 0 0 0 0 0 0 0 0 0 0 0 0 0 0 0 0 0 0 0
22	0 0 0 0 0 0 0 0 0 0 0 0 0 0 0
26	0 0 0 0 0 0 0 0 0 0
28	0 0 0 0 0 0 0 0 0 0 0 0 0 0 0 0 0 0 0 0 0 0
29	0
34	0 0 0 0 0 0 0 0 0 0 0 0 0 0 0 0 0 0 0 0 0 0 0 0 0 0 0 0
41	0 0 0 0 0 0 0 0 0 0 0 0 0 0
46	/
48	0 0 0 0 0 0 0
51	0 0 0 0 0 0 0 0 0 0 0 0 0 0 0 0 0 0 0 0 0 0 0 0 0 0 0 0 0 0
52	0 0 0 0 0 0 0 0 0 0 0 0 0 0 0 0 0 0 0 0 0 0 0 0 0 0 0 0 0
53	0 0 0 0 0 0 0 0 0 0 0 0 0 0 0 0 0 0 0 0 0 0 0 0 0 0 0 0 0 0
59	0 0 0 0 0 0 / /
60	0 0 0 0 0 0 0 0 0 0 0 0 0 0 /
61	0
62	0 0 0 0 0 0 0 0 0 0 0 0 0 0 0 0 0 0 0 0 0 0 0 0 0 0 0 0 0 0
63	/ 0 0 0 0 0 0 0 0 0 0 0 0 0 0 0 0 0 0 0 0 0 0

portfolio is the (weighted) average of the volatilities of its component securities; and it is usually far easier to predict an average than to predict the value of a single item.

This concludes the examination of the record. The overall view is one of a remarkably efficient market—one in which few securities are likely to be seriously underpriced or overpriced for long. Clearly inferior portfolios can easily be avoided by undertaking modest amounts of diversification. And clearly superior portfolios are hard to find; some highly paid investment managers are unable to consistently outperform portfolios selected using the most simple rules.

If the market is efficient, and if an investor is privy to no special information or predictive power, what should he do? First, and most important: diversify. Second, select an appropriate risk class (perhaps based on past trade-offs between risk and expected return),

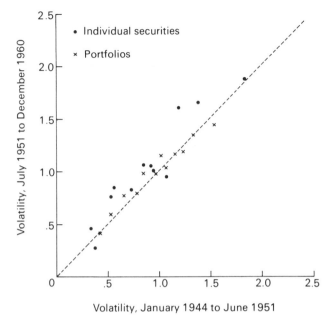

FIGURE 8-32

Volatility, January 1944 to June 1951

then restrict attention to portfolios of the appropriate type. The record may be invoked at this point, since past volatility appears to provide a useful guide for predicting volatility in the future (i.e., risk).

Given b_i values, it is a simple matter to find one of the many portfolios with some desired value of b_p. But which of the many portfolios should be chosen? In a perfect market, there is no basis for choice—one of the set can be chosen at random. However, on the outside chance that the past record might contain evidence of (still) mispriced securities, an investor could select the portfolio with the greatest average return during some past period. In other words,

$$\text{maximize } \sum_{i=1}^{N} X_i E_i$$

$$\text{subject to } \sum_{i=1}^{N} X_i b_i = b_p^*$$

$$\text{and } 0 \leq X_i \leq \frac{1}{n}$$

for every security (i).

where E_i—is assumed to equal the average return of security i over some past period

b_i—is assumed to equal the actual volatility of security i over some past period

$b_p^* =$ some desired level of volatility

$n =$ a number large enough to force adequate diversification (i.e., at least 20)

This is the simplest type of portfolio-analysis problem; it can even be solved graphically, using the method described in Chap. 7. At the very least, no harm should result from the consideration of *both* expected return and volatility. In a perfect market, information about one is redundant, since all values will lie along the security market line (b_i can thus be used as a surrogate for E_i, or E_i can be used as a surrogate for b_i). But it is better to look at relevant information twice than to look at irrelevant information once.

9.

UTILITY

Portfolio theory assumes that investors consider only expected return and standard deviation of return when comparing alternative portfolios. This may or may not be too simple a view. To assess it, one must consider a more general theory of choice under conditions of uncertainty. This is the task of the present chapter.

Consider Mr. *I*, an investor. To simplify the exposition, assume that he is concerned only with wealth at some future date (i.e., *later*). Can his preferences be summarized concisely? In other words, can his choices be predicted from some simple representation of his feelings? Yes, if he conforms to a few perfectly reasonable rules of behavior.

EXPECTED UTILITY[1]

[1] This section draws heavily on the presentation in an excellent book by Howard Raiffa, *Decision Analysis, Introductory Lectures on Choices Under Uncertainty,* Addison-Wesley Publishing Company, Inc., Reading, Mass., 1968.

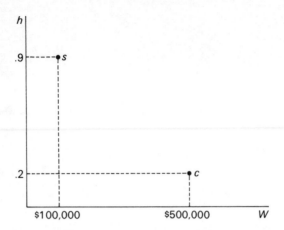

FIGURE 9-1

The horizontal axis in Fig. 9-1 plots alternative amounts of Mr. *I*'s future wealth. For convenience, assume that no choice he can make will leave him with less than nothing or more than $1 million. These values (a lower and an upper bound) can be used to construct a series of hypothetical securities. For example,

Security .5 gives:
   $1 million with probability .5, or nothing with probability .5
Security .7 gives:
   $1 million with probability .7, or nothing with probability .3
Security *h* gives:
   $1 million with probability *h*, or nothing with probability $(1 - h)$

Each point on the vertical axis of Fig. 9-1 represents a hypothetical security of this type.

Assume that Mr. *I* prefers (i.e., would choose) (1) a security offering $1 million with probability .9, or nothing with probability .1 over (2) $100,000 for certain. This is shown by point *s* (security preferred) in Fig. 9-1. Assume that he would prefer (1) $500,000 for certain over (2) a security offering $1 million with probability .2, or nothing with probability .8. This is shown by point *c* (certain wealth preferred) in Fig. 9-1.

In Fig. 9-2, the diagram has been divided into two regions. At any point in the upper region, the security is preferred; at any point in the lower region, the certain wealth is preferred. At any point on the boundary, the investor considers the security and the certain amount of wealth equally attractive. Such a boundary can be used to summarize the feelings of any investor. It will be termed his *preference curve*. To summarize:

An investor's preferences can be represented by a curve relating

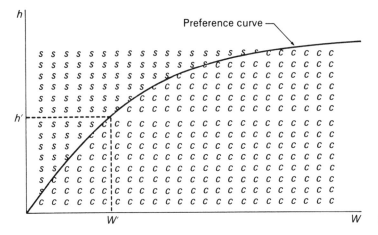

FIGURE 9-2

h to W. Let (h', W') be a point on such a curve. The investor has said that he is indifferent between:

1. W' dollars for certain
2. $1 million with probability h' or nothing with probability $(1 - h')$

It is useful at this point to introduce a graphic representation for chance events. For example:

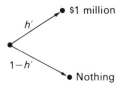

This indicates that there is a probability of h' that the investor will follow the upper path to $1 million and a probability of $1 - h'$ that he will follow the lower path to nothing.

Now consider a portfolio with K possible outcomes: $W_1, W_2, \ldots, W_K$. Let the respective probabilities be $p_1, p_2, \ldots, p_K$. Graphically:

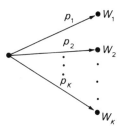

The investor's preference curve may be used to construct another portfolio—one that he should consider equally desirable. Let h_1 be the value of h corresponding to W_1 [that is, (h_1, W_1) is a point on the investor's preference curve]. Let h_2 be the value of h corresponding to W_2, etc. The investor has said that he is indifferent between

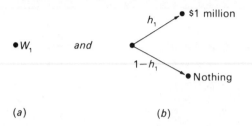

$\bullet W_1$ and

(a)   (b)

His feelings about a portfolio should thus be unaffected if b is substituted for a. Making this substitution and others of the same type gives

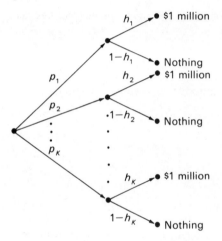

This is a particularly simple set of prospects. There are only two possible outcomes: $1 million and nothing. The probability of obtaining $1 million is

$$H = p_1 h_1 + p_2 h_2 + \cdots + p_K h_K$$

The probability of obtaining nothing is 1 minus this sum.

Now consider two portfolios. Portfolio A offers outcomes $W_1, W_2, \ldots, W_K$ with probabilities $p_1^A, p_2^A, \ldots, p_K^A$. Portfolio B offers outcomes $W_1, W_2, \ldots, W_K$ with probabilities $p_1^B, p_2^B, \ldots, p_K^B$. The investor should be indifferent between portfolio A and

$$H^A = p_1^A h_1 + p_2^A h_2 + \cdots + p_K^A h_K$$

$\widehat{A'}$ ———————————————● $1 million

                $1 - H^A$ ———————————————➤● Nothing

He should also be indifferent between portfolio B and

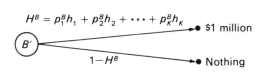

It is a simple matter to predict the investor's feelings about A' and B'. He will prefer the one with the larger value of H. Assume that H^A is larger than H^B. If Mr. I is at all reasonable (rational), he will prefer portfolio A to portfolio B. This follows from simple transitivity of preferences:

If : A is as good as A', which is preferred to B', which is as good as B

Then : A should be preferred to B.

To generalize,

Given any number of alternative portfolios, an investor will choose the one for which

$$H = \sum_{k=1}^{K} p_k h_k \qquad \text{is the largest}$$

where $H =$ a measure of desirability of a portfolio

$p_k =$ the probability that a portfolio will give the investor wealth W_K

$h_k =$ value of h associated with wealth W_K along investor's preference curve

$K =$ number of possible outcomes

The procedure used to represent Mr. I's preferences may seem rather arbitrary. In a sense it is. Different hypothetical securities could have been used. For example:

1. Hypothetical security h might give:
    $2 million with probability h, or nothing with probability $(1 - h)$
2. Hypothetical security h might give:
    $2 million with probability h, or $1 million with probability $(1 - h)$

The first alternative would involve a change in scale; the second would involve a change in origin.

Consider a function relating u to h in the following manner:

$$u_k = c_o + c_s h_k$$

where $c_o =$ constant (indicating origin)

$c_s =$ positive constant (indicating scale)

$u_k =$ value of u corresponding to h_k (value of h)

Define $EU = \sum\limits_{k=1}^{K} p_k u_k$

Substituting,

$$EU = \sum_{k=1}^{K} p_k (c_o + c_s h_k)$$

$$= c_o \sum_{k=1}^{K} p_k + c_s \sum_{k=1}^{K} p_k h_k$$

$$= c_o + c_s H$$

Obviously the portfolio with the largest possible value of H will also have the largest possible value of EU.

A preference curve may be obtained by arbitrarily defining hypothetical securities, then asking the investor to express his preferences for such securities vis-à-vis certain wealth. A curve relating u to W may then be obtained, using any desired origin (c_o) and scale (c_s). The original preference curve is one possibility:

$$u_k = 0 + 1h_k$$

Bowing to historical precedent, the value of u will be termed the investor's *utility*. A curve relating u to W will be termed a *utility function* or *utility curve*. In general an investor will choose the portfolio that maximizes

$$EU_p = \sum_{k=1}^{K} p_k u_k$$

where EU_p = expected utility of portfolio
p_k = probability that portfolio will give the investor wealth W_k
u_k = utility associated with wealth W_k along investor's utility curve

This is termed the *expected-utility maxim*.

The conclusion is both powerful and simple. Its derivation deserves restatement. Mr. I was assumed to behave in ways that seem so natural they hardly warrant discussion. In particular, it was assumed that:

1. He could identify some gamble that was neither better nor worse than each possible amount of wealth (i.e., his preference curve existed).
2. His preferences among portfolios would not be affected if money outcomes were replaced by equally desirable gambles (i.e., those on his preference curve).

FIGURE 9-3

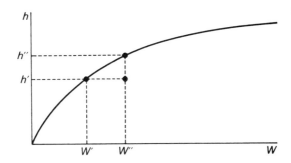

3. His feelings about each portfolio depended only on the probabilities of various outcomes (amounts of wealth).

4. His preferences were transitive (e.g., if he would choose X over Y and was indifferent between Y and Z, then he would choose X over Z).

The preferences of *any* investor with similar characteristics can be represented by (1) some function relating his *utility* to wealth plus (2) the assertion that he will always choose the portfolio with the greatest expected utility.

What about an investor who makes choices that cannot be characterized in this manner? He must behave in rather strange ways. One might call him unthinking, inconsistent, or even irrational. In any event, the theory described in this chapter does not apply to him.

RISK AVERSION

A utility function represents someone's preferences. To find a function for a particular person, one must determine his responses when faced with various choices. But some characteristics of an investor's utility function can be predicted. Utility curves have similarities as well as differences.

First, they are upward-sloping. This must be the case if both W and h are goods. All other things equal, an investor can be assumed to prefer more wealth to less. He can also be assumed to prefer a higher probability of receiving $1 million to a lower probability. Consider Fig. 9-3. The investor will prefer W″ to W′, since the former is greater. He will also prefer W″ to h′ (since W′ and h′ are equally desirable). Thus point (W″,h′) must lie under the investor's preference (utility) curve.

If an investor is risk averse, his utility curve will slope upward in a particular way—it will increase at a decreasing rate.

Thus far, risk aversion has been characterized in terms of attitudes toward the standard deviation of rate of return. A risk-averse investor considers σ_p bad; other things equal, he prefers less σ_p to more. Such an investor will hold a risky portfolio only if it offers a sufficiently greater expected return than a riskless one.

Consider portfolio p. In the eyes of a particular investor, some riskless portfolio would be just as desirable. Such a portfolio would provide some amount of wealth with certainty. The investor's feelings about portfolio p can usefully be summarized with this value:

CE_p = certainty-equivalent wealth of portfolio p

The investor in question would as soon have CE_p dollars for certain as the set of prospects associated with portfolio p.

The actual prospects of a portfolio can be summarized with an expected value:

EW_p = expected wealth of portfolio p

$$= \sum_{k=1}^{K} p_k W_k$$

A riskless portfolio offers some amount of wealth with certainty. Both its certainty-equivalent wealth and its expected wealth must equal this amount. Thus for a riskless portfolio,

$CE_p = EW_p$ for all investors

What about risky portfolios? Investors indifferent to risk would evaluate them as if they were riskless. Risk-averse investors would consider such portfolios less desirable than comparable riskless portfolios. Investors who prefer risk would consider them more desirable. These differences serve to define the three possible attitudes toward risk. For a risky portfolio:

$CE_p < EW_p$ for risk-averse investors
$CE_p = EW_p$ for investors indifferent to risk
$CE_p > EW_p$ for investors who prefer risk

This is consistent with the definition of risk aversion used in previous chapters. Consider two portfolios with the same expected wealth — one risky, the other riskless. A risk-averse investor would assign a smaller certainty-equivalent wealth to the risky portfolio. He would be willing to hold it only if it were cheaper. But if it were cheaper, the risky portfolio would offer a greater expected rate of return. In other words, a risk-averse investor requires a higher expected return from a risky portfolio than from a riskless one.

A risk-averse investor considers a risky portfolio less desirable than a

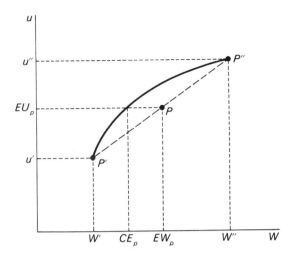

FIGURE 9-4

riskless portfolio with the same expected wealth. This attitude defines risk aversion. It also implies that the investor's utility curve increases at a decreasing rate.

Consider Fig. 9-4. W' and W'' are two possible amounts of wealth; u' and u'' are the corresponding amounts of utility for some investor (points P' and P'' lie on his utility curve). Now imagine a portfolio offering a 50-50 chance to receive either W' or W''. Diagramatically,

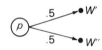

The expected utility of the portfolio is

$$EU_p = .5u' + .5u''$$

Its expected wealth is

$$EW_p = .5W' + .5W''$$

Point P in Fig. 9-4 represents these two values; it must lie on the straight line connecting points P' and P''.

The certainty-equivalent wealth of portfolio P is defined as the certain amount of wealth the investor considers as desirable as the portfolio. It must thus have the same expected utility. Clearly, the certainty-equivalent wealth of portfolio P is the value of W for which $u = EU_p$ (i.e., the point on the investor's utility curve at which utility equals EU_p).

A risk-averse investor considers the certainty-equivalent wealth of a risky portfolio to be less than its expected wealth. This implies that the utility curve must lie to the left of point P in Fig. 9-4, as shown. In fact, the curve must lie to the left of line $P'P''$ at all points other than P' and P''. This can be proven by considering portfolios with different odds of receiving W' and W''.

The values of W' and W'' used in the example are arbitrary. Any values could have been chosen. This leads to the general conclusion:

Risk aversion = a utility curve that increases at a decreasing rate

No fundamental law of nature requires all investors to be risk averse. In fact, a single investor might be averse to risk concerning decisions likely to result in one range of outcomes but actually prefer risk for decisions likely to result in outcomes in another range. For analyzing major investment decisions, such cases are of relatively little importance. The remainder of the chapter thus deals with investors who are risk averse.

QUADRATIC UTILITY FUNCTIONS

Risk-averse investors are characterized by utility curves that increase at a decreasing rate. The precise form of any particular curve will depend on the attitudes of the investor in question.

To carry the analysis further, some sort of simplifying assumption must be invoked. A number of alternatives have been proposed. Only one is completely consistent with choices based solely on expected return and standard deviation of return: the assumption that utility is a quadratic function of wealth.

Imagine a person who has chosen to invest some amount (W_o) now. Every possible amount of his wealth *later* can be related to a particular rate of return on his investment. Thus utility can be made a function of either wealth or rate of return, as indicated in Fig. 9-5. For present purposes, it is convenient to use rate of return.

Consider a *quadratic utility function* of the form

$$u = a + br - cr^2$$

where u = utility
r = rate of return
a = constant
b = positive constant
c = positive constant

The general appearance of such a function is shown in Fig. 9-5;

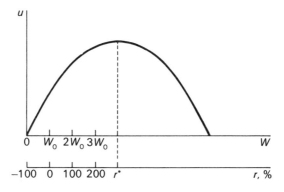

FIGURE 9-5

the exact shape of the curve will depend on the values of the parameters (a, b, and c).

This type of function reaches maximum at some value of r—call it r^*. Beyond that point, utility actually decreases as rate of return increases. This is clearly unacceptable. Such a curve should never be used for decisions with outcomes above r^*. In general one must:

Assume that over some *relevant range* of rate of return an investor's actual utility curve can be adequately approximated by a quadratic curve of the form

$$u = a + br - cr^2$$

Figure 9-6 provides an illustration.

The footnote[1] proves that if an investor's utility curve is of the form

$$u = a + br - cr^2$$

---

[1] Assume that a portfolio can give any one of K rates of return (r_1, r_2, . . . , r_K) with probabilities p_1, p_2, . . . , p_K, respectively. Let u_k be the utility associated with rate of return r_k. The utility curve is quadratic. Thus

$$u_k = a + br_k - cr_k^2$$

The expected utility of the portfolio will be

$$EU_p = \sum_{k=1}^{K} p_k u_k$$

$$= \sum_{k=1}^{K} p_k(a + br_k - cr_k^2)$$

$$= a \sum_{k=1}^{K} p_k + b \sum_{k=1}^{K} p_k r_k - c \sum_{k=1}^{K} p_k r_k^2$$

The first two sums should be familiar:

$$\sum_{k=1}^{K} p_k = 1$$

$$\sum_{k=1}^{K} p_k r_k = E_p$$

(Footnote continued on next page)

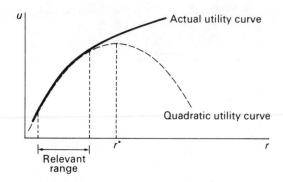

FIGURE 9-6

the expected utility of a portfolio will be

$$EU_p = a + bE_p - cE_p^2 - c\sigma_p^2$$

The expected-utility maxim implies that an investor will be indifferent among portfolios with the same expected utility. Consider all portfolios with a given expected utility—call it EU^*; each one must have an expected return and standard deviation of return consistent with the equation

$$EU^* = a + bE_p - cE_p^2 - c\sigma_p^2$$

Values of E_p and σ_p meeting this requirement lie on the same indifference curve. Viewing E_p and σ_p as variables, this *is* the equation of an indifference curve.

What sort of equation is it? That of a circle—one with a center at $E_p = r^*$ and $\sigma_p = 0$. Figure 9-7 provides an illustration. Two indifference curves are shown—one indicating all E_p, σ_p combinations with expected utility EU^*, the other indicating all combinations with

---

The last sum can be turned into something familiar with a little effort:

$$\sum_{k=1}^{K} p_k r_k^2 = \sum_{k=1}^{K} p_k [(r_k - E_p) + E_p]^2$$

$$= \sum_{k=1}^{K} p_k [(r_k - E_p)^2 + 2E_p(r_k - E_p) + E_p^2]$$

$$= \sum_{k=1}^{K} p_k (r_k - E_p)^2 + 2E_p \sum_{k=1}^{K} p_k (r_k - E_p) + E_p^2 \sum_{k=1}^{K} p_k$$

In the latter expression, the first sum equals σ_p^2 (by definition). The second sum equals 0. And the last sum equals 1. Thus,

$$\sum_{k=1}^{K} p_k r_k^2 = \sigma_p^2 + E_p^2$$

The expression for expected utility can thus be rewritten as

$$EU_p = a + bE_p - cE_p^2 - c\sigma_p^2$$

This shows that the expected utility of a portfolio can be determined once its expected return and standard deviation of return are known. But expected utility provides a complete measure of the desirability of a portfolio. Thus only E_p and σ_p are needed to evaluate a portfolio if the investor's utility is a quadratic function of rate of return.

some greater expected utility (EU^{**}). The footnote[1] provides proof that Fig. 9-7 is representative.

As indicated earlier, an investor's utility curve can (at best) be approximated by a quadratic function only over some relevant range. In particular, outcomes exceeding r^* must not be considered. Thus only the portions of the indifference curves lying southeast of point r^* in Fig. 9-7 are relevant. Within that region, each curve increases at an increasing rate, as expected.

A quadratic utility curve implies decisions based only on E_p and σ_p; it also implies a somewhat rigid but seemingly acceptable pattern of indifference curves. Unfortunately, further examination reveals some drawbacks.

There is not much latitude for expressing differences in investors' preferences. The attitude of any single person can be completely described with one number (r^*). Moreover, as soon as two equally desirable alternatives have been identified, all other choices can be predicted. This is easily proven. If two points must lie on a circle centered at some higher point along the vertical axis, there can be

---

[1] The equation of an indifference curve can be written as

$$cE_p^2 - bE_p + c\sigma_p^2 = a - EU^*$$

Dividing by c,

$$E_p^2 - \frac{b}{c}E_p + \sigma_p^2 = \frac{a - EU^*}{c}$$

Adding $b^2/4c^2$ to both sides,

$$E_p^2 - \frac{b}{c}E_p + \frac{b^2}{4c^2} + \sigma_p^2 = \frac{a - EU^*}{c} + \frac{b^2}{4c^2}$$

Rewriting,

$$\left(E_p - \frac{b}{2c}\right)^2 + \sigma_p^2 = \frac{a - EU^*}{c} + \frac{b^2}{4c^2}$$

This is the equation of a circle centered at

$$E_p = \frac{b}{2c} \qquad \sigma_p = 0$$

To complete the proof, the equality of $b/2c$ with r^* must be shown. The utility curve is

$$u = a + br - cr^2$$

Taking the derivative of u with respect to r,

$$\frac{du}{dr} = b - 2cr$$

This must equal zero at r^*:

$$b - 2cr^* = 0$$
$$r^* = b/2c$$

Thus the indifference curve is a circle centered at $E_p = r^*$ and $\sigma_p = 0$, as asserted in the text.

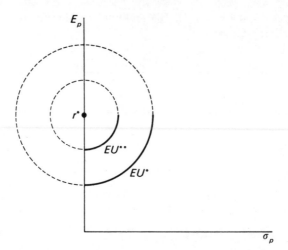

FIGURE 9-7

only one possible location for the center of the circle. The center, and therefore all possible indifference curves, can then be determined.[1]

Limited flexibility is one thing; implied behavior inconsistent with reality is another. Consider an investor faced with prospects along a capital market line. In Fig. 9-8, let CML′ represent the available alternatives and P' the preferred point. The investor undertakes risk equal to σ_p' for an expected return of E_p'. Now assume that the expected return of every security (including riskless securities) increases by 5 percent. The investor is wealthier in real terms. How will he react? By taking less risk. In Fig. 9-8, the new capital market line is CML″, and point P'' is now preferred; it involves risk equal to σ_p'' and an expected return of E_p''.

Is such a reaction likely? Many think not. Risky securities are asserted to be *normal goods*—things purchased in larger quantities as one grows wealthier. But simple graphics rule out such behavior as long as indifference curves are concentric circles centered on the vertical axis.[2]

The argument has now run its course. Minimal assumptions about choice under uncertainty imply behavior consistent with the maximization of expected utility. Concern with only E_p and σ_p is consistent

---

[1] If the two points are (E_p', σ_p') and (E_p'', σ_p''), the center lies at

$$\sigma_p = 0 \qquad E_p = \frac{(\sigma_p'')^2 - (\sigma_p')^2 + (E_p'')^2 - (E_p')^2}{2(E_p'' - E_p')}$$

[2] The preferred combination lies at a point at which an indifference curve is tangent to the capital market line. This must occur at a point at which the capital market line is perpendicular to a line from the point to the center of the circle (r^*). Since the slope of the new capital market line equals that of the previous one, both points must lie along a line extending downward from point r^*.

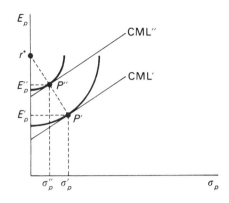

FIGURE 9-8

with a quadratic utility function. But a quadratic utility function implies indifference curves that plot as concentric circles centered on the vertical axis. And such curves cannot represent the preferences of some investors in a wholly satisfactory manner.

In some instances, investors will be concerned with more than the expected return and standard deviation of return. In such cases a quadratic utility curve will imperfectly approximate an investor's actual utility curve. If portfolios with radically different prospects are considered by an investor, too much reality may be omitted if his decision is assumed to depend only on expected return and standard deviation of return.

But few investors seriously consider portfolios with radically different prospects. Most people prefer well-diversified portfolios. The return on such a portfolio is likely to be highly correlated with the return on the market portfolio; and the entire probability distribution of the rate of return on such a portfolio may be summarized with two numbers: the expected return and standard deviation of return suffice.

Each point in an E_p, σ_p diagram may be interpreted as representing a specific probability distribution—that of the rate of return on a well-diversified portfolio. Any investor should be able to rank all such possibilities. Putting it another way, a set of indifference curves reflecting an investor's preferences among such alternatives can be constructed. And the curves can have any shape (i.e., they need not be circular).

In the final analysis, it is necessary to appeal to the original justification for assuming that investors choose among portfolios solely on the basis of expected return and standard deviation of return. It is a convenient simplifying assumption. Together with other assumptions, it leads to important and useful implications. Little more need be said in its behalf.

10.

STATE-PREFERENCE THEORY

Capital market theory depends on a simplifying assumption about investors. Each is assumed to choose among portfolios on the basis of expected return and standard deviation of return. As indicated in the previous chapter, this is an heroic assumption—one justified primarily by its ability to produce useful implications.

This chapter deals with a different model of investor choice and with its implications for the capital market. The theory of Part II can be considered a special case of the more general approach presented here.

No attempt will be made to assess the advantages and disadvantages of the two approaches. It suffices to present the more general model and relate it to the conclusions reached earlier.

Key to the state-preference approach is the notion of the future *state*
of the world. At any point in time, one (and only one) of a number
of alternatives must prevail. States may be defined very broadly; for
example:

State 1: depression
State 2: inflation
State 3: price level unchanged

Alternatively, states may be defined very narrowly:

State 593: General Motors sales are up 10 percent, Mr. *I*'s aunt dies,
leaving him a modest fortune, etc.

However defined, states are *mutually exclusive* and *exhaustive*. The
existence of one state precludes any other; and together, the states
cover all possibilities.

For convenience, only two periods (*now* and *later*) will be considered. Investors are presumed to have preferences regarding the
future state of the world. Hence the name *state-preference theory*.
The approach can easily be applied to cases involving more than two
time periods; thus it is sometimes termed *time-state-preference
theory*. The shorter name (and simpler case) will be employed here.

An investor's prospects can be described as a set of contingent
future wealth positions. In particular, let

W_1 = investor's wealth if state 1 occurs
W_2 = investor's wealth if state 2 occurs

$\vdots$

W_N = investor's wealth if state N occurs

In its most elegant form, state-preference theory deals with individual commodities. But elegance leads to complexity. Thus most
expositions deal with a single commodity (corn is the economist's
traditional example). For present purposes it is preferable to express
wealth in dollars, with the understanding that the term refers to
real dollars of equal purchasing power (i.e., dollars able to purchase
identical quantities of some representative basket of commodities).

There is no need to assume that a (real) dollar in one state is as
desirable as a (real) dollar in another state. For example, money may
be more desirable in the state *investor ill* than in the state *investor well*.
One of the advantages of state-preference theory is its ability to
accommodate different attitudes towards dollars in various states.

Figure 10-1 shows an investor's preferences in a situation involving

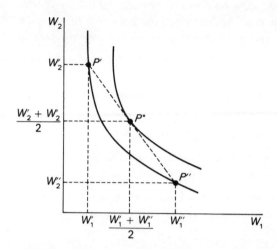

FIGURE 10-1

only two alternative future states. Consider point P'. It represents a guarantee that the investor will have wealth W_1' if state 1 occurs and wealth W_2' if state 2 occurs. Point P'' represents a guarantee that the investor will have wealth W_1'' if state 1 occurs and wealth W_2'' if state 2 occurs. The investor in question considers these alternatives equally desirable—points P' and P'' lie on the same indifference curve.

Both W_1 and W_2 are considered to be goods. Points below or to the left of an indifference curve represent inferior combinations; points above or to the right are superior. In general, indifference curves are convex to the origin; thus in Fig. 10-1, each curve becomes flatter moving from left (top) to right (bottom).

Convexity is analogous to risk aversion. Consider point P^*, midway between points P' and P''. It is preferred to either point P' or point P''. In general:

If an investor is indifferent between

1. $W_1', W_2', \ldots, W_N'$
   and
2. $W_1'', W_2'', \ldots, W_N''$

then he will prefer

3. $\dfrac{W_1' + W_1''}{2}, \dfrac{W_2' + W_2''}{2}, \ldots, \dfrac{W_N' + W_N''}{2}$

to either 1 or 2.

It is natural to term an investor with such preferences *risk averse*. Each of the combinations can be considered a security. The relationship can then be stated:

If an investor is indifferent between

1. security 1 and
2. security 2

then he will prefer

3. a portfolio invested equally in securities 1 and 2 to either security 1 or security 2

All other things equal, a risk-averse investor prefers to diversify.

What factors determine an investor's preferences? The relative desirabilities of wealth in various states are clearly relevant. So are the investor's estimates of the probabilities that each state will in fact occur. But state-preference theory does not require explicit assumptions about the formation of preferences—only their essential characteristics (e.g., convex indifference curves). In particular, investors may have different beliefs about the probabilities of various states. Probabilities (real or imagined) do not enter the analysis explicitly; they are implicit in the preferences (indifference curves) of the individual investors.

A security may be described in terms of payments received by its owner in all possible states. The (real) dollars received by the holder of one share of security i if state j occurs will be denoted D_{ij}. Consider security a, each share of which will pay $10 if state 1 occurs and $20 if state 2 occurs:

$$D_{a1} = 10$$
$$D_{a2} = 20$$

Assume that security b has the following prospects:

$$D_{b1} = 30$$
$$D_{b2} = 10$$

Finally, assume that one share of security a costs $15, as does one share of security b.

Now consider a person who has decided to invest $900. What are his alternatives? He can buy 60 shares of security a; if he does, his prospects will be

$$W_1 = 600$$
$$W_2 = 1,200$$

This is shown by point a in Fig. 10-2. Alternatively, he can buy 60 shares of security b; if he does, his prospects will be

$$W_1 = 1,800$$
$$W_2 = 600$$

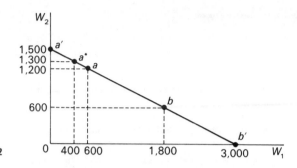

FIGURE 10-2

This is shown by point *b* in Fig. 10-2.

There are other possibilities. The investor can divide his money between the two securities. If he does, his prospects will plot at some point along the line connecting points *a* and *b* in Fig. 10-2. By issuing securities, he can even obtain prospects lying between points *a'* and *a* or between points *b* and *b'*.

Assume that the investor issues 10 shares of security *b*, using the proceeds as well as his own money to buy shares of security *a*. His prospects will be

State	Proceeds from 70 shares of security *a*	Less payment to holders of 10 shares of security *b*	Equals net proceeds
1	$ 700	$300	$W_1 = \$ 400$
2	1,400	100	$W_2 = 1,300$

This is shown by point *a** in Fig. 10-2.

It is perfectly reasonable to suppose that an investor can issue securities as long as doing so will not cause his overall prospects to include a negative amount of wealth if some state occurs. As long as $W_1, W_2, W_3, \ldots,$ to W_N are all greater than or equal to zero, the investor can meet the obligations incurred by issuing securities, no matter which state occurs.

Clearly an investor can choose to have as much wealth as possible if one state occurs (at the cost of having none in any other event). Needless to say, such an alternative is of more interest analytically than practically. In Fig. 10-2, point *a'* represents one such strategy, and point *b'* another. The prospects are

$$a' : \quad \begin{aligned} W_1 &= 0 \\ W_2 &= 1{,}500 \end{aligned}$$

$$b' : \quad \begin{aligned} W_1 &= 3{,}000 \\ W_2 &= 0 \end{aligned}$$

The investor's alternatives lie along line $a'b'$ in Fig. 10-2; this is his *budget line*. Its location depends on the amount invested and the prices and prospects of securities a and b.

An alternative view characterizes a situation of this sort in terms of securities that are seldom traded explicitly:

One share of *pure security 1* pays $1 if state 1 occurs and nothing if any other state occurs.

One share of *pure security 2* pays $1 if state 2 occurs and nothing if any other state occurs.

. . . .

One share of *pure security N* pays $1 if state N occurs and nothing if any other state occurs.

In Fig. 10-2 point b' can be considered the purchase of 3,000 shares of pure security 1. The cost is $900. Denote:

$P_j =$ the price of one share of pure security j (i.e., the cost of a claim to receive $1 if state j occurs and nothing if any other state occurs)

In this case,

$$P_1 = \frac{\$900}{3{,}000} = \$.30$$

Point a' can be considered the purchase of 1,500 shares of pure security 2. The cost is $900. Thus

$$P_2 = \frac{\$900}{1{,}500} = \$.60$$

The investor can be assumed to face a situation in which he can buy shares of pure security 1 at 30 cents each and/or shares of pure security 2 at 60 cents each. Given these prices and a budget of $900, his alternatives lie along line $a'b'$ in Fig. 10-2.

It may prove useful to summarize the analysis to this point. Given an amount to be invested and the prices and prospects of two securities (a and b), an investor's alternatives can be characterized by a budget line. It is constructed by connecting the points representing invest- ment in each security, but extends throughout the region in which neither W_1 nor W_2 is negative. A useful characterization describes the budget line in terms of its intercepts. The investor is assumed to be able to buy (but not sell) *pure securities*—each promising payment if one (and only one) state occurs. The investor's alternatives can then be calculated directly, given the amount to be invested and the prices of the pure securities.

Figure 10-3 shows a typical situation for a case involving only two states. The investor chooses the preferred point on his budget line. In Fig. 10-3 it is point x. At the preferred point, an indifference curve is tangent to the budget line.

Returning to the example, consider the introduction of a new security—call it c. Assume that each share will pay $20 if state 1 occurs and $10 if state 2 occurs:

$$D_{c1} = 20$$
$$D_{c2} = 10$$

How much should security c cost? The answer is $12. To see why this must be the case, consider some other possibilities (counter-examples).

Assume that a share of security c costs $18. The investor could buy 50 shares for $900, obtaining the following prospects:

$$W_1 = 1,000$$
$$W_2 = 500$$

This is shown by point c' in Fig. 10-4. Clearly, no one would be willing to hold security c under these conditions. Several combinations of securities a and b costing $900 provide more wealth no matter which state occurs (i.e., lie to the northeast of point c').

FIGURE 10-3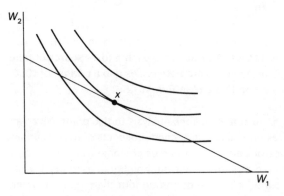

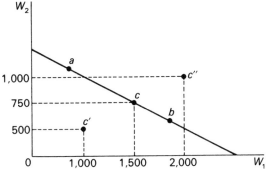
FIGURE 10-4

The price of security c will fall as people attempt to get rid of their holdings (the prices of a and b may also rise).

Assume next that a share of security c costs $9. The investor could buy 100 shares for $900, obtaining the following prospects:

$W_1 = 2,000$
$W_2 = 1,000$

This is shown by point c'' in Fig. 10-4. Security c now dominates combinations of a and b. In fact, by issuing combinations of a and b, and investing the proceeds in c, the investor could in theory obtain any desired amount of wealth in *every* state. The result is not hard to predict. The price of security c will rise as people attempt to purchase more and more of it (the prices of a and b may also fall).

The conclusion is obvious. In equilibrium, all such securities must plot along a single budget line. This means that the price of any security can be calculated by *pricing out* its prospects, using the prices of the relevant pure securities. In this example,

$P_1 = \$.30$
$P_2 = \$.60$

The price of security c must be:

$$P_1 D_{c1} + P_2 D_{c2} = (\$.30 \times 20) + (\$.60 \times 10)$$
$$= \$12$$

For $900, the investor can buy 75 shares, obtaining the following prospects:

$W_1 = 1,500$
$W_2 = 750$

This is shown by point c in Fig. 10-4. As intended, it plots on the budget line.

This relationship in no way depends on the investor's preferences. It follows directly from the requirement that similar things be traded on similar terms. To make the point even more obvious, consider the following analogy. Certain growers prepare *California fruit baskets*. Assume that one basket (*a*) contains 10 oranges and 20 grapefruit, while another (*b*) contains 30 oranges and 10 grapefruit. Each sells for $15. Buying and/or selling such packages, a consumer can obtain any desired ratio of oranges to grapefruit. A little calculation shows that the implicit price of an orange is 30 cents, while that of a grapefruit is 60 cents. If a grower plans to sell a new package (*c*) containing 20 oranges and 10 grapefruit, he should use the prevailing (implicit) prices:

        20 oranges at $.30 each   = $ 6
        10 grapefruit at $.60 each =   6
        Price of package   = $12

This is the equilibrium price for the new package.

The principle can be extended to a case involving many states. The equilibrium price of a security will be

$$\pi_i = \sum_{j=1}^{N} P_j D_{ij}$$

where π_i = equilibrium price of one share of security i

P_j = price of one share of pure security j (i.e., the cost of a claim to receive one [real] dollar if state j occurs and nothing if any other state occurs)

D_{ij} = (real) dollars received by the holder of one share of security i if state j occurs

An investor can be assumed to divide his investment budget among N pure securities. His opportunities can be described by his budget and the prices of the pure securities (that is, $P_1, P_2, \ldots, P_N$). At the preferred point, one of his indifference surfaces will be tangent to his budget surface. The situation is thus comparable to the standard economic analysis of choice under conditions of certainty.

But there are differences. Pure securities are not bought and sold on the New York Stock Exchange. Real securities represent complex bundles of many pure securities. This may be explained (rationalized) relatively easily. Few investors want to stake their future on the occurrence of one state (e.g., in Fig. 10-2, few prefer points between *a* and *a'* or between *b* and *b'*). It may be more convenient to deal in packages that are not too extreme. In theory, one can always compute the implicit prices of the pure securities, given the prices and prospects of real securities.[1]

A more serious problem concerns the true nature of real securities. In terms of the analogy, the packages are wrapped in very thick cellophane, the precise number of oranges and grapefruit is uncertain, and individuals may disagree about the quantities.

Finally, it may be impossible to obtain different outcomes in states that an investor considers significantly different. Again the analogy, assume that all packages include precisely the same number of pears and peaches. A consumer who prefers pears to peaches is powerless to obtain a preferred mix. Similarly, real securities are likely to provide the same outcome, regardless of a particular investor's marital bliss. It is difficult to arrange for different prospects if *investor happily married* applies than if it does not.

Having acknowledged these deficiencies, it is now possible to proceed. Henceforth it will be assumed that there are M real securities and N states, that M exceeds N, and that the securities' prospects differ sufficiently to allow investors to obtain any desired proportional mix of the N pure securities.

THE RISKLESS PORTFOLIO

The holder of a riskless security knows that he will receive a certain amount, no matter what happens. In the current context: the payment in real dollars will be the same, regardless of the state that actually occurs. A riskless security is thus equivalent to a portfolio made up of equal parts of every pure security.

Consider a portfolio that includes one share of every pure security. The holder is certain to receive $1, no matter which state occurs.

[1] Any N securities that are independent of one another may be used. Assume that securities 1 to N are satisfactory. Construct the following set of simultaneous equations:

$$P_1 D_{1,1} + P_2 D_{1,2} + \cdots + P_N D_{1N} = \pi_1$$

$$P_1 D_{2,1} + P_2 D_{2,2} + \cdots + P_N D_{2N} = \pi_2$$

$$\vdots$$

$$P_1 D_{N1} + P_2 D_{N2} + \cdots + P_N D_{NN} = \pi_N$$

The method described in Sec. A of the Supplement can be used to find the values of $P_1, P_2, \ldots,$ to P_N consistent with this set of equations. If the situation is one of equilibrium, the set of prices so determined will be consistent with the prices and prospects of the other securities.

The cost of such a portfolio is simply the sum of the costs of its component pure securities:

$$\sum_{j=1}^{N} P_j$$

Thus $\sum_{j=1}^{N} P_j$ now equals \$1 *later* with certainty. As usual, the pure interest rate will be denoted p. By definition, \$1 *now* equals $(1 + p)$ *later* with certainty.

$$\text{Thus } p = \left(\frac{1}{\sum_{j=1}^{N} P_j}\right) - 1$$

The previous example provides an illustration. P_1, the cost of insuring payment of \$1 if state 1 occurs, is 30 cents; P_2, the cost of insuring payment of \$1 if state 2 occurs, is 60 cents. Thus for 90 cents ($= P_1 + P_2$), an investor can be certain to receive \$1 no matter which state occurs. The pure interest rate is

$$p = \frac{1}{.90} - 1 = .111 = 11.1\%$$

Riskless transactions are usually represented by a single security (note, contract, etc.). For present purposes, it is more convenient to regard them as portfolios of pure securities. The term *riskless portfolio* will be used to denote any portfolio containing equal parts of all N pure securities.

If an investor puts all his funds in riskless securities, what will his prospects be? Let $\overline{W}$ represent his guaranteed future wealth. To assure $\overline{W}$ in state 1 costs $P_1\overline{W}$; to assure $\overline{W}$ in state 2 costs $P_2\overline{W}$; etc. The total cost will equal the investor's budget (B):

$$B = \sum_{j=1}^{N} P_j\overline{W}$$

Given a budget and the prices of pure securities, an investor holding only riskless securities will be certain to receive $\overline{W}$ (real) dollars, where

$$\overline{W} = \frac{B}{\sum_{j=1}^{N} P_j}$$

This is his riskless portfolio. It will be denoted R.

The market portfolio represents the totality of all existing (real)
securities. But every real security may be considered a combination
of various pure securities. It is thus possible to redefine the market
portfolio as the totality of all existing pure securities. In other words,
the market portfolio represents a claim to everything that exists,
regardless of the state of the world. Of course, no single investor
can hold such a claim. But an investor can hold a proportional share.
As before, the term *market portfolio* will be used to refer to any
portfolio in which holdings are proportional to the amounts of
existing securities.

Let W_1^T = total available wealth if state 1 occurs
$\quad W_2^T$ = total available wealth if state 2 occurs
$$\vdots$$
$\quad W_N^T$ = total available wealth if state N occurs

The holder of a *market portfolio* will receive

$\alpha W_1^T \qquad$ if state 1 occurs
$\alpha W_2^T \qquad$ if state 2 occurs
$$\vdots$$
$\alpha W_N^T \qquad$ if state N occurs

where α is some constant.

It is a simple matter to determine the composition of any investor's
market portfolio. To assure αW_1^T in state 1 costs $P_1 \alpha W_1^T$; to assure αW_2^T
in state 2 costs $P_2 \alpha W_2^T$; etc. The total cost will equal the investor's
budget (B):

$$B = \sum_{j=1}^{N} P_j \alpha W_j^T$$

Given a budget, the prices of pure securities, and the society's total
wealth in each state, the proportional share that can be obtained by
an investor holding a market portfolio is

$$\alpha = \frac{B}{\sum\limits_{j=1}^{N} P_j W_j^T}$$

The result is not surprising. The denominator indicates the cost (in
present value) of all future wealth. The investor's share of wealth
equals the ratio of his budget to that sum. He can obtain a similar
proportion of future wealth in every contingency. The portfolio that
allows him to do so is his market portfolio. It will be denoted M.

One of the key implications of capital market theory under conditions of agreement is the notion that every investor will choose a portfolio plotting along the capital market line. Put somewhat differently, every investor will choose a portfolio that is equivalent to some combination of the market portfolio and the riskless portfolio. In the context of capital market theory, a portfolio is equivalent to another if it has the same expected return and standard deviation of return.

An analogous situation may be defined in the context of state-preference theory. Two portfolios may be said to be equivalent if both are equivalent to the same mix of pure securities (i.e., promise the same payments in various states). Portfolios equivalent to combinations of an investor's market portfolio and his riskless portfolio lie along a *market line* on his budget surface.

Figure 10-5 provides an illustration for a case involving three states. The plane *abc* represents an investor's budget surface. Point R represents a riskless portfolio, giving the same wealth in every state (that is, $W_1 = W_2 = W_3 = \overline{W}$). Point M represents a market portfolio, giving wealth in every state proportional to the total amount available (that is, $W_1 = \alpha W_1^T$, $W_2 = \alpha W_2^T$, $W_3 = \alpha W_3^T$). RMQ is the investor's

FIGURE 10-5

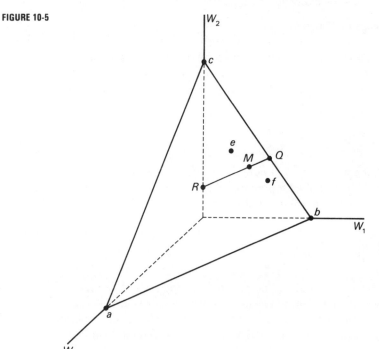

market line : any portfolio plotting on it is equivalent to borrowing or lending plus investment in the market. Point R corresponds to lending only. Points between R and M correspond to combinations of lending plus investment in the market. Point M corresponds to investment in the market. And points between M and Q correspond to borrowing plus investment in the market.

Collectively, investors must hold all existing securities. Thus *on the average*, they must hold market portfolios. This in no way implies that every investor must choose a market portfolio. For example, one investor with a budget surface similar to that shown in Fig. 10-5 could select the combination shown by point e, while another could select the combination shown by point f. Although neither chooses a point on his market line, the collective holdings can still average out to point M.

As shown in Chap. 6, when investors disagree about the future, very little can be said about their holdings. State-preference theory allows people to disagree. It is hardly surprising that the theory does *not* imply that every investor will select a market-based portfolio (i.e., one on his market line).

But many investors do hold market-based portfolios, as the empirical evidence in Chap. 8 shows. Such investors do select points along their market lines. And the points can be succinctly described, as the next section indicates.

It is convenient to characterize points along the market line by their proximity to the market portfolio. A reasonable scale assigns a value of 0 to the riskless portfolio and a value of 1 to the market portfolio. The resulting measure indicates the similarity of the portfolio to the market portfolio—it will be denoted β. Figure 10-6 provides an illustration :

MARKET SIMILARITY

$\beta = 0$ for the riskless portfolio (point R)
$\beta = 1$ for the market portfolio (point M)
$\beta = .5$ for a portfolio made up of equal parts of riskless and market portfolios (point x)
$\beta = 2$ for a portfolio obtained by borrowing an amount equal to the investor's budget and placing all funds in the market (point y)

Market similarity (β) plays a role in state-preference theory similar to that of volatility in capital market theory. In fact, for combinations of the riskless and market portfolios, the two values are identical.

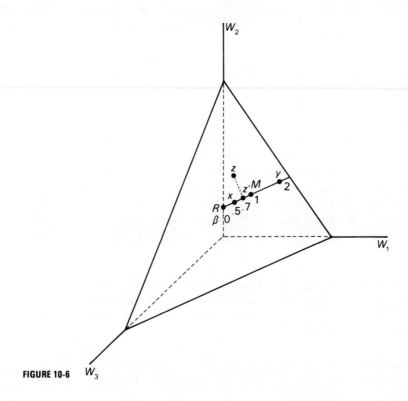

FIGURE 10-6 W_3

The concept of market similarity can be applied to any security or portfolio. The definition is straightforward:

The market similarity of a security or portfolio equals the value of β at the nearest point along the market line.

Point z in Fig. 10-6 provides an illustration. The nearest point along the market line is z'. Thus the market similarity of security or portfolio z is .7.

Market similarity can be calculated directly.[1]

Define r_{ij} = rate of return on security or portfolio i if state j occurs
$\qquad r_{Mj}$ = rate of return on market portfolio if state j occurs
$\qquad p$ = pure interest rate
$\qquad \beta_i$ = market similarity of security or portfolio i

---

[1] The formula was first derived by Nancy Jacob, of the University of Washington. The proof given in the following footnote is less direct than hers, but more appropriate in the present context.

The footnote[1] shows that

$$\beta_i = \frac{\sum\limits_{j=1}^{N} (r_{ij} - p)(r_{Mj} - p)}{\sum\limits_{j=1}^{N} (r_{Mj} - p)^2}$$

The market similarity of a portfolio is simply the weighted average

[1] No matter which state occurs, an investor holding a riskless portfolio will receive

$$\overline{W} = B(1 + p)$$

If state j occurs, an investor holding a market portfolio will receive

$$\alpha W_j^T = B(1 + r_{Mj})$$

If state j occurs, an investor holding a portfolio on the market line with market similarity β will receive

$$
\begin{aligned}
W_j^\beta &= (1 - \beta)\overline{W} + \beta(\alpha W_j^T) \\
&= (1 - \beta)B(1 + p) + \beta B(1 + r_{Mj}) \\
&= B[(1 + p) + \beta(r_{Mj} - p)]
\end{aligned}
$$

If state j occurs, an investor holding security or portfolio i will receive

$$W_j^i = B(1 + r_{ij})$$

The point representing security or portfolio i has coordinates: $W_1^i,\ W_2^i,\ \ldots,\ W_N^i$. The point on the market line with market similarity β has coordinates: $W_1^\beta,\ W_2^\beta,\ \ldots,\ W_N^\beta$. Let D be the distance between the two points:

$$
\begin{aligned}
D^2 &= (W_1^i - W_1^\beta)^2 + (W_2^i - W_2^\beta)^2 + \cdots + (W_N^i - W_N^\beta)^2 \\
&= \sum\limits_{j=1}^{N} (W_j^i - W_j^\beta)^2
\end{aligned}
$$

The parenthesized expression can be simplified:

$$
\begin{aligned}
(W_j^i - W_j^\beta) &= B(1 + r_{ij}) - B[(1 + p) + \beta(r_{Mj} - p)] \\
&= B[(r_{ij} - p) - \beta(r_{Mj} - p)]
\end{aligned}
$$

Substituting,

$$D^2 = \sum\limits_{j=1}^{N} B^2[(r_{ij} - p)^2 - 2\beta(r_{ij} - p)(r_{Mj} - p) + \beta^2(r_{Mj} - p)^2]$$

The goal is to select a value of β that minimizes D. A sufficient condition requires the derivative of D^2 with respect to β to be zero:

$$\frac{dD^2}{d\beta} = \sum\limits_{j=1}^{N} B^2[-2(r_{ij} - p)(r_{Mj} - p) + 2\beta(r_{Mj} - p)^2] = 0$$

Simplifying,

$$\beta = \frac{\sum\limits_{j=1}^{N} (r_{ij} - p)(r_{Mj} - p)}{\sum\limits_{j=1}^{N} (r_{Mj} - p)^2}$$

which is the formula for β_i given in the text.

of the corresponding values for its component securities, using the proportions invested as weights:[1]

$$\beta_p = \sum_{i=1}^{N} X_i \beta_i$$

As suggested in Chap. 8, volatility can be measured after the fact by treating each observation as an equally likely outcome. More precisely,

$$b'_i = \frac{\sum_{i=1}^{N'} (r'_{ij} - A_i)(r'_{Mj} - A_M)}{\sum_{j=1}^{N'} (r'_{Mj} - A_M)^2}$$

where b'_i = actual volatility of security or portfolio i

[1] Let r_{pj} = the rate of return on portfolio p if state j occurs.

Then $r_{pj} = \sum_{i=1}^{N} X_i r_{ij}$

where X_i = the proportion invested in (pure) security i.

By definition,

$$\beta_p = \frac{\sum_{i=1}^{N} (r_{pj} - p)(r_{Mj} - p)}{\sum_{j=1}^{N} (r_{Mj} - p)^2}$$

Note that

$$r_{pj} - p = \sum_{i=1}^{N} X_i r_{ij} - p$$

Since the X_i's must sum to 1:

$$r_{pj} - p = \sum_{i=1}^{N} X_i r_{ij} - \sum_{i=1}^{N} X_i p$$

$$= \sum_{i=1}^{N} X_i (r_{ij} - p)$$

Substituting,

$$\beta_p = \frac{\sum_{j=1}^{N} \sum_{i=1}^{N} X_i (r_{ij} - p)(r_{Mj} - p)}{\sum_{j=1}^{N} (r_{Mj} - p)^2}$$

Rearranging,

$$\beta_p = \frac{\sum_{i=1}^{N} X_i \sum_{j=1}^{N} (r_{ij} - p)(r_{Mj} - p)}{\sum_{j=1}^{N} (r_{Mj} - p)^2}$$

$$= \sum_{i=1}^{N} X_i \beta_i$$

which is the formula given in the text.

r'_{ij} = actual rate of return on security or portfolio i in period j
r'_{Mj} = actual rate of return on market portfolio in period j
A_i = average rate of return on security or portfolio i
A_M = average rate of return on market portfolio
N' = number of periods (observations)

A comparable procedure can be used to measure market similarity. The observations are assumed to represent the possible states:

$$\beta'_i = \frac{\sum\limits_{j=1}^{N'} (r'_{ij} - p')(r'_{Mj} - p')}{\sum\limits_{j=1}^{N'} (r'_{Mj} - p')^2}$$

where β'_i = actual market similarity of security or portfolio i
r'_{ij} = actual rate of return on security or portfolio i in period j
r'_{Mj} = actual rate of return on market portfolio in period j
p' = actual pure rate of interest
N' = number of periods (observations)

These two measures are closely related. Consider Fig. 10-7. Each point represents a pair of actual rates of return. How should a characteristic line be "fit" to the data? The usual criterion involves the minimization of the sum of the squared deviations of the actual rates of return on the security from the values implied by the line. A line that accomplishes this must pass through point A, at which both rates of return equal their average values. The formula for the slope of such a line (i.e., volatility) emphasizes the fact that the point of reference involves both A_i and A_M.

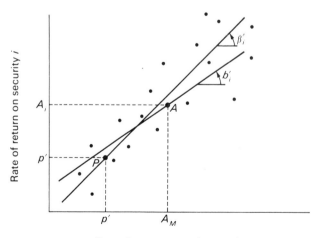

FIGURE 10-7

Rate of return on market portfolio

Only by chance will a characteristic line estimated in the usual manner pass through point P, at which both rates of return equal the pure interest rate. But equilibrium conditions may imply that the true characteristic line does go through point P. It might thus be desirable to force the estimated line to do so too. The slope could be selected (as before) to minimize the sum of the squared deviations of actual rate of return on the security from the values implied by the line. Happily, the formula for the slope of such a line is precisely that given earlier for actual market similarity (β_i'), as the footnote[1] shows.

There are other alternatives. For example, it may be better to minimize the sum of the absolute deviations than to minimize the sum of the squared deviations. The selection of the best measure is, in essence, an empirical issue. Note, however, that the usefulness of the characteristic line and the importance of its slope are *not* at issue. The only question concerns the best method for estimating such a line from actual data.

[1] The objective is to minimize

$$\sum_{j=1}^{N'} [(r_{ij} - p') - \beta_i'(r_{Mj} - p')]^2$$

The derivative with respect to β_i' is

$$\sum_{j=1}^{N'} [-2(r_{ij} - p')(r_{Mj} - p') + 2\beta_i'(r_{Mj} - p')^2]$$

Setting this equal to zero

$$-2 \sum_{j=1}^{N'} (r_{ij} - p')(r_{Mj} - p') + 2\beta_i' \sum_{j=1}^{N'} (r_{Mj} - p')^2 = 0$$

Rearranging,

$$\beta_i' = \frac{\displaystyle\sum_{j=1}^{N'} (r_{ij} - p')(r_{Mj} - p')}{\displaystyle\sum_{j=1}^{N'} (r_{Mj} - p')^2}$$

which is the formula for actual market similarity.

SUPPLEMENT
THE MATHEMATICAL FOUNDATION

A.

ESSENTIAL INGREDIENTS

This section presents a few mathematical techniques that are essential for the material in the subsequent sections. The goal is not to present the techniques completely and rigorously, only to provide a minimum foundation for what follows.

The reader is assumed to either know the rudiments of differential calculus or to be willing to accept on faith the summary description included here.

The essential problem in portfolio theory is of the form:

Minimize $Z = V_p - \lambda E_p$

where $V_p = \displaystyle\sum_{i=1}^{N}\sum_{j=1}^{N} X_i X_j C_{ij}$

and $E_p = \displaystyle\sum_{i=1}^{N} X_i E_i$

subject to $\displaystyle\sum_{i=1}^{N} X_i = 1$

and (perhaps) other constraints.

More succinctly,

minimize $Z = \displaystyle\sum_{i=1}^{N}\sum_{j=1}^{N} X_i X_j C_{ij} - \lambda\left(\sum_{i=1}^{N} X_i E_i\right)$

subject to $\displaystyle\sum_{i=1}^{N} X_i = 1$

and (perhaps) other constraints.

The problem is to select values for the decision variables (X_i's) that will minimize the objective function (Z).

To understand the nature of such a problem it is convenient to think graphically. And since most people have difficulty visualizing more than three dimensions, it is convenient to consider a simple problem.

Figure A-1 shows the relationship between Z and two decision variables, X_1 and X_2. Think of changing X_1 as moving in an east-west direction. Think of changing X_2 as moving in a north-south direction. Let Z represent height.

FIGURE A-1

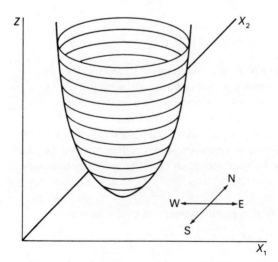

Any pair of X_1, X_2 values corresponds to a location (latitude and longitude). The problem is to find the lowest (least-Z) location—the bottom of the lowest valley.

Consider some location at which $X_1 = X_1^*$ and $X_2 = X_2^*$; call it (X_1^*, X_2^*). Let Z^* be the height at that location. Now consider a move to a new location: $(X_1^* + \Delta X_1, X_2^*)$. If ΔX_1 is positive, this is a move to the east; if ΔX_1 is negative, it is a move to the west. Let the height at the new location be $Z^* + \Delta Z$. If ΔZ is positive, it is higher than the old location; if ΔZ is negative, it is lower; if ΔZ equals zero, the heights are the same.

By moving ΔX_1 units east or west, one moves ΔZ units up or down. The change in height per unit traveled in the X_1 (east-west) direction will be

$$\frac{\Delta Z}{\Delta X_1}$$

Now consider a different kind of move—one in the north-south direction; from (X_1^*, X_2^*), move to $(X_1^*, X_2^* + \Delta X_2)$. If ΔX_2 is positive, the move is northward; if ΔX_2 is negative, the move is southward. Let the height at the new location be $Z^* + \Delta Z$. The change in height per unit traveled in the X_2 (north-south) direction will be

$$\frac{\Delta Z}{\Delta X_2}$$

The slope of a curve at a precise point is measured by a *partial derivative*. By definition,

$$\frac{\partial Z}{\partial X_i} = \lim_{\Delta X_i \to 0} \left(\frac{\Delta Z}{\Delta X_i} \right)$$

The symbol $(\partial Z / \partial X_i)$ is read "the partial derivative of Z with respect to X_i." It is the value approached by $(\Delta Z / \Delta X_i)$ as ΔX_i takes on successively smaller values. For such a derivative to exist, the ratio must approach the same value as ΔX_i takes on successively larger (algebraically) negative values.

What characteristics does a valley bottom have? Most notably, it does not slope up or down in any direction. What is true in general must be true in particular. In the example, the curve must have a zero slope in both the east-west and north-south directions:

If Z is minimum at (X_1^*, X_2^*),

then $\dfrac{\partial Z}{\partial X_1} = 0$

and $\dfrac{\partial Z}{\partial X_2} = 0$

These remarks extend naturally to a more general case. One must think in N dimensions. Instead of east-west and north-south there is an X_1 direction, an X_2 direction, etc. A location is described by a set of N coordinates. As before, the objective is minimized at a valley bottom. In other words, if Z is minimum at $(X_1^*, X_2^*, \ldots, X_N^*)$,

then $\dfrac{\partial Z}{\partial X_1} = 0$

$\dfrac{\partial Z}{\partial X_2} = 0$

$\vdots$

$\dfrac{\partial Z}{\partial X_N} = 0$

The terrain of portfolio theory has an extremely useful feature: one and only one location has these essential characteristics. The conditions are thus both necessary and sufficient. The previous statement may therefore be turned around:

If $\dfrac{\partial Z}{\partial X_1} = 0$

$\dfrac{\partial Z}{\partial X_2} = 0$

$\vdots$

$\dfrac{\partial Z}{\partial X_N} = 0$

at $(X_1^*, X_2^*, \ldots, X_N^*)$, then Z is minimum.

DERIVATIVES A partial derivative indicates the effect of one variable on another. It may be considered the slope of a curve. Consider the following function:

$$Z = 10 - 2X_1 - X_2 + 2X_1X_2 + (X_1)^2 + \tfrac{1}{4}(X_2)^2$$

What is the partial derivative of Z with respect to X_2 at the location $(X_1 = 5, X_2 = 10)$?

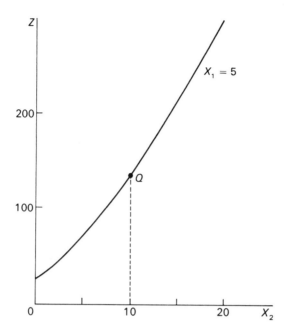

FIGURE A-2

Since the relationship between Z and X_2 is of interest, the relevant value of X_1 (5) may be substituted:

$$Z = 10 - 2(5) - X_2 + 2(5)X_2 + (5)^2 + \tfrac{1}{4}(X_2)^2$$

Simplifying,

$$Z = 25 + 9X_2 + \tfrac{1}{4}(X_2)^2$$

This relationship is shown in Fig. A-2. The partial derivative of Z with respect to X_2 at $(X_1 = 5, X_2 = 10)$ is simply the slope of this curve at point Q, where X_2 equals 10.

Needless to say, one cannot always draw graphs and measure slopes. Precise values will sometimes be needed. The remainder of this discussion provides formulas for the partial derivatives of simple functions. All the problems considered in the subsequent sections can be solved with these few formulas.

Consider first the case shown in Fig. A-3a: Z is totally unaffected by changes in X_i. The relationship can be represented by

$$Z = K$$

where K is a constant.

Obviously $\Delta Z = 0$ for any change in X_i, large or small. Thus:

If $Z = K$

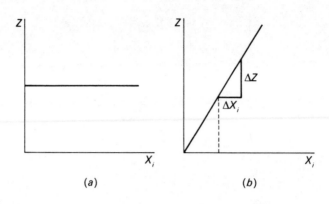

(a)   (b)

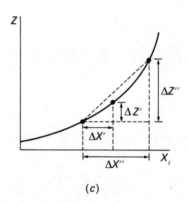

(c)

then $\dfrac{\partial Z}{\partial X_i} = 0$

Consider next the case shown in Fig. A-3b: The ratio of Z to X_i is constant. The formula is

$Z = KX_i$

where K is a constant.

Let X_i be changed by some amount ΔX_i. The new value of Z will be

$K(X_i + \Delta X_i) = KX_i + K(\Delta X_i)$

The first term is the original value of Z. Thus the change is

$\Delta Z = K(\Delta X_i)$

and the ratio is

$\dfrac{\Delta Z}{\Delta X_i} = \dfrac{K(\Delta X_i)}{\Delta X_i} = K$

As this formula indicates, the ratio does not depend on the distance moved. This is not surprising—the slope of a straight line is constant. Thus:

If $Z = KX_i$

then $\dfrac{\partial Z}{\partial X_i} = K$

Figure A-3c presents a more complex case. The formula is

$Z = KX_i^2$

where K is a constant.

Obviously the ratio of ΔZ to ΔX_i will depend on the distance traveled (i.e., the size of ΔX_i). As the figure shows, the ratio is greater when ΔX_i is $\Delta X_i''$ than when it is $\Delta X_i'$. In general, after a change in X_i, the value of Z will be

$$K(X_i + \Delta X_i)^2 = K[X_i^2 + 2X_i\,\Delta X_i + (\Delta X_i)^2]$$
$$= KX_i^2 + 2KX_i\,\Delta X_i + K(\Delta X_i)^2$$

The first term is the original value of Z. The change in Z brought about by the change in X_i is thus

$$\Delta Z = 2KX_i\,\Delta X_i + K(\Delta X_i)^2$$

And the ratio is

$$\frac{\Delta Z}{\Delta X_i} = \frac{2KX_i\,\Delta X_i + K(\Delta X_i)^2}{\Delta X_i}$$
$$= 2KX_i + K(\Delta X_i)$$

The partial derivative indicates the value this ratio approaches as ΔX_i becomes smaller and smaller. In such a case only the first term is important.[1] Thus:

If $Z = KX_i^2$

then $\dfrac{\partial Z}{\partial X_i} = 2KX_i$

These three examples can be considered special cases of a more general rule:

If $Z = KX_i^n$

where K and n are constants,

then $\dfrac{\partial Z}{\partial X_i} = nKX_i^{n-1}$

[1] More properly, the second term vanishes (approaches zero) as ΔX_i approaches zero.

One more rule is needed. Assume that Z is the sum of three values:

$$Z = Z_1 + Z_2 + Z_3$$

Now consider a change in X_i. Let the corresponding changes be ΔZ_1, ΔZ_2, and ΔZ_3. Obviously the total change will equal the sum of the individual changes:

$$\Delta Z = \Delta Z_1 + \Delta Z_2 + \Delta Z_3$$

Dividing by the change in X_i that caused it all:

$$\frac{\Delta Z}{\Delta X_i} = \frac{\Delta Z_1}{\Delta X_i} + \frac{\Delta Z_2}{\Delta X_i} + \frac{\Delta Z_3}{\Delta X_i}$$

This relationship holds as ΔX_i becomes smaller and smaller. In general,

if $Z = Z_1 + Z_2 + \cdots + Z_n$

then $\dfrac{\partial Z}{\partial X_i} = \dfrac{\partial Z_1}{\partial X_i} + \dfrac{\partial Z_2}{\partial X_i} + \cdots + \dfrac{\partial Z_n}{\partial X_i}$

In other words, the derivative of a sum is the sum of the derivatives.

This completes the set of required rules. To show how they are applied, consider the function given earlier:

$$Z = 10 - 2X_1 - X_2 + 2X_1 X_2 + (X_1)^2 + \tfrac{1}{4}(X_2)^2$$

It is useful to express each derivative in terms of the relevant variables instead of substituting numeric values at the outset. The value of the derivative at any point can then be found by substituting the values of the variables in the formula for the derivative itself.

Note that Z is the sum of a number of terms. Each can thus be treated separately and the resulting derivatives summed.

Consider first the partial derivative of Z with respect to X_2:

(10) is a constant. Its derivative with respect to X_2 is zero.

$(-2X_1)$ is a constant in this case (the term does not include X_2). Its derivative with respect to X_2 is zero.

$(-X_2)$ is a constant (-1) times X_2. Its derivative with respect to X_2 is (-1).

$(2X_1 X_2)$ is a constant $(2X_1)$ times X_2. Its derivative with respect to X_2 is $(2X_1)$.

$(X_1)^2$ is a constant in this case. Its derivative with respect to X_2 is zero.

$\tfrac{1}{4}(X_2)^2$ is a constant $(\tfrac{1}{4})$ times $(X_2)^2$. Its derivative with respect to X_2 is $(\tfrac{1}{2}X_2)$.

The result is

$$\frac{\partial Z}{\partial X_2} = 0 + 0 - 1 + 2X_1 + 0 + \tfrac{1}{2}X_2$$

At $(X_1 = 5, X_2 = 10)$ the value is

$$-1 + 2(5) + \tfrac{1}{2}(10) = 14$$

The partial derivative with respect to X_1 is

$$\frac{\partial Z}{\partial X_1} = 0 - 2 + 0 + 2X_2 + 2X_1 + 0$$

At $(X_1 = 5, X_2 = 10)$ the value is

$$-2 + 2(10) + 2(5) = 28$$

Clearly, the location investigated is not the bottom of a valley. At $(X_1 = 5, X_2 = 10)$ height rises with increases and falls with decreases in either X_1 or X_2. It is an uphill climb going either east or north and downhill going either west or south.

If the valley bottom is not at $(X_1 = 5, X_2 = 10)$, where is it? To answer such a question, a process of elimination is required. But the elimination can be performed very efficiently in cases such as this.

SIMULTANEOUS EQUATIONS

Consider first all locations that have zero slope in the east-west (X_1) direction. Any location with this characteristic must "fit" the equation

$$\frac{\partial Z}{\partial X_1} = 0$$

In other words, the values of X_1 and X_2 must *satisfy* the equation. In this example,

$$\frac{\partial Z}{\partial X_1} = -2 + 2X_2 + 2X_1 = 0$$

Simplifying and rearranging,

$$X_1 + X_2 = 1$$

Any location with coordinates summing to 1 will have 0 slope in the east-west (X_1) direction. Any other will not. Line 1 in Fig. A-4 shows the coordinates of all locations that satisfy this requirement.

Now consider all locations that have zero slope in the north-south (X_2) direction. Such a location will "fit" the equation,

$$\frac{\partial Z}{\partial X_2} = 0$$

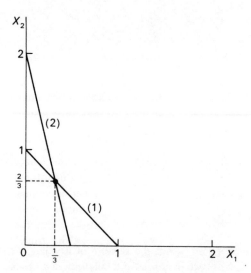

In this example, the values of X_1 and X_2 must satisfy

$$\frac{\partial Z}{\partial X_2} = -1 + 2X_1 + \tfrac{1}{2}X_2 = 0$$

Simplifying and rearranging,

$$2X_1 + \tfrac{1}{2}X_2 = 1$$

Line 2 in Fig. A-4 shows the coordinates of all locations that satisfy this requirement.

The goal is to find a location that has zero slope in both directions. Obviously, it lies at the intersection of the two lines. To determine its coordinates exactly requires the solution of a system of two simultaneous equations. In other words, values for X_1 and X_2 must be found that will *simultaneously* satisfy both equations.

In this case the answer can be found by simple substitution. The equations are

(1) $X_1 + X_2 = 1$
(2) $2X_1 + \tfrac{1}{2}X_2 = 1$

From (1),

$$X_2 = 1 - X_1$$

Substituting in (2),

$$2X_1 + \tfrac{1}{2}(1 - X_1) = 1$$

Thus, $X_1 = \tfrac{1}{3}$

and $X_2 = 1 - X_1 = \tfrac{2}{3}$

The valley bottom has been found. Its coordinates are ($X_1 = \frac{1}{3}$, $X_2 = \frac{2}{3}$).

In general there will be as many equations as there are unknowns (decision variables). Each will state that a partial derivative must equal zero. If all are satisfied simultaneously, the associated location meets all the requirements. The set of equations may be satisfied by just one location (as in the example), by many, or by none.

The problems of interest to portfolio theorists involve only linear partial derivatives. Thus the search for a minimum value of the objective requires only the solution of a system of linear equations. One set of values will typically satisfy all the equations simultaneously; the solution will be unique. And the structure of the problem (nature of the terrain) insures that it will be the (only) valley bottom.

Conditions under which this would not be true are easily identified. Consider a problem involving only two decision variables. The three possible cases are shown in Fig. A-5a to c.

FIGURE A-5

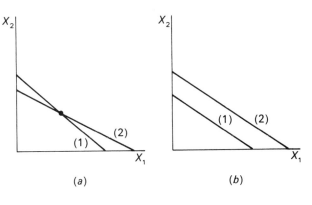

(a)   (b)

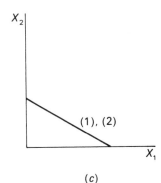

(c)

In Fig. A-5a, the two lines cross; the equations are said to be *independent*. Only one location (the intersection of the lines) satisfies both conditions. In Fig. A-5b the lines are parallel. No location has zero slope in both directions. No solution simultaneously satisfies both equations. In Fig. A-5c the lines are the same. A great many locations satisfy both requirements. The solution is not unique.

How can situations such as those shown in Fig. A-5b and c be identified? Consider first the case shown in Fig. A-5c. The two equations are the same. This may not be immediately apparent, since one may be a multiple of the other. For example,

(1) $X_1 + X_2 = 1$
(2) $2X_1 + 2X_2 = 2$

In general, two equations are the same if every coefficient in one is some constant times the corresponding coefficient in the other.

Now consider the case shown in Fig. A-5b. Here the equations differ by some constant amount. For example,

(1) $X_1 + X_2 = 1$
(2) $X_1 + X_2 = 2$

Of course this may be partially hidden if one of the equations is multiplied by a constant. For example,

(1) $X_1 + X_2 = 1$
(2) $2X_1 + 2X_2 = 4$

In general, two linear equations represent parallel lines if every coefficient on the left-hand side of one is some constant times the corresponding coefficient of the other.

In the cases shown in Fig. A-5b and c the equations are not independent:

Two equations are not independent if every coefficient on the left-hand side of one equals a constant times the corresponding coefficient of the other.

In general:

There will be a unique solution for a system of N independent linear equations in N unknowns.

A system of equations is said to be independent if every equation is independent of every other equation and every linear combination of the other equations.

There are several methods for solving simultaneous linear equations. Only one will be described here. It is based on the following principles:

1. If a set of values satisfies an equation, it will also satisfy an equation obtained by multiplying or dividing every coefficient by the same value.

2. If a set of values satisfies each of two equations, it will also satisfy an equation obtained by adding the two together or by subtracting one from the other.

To simplify both the description and the computation, it is convenient to write the coefficients in tabular form. For example, instead of

(1) $1X_1 + 1X_2 = 1$
(2) $2X_1 + \frac{1}{2}X_2 = 1$

write

	X_1	X_2	= constant
(1)	1	1	1
(2)	2	$\frac{1}{2}$	1

In general,

	X_1	X_2	X_3	$\cdots$	X_N	= constant
(1)						
(2)						
(3)						
$\vdots$						
(N)						

Each row represents an equation. The object is to obtain a set of equations of the form:

	X_1	X_2	X_3	$\cdots$	X_N	$=$ constant
(1)	1	c	c	$\cdots$	c	c
(2)	0	1	c	$\cdots$	c	c
(3)	0	0	1	$\cdots$	c	c
$\vdots$	$\vdots$	$\vdots$	$\vdots$	$\vdots$	$\vdots$	$\vdots$
(N)	0	0	0	$\cdots$	1	c

where the c's represent coefficients of any type. Given such a system of equations, it is a simple matter to find the solution. The last row immediately gives the value of X_N:

$$(1)X_N = c$$

This value can be used to obtain the value of X_{N-1}, using the next-to-last row:

$$(1)X_{N-1} + (c)X_N = c$$

By working backward, all values (X_i's) can be calculated.

A system of equations in the desired form can be obtained by performing *row operations* on the table obtained from the original set of equations. Such operations include:

1. Multiplying or dividing all coefficients in a row by the same value
2. Adding (or subtracting) every coefficient in one row to (or from) the corresponding coefficient in another row
3. Switching the positions of two rows

Consider the example. The table is

1	1		1
2	$\frac{1}{2}$		1

The first row is already in the desired form. Now, divide each coefficient in the second row by 2. This gives

1	1	1
1	$\frac{1}{4}$	$\frac{1}{2}$

Next, subtract each coefficient in the second row from the corresponding coefficient in the first row, putting the result in the second row. This gives

1	1	1
0	$\frac{3}{4}$	$\frac{1}{2}$

Finally, divide each coefficient in the second row by $\frac{3}{4}$. This gives

1	1	1
0	1	$\frac{2}{3}$

The solution can now be found by working backward. Row 2 requires that

$$0X_1 + 1X_2 = \tfrac{2}{3}$$
Thus, $X_2 = \tfrac{2}{3}$

Row 1 requires

$$1X_1 + 1X_2 = 1$$

But $X_2 = \tfrac{2}{3}$; thus,

$$1X_1 + (1)\tfrac{2}{3} = 1$$
and $X_1 = \tfrac{1}{3}$

Although the procedure may seem cumbersome, it is easily automated.

The discussion thus far has dealt with problems for which there is a unique numeric solution. In terms of the simultaneous equations,

PARAMETRIC SOLUTIONS

$$a_{1,1}X_1 + a_{1,2}X_2 + \cdots + a_{1N}X_N = b_1$$
$$a_{2,1}X_1 + a_{2,2}X_2 + \cdots + a_{2N}X_N = b_2$$
$$\vdots$$
$$a_{N1}X_1 + a_{N2}X_2 + \cdots + a_{NN}X_N = b_N$$

where the a's and b's are constants. The first subscript for each a coefficient indicates the equation, the second the variable. The subscript for each b coefficient indicates the equation. In tabular form:

X_1	X_2	$\cdots$	X_N	$=$	constant
$a_{1,1}$	$a_{1,2}$	$\cdots$	a_{1N}		b_1
$a_{2,1}$	$a_{2,2}$	$\cdots$	a_{2N}		b_2
$\vdots$	$\vdots$	$\vdots$	$\vdots$		$\vdots$
a_{N1}	a_{N2}	$\cdots$	a_{NN}		b_N

The subscripts for each a coefficient indicate its row and column; the subscript for each b coefficient indicates its row.

Now consider a situation in which the value of each right-hand side depends on the value of some parameter λ. For example,

$$a_{1,1}X_1 + a_{1,2}X_2 + \cdots + a_{1N}X_N = b_1 + \beta_1\lambda$$
$$a_{2,1}X_1 + a_{2,2}X_2 + \cdots + a_{2N}X_N = b_2 + \beta_2\lambda$$
$$\vdots$$
$$a_{N1}X_1 + a_{N2}X_2 + \cdots + a_{NN}X_N = b_N + \beta_N\lambda$$

where $\beta_1, \beta_2, \ldots, \beta_N$ are constants.
Obviously the solution (set of X_i values) will depend on the value of λ. The goal is to determine the relationship explicitly.

The procedure described earlier requires only a slight modification. The table of coefficients is expanded by one column:

X_1	X_2	$\cdots$	X_N	$=$	constant	λ
$a_{1,1}$	$a_{1,2}$	$\cdots$	a_{1N}		b_1	β_1
$a_{2,1}$	$a_{2,2}$	$\cdots$	a_{2N}		b_2	β_2
$\vdots$	$\vdots$	$\vdots$	$\vdots$		$\vdots$	$\vdots$
a_{N1}	a_{N2}	$\cdots$	a_{NN}		b_N	β_N

As before, row operations are used to obtain a table with 1s along the diagonal and 0s below it. Of course all coefficients, including the one in the right-most column, are altered when performing such operations. When the job is done, the last row will state the value of X_N as some constant plus another constant times λ. Working backward in this manner gives an entire solution of the form:

$$X_1 = K_1 + k_1\lambda$$
$$X_2 = K_2 + k_2\lambda$$
$$\vdots$$
$$X_N = K_N + k_N\lambda$$

where $K_1, K_2, \ldots, K_N$ and $k_1, k_2, \ldots, k_N$ are constants.

Given a value of λ, the values of the X_i's satisfying the original set of equations can be immediately determined.

A solution of this type is called *parametric* because each value (X_i) is stated in terms of the value of some parameter (λ). A parameter is neither a decision variable nor a constant. One is typically interested in more than one possible value that it might assume. A parametric solution shows explicitly the relationship between the value of the parameter and the values of the decision variables.

LAGRANGE MULTIPLIERS

It is almost enough to know how to find a valley bottom. But one must be on the appropriate terrain. Most problems involve constraints; the original valley bottom may thus be illegal. The trick is to rearrange the problem so that the solution lies at the bottom of a valley once again. This may require a redefinition of the relevant terrain.

Consider the example used in the previous discussions, with a constraint added:

Minimize $Z = 10 - 2X_1 - X_2 + 2X_1X_2 + (X_1)^2 + \frac{1}{4}(X_2)^2$
Subject to $X_1 + 2X_2 = 4$

The valley bottom of the original terrain (showing Z as a function of X_1 and X_2) is illegal since $[\frac{1}{3} + 2(\frac{2}{3})]$ does not equal 4 as required.

What to do? First, rearrange the constraint so that the left-hand side is zero:

$$0 = 4 - X_1 - 2X_2$$

Next, make up a new objective function by adding the right-hand side of the constraint, multiplied by a new variable, to the original function:

$$Z' = 10 - 2X_1 - X_2 + 2X_1X_2 + (X_1)^2 + \tfrac{1}{4}(X_2)^2$$
$$+ \lambda_c(4 - X_1 - 2X_2)$$

The new variable (λ_c) is a *Lagrange multiplier* associated with the constraint. The problem has now been transformed. The initial version was:

Select X_1 and X_2

    to minimize $Z = 10 - 2X_1 - X_2 + 2X_1X_2 + (X_1)^2 + \tfrac{1}{4}(X_2)^2$
    subject to $X_1 + 2X_2 = 4$

The new version is:

Select X_1, X_2, and λ_c

    to minimize $Z' = 10 - 2X_1 - X_2 + 2X_1X_2 + (X_1)^2 + \tfrac{1}{4}(X_2)^2$
    $+ \lambda_c(4 - X_1 - 2X_2)$

The latter form can be solved using the techniques described in the previous discussions. Each of the three partial derivatives must equal zero. This provides a system of three equations in three unknowns to be solved in the usual way.

But why does it work? The simple answer is that the true solution does lie at the bottom of a valley in the terrain relating Z' to X_1, X_2, and λ_c. By finding the location at which the surface has zero slope in all three directions, one can determine the solution to the original problem.

This explanation tends to beg the question. Consideration of the procedure will show why it really works. Assume for the moment that only values of X_1 and X_2 satisfying the original constraint will be considered. Then $(4 - X_1 - 2X_2)$ will in fact equal zero. And Z' will equal Z. As long as attention is restricted to such locations, the minimum value of Z' will in fact be the minimum legal value of Z.

Recall the manner in which a minimization problem of this type is solved. All partial derivatives are required to equal zero. In this case,

$$\frac{\partial Z'}{\partial X_1} = 0$$

$$\frac{\partial Z'}{\partial X_2} = 0$$

$$\frac{\partial Z'}{\partial \lambda_c} = 0$$

The latter requirement is

$$\frac{\partial Z'}{\partial \lambda_c} = 4 - X_1 - 2X_2 = 0$$

But this *is* the original constraint. It was added to the objective function in a manner that guarantees it will "fall out" when the partial derivatives are required to be zero. Thus only legal values of X_1 and X_2 will be considered. The solution to the new problem will be the solution to the original problem.

The full set of (three) equations is

$$\frac{\partial Z'}{\partial X_1} = -2 + 2X_2 + 2X_1 - \lambda_c = 0$$

$$\frac{\partial Z'}{\partial X_2} = -1 + 2X_1 + \tfrac{1}{2}X_2 - 2\lambda_c = 0$$

$$\frac{\partial Z'}{\partial \lambda_c} = 4 - X_1 - 2X_2 = 0$$

In tabular form :

X_1	X_2	λ_c	=	constant
2	2	-1		2
2	$\frac{1}{2}$	-2		1
-1	-2	0		-4

Applying the rules for row operations, this may be converted to

X_1	X_2	λ_c	=	constant
1	1	$-\frac{1}{2}$		1
0	1	$\frac{2}{3}$		$\frac{2}{3}$
0	0	1		-14

The solution is thus

$$X_1 = -16$$
$$X_2 = 10$$
$$\lambda_c = -14$$

The values of X_1 and X_2 constitute the solution to the original problem (the legal location giving the minimum possible value of Z).

The value of λ_c is, in a sense, an artifact of the solution method. However it does have a meaning. It indicates the effect of a small change in the right-hand side of the constraint on the optimal value of Z. Let Z^{opt} represent the optimal legal value of Z and R_c the right-hand side of the constraint (in this example, it equals 4). If λ_c^* is the solution value of λ_c,

$$\lambda_c^* = \frac{\partial Z^{opt}}{\partial R_c}$$

The method may be employed for any problem involving constraints expressed as equalities. Assume that there are N decision variables $(X_1, X_2, \ldots, X_N)$ and M equality constraints. Let the latter be represented by

$$d_{1,1}X_1 + d_{1,2}X_2 + \cdots + d_{1N}X_N = R_1$$
$$d_{2,1}X_1 + d_{2,2}X_2 + \cdots + d_{2N}X_N = R_2$$
$$\vdots$$
$$d_{M1}X_1 + d_{M2}X_2 + \cdots + d_{MN}X_N = R_M$$

Form a new objective function:

$$Z' = Z + \lambda_1 (R_1 - d_{1,1}X_1 - d_{1,2}X_2 - \cdots - d_{1N}X_N)$$
$$+ \lambda_2 (R_2 - d_{2,1}X_1 - d_{2,2}X_2 - \cdots - d_{2N}X_N)$$
$$\vdots$$
$$+ \lambda_M (R_M - d_{M1}X_1 - d_{M2}X_2 - \cdots - d_{MN}X_N)$$

Then solve the problem by finding the set of values $(X_1, X_2, \ldots, X_N, \lambda_1, \lambda_2, \ldots, \lambda_M)$ that simultaneously satisfies

$$\frac{\partial Z'}{\partial X_1} = 0$$

$$\frac{\partial Z'}{\partial X_2} = 0$$

$$\vdots$$

$$\frac{\partial Z'}{\partial X_N} = 0$$

$$\frac{\partial Z'}{\partial \lambda_1} = 0$$

$$\frac{\partial Z'}{\partial \lambda_2} = 0$$

$$\vdots$$

$$\frac{\partial Z'}{\partial \lambda_M} = 0$$

THE MATHEMATICAL FOUNDATION

If each of these is a linear equation, the solution will be unique (as long as each is independent of every other).

This completes the set of essential ingredients. It is now possible to come to grips with portfolio-analysis problems. Section B deals with basic problems. Standard problems (involving upper and lower bounds) are considered in Sec. C.

B.

SOLVING A BASIC PROBLEM

THE SOLUTION As defined in Chap. 4, a *basic* problem has the form:

Minimize $Z = -\lambda E_p + V_p$

where $E_p = \sum_{i=1}^{N} X_i E_i$

and $V_p = \sum_{i=1}^{N} \sum_{j=1}^{N} X_i X_j C_{ij}$

subject to $\sum_{i=1}^{N} X_i = 1$

To solve it, a new objective function must be considered:

$$Z' = Z + \lambda_f \left(1 - \sum_{i=1}^{N} X_i\right)$$

where λ_f = a Lagrange multiplier associated with the constraint that

funds must be fully invested (i.e., $\sum_{i=1}^{N} X_i = 1$).

The transformed problem is to select X_1, X_2, . . ., X_N and λ_f to minimize Z'. To solve it, each of the partial derivatives of Z' must be set to zero. In other words, a set of values must be found that will simultaneously satisfy

$$\frac{\partial Z'}{\partial X_1} = 0$$

$$\frac{\partial Z'}{\partial X_2} = 0$$

$$\vdots$$

$$\frac{\partial Z'}{\partial X_N} = 0$$

$$\frac{\partial Z'}{\partial \lambda_f} = 0$$

The last equation is the simplest:

$$\frac{\partial Z'}{\partial \lambda_f} = 1 - \sum_{i=1}^{N} X_i = 0$$

As intended, this is just the original constraint—the requirement that the sum of the X_i's be 1.

Each of the first N equations is of the same form. By considering the ith one (where i can be any number between 1 and N inclusive), the nature of each can be determined.

The modified objective function is the sum of three terms:

$$Z' = -\lambda E_p + V_p + \lambda_f(1 - \sum_{i=1}^{N} X_i)$$

The desired partial derivative will equal the sum of three derivatives:

$$\frac{\partial Z'}{\partial X_i} = \frac{\partial(-\lambda E_p)}{\partial X_i} + \frac{\partial V_p}{\partial X_i} + \frac{\partial\left[\lambda_f(1 - \sum_{i=1} X_i)\right]}{\partial X_i}$$

The first term is simple enough:

$$-\lambda E_p = -\lambda(\sum_{i=1}^{N} X_i E_i)$$

$$= -\lambda X_1 E_1 - \lambda X_2 E_2 - \cdots - \lambda X_N E_N$$

Thus,

$$\frac{\partial(-\lambda E_p)}{\partial X_i} = -\lambda E_i$$

The second term is not as simple. Its consideration will be deferred temporarily.

The third term causes no difficulty:

$$\lambda_f(1 - \sum_{i=1}^{N} X_i) = \lambda_f - \lambda_f X_1 - \lambda_f X_2 - \cdots - \lambda_f X_N$$

Thus $\dfrac{\partial\left[\lambda_f(1 - \sum_{i=1}^{N} X_i)\right]}{\partial X_i} = -\lambda_f$

The results obtained thus far may be summarized:

$$\frac{\partial Z'}{\partial X_i} = -\lambda E_i + \frac{\partial V_p}{\partial X_i} - \lambda_f$$

Now to come to grips with the middle term. The relationship between V_p and the values of the X's is, of course,

$$V_p = \sum_{i=1}^{N} \sum_{j=1}^{N} X_i X_j C_{ij}$$

Arrayed in a tabular format:

$$V_p = \begin{cases} X_1 X_1 C_{1,1} + X_1 X_2 C_{1,2} + \cdots + X_1 X_N C_{1N} \\ + X_2 X_1 C_{2,1} + X_2 X_2 C_{2,2} + \cdots + X_2 X_N C_{2N} \\ \quad\vdots \\ + X_N X_1 C_{N1} + X_N X_2 C_{N2} + \cdots + X_N X_N C_{NN} \end{cases}$$

Note that all terms involving X_1 are in the first row and column. All terms involving X_2 are in the second row and column. In general, all terms involving X_i are in the ith row and column. And when the derivative with respect to X_i is being considered, only terms involving X_i are of interest—all others can be considered constants, with a derivative of zero.

The terms that are relevant for determining the partial derivative of V_p with respect to X_i, shown as they appear in the tabular format, are

$$+ X_1 X_i C_{1i}$$
$$+ X_2 X_i C_{2i}$$
$$\vdots$$
$$+ X_i X_1 C_{i1} + \cdots + X_i X_i C_{ii} + \cdots + X_i X_N C_{iN}$$
$$\vdots$$
$$+ X_N X_i C_{Ni}$$

Every term but the one at the intersection involves the product of two values times X_i. For example,

$$X_2 X_i C_{2i} = (X_2 C_{2i}) X_i$$

The derivative with respect to X_i is simply the product of the two values by which X_i is multiplied. For example,

$$\frac{\partial [(X_2 C_{2i}) X_i]}{\partial X_i} = X_2 C_{2i}$$

The term at the intersection is

$$X_i X_i C_{ii} = X_i^2 C_{ii}$$

Its derivative with respect to X_i is

$$\frac{\partial (X_i^2 C_{ii})}{\partial X_i} = 2 X_i C_{ii}$$

The derivatives, arranged in the same format as the terms from which they come, are

$$X_1 C_{1i}$$
$$+ X_2 C_{2i}$$
$$\vdots$$
$$X_1 C_{i1} + \cdots + 2 X_i C_{ii} + \cdots + X_N C_{iN}$$
$$\vdots$$
$$+ X_N C_{Ni}$$

Note that every term except the one at the intersection equals some other term. For example:

$$C_{i1} = C_{1i}$$
$$\text{thus } X_1 C_{i1} = X_1 C_{1i}$$

Combining such terms and rewriting:

$$\frac{\partial V_p}{\partial X_i} = 2 C_{i1} X_1 + 2 C_{i2} X_2 + \cdots + 2 C_{ii} X_i + \cdots + 2 C_{iN} X_N$$

It is now possible to write the partial derivative of Z' with respect to X_i explicitly:

$$\frac{\partial Z'}{\partial X_i} = -\lambda E_i + 2C_{i1}X_1 + \cdots + 2C_{iN}X_N - \lambda_f$$

This must equal zero:

$$-\lambda E_i + 2C_{i1}X_1 + \cdots + 2C_{iN}X_N - \lambda_f = 0$$

Rewriting,

$$2C_{i1}X_1 + \cdots + 2C_{iN}X_N - \lambda_f = \lambda E_i$$

The full set of equations can now be written in tabular form:

X_1	X_2		X_N	λ_f	= constant	λ
$2C_{1,1}$	$2C_{1,2}$	$\cdots$	$2C_{1N}$	-1	0	E_1
$2C_{2,1}$	$2C_{2,2}$	$\cdots$	$2C_{2N}$	-1	0	E_2
$\vdots$	$\vdots$	$\vdots$	$\vdots$	$\vdots$	$\vdots$	$\vdots$
$2C_{N1}$	$2C_{N2}$	$\cdots$	$2C_{NN}$	-1	0	E_N
1	1	$\cdots$	1	0	1	0

To solve a basic problem, one need only place the relevant data in the format shown above. The bulk of the entries are the covariances (doubled). The remaining entries are 1s, minus 1s, 0s, and the expected returns.

Once a problem has been cast in this form, a standard method for finding a (parametric) solution can be invoked. The result will be a series of equations of the form

$$X_1 = K_1 + k_1\lambda$$
$$X_2 = K_2 + k_2\lambda$$
$$\vdots$$
$$X_N = K_N + k_N\lambda$$
$$\lambda_f = \lambda_f^* + (\lambda_f^{**})\lambda$$

where $K_1, \ldots, K_N$; $k_1, \ldots, k_N$; λ_f^* and λ_f^{**} are constants, and λ is a parameter.

For any given value of λ, the corresponding values of the variables can be computed directly.

It is a relatively simple matter to handle a basic problem with additional constraints, as long as each is expressed by an equation. Let there be M such constraints (in addition to the regular *full-investment* requirement):

$$d_{1,1}X_1 + d_{1,2}X_2 + \cdots + d_{1N}X_N = R_1$$
$$d_{2,1}X_1 + d_{2,2}X_2 + \cdots + d_{2N}X_N = R_2$$
$$\vdots$$
$$d_{M1}X_1 + d_{M2}X_2 + \cdots + d_{MN}X_N = R_M$$

The new objective function is

$$Z' = -\lambda E_p + V_p$$
$$+ \lambda_1(R_1 - d_{1,1}X_1 - d_{1,2}X_2 - \cdots - d_{1N}X_N)$$
$$+ \lambda_2(R_2 - d_{2,1}X_1 - d_{2,2}X_2 - \cdots - d_{2N}X_N)$$
$$\vdots$$
$$+ \lambda_M(R_M - d_{M1}X_1 - d_{M2}X_2 - \cdots - d_{MN}X_N)$$
$$+ \lambda_f(1 - \sum_{i=1}^{N} X_i)$$

There are $M + N + 1$ variables:

$$X_1, X_2, \ldots, X_N$$
$$\lambda_1, \lambda_2, \ldots, \lambda_M$$
$$\lambda_f$$

The solution requires that

$$\frac{\partial Z'}{\partial X_1} = 0$$
$$\vdots$$
$$\frac{\partial Z'}{\partial X_N} = 0$$
$$\frac{\partial Z'}{\partial \lambda_1} = 0$$
$$\vdots$$
$$\frac{\partial Z'}{\partial \lambda_M} = 0$$
$$\frac{\partial Z'}{\partial \lambda_f} = 0$$

The final equation is, of course, the full-investment constraint. The previous M equations are the M other constraints. The first N equations are the partial derivatives with respect to the original variables. In general,

$$\frac{\partial Z'}{\partial X_i} = -\lambda E_i + 2C_{i1}X_1 + \cdots + 2C_{iN}X_N - d_{1i}\lambda_1 - \cdots - d_{Mi}\lambda_M - \lambda_f$$

The full set of equations in tabular form is thus:

X_1	$\cdots$	X_N	λ_1	$\cdots$	λ_M	λ_f		$=$ constant	λ
$2C_{1,1}$	$\cdots$	$2C_{1N}$	$-d_{1,1}$	$\cdots$	$-d_{M1}$	-1		0	E_1
$\vdots$		$\vdots$	$\vdots$		$\vdots$	$\vdots$		$\vdots$	$\vdots$
$2C_{N1}$	$\cdots$	$2C_{NN}$	$-d_{1N}$	$\cdots$	$-d_{MN}$	-1		0	E_N
$d_{1,1}$	$\cdots$	d_{1N}	0	$\cdots$	0	0		R_1	0
$\vdots$		$\vdots$	$\vdots$		$\vdots$	$\vdots$		$\vdots$	$\vdots$
d_{M1}	$\cdots$	d_{MN}	0	$\cdots$	0	0		R_M	0
1	$\cdots$	1	0	$\cdots$	0	0		1	0

Such a problem can be solved directly once the required coefficients have been arranged in the format above. Each of the coefficients from the left-hand side of a constraint is entered twice—once in the appropriate row and again (with its sign reversed) in the appropriate column.

As before, any standard technique for solving a set of simultaneous linear equations can be utilized. The solution will be a series of equations of the form:

$$X_1 = K_1 + k_1\lambda$$
$$X_2 = K_2 + k_2\lambda$$
$$\vdots$$

$$X_N = K_N + k_N\lambda$$
$$\lambda_1 = \lambda_1^* + (\lambda_1^{**})\lambda$$
$$\lambda_2 = \lambda_2^* + (\lambda_2^{**})\lambda$$
$$\vdots$$

$$\lambda_M = \lambda_M^* + (\lambda_M^{**})\lambda$$
$$\lambda_f = \lambda_f^* + (\lambda_f^{**})\lambda$$

where $K_1, \ldots, K_N$; $k_1, \ldots, k_N$; $\lambda_1^*, \ldots, \lambda_M^*$; $\lambda_1^{**}, \ldots, \lambda_M^{**}$; λ_f^*; and λ_f^{**} are constants, and λ is a parameter.

The procedures described in the previous discussions apply generally. Thus they may be used without modification when a riskless security is included in the analysis. However, it is instructive to consider the nature of such a problem. In the absence of additional constraints, it is possible to simplify the analysis. And the simplification is directly related to the *separation theorem* described in Chap. 4.

Consider a basic problem with no additional constraints. Let security 1 be riskless. This implies,

$$C_{1,1}(= \sigma_1^2) = 0$$
$$C_{1,2} = C_{2,1} = 0$$
$$\vdots \qquad \vdots$$
$$C_{1N} = C_{N1} = 0$$
$$E_1 = p$$

where p = the pure interest rate.

Utilizing this information, the table of coefficients for the simultaneous equations that yield the solution can be written as follows:

X_1	X_2	$\cdots$	X_N	λ_f	= constant	λ
0	0	$\cdots$	0	-1	0	p
0	$2C_{2,2}$	$\cdots$	$2C_{2N}$	-1	0	E_2
$\vdots$	$\vdots$	$\vdots$	$\vdots$	$\vdots$	$\vdots$	$\vdots$
0	$2C_{N2}$	$\cdots$	$2C_{NN}$	-1	0	E_N
1	1	$\cdots$	1	0	1	0

The first row requires the values of λ_f to be related directly to that of λ:

$$(-1)\lambda_f = 0 + p\lambda$$

Simplifying,

$$\lambda_f = -p\lambda$$

Now consider the second to Nth rows. In general, the ith row requires that

$$2C_{i1}X_1 + 2C_{i2}X_2 + \cdots + 2C_{iN}X_N - \lambda_f = 0 + E_i\lambda$$

But λ_f must equal $-p\lambda$. Substituting,

$$2C_{i1}X_1 + 2C_{i2}X_2 + \cdots + 2C_{iN}X_N - (-p\lambda) = 0 + E_i\lambda$$

Simplifying and rearranging,

$$2C_{i1}X_1 + 2C_{i2}X_2 + \cdots + 2C_{iN}X_N = 0 + (E_i - p)\lambda$$

The problem can thus be considered one involving only N variables $(X_1$ to $X_N)$ since the value of λ_f will always equal $-p\lambda$. The new version in tabular form is:

X_1	X_2	$\cdots$	X_N	= constant	λ
0	$2C_{2,2}$	$\cdots$	$2C_{2N}$	0	$E_2 - p$
0	$2C_{3,2}$	$\cdots$	$2C_{3N}$	0	$E_3 - p$
$\vdots$	$\vdots$	$\cdots$	$\vdots$	$\vdots$	$\vdots$
0	$2C_{N2}$	$\cdots$	$2C_{NN}$	0	$E_N - p$
1	1	$\cdots$	1	1	0

Note that the table differs from the original in two respects: the λ_f column and the first row have been omitted.

Formally, this represents a system of N equations in N unknowns and can be solved as such. However, its structure allows further simplification.

Consider the outlined portion of the table. It describes a subproblem involving $N - 1$ variables: X_2 to X_N. There are $N - 1$ equations. This portion of the problem will determine the values of X_2 to X_N. The value of X_1 will be a residual, determined by the last row in the full table: X_1 must take on whatever value (positive, zero, or negative) is required to make the sum of the X's equal 1.

The values of X_2 to X_N can be found by solving the set of outlined equations. Note that each row has a zero entry in the *constant* column. The solution procedure involves (1) multiplication and division of the coefficients by a constant, (2) the addition or subtraction of corresponding coefficients in different rows, and (3) the interchange of rows. In a case such as this, the procedure can in no way result in a nonzero entry in the constant column. Thus the solution for X_2 to X_N must be of the form:

$$X_2 = 0 + k_2\lambda$$
$$X_3 = 0 + k_3\lambda$$
$$\vdots$$
$$X_N = 0 + k_N\lambda$$

This leads directly to the separation theorem. It asserts that the proportionate holdings of risky securities are the same for all efficient portfolios (i.e., for all values of λ). The portion of the portfolio *at risk* will be

$$\sum_{j=2}^{N} X_j = \sum_{j=2}^{N} k_j\lambda = \lambda \sum_{j=2}^{N} k_j$$

The proportion of such funds invested in security i will be

$$\frac{X_i}{\sum_{j=2}^{N} X_j} = \frac{k_i\lambda}{\lambda \sum_{j=2}^{N} k_j} = \frac{k_i}{\sum_{j=2}^{N} k_j}$$

which is unrelated to λ.

The separation theorem thus holds if a riskless security is included in a basic problem without additional constraints. The optimal combination of risky securities can be found by solving the following set of $N-1$ simultaneous equations:

X_2	X_3	$\ldots$	X_N	$=$	λ
$2C_{2,2}$	$2C_{2,3}$	$\ldots$	$2C_{2N}$		$E_2 - p$
$2C_{3,2}$	$2C_{3,3}$	$\ldots$	$2C_{3N}$		$E_3 - p$
$\vdots$	$\vdots$	$\ldots$	$\vdots$		$\vdots$
$2C_{N2}$	$2C_{N3}$	$\ldots$	$2C_{NN}$		$E_N - p$

The separation theorem will usually not hold when constraints are added to a basic problem. Consideration of the resulting set of simultaneous equations shows why this is so. The coefficients associated with the left-hand sides of the constraints (the d's) appear in every row. The coefficients from the right-hand sides (the R's) appear in the constant column. These entries serve to tie the elements of the overall problem together in such a way that it is usually impossible to separate out the determination of the proportionate holdings of risky assets. The proportions for one efficient portfolio will usually differ from those of another.

Under what conditions will the separation theorem hold? Consideration of the nature of the solution provides the answer.

The solution to a basic problem with additional constraints will be of the form:

$$X_1 = K_1 + k_1\lambda$$
$$X_2 = K_2 + k_2\lambda$$
$$\vdots$$
$$X_N = K_N + k_N\lambda$$
$$\lambda_1 = \lambda_1^* + (\lambda_1^{**})\lambda$$
$$\vdots$$
$$\lambda_M = \lambda_M^* + (\lambda_M^{**})\lambda$$
$$\lambda_f = \lambda_f^* + (\lambda_f^{**})\lambda$$

As usual, a portfolio consisting solely of the riskless security will have a variance of zero; all others will have a positive variance. If an all-X_1 portfolio is feasible (i.e., does not violate any of the constraints), it will clearly be the minimum-variance efficient portfolio. Under such conditions, when λ equals 0, X_1 will equal 1, and X_2 to X_N will equal 0. The equations for the X_i's thus become

$$X_1 = 1 + k_1\lambda$$
$$X_2 = 0 + k_2\lambda$$
$$\vdots$$
$$X_N = 0 + k_N\lambda$$

As shown earlier, the separation theorem follows immediately from this set of relationships.

Unfortunately, additional constraints typically make an all-X_1 portfolio illegal (i.e., infeasible). Thus X_1 will not equal 1 when λ equals 0. This implies that at least one of the other constant terms (i.e., $K_2, K_3, \ldots, K_N$) will not equal zero. And this implies that the separation theorem will not hold.

It is a simple matter to determine whether or not the separation theorem applies to a specific (basic) problem. Just check each constraint to see if it is satisfied when X_1 equals 1 and all other X_i's equal 0. Some will be. For example,

$$X_2 - X_3 = 0$$
$$X_2 + 3X_3 = 0$$

Most will not. For example,

$$X_2 + X_3 = .05$$
$$X_2 + 2X_3 - X_5 = .09$$

It takes only one constraint of this type to make the theorem inapplicable. Thus:

The separation theorem may not (and typically will not) apply to a basic problem with additional constraints.

UNIQUENESS

Thus far it has been assumed that every problem has a unique solution. This will be the case if (1) there are as many linear equations as there are variables and (2) the equations are independent. Every set of equations discussed in this section meets the first requirement. Except for unusual cases, each will also meet the second.

Two equations will not be independent if every coefficient on the left-hand side of one equals some constant times the corresponding coefficient of another.

Consider a basic problem. The left-hand side coefficients for rows i and j (where i and j can represent any values from 1 to N) will be:

Row i: $2C_{i1}$ $2C_{i2} \cdots 2C_{iN}$ -1

Row j: $2C_{j1}$ $2C_{j2} \cdots 2C_{jN}$ -1

Since the coefficients in the final column are the same, the two equations will be dependent only if every other column contains identical coefficients in the two rows.

Consider next a problem for which the separation theorem holds. The subproblem which determines the optimal combination of risky securities will have the following coefficients on the left-hand sides of the two rows:

Row i: $2C_{i2}$ $2C_{i3} \cdots 2C_{iN}$

Row j: $2C_{j2}$ $2C_{j3} \cdots 2C_{jN}$

In such a case the two equations will be dependent if every coefficient in one row is some multiple of the corresponding coefficient in the other. Letting k represent any column,

$$C_{ik} = mC_{jk}$$

where m is some constant. The first example represents a special case in which m must equal 1.

In either case, two equations will be dependent only if the returns of the corresponding securities are perfectly correlated.

This is easily shown. Assume that

$$C_{ik} = mC_{jk} \qquad \text{for every } k$$

Substituting,

$$\rho_{ik}\sigma_i\sigma_k = m\rho_{jk}\sigma_j\sigma_k$$

Simplifying and rearranging,

$$\frac{\rho_{ik}}{\rho_{jk}} = \frac{m\sigma_j}{\sigma_i}$$

This relationship is assumed to hold for every column (k), including the ith and jth columns. For $k = j$,

$$\frac{\rho_{ij}}{\rho_{jj}} = \frac{m\sigma_j}{\sigma_i}$$

But $\rho_{jj} = 1$, thus

$$\rho_{ij} = \frac{m\sigma_j}{\sigma_i}$$

For $k = i$,

$$\frac{\rho_{ii}}{\rho_{ji}} = \frac{m\sigma_j}{\sigma_i}$$

But $\rho_{ii} = 1$, and $\rho_{ji} = \rho_{ij}$. Thus,

$$\frac{1}{\rho_{ij}} = \frac{m\sigma_j}{\sigma_i}$$

How can ρ_{ij} and its reciprocal equal the same value? They cannot, unless ρ_{ij} equals plus or minus 1. The conclusion is clear: Securities i and j must be perfectly correlated.

In general, a portfolio-analysis problem may not have a unique solution if two securities' rates of return are perfectly correlated with one another. Fortunately, such a situation is unlikely.

C.

SOLVING A STANDARD PROBLEM

As described in Chap. 4, a *standard problem* involves the addition of upper- and lower-bound constraints to either a basic problem or an augmented basic problem. In general, it has the form: **THE KUHN-TUCKER CONDITIONS**

$$\text{Minimize } -\lambda \sum_{i=1}^{N} X_i E_i + \sum_{i=1}^{N} \sum_{j=1}^{N} X_i X_j C_{ij}$$

for all possible values of λ from infinity to zero subject to

$$\sum_{i=1}^{N} X_i = 1$$

plus any other linear *equality* constraints, plus $L_1 \leqq X_1 \leqq U_1$
$$L_2 \leqq X_2 \leqq U_2$$
$$\vdots$$
$$L_N \leqq X_N \leqq U_N$$

For any given value of λ, the solution will involve:

1. Variables that are *down* (at their lower bounds):
   $X_i = L_i$
2. Variables that are *in* (between bounds):
   $L_i < X_i < U_i$
3. Variables that are *up* (at their upper bounds):
   $X_i = U_i$

Every portfolio-analysis problem requires the selection of a set of values that will minimize some objective function, subject to relevant constraints. Equality constraints can always be included in an expanded objective function, with associated Lagrange multipliers. As shown in the previous section, if there are no inequality constraints, the problem can be solved by selecting a set of values that makes the partial derivative of the new objective function (Z') with respect to each of the variables equal zero.

But a standard problem does have inequality constraints. A value of X_i for which $\partial Z'/\partial X_i$ equals zero may not be legal (i.e., it may lie outside the permissible range).

Figure C-1*a* to *c* illustrates three possible relationships between Z' and X_i. In Fig. C-1*a* the value of X_i for which $\partial Z'/\partial X_i$ equals zero is legal. The variable should be *in* the solution. And at the optimal point the partial derivative equals zero.

In Fig. C-1*b*, the value for which the partial derivative is zero is illegal. Obviously X_i should be set at its lower bound—the variable should be *down*. Note that at this point, the partial derivative is positive.

In the case shown in Fig. C-1*c*, the optimal legal value of X_i is its upper bound—the variable should be *up*. In this case the partial derivative is negative at the optimal point.

The conditions for an optimal solution with upper and lower bounds are special cases of a set of relationships termed the *Kuhn-Tucker conditions*. To summarize:

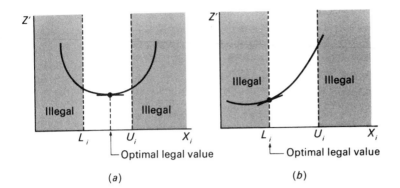

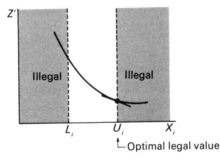

(c)

FIGURE C-1

1. If security i is *down*:

   a. $X_i = L_i$

   b. $\dfrac{\partial Z'}{\partial X_i} > 0$

2. If security i is *in*:

   a. $L_i \leqq X_i \leqq U_i$

   b. $\dfrac{\partial Z'}{\partial X_i} = 0$

3. If security i is *up*:

   a. $X_i = U_i$

   b. $\dfrac{\partial Z'}{\partial X_i} < 0$

Assume that you want to solve a standard problem for a specific
value of λ. Assume moreover that a friendly angel tells you the correct
status for each variable (i.e., whether it should be *down*, *in*, or *up*).
Given this information, the Kuhn-Tucker conditions provide a
strategy for solving the problem in a simple and straightforward
manner.

As usual, the first step involves the formation of an expanded
objective function: Each equality constraint is included, along with
an associated Lagrange multiplier. The second step is similar (but
not identical) to that employed for a basic problem. A set of linear
equations is formed and values found that simultaneously satisfy
every equation. The only difference concerns the set of equations.

As usual, one equation will be included for each equality constraint:

$$\frac{\partial Z'}{\partial \lambda_f} = 0$$

$$\frac{\partial Z'}{\partial \lambda_1} = 0$$

$$\vdots$$

$$\frac{\partial Z'}{\partial \lambda_M} = 0$$

Each decision variable will generate an additional equation, with the
form depending on the variable's status:

If variable i is to be *down*,

$$X_i = L_i$$

If variable i is to be *in*,

$$\frac{\partial Z'}{\partial X_i} = 0$$

If variable i is to be *up*,

$$X_i = U_i$$

The rules insure that there will be as many equations as there are
variables. Moreover, every equation will be linear. Barring unusual
circumstances, the full set will be satisfied by only one set of values
for the X_i's and the Lagrange multipliers. If the angel spoke truth,
the solution will be legal (i.e., each *in* variable will be assigned a
value lying between its upper and lower bound).

The set of equations can be shown in tabular form. If all variables were to be *in*, the table would have its usual appearance:

X_i	$\cdots$	X_N	λ_1	$\cdots$	λ_M	λ_f	= constant	λ
$2C_{1,1}$	$\cdots$	$2C_{1N}$	$-d_{1,1}$	$\cdots$	$-d_{M1}$	-1	0	E_1
$\vdots$		$\vdots$	$\vdots$		$\vdots$	$\vdots$	$\vdots$	$\vdots$
$2C_{N1}$	$\cdots$	$2C_{NN}$	$-d_{1N}$	$\cdots$	$-d_{MN}$	-1	0	E_N
$d_{1,1}$	$\cdots$	d_{1N}	0	$\cdots$	0	0	R_1	0
$\vdots$		$\vdots$	$\vdots$		$\vdots$	$\vdots$	$\vdots$	$\vdots$
d_{M1}	$\cdots$	d_{MN}	0	$\cdots$	0	0	R_M	0
1	$\cdots$	1	0	$\cdots$	0	0	1	0

To solve a problem in which some variables are to be *down* and others *up* merely requires the modification of the corresponding rows. If variable i is to be *down*, row i becomes:

X_1	$\cdots$	X_{i-1}	X_i	X_{i+1}	$\cdots$	X_N	λ_1	$\cdots$	λ_M	λ_f	= constant	λ
0	$\cdots$	0	1	0	$\cdots$	0	0	$\cdots$	0	0	L_i	0

If variable i is to be *up*, row i becomes:

X_1	$\cdots$	X_{i-1}	X_i	X_{i+1}	$\cdots$	X_N	λ_1	$\cdots$	λ_M	λ_f	= constant	λ
0	$\cdots$	0	1	0	$\cdots$	0	0	$\cdots$	0	0	U_i	0

Once the table has been modified, the standard procedure can be used to find the set of values that simultaneously satisfies all the equations.

The time required to obtain a solution will typically be longer, the greater the number of *in* variables. The solution process requires row operations to be performed until (1) all elements along the diagonal from the upper-left corner to the lower-right corner are 1 and (2) all elements to the left of this diagonal are 0. Any row that has been modified to account for a variable that is to be *down* or *up* automatically fulfills this requirement. Only the rows corresponding to variables that are to be *in* need any modification.

It is important that the relationship of the method to the Kuhn-Tucker conditions be clearly understood. The problem is to find the optimal set of X_i's for a specific value of λ. An angel is assumed to indicate the appropriate status for each variable. Given this information, three of the Kuhn-Tucker conditions are utilized to find a set of values.

For every security assigned to be *down*,

1*a*. $X_i = L_i$

For every security assigned to be *in*,

2*b*. $\dfrac{\partial Z'}{\partial X_i} = 0$

For every security assigned to be *up*,

3*a*. $X_i = U_i$

If the angel was right (suggested the correct status for each variable), the remaining Kuhn-Tucker conditions will also be fulfilled.

For every security assigned to be *down*,

1*b*. $\dfrac{\partial Z'}{\partial X_i} > 0$

For every security assigned to be *in*,

2*a*. $L_i \leqq X_i \leqq U_i$

For every security assigned to be *up*,

3*b*. $\dfrac{\partial Z'}{\partial X_i} < 0$

How can the angel's accuracy be tested? Simply. If each variable was assigned the correct status, these conditions will all be fulfilled. If any one is violated, some variable or variables must be assigned a different status.

FINDING THE NEXT SOLUTION

Assume that the method described above was used to find a solution for a specific value of λ—call it λ'. As usual, the result is expressed as a series of equations relating the variables to λ (where relevant).

For every security that is *down*,

$X_i = L_i$

For every security that is *in*,

$X_i = K_i + k_i \lambda$

For every security that is *up*,

$X_i = U_i$

For λ_f,

$$\lambda_f = \lambda_f^* + (\lambda_f^{**})\lambda$$

and for λ_1 to λ_M,

$$\lambda_1 = \lambda_1^* + (\lambda_1^{**})\lambda$$

$$\vdots$$

$$\lambda_M = \lambda_M^* + (\lambda_M^{**})\lambda$$

The specific solution for λ' is, of course, found by substituting λ' for λ in each of the equations in which λ appears.

Now consider a variable that is either *down* or *up*. The partial derivative of Z' with respect to such a variable will, of course, depend on the values of all the variables. For security i,

$$\frac{\partial Z'}{\partial X_i} = -\lambda E_i + 2C_{i1}X_1 + \cdots + 2C_{iN}X_N - d_{1i}\lambda_1 - \cdots - d_{Mi}\lambda_M - \lambda_f$$

It is possible to relate the value of such a derivative directly to the value of λ, using the results obtained by solving the set of simultaneous equations:

1. For every security that is *down*, substitute L_i for X_i.
2. For every security that is *in*, substitute $(K_i + k_i\lambda)$ for X_i.
3. For every security that is *up*, substitute U_i for X_i.
4. For λ_1 to λ_M, substitute $[\lambda_1^* + (\lambda_1^{**})\lambda]$ to $[\lambda_M^* + (\lambda_M^{**})\lambda]$.
5. For λ_f, substitute $[\lambda_f^* + (\lambda_f^{**})\lambda]$.

After making such substitutions and collecting terms, the partial derivative of Z' with respect to X_i can be written as a simple linear function of λ:

$$\frac{\partial Z'}{\partial X_i} = P_i + p_i\lambda$$

where P_i and p_i are constants.

Assume a reliable angel. This means that for $\lambda = \lambda'$:

1. Every *in* variable is legal; i.e.,
    $$L_i \leq (K_i + k_i\lambda) \leq U_i$$
2. The partial derivative of Z' with respect to every *down* variable is positive; i.e.,
    $$(P_i + p_i\lambda) > 0$$
3. The partial derivative of Z' with respect to every *up* variable is negative; i.e.,
    $$(P_i + p_i\lambda) < 0$$

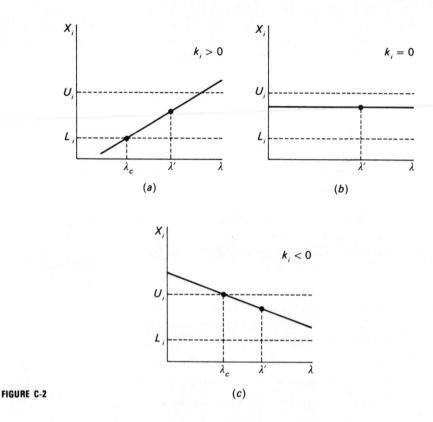

FIGURE C-2

Now consider a slightly smaller value of λ—call it λ''. It is just possible that the status assigned to each variable will "work" for this value as well. The test is straightforward; substitute the new value instead of λ' and see if every required relationship holds. If so, the problem is solved for $\lambda = \lambda''$.

The situation can be shown graphically. One of the relationships in Fig. C-2a to c will apply to every *in* variable. One of the relationships in Fig. C-3a to c will apply to every *down* variable. And one of the relationships in Fig. C-4a to c will apply to every *up* variable.

As successively smaller values of λ are considered, the values assigned to *in* variables may or may not change. In a case such as that shown in Fig. C-2a, X_i will eventually reach the specified lower bound. The corresponding value of λ (λ_c in the figure) is the *critical* value of λ for that variable—values below λ_c would yield an illegal solution. In a case such as that shown in Fig. C-2c, the critical value of λ is reached when X_i reaches its upper bound. In Fig. C-2b there is no critical value of λ.

Cases such as those shown in Figs. C-3a and C-4c yield critical values of λ for variables that are (respectively) *down* and *up*. In Figs. C-3b, C-3c, C-4a, and C-4b there is no critical value of λ.

The categories (*down, in,* and *up*) that are correct for $\lambda = \lambda'$ are also correct for all smaller values of λ down to and including the largest critical value. At that point, some variable must change status. Which one? Clearly, the one that has reached its critical value. How should its status be changed? The answer depends on the condition reached:

1. If an *in* variable has reached its upper bound, it should be reassigned to be an *up* variable.

2. If an *in* variable has reached its lower bound, it should be reassigned to be a *down* variable.

3. If the partial derivative of Z' with respect to a *down* variable has reached a value of zero, the variable should be reassigned to be an *in* variable.

4. If the partial derivative of Z' with respect to an *up* variable has reached a value of zero, the variable should be reassigned to be an *in* variable.

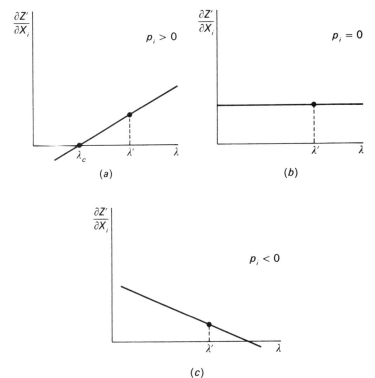

FIGURE C-3

(a)

(b)

(c)

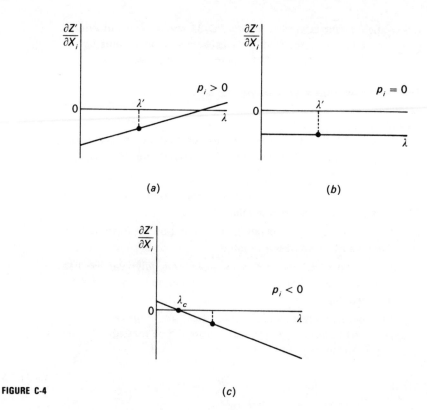

FIGURE C-4

(c)

Let C' represent the categories assigned by the angel for $\lambda = \lambda'$. The solution for $\lambda = \lambda'$ can be denoted

$$X_1 = K'_1 + k'_1 \lambda'$$
$$\vdots$$
$$X_N = K'_N + k'_N \lambda'$$

(Of course k'_i will be zero for variables that are assigned to be either *up* or *down*.) Let E' denote this entire set of equations.

Now, let λ'' denote the largest critical value of λ below λ'. The solution equation set (E') will apply for all values of λ between λ' and λ''. But it will not apply for values below λ''. The set of securities associated with λ'' is thus a *corner* portfolio; at λ'' some variable changes status. The four possibilities are shown in Fig. C-5a to d.

How can portfolios corresponding to values of λ below λ'' be found? The appropriate categories are simply those utilized before, with one modification—that required for the variable reaching its critical point at λ''. Let C'' represent this new set of categories. Using C'', a new set of solution equations can be found, following the procedure described earlier. The result will be a new set of relationships:

For every *down* variable,

$$\frac{\partial Z'}{\partial X_i} = P_i'' + p_i''\lambda$$

For every *in* variable,

$$X_i = K_i'' + k_i''\lambda$$

and for every *up* variable,

$$\frac{\partial Z'}{\partial X_i} = P_i'' + p_i''\lambda$$

Each of these relationships will satisfy its required condition for $\lambda = \lambda''$. As successively smaller values of λ are considered, one will eventually reach a critical point. Let λ''' denote the largest critical value of λ below λ''. The associated portfolio will be the next corner portfolio. For smaller values of λ, another set of equations must be found. A new set of categories is obtained by modifying the status of the variable reaching its critical point at λ''' and the associated system of equations is solved once again.

FIGURE C-5

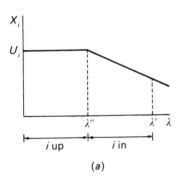

(a)

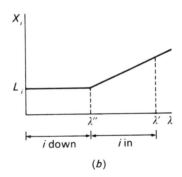

(b)

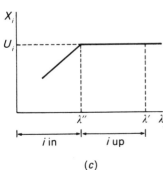

(c)

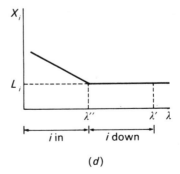

(d)

The procedure described in the previous discussion constitutes the core of the *critical-line algorithm* (an algorithm is a set of rules guaranteed to solve a problem, usually in an efficient manner). Given a solution for some specific value of λ, the procedure can be used to find solutions for every smaller value.

Recall the nature of the portfolio problem. The goal is to find efficient portfolios for all values of λ from infinity down to (and including) zero. The latter requirement suggests the condition for stopping the computations:

Terminate if the next critical value of λ is less than or equal to zero.

The condition for beginning the computations is equally obvious:

The first portfolio is the efficient portfolio for $\lambda = +\infty$.

The objective function, which is to be minimized, includes the term $(-\lambda E_p)$. When λ equals infinity, this term completely dominates all others. Thus:

The first portfolio is the one that maximizes E_p, subject to all relevant constraints.

To begin, the composition of this portfolio (or the status of every security in it) must be known. Thus far, this kind of information has been assumed to be provided by a friendly angel. But angels have more important things to do. Some means must be found to dispense with such services.

For $\lambda = +\infty$, the portfolio problem can be written:

$$\text{Maximize} \sum_{i=1}^{N} X_i E_i$$

$$\text{subject to} \sum_{i=1}^{N} X_i = 1$$

plus any other equality constraints,

$$\text{plus } L_1 \leqq X_1 \leqq U_1$$
$$\vdots$$
$$L_N \leqq X_N \leqq U_N$$

This is a linear-programming problem; whatever the constraints, such a problem can be solved easily using any one of several available computer programs. In many cases, however, the first (max-E_p) portfolio can be found directly. If all lower bounds equal 0 and all upper bounds equal 1, and if the only equality constraint is the full-investment constraint, the first portfolio will consist of one security only—the one with the greatest expected return. If more con-straining upper and lower bounds are imposed, but no equality constraints are added, the procedure is only slightly more complex. Barring cases in which certain securities have identical expected returns, the following procedure will suffice:

1. Assign all securities to be *down*; i.e.,

    $X_i = L_i$

2. Find the *down* security with the highest expected return (E_i). Assign it to be *up*; i.e.,

    $X_i = U_i$

3. Compute the sum of all the X_i's.

    a. If it is less than 1, return to step 2.

    b. If it equals 1, the procedure is complete.

    c. If it exceeds 1, reassign the last security to be *in* instead of *up*; the specific value (X_i) will be the amount required to bring the sum to 1. The procedure is now complete.

Figure C-6 shows the algorithm in its entirety. The equations obtained in step ($b2$) the first time through apply for values of λ from infinity down to the value (λ_c) found in step $b3$. The equations obtained in each subsequent set of computations apply for values of λ from the previously found critical value (λ_c) down to and including the next critical value (λ_c). Substitution of either of these critical values in the set of equations will provide the composition of a corner portfolio. The minimum-risk efficient portfolio is found by sub-stituting zero for λ in the final set of equations.

Figure C-7 provides the details for step ($b3$). Only securities that could lead to a critical value of λ need to be considered in detail. In each such case, the critical value can be computed directly. An *in* variable will reach its lower bound when

$X_i = L_i$

Substituting ($K_i + k_i \lambda$) for X_i,

$K_i + k_i \lambda = L_i$

The critical value of λ will thus be

$$\lambda_c = \frac{L_i - K_i}{k_i}$$

Similar reasoning leads to the conclusion that an *in* variable will reach its upper bound when

$$\lambda_c = \frac{U_i - K_i}{k_i}$$

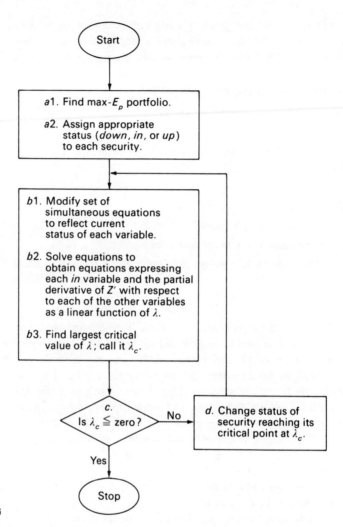

FIGURE C-6

A critical point for a *down* or *up* variable is reached when the corresponding partial derivative equals zero:

$$\frac{\partial Z'}{\partial X_i} = P_i + p_i \lambda = 0$$

The critical value of λ will thus be

$$\lambda_c = -\frac{P_i}{p_i}$$

DEGENERACY Thus far, the discussion has assumed (implicitly) that only one variable or partial derivative reaches a critical point at any given value of λ. In terms of the usual diagram, this is equivalent to

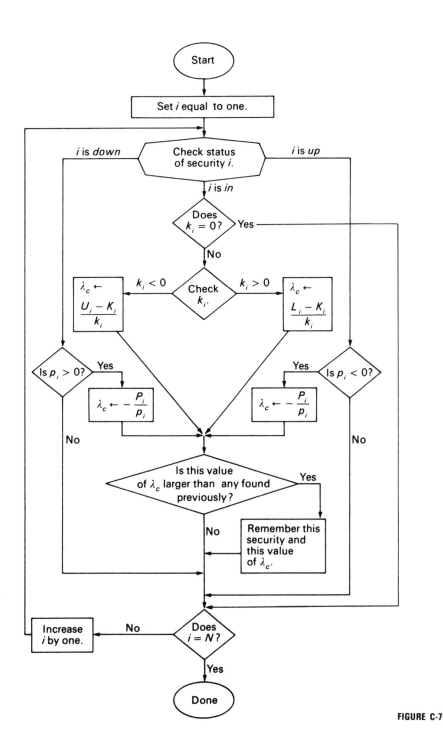

FIGURE C-7

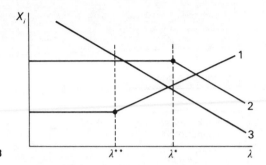

FIGURE C-8

assuming that only one security's line turns a corner at each value of λ corresponding to a corner portfolio. Figure C-8 provides an example. At λ^* only security 2 changes status; at λ^{**} only security 1 changes status. The portfolios corresponding to λ^* and λ^{**} are corner portfolios. As λ goes from a value slightly above that associated with a corner portfolio to a value slightly below it, only one variable changes status.

Figure C-9 provides an example in which the assumption is violated. At λ^* two securities (numbers 1 and 3) change status. In mathematical-programming terms, there is *degeneracy* at this point.

In many cases the critical-line algorithm will work even when degeneracy is encountered. Since only one variable may change status each time through the procedure, the result may involve a set of equations that is relevant only at a point. Putting it another way, two or more adjacent corner portfolios may be the same in fact (though not in theory). For example, in the case shown in Fig. C-9, the algorithm might provide the following adjacent corner portfolios:

Portfolio a: security 1—*down*
   security 2—*in*
   security 3—*in* at an amount equal to its upper bound
   value of λ: λ^*

Portfolio b: security 1—*down*
   security 2—*in*
   security 3—*up*
   value of λ: λ^*

In such a case one set of equations relating each of the variables to the value of λ would apply only for values from λ^* to λ^*.

The likelihood of encountering difficulties with procedures such as the critical-line algorithm may depend on the precision with which

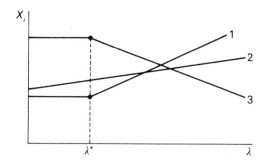

FIGURE C-9

the calculations are performed. The larger the errors introduced through rounding, the smaller the chance of complete success.

Fortunately, the critical-line algorithm usually works with no complications.

OTHER METHODS

The standard portfolio-analysis problem is one of the broader class of parametric quadratic programming problems. Several algorithms have been developed to solve such problems.

A particularly reliable computer program has been prepared by Leola Cutler and Philip Wolfe for the RAND Corporation.[1] Although the method utilized differs significantly from the critical-line algorithm, the program provides similar results (i.e., a series of adjacent corner portfolios). Needless to say, the terminology used to describe the results is not identical to that used here, but the output is not difficult to interpret.

In the final analysis, the choice of a method for solving any large problem will (and should) depend upon the efficiency, reliability, and availability of computer programs capable of doing the job.

[1] The RAND Corporation, Product Form Quadratic Programming Code (RS QPF4), SHARE Distribution Code 3326.

D.

SECURITY PRICES

MAKING THE MARKET PORTFOLIO AN OPTIMAL COMBINATION OF RISKY SECURITIES

This section deals with the central issue of capital market theory—the determination of security prices. How are such prices related to (determined by) people's preferences and predictions? Under what conditions will a set of prices lead to an equilibrium situation—one which, once attained, will tend to be maintained? With the exception of the final discussion in this section, complete agreement is assumed throughout the section.

This discussion is concerned with one of the requirements for equilibrium in a world of complete agreement. In such a world, prices must adjust until the market portfolio is an optimal combination of risky securities. Is there a set of prices that fulfills this requirement? In fact, there are many. Other equilibrium requirements rule out many of them; such considerations will be treated later. This discussion concentrates on the relationship between security prices and predictions, when prices are required to make the market portfolio efficient.

Assume that the stock of risky securities is given. There are Q_2 units of security 2, Q_3 units of security 3, etc. (As always, security 1 represents riskless transactions.) The objective is to find a set of prices $(P_2, P_3, \ldots, P_N)$ such that

$$X_2^* = k(P_2 Q_2)$$
$$X_3^* = k(P_3 Q_3)$$
$$\vdots$$
$$X_N^* = k(P_N Q_N)$$

where $(X_2^*, X_3^*, \ldots, X_N^*)$ represent the proportionate holdings constituting an optimal combination of risky securities, and k is some constant. In other words, the goal is to find a set of prices that make it efficient to invest all funds *at risk* in amounts proportionate to the relative values of the various securities in the market as a whole.

As usual, the investor is assumed to be able to borrow or lend any desired amount at a common pure rate of interest (p).

Following the terminology of Chap. 5, define a unit of a security as a *share*. Let $A_i^\$$ be the amount actually paid to the holder of one share of security i. Investors are assumed to agree on the following values:

$E_i^\$$ = expected dollar amount per share of security i (i.e., the expected value of $A_i^\$$)

$\sigma_i^\$$ = standard deviation of the dollar amount paid per share of security i (i.e., the standard deviation of the probability distribution of $A_i^\$$)

$\rho_{ij}^\$$ = the correlation coefficient between $A_i^\$$ and $A_j^\$$

Given a set of prices, the data required for a standard portfolio analysis are easily obtained. As shown in Chap. 5,

$$E_i = \frac{E_i^\$}{P_i} - 1$$

$$\sigma_i = \frac{\sigma_i^\$}{P_i}$$

$$\rho_{ij} = \rho_{ij}^\$$$

Assume for the moment that a set of prices has been selected. Under the assumed conditions (unlimited ability to borrow or lend at the pure interest rate), the separation theorem implies that

$$X_2^* = k_2 \lambda$$
$$X_3^* = k_3 \lambda$$
$$\vdots$$
$$X_N^* = k_N \lambda$$

where $(X_2^*, X_3^*, \ldots, X_N^*)$ represent the proportionate holdings of risky securities in an efficient portfolio, and λ is a parameter. Some specific value of λ will, of course, make these proportions sum to 1 (and X_1^* equal 0): The corresponding portfolio will be the optimal combination of risky securities.

Now, assume that there is a set of prices for which

$$X_2^* = k_2 \lambda = P_2 Q_2$$
$$X_3^* = k_3 \lambda = P_3 Q_3$$
$$\vdots$$
$$X_N^* = k_N \lambda = P_N Q_N$$

for *some* value of λ. Under such conditions, the optimal combination of risky securities will involve amounts proportionate to the market values of the various securities, for changes in λ lead to strictly proportionate changes in the amounts invested.

This discussion suggests a useful strategy for selecting a set of prices that will make the market portfolio an optimal combination of risky securities.

Find a set of prices such that

$$X_2^* = P_2 Q_2$$
$$X_3^* = P_3 Q_3$$
$$\vdots$$
$$X_N^* = P_N Q_N$$

for some value of λ.

As shown in Sec. B the separation theorem implies that an investor may devote his attention to the relationships among risky securities. In tabular form:

X_2	$\cdots$	X_N	$=$	λ
$2C_{2,2}$	$\cdots$	$2C_{2N}$		$E_2 - p$
$\vdots$		$\vdots$		$\vdots$
$2C_{N2}$	$\cdots$	$2C_{NN}$		$E_N - p$

The solution to this problem provides efficient values for X_2 to X_N (in the terminology of the present discussion—X_2^* to X_N^*). Each will equal some constant times λ.

Security prices are implicit in this formulation; it is necessary now to make them explicit. The changes are straightforward. Recall that

$$C_{ij} = \rho_{ij}\sigma_i\sigma_j$$

Substituting security prices and predictions concerning dollar payments,

$$C_{ij} = \rho_{ij}\sigma_i\sigma_j = \frac{\rho_{ij}^\$\sigma_i^\$\sigma_j^\$}{P_iP_j}$$

The values on the right-hand side of the table are also dependent upon security prices and predictions about dollar payments:

$$E_i - p = \frac{E_i^\$}{P_i} - 1 - p = \frac{E_i^\$}{P_i} - (1 + p)$$

The ith row of the table can thus be written,

X_2	$\cdots$	X_N	$=$	λ
$\dfrac{2\rho_{i2}^\$\sigma_i^\$\sigma_2^\$}{P_iP_2}$	$\cdots$	$\dfrac{2\rho_{iN}^\$\sigma_i^\$\sigma_N^\$}{P_iP_N}$		$\dfrac{E_i^\$}{P_i} - (1 + p)$

Some simplification is possible. Multiplying each term by P_i gives

X_2	$\cdots$	X_N	$=$	λ
$\dfrac{2\rho_{i2}^\$\sigma_i^\$\sigma_2^\$}{P_2}$	$\cdots$	$\dfrac{2\rho_{iN}^\$\sigma_i^\$\sigma_N^\$}{P_N}$		$E_i^\$ - (1 + p)P_i$

It is now possible to address the question directly. Is there a set of

prices that will make $X_2 = P_2 Q_2$, $X_3 = P_3 Q_3$, etc., for some value of λ?
In tabular form:

$P_2 Q_2$	$\cdots$	$P_N Q_N$	$=$	λ
$\dfrac{2\rho_{2,2}^{\$}\sigma_2^{\$}\sigma_2^{\$}}{P_2}$	$\cdots$	$\dfrac{2\rho_{2N}^{\$}\sigma_2^{\$}\sigma_N^{\$}}{P_N}$		$E_2^{\$} - (1+p)P_2$
$\vdots$		$\vdots$		$\vdots$
$\dfrac{2\rho_{N2}^{\$}\sigma_N^{\$}\sigma_2^{\$}}{P_2}$	$\cdots$	$\dfrac{2\rho_{NN}^{\$}\sigma_N^{\$}\sigma_N^{\$}}{P_N}$		$E_N^{\$} - (1+p)P_N$

Needless to say, this is not the appropriate table for actually solving the problem, since the decision variables (the P_i's) appear in the body while some of the given values (the Q_i's) appear in the column headings. However, the table does provide a correct statement of the required relationships.

Any acceptable set of prices must simultaneously satisfy every one of the equations represented by the rows of this table. Consider the ith equation (row). It requires that

$$\frac{2\rho_{i2}^{\$}\sigma_i^{\$}\sigma_2^{\$}}{P_2}P_2 Q_2 + \cdots + \frac{2\rho_{iN}^{\$}\sigma_i^{\$}\sigma_N^{\$}}{P_N}P_N Q_N$$

$$= [E_i^{\$} - (1+p)P_i]\lambda$$

Simplifying,

$$2\rho_{i2}^{\$}\sigma_i^{\$}\sigma_2^{\$}Q_2 + \cdots + 2\rho_{iN}^{\$}\sigma_i^{\$}\sigma_N^{\$}Q_N = [E_i^{\$} - (1+p)P_i]\lambda$$

The terms on the left are all given values; they represent predictions ($\rho_{ij}^{\$}$'s, $\sigma_i^{\$}$'s) and quantities ($Q_i$'s). For convenience denote their sum $S_i^{\$}$:

$$S_i^{\$} = \sum_{j=2}^{N} 2\rho_{ij}^{\$}\sigma_i^{\$}\sigma_j^{\$}Q_j$$

The ith row requires that

$$S_i^{\$} = [E_i^{\$} - (1+p)P_i]\lambda$$

Rewriting,

$$P_i = \frac{E_i^{\$}}{1+p} - \frac{S_i^{\$}}{(1+p)\lambda}$$

Note that this equation involves only one price, P_i. The entire system of equations is thus

$$P_2 = \frac{E_2^\$}{1+p} - \frac{S_2^\$}{(1+p)\lambda}$$

$$P_3 = \frac{E_3^\$}{1+p} - \frac{S_3^\$}{(1+p)\lambda}$$

$$\vdots$$

$$P_N = \frac{E_N^\$}{1+p} - \frac{S_N^\$}{(1+p)\lambda}$$

Obviously this set of simultaneous equations has a unique solution for any given value of λ. No further row operations are required; each price can be calculated directly.

What does the set of equations imply? The desired result. Select a pure interest rate (p) and a value for λ. Then let

$$P_2 = \frac{E_2^\$}{1+p} - \frac{S_2^\$}{(1+p)\lambda}$$

$$P_3 = \frac{E_3^\$}{1+p} - \frac{S_3^\$}{(1+p)\lambda}$$

etc.

The resulting set of prices will meet one of the requirements for equilibrium in a world of complete agreement—the market portfolio will be an optimal combination of risky securities.

A numerical example may help clarify the situation. Assume that there are two risky securities. Each share of security 2 is expected to pay \$20 at end of the period with a risk (standard deviation) of \$5. Each share of security 3 is expected to pay \$30 with a risk (standard deviation) of \$10. Five shares of security 2 and ten shares of security 3 are outstanding. The correlation coefficient between their payoffs is .5. In standard notation,

$$E_2^\$ = 20 \qquad\qquad E_3^\$ = 30$$

$$\sigma_2^\$ = 5 \qquad\qquad \sigma_3^\$ = 10$$

$$Q_2 = 5 \qquad\qquad Q_3 = 10$$

$$\rho_{2,3}^\$ = .5$$

Substituting these values into the formulas gives

$$P_2 = \frac{20}{1+p} - \frac{750}{(1+p)\lambda}$$

$$P_3 = \frac{30}{1+p} - \frac{2,250}{(1+p)\lambda}$$

Now let $p = .1$ (10 percent) and $\lambda = 300$. This implies

$$P_2 = \frac{20}{1.1} - \frac{750}{(1.1)(300)} \approx 15.91$$

$$P_3 = \frac{30}{1.1} - \frac{2,250}{(1.1)(300)} \approx 20.45$$

With these prices, an investor would be faced with the following prospects concerning rate of return:

$p = .10$
$E_2 \approx .257$
$E_3 \approx .467$
$\sigma_2 \approx .314$
$\sigma_3 \approx .489$
$\rho_{2,3} = .5$

Given such estimates, the optimal combination of risky securities could be found by solving the corresponding portfolio-analysis problem in the usual way. The result would be

$X_2 = .28$
$X_3 = .72$

But this is equivalent to "investment in the market." Each of the five shares of security 2 is worth $15.91, and each of the 10 shares of security 3 is worth $20.45. The total market value of risky securities is thus $284.05. Security 2 constitutes 28 percent of the total market by value and security 3 the remaining 72 percent.

Figure D-1a shows the situation facing an investor given this particular set of predictions, security prices, and pure interest rate.

Needless to say, other sets of prices fulfill the desired condition. A variation in p or λ (or both) will yield a completely new set of prices. For example, let $p = .1$ and $\lambda = 150$. Then,

$$P_2 = \frac{20}{1.1} - \frac{750}{(1.1)(150)} \approx 13.63$$

$$P_3 = \frac{30}{1.1} - \frac{2,250}{(1.1)(150)} \approx 13.63$$

Figure D-1b shows the situation facing an investor given this particular set of predictions, security prices, and pure interest rate. The market portfolio again is an optimal combination of risky securities. In this case, security 2 constitutes one-third of the total

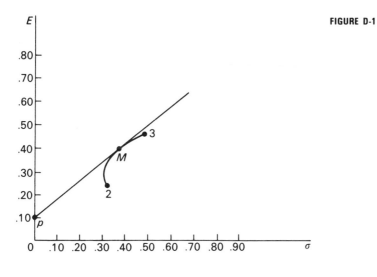

(a)

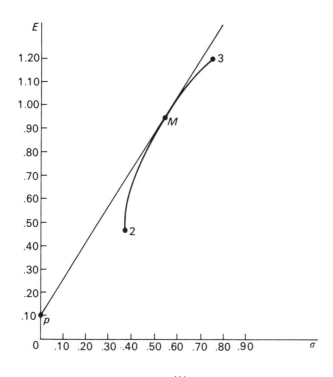

(b)

market value of risky securities and security 3 the remaining two-thirds.

EXPECTED RETURN, RISK, AND SECURITY PRICES The results of the previous discussion on the market portfolio shed considerable light on the determination of security prices in a world of complete agreement. In general, the price of risky security i is related to its expected payoff and risk as follows:

$$P_i = \frac{E_i^\$}{1 + p} - \frac{S_i^\$}{(1 + p)\lambda}$$

This formula can also be applied to the first (riskless) security. Recall the definition of S_i:

$$S_i^\$ = \sum_{j=2}^{N} 2\rho_{ij}^\$ \sigma_i^\$ \sigma_j^\$ Q_j$$

The payoff from a riskless security is, of course, uncorrelated with that of any other. Thus,

$$S_1^\$ = 0$$

$S_i^\$$ can be interpreted as the risk associated with a share of security i. Define $C_{ij}^\$$ as the covariance between the payoff from a share of security i and the payoff from a share of security j. Obviously,

$$C_{ij}^\$ = \rho_{ij}^\$ \sigma_i^\$ \sigma_j^\$$$

Substituting this into the formula for S_i,

$$S_i^\$ = 2 \sum_{j=2}^{N} C_{ij}^\$ Q_j$$

This is twice the covariance between the payoff from a share of security i and the payoff from a portfolio composed of all outstanding securities. It thus provides a measure of risk closely related to that indicated by the covariance between the rate of return on a security and the rate of return on the market portfolio.[1]

The general formula for the price of a security can now be given a more useful interpretation. Rewriting,

$$P_i = \frac{E_i^\$ - \dfrac{S_i^\$}{\lambda}}{1 + p}$$

The numerator represents the value of the security in *future* dollars. Dividing by $1 + p$ gives the value in *present* dollars (i.e., the present

[1] Let P_M = the total market value of risky securities. Then,

$$\sum_{j=2}^{M} C_{ij}^\$ Q_j = (P_M P_i) C_{im}$$

value of the security's future prospects). The pure interest rate thus serves its usual purpose, relating present to future value (and vice versa).

The value of security i, stated in future dollars, is

$$E_i^\$ - \frac{S_i^\$}{\lambda}$$

The first term is simply the expected payoff from the security. In the absence of risk (or risk aversion), it would be the value of the security. In general, however, the value is smaller. The second term shows how much. $S_i^\$$ measures security i's risk; the greater the risk, the smaller the security's value. The reciprocal of λ indicates the reduction in value per unit of risk. Future value thus equals expected value minus the product of (1) the reduction in value per unit risk times (2) the amount of risk:

$$E_i^\$ - \frac{1}{\lambda} S_i^\$$$

Present value (price) equals future value divided by $1 + p$.

The impact of the value of λ on the set of security prices can easily be seen. Recall the meaning of λ; it indicates the relative importance of expected return vis-à-vis risk (variance of return). Its reciprocal thus indicates the relative importance of (distaste for) risk vis-à-vis expected return. A value of zero for $1/\lambda$ would reflect a complete lack of concern for risk. Under such conditions, every security would sell for a price equal to its expected payoff, discounted by $1 + p$. The larger the value of $1/\lambda$, the greater the concern for risk (extent of risk aversion) and the smaller the price of every risky security.

Figure D-2 shows the impact of the degree of risk aversion on the price of each of the two securities in the previous example. Price is stated in terms of the pure interest rate; the horizontal axis is based on the value of $1/\lambda$, with corresponding values of λ shown in Fig. D-2 for convenience.

Given a pair of values for p and λ, there is a unique set of prices that will make the market portfolio an optimal combination of risky securities. Each such set of prices corresponds to a different capital market line, and vice versa.

SECURITY PRICES AND THE CAPITAL MARKET LINE

Consider a portfolio composed of all outstanding risky securities. The expected dollar payoff will be

$$E_M^\$ = \sum_{i=2}^{N} E_i^\$ Q_i$$

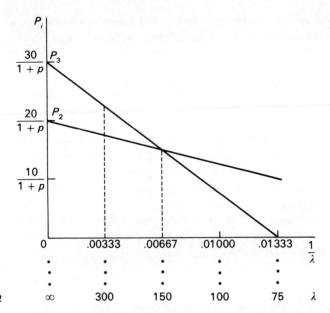

FIGURE D-2

The standard deviation of dollar payoff will be

$$\sigma_M^\$ = \sqrt{V_M^\$}$$

where $V_M^\$ = \sum_{i=2}^{N} \sum_{j=2}^{N} (C_{ij}^\$ Q_i Q_j)$

The market value will be

$$P_M = \sum_{i=2}^{N} P_i Q_i$$

The expected rate of return on the market portfolio will be

$$E_M = \frac{E_M^\$}{P_M} - 1$$

While the standard deviation of return will be

$$\sigma_M = \frac{\sigma_M^\$}{P_M}$$

It thus follows that

$$\frac{E_M + 1}{\sigma_M} = \frac{\dfrac{E_M^\$}{P_M}}{\dfrac{\sigma_M^\$}{P_M}} = \frac{E_M^\$}{\sigma_M^\$}$$

The market value of a portfolio composed of all outstanding securities thus does not affect the ratio of its expected return (plus 1) to its risk. This must also hold for any portfolio in which securities are included in proportion to their market value. Therefore the market portfolio must plot along a ray that (1) begins at the point at which $E_p = -1$ and $\sigma_p = 0$ and (2) has a slope of $E_M^\$/\sigma_M^\$$. The smaller the market value of all outstanding risky securities, the farther along the ray will be the point representing the market portfolio.

This point lies on the capital market line. So does that representing the pure interest rate. Together, they determine the position of the line. The value of p indicates the location of one point. Given a value of p, the value of λ indicates the location of the other.

Recall the relationship between the value of a security and the value of $1/\lambda$:

$$F_i = E_i^\$ - \frac{1}{\lambda}(S_i^\$)$$

where F_i = the value of security i in future dollars and

$$P_i = \frac{F_i}{1+p}$$

The value of all risky securities, in future dollars, is

$$F_M = \sum_{i=2}^{N} F_i Q_i$$

$$= \sum_{i=2}^{N} \left[E_i^\$ - \frac{1}{\lambda}\left(S_i^\$\right) \right] Q_i$$

$$= \left(\sum_{i=2}^{N} E_i^\$ Q_i \right) - \frac{1}{\lambda}\left(\sum_{i=2}^{N} S_i^\$ Q_i \right)$$

Each of the parenthesized sums can be regarded as a constant. The value of the market portfolio in future dollars is thus a linear function of $1/\lambda$. Given a value of p, so is the value in present dollars:

$$P_M = \left(\frac{\sum_{i=2}^{N} E_i^\$ Q_i}{1+p} \right) - \frac{1}{\lambda}\left(\frac{\sum_{i=2}^{N} S_i^\$ Q_i}{1+p} \right)$$

Figure D-3 provides an illustration of these relationships. Three possible capital market lines are shown. All are based on the same pure rate of interest (represented by point p).

In the first case, $1/\lambda$ equals zero; there is no risk aversion. Every security sells at a price equal to its expected payoff, discounted by $1+p$. The expected return on the market portfolio (or any other,

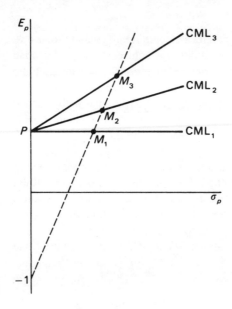

FIGURE D-3

for that matter) equals the pure interest rate. The market portfolio is represented by point M_1, and the capital market line (CML) is horizontal.

In the second case, $1/\lambda$ is greater than zero; there is risk aversion. The market value of all outstanding risky securities is less, and the capital market line slopes upward. The market portfolio is represented by point M_2.

In the third case, $1/\lambda$ is larger yet, indicating even greater risk aversion. The market value of all outstanding risky securities is smaller, and the capital market line is steeper than in the second case.

There is a one-to-one correspondence between the location of the capital market line and the values of p and λ. Given (1) predictions about the dollar payoffs from risky securities and (2) the number of shares of each outstanding, the market (in equilibrium) can be described:

1. By the location of the capital market line; or
2. By the values of p and λ; or
3. By the pure interest rate (p) and the market value of all outstanding risky securities.

BORROWING AND LENDING

Every possible capital market line is associated with a unique set of security prices that will make the market portfolio an optimal combination of risky securities. Not all can be consistent with the full set of conditions required for equilibrium. This portion of the section is concerned with the demand and supply for shares of security number 1—factors ignored in the previous discussions.

The total dollar amount people wish to borrow must equal the total dollar amount others wish to lend. Given a capital market line, every investor will choose to borrow, to lend, or to do neither. Figure D-4a to c illustrates the three possibilities. The location of the preferred point along the capital market line (CML) indicates each individual's position in the market for risk-free funds. Those choosing a point above and to the right of the point representing the market portfolio will demand such funds (borrow); those choosing a point below and to the left will supply funds (lend). Equilibrium requires that the quantity demanded equal the quantity supplied.

How can such an equilibrium be found? Consider capital market line 1 in Fig. D-5. Given the alternatives it represents, the individual whose preferences are shown by the set of indifference curves will choose to borrow sufficient funds to reach point 1. Now consider capital market line 2, with a smaller slope, but constructed to pass through point M. The individual in question chooses to borrow

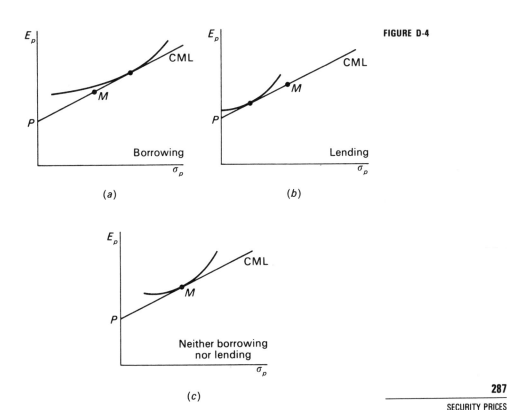

(a)   (b)

(c)

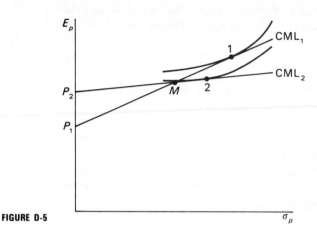

FIGURE D-5

less in this case, preferring to only reach point 2. This is not sur-prising. The change from line 1 to line 2 entails an increase in the pure interest rate (cost of borrowing) with no change in the price of the market portfolio. An individual generally will purchase less of an item following an increase in its price relative to that of other items (this is the economist's *law of demand*).

Without placing some restrictions on the nature of indifference curves, such a reaction cannot be *proven*. A rise in the cost of borrowing makes a borrower poorer in real terms. The associated loss of real income could conceivably lead to increased purchases of risk-free funds, in spite of substantial reasons for purchasing less of the now relatively more expensive item. However, cases in which such an *income effect* overwhelms the *substitution effect* are likely to be exceedingly rare.

In general, a rise in the pure interest rate, with no change in the price of the market portfolio, should lead to a decrease in the quantity of risk-free funds demanded. The effect on the other side of the market is equally predictable. A rise in the pure interest rate (*ceteris paribus*) should lead to an increase in the quantity of risk-free funds supplied. In general, for any market value of risky securities, one (and only one) pure interest rate will equate the quantity of risk-free funds demanded with the quantity supplied.

PRESENT VERSUS FUTURE CONSUMPTION Assume that some capital market line fulfills both equilibrium requirements considered thus far: (1) The market portfolio is an optimal combination of risky securities, and (2) the quantity of risk-free funds demanded equals the quantity supplied. What can be

THE MATHEMATICAL FOUNDATION

said about other capital market lines—in particular, those that are parallel to the one that meets the required conditions?

Recall the relationship between the market value of risky securities and the relevant values in equilibrium:

$$P_M = \left(\frac{\sum\limits_{i=2}^{N} E_i^\$ Q_i}{1 + p} \right) - \frac{1}{\lambda} \left(\frac{\sum\limits_{i=2}^{N} S_i^\$ Q_i}{1 + p} \right)$$

Recall also that

$$E_M = \frac{E_M^\$}{P_M} - 1 \qquad \text{and} \qquad \sigma_M = \frac{\sigma_M^\$}{P_M}$$

The slope of a capital market line (S_M) equals the ratio of (1) the excess expected return on the market portfolio over and above the pure interest rate to (2) the standard deviation of return:

$$S_M = \frac{E_M - p}{\sigma_M}$$

In terms of predicted values and P_M,

$$S_M = \frac{\dfrac{E_M^\$}{P_M} - 1 - p}{\dfrac{\sigma_M^\$}{P_M}} = \frac{E_M^\$ - (1 + p)P_M}{\sigma_M^\$}$$

Substituting the equilibrium relationship for P_M,

$$S_M = \frac{E_M^\$ - (1 + p) \left[\left(\dfrac{\sum\limits_{i=2}^{N} E_i^\$ Q_i}{1 + p} \right) - \dfrac{1}{\lambda} \left(\dfrac{\sum\limits_{i=2}^{N} S_i^\$ Q_i}{1 + p} \right) \right]}{\sigma_M^\$}$$

Simplifying,

$$S_M = \frac{E_M^\$ - \sum\limits_{i=2}^{N} E_i^\$ Q_i + \dfrac{1}{\lambda} \sum\limits_{i=2}^{N} S_i^\$ Q_i}{\sigma_M^\$}$$

This can be further simplified,[1] but for present purposes this form suffices. The important point is that:

The slope of the capital market line is unaffected by changes in p, if λ remains constant.

Any change in the pure interest rate, *ceteris paribus*, is thus equivalent to a parallel shift in the capital market line.

[1] To $2/\lambda$

Consider the effect of a decrease in the pure interest rate from p_1 to p_2. Initially, the price of security i would be

$$\frac{1}{1+p_1}\left(E_i^\$ - \frac{1}{\lambda}(S_i^\$)\right)$$

After the change, its price would be

$$\frac{1}{1+p_2}\left(E_i^\$ - \frac{1}{\lambda}(S_i^\$)\right)$$

Giving a ratio of the final price to initial price of

$$\frac{\dfrac{1}{1+p_2}\left[E_i^\$ - \dfrac{1}{\lambda}(S_i^\$)\right]}{\dfrac{1}{1+p_1}\left[E_i^\$ - \dfrac{1}{\lambda}(S_i^\$)\right]} = \frac{1+p_1}{1+p_2}$$

This result applies to all securities, whether risky or not. Thus:

A parallel shift in the capital market line reflects an equal percentage change in the price of every security (risky and risk free).

Putting it another way:

A parallel shift in the capital market line leaves the relative prices of securities unchanged.

It would appear that any one of a number of parallel capital market lines could fulfill all the requirements for equilibrium, since each would represent the same set of relative security prices. Given a stock of risky securities to be held regardless of price, this would be the case.

But the world does not operate this way. Risky securities represent risky assets. These, in turn, represent foregone consumption. It is time to come to grips with a third equilibrium requirement. Prices must adjust until people are willing to hold the securities representing assets that others are willing to create by foregoing present consumption.

The process is most easily seen by considering parallel shifts in the capital market line. An upward shift is equivalent to an equal percentage decrease in the price of every risky security. Such a shift will increase the quantity of such securities demanded and decrease the quantity supplied. In more basic terms, it will lead to an increase in the quantity of future consumption demanded by some and a decrease in the quantity supplied by others.

The height of the capital market line represents the relative price of future consumption vis-à-vis that of present consumption. Its slope represents the relative price of risk vis-à-vis expected return when present consumption is foregone in order to obtain (prospects for) future consumption. In general, only one capital market line will be consistent with the last two equilibrium requirements considered:

2. Borrowing must equal lending.[1]

3. The quantity of present consumption demanded must equal the quantity supplied.

Given a capital market line, of course, only one set of security prices is consistent with the first requirement:

1. The market portfolio must be an optimal combination of risky securities.

In a somewhat superficial sense, the equilibrium relationships derived for a world of complete agreement can be said to apply to a world in which there is disagreement, if certain values are considered to be averages. This result is not exceptionally useful, but it does reveal both similarities and differences in the two approaches.

EQUILIBRIUM WITH DISAGREEMENT

Recall the key result obtained earlier in this section. In equilibrium, each investor able to either purchase or issue securities will adjust his holdings until the following relationship holds for every security:

$$P_i = \frac{E_i^\$}{1 + p} - \frac{S_i^\$}{(1 + p)\lambda}$$

where $S_i^\$ = \sum_j 2\rho_{ij}^\$ \sigma_i^\$ \sigma_j^\$ Q_j$

Rearranging, and substituting covariances for correlation coefficients and standard deviations,

$$P_i = \frac{1}{1 + p}\left[E_i^\$ - 2\sum_j \left(\frac{C_{ij}^\$}{\lambda}\right)Q_j\right]$$

To accommodate disagreement, the investor must be specified. Using superscripts:

Every investor (k) will adjust his holdings until the following relationship holds for every security (i):

$$P_i = \frac{1}{1 + p}\left[E_i^{\$k} - 2\sum_j \left(\frac{C_{ij}^{\$k}}{\lambda^k}\right)Q_i^k\right]$$

[1] Assuming that there are no riskless capital assets. A more general statement requires that the quantity of each asset demanded equal the quantity supplied.

where P_i = price of security i

p = pure interest rate

$E_i^{\$k}$ = investor k's prediction concerning the expected dollar payoff from a share of security i

$C_{ij}^{\$k}$ = investor k's predicted covariance between the dollar payoff of one share of security i and that of one share of security j

λ^k = investor k's attitude towards risk vis-à-vis expected return

Q_j^k = number of shares of security j held by investor k

Consider security i. For investor 1, the following relationship will hold:

$$P_i = \frac{1}{1+p}\left[E_i^{\$1} - 2\sum_j \left(\frac{C_{ij}^{\$1}}{\lambda^1}\right)Q_j^1\right]$$

For investor 2,

$$P_i = \frac{1}{1+p}\left[E_i^{\$2} - 2\sum_j \left(\frac{C_{ij}^{\$2}}{\lambda^2}\right)Q_j^2\right]$$

And so on. Let there be K investors. There will be K equations of this type.

Consider the sum of the items on the left-hand sides of all K equations. It will obviously be

$$KP_i$$

But this must equal the sum of the items on the right-hand sides. The latter sum will be

$$\frac{1}{1+p}\left[\sum_k E_i^{\$k} - 2\sum_k \sum_j \left(\frac{C_{ij}^{\$k}}{\lambda^k}\right)Q_j^k\right]$$

Dividing both sums by K,

$$P_i = \frac{1}{1+p}\left[\frac{1}{K}\sum_k E_i^{\$k} - \frac{2}{K}\sum_k \sum_j \left(\frac{C_{ij}^{\$k}}{\lambda^k}\right)Q_j^k\right]$$

Consider the first term in the brackets. It is clearly the average value of the $E_i^{\$k}$'s. Define

$$E_i^{\$\,avg} = \frac{1}{K}\sum_k E_i^{\$k}$$

Substituting,

$$P_i = \frac{1}{1+p}\left[E_i^{\$\,avg} - \frac{2}{K}\sum_k \sum_j \left(\frac{C_{ij}^{\$k}}{\lambda^k}\right)Q_j^k\right]$$

Now consider the second term,

$$\frac{2}{K}\sum_{k}\sum_{j}\left(\frac{C_{ij}^{\$k}}{\lambda^{k}}\right)Q_{j}^{k}$$

Since the order in which a sum is taken is irrelevant, the term may be rewritten as

$$2\sum_{j}\left[\frac{1}{K}\sum_{k}\left(\frac{C_{ij}^{\$k}}{\lambda^{k}}\right)Q_{j}^{k}\right]$$

Let Q_{j}^{T} be the total number of shares of security j outstanding:

$$Q_{j}^{T}=\sum_{k}Q_{j}^{k}$$

Dividing and multiplying the term by Q_{j}^{T} gives

$$2\sum_{j}\left[\frac{Q_{j}^{T}}{K}\sum_{k}\left(\frac{C_{ij}^{\$k}}{\lambda^{k}}\right)\left(\frac{Q_{j}^{k}}{Q_{j}^{T}}\right)\right]$$

The sum on the right is simply a weighted average value of $\frac{C_{ij}^{\$k}}{\lambda^{k}}$, with each investor's ratio weighted by his proportionate holding of security j. Thus it is not unreasonable to define

$$\left(\frac{C_{ij}^{\$}}{\lambda}\right)^{avg}=\sum_{k}\left(\frac{C_{ij}^{\$k}}{\lambda^{k}}\right)\left(\frac{Q_{j}^{k}}{C_{j}^{T}}\right)$$

Finally, consider the ratio

$$\frac{Q_{j}^{T}}{K}$$

This is simply the average holding of security j. Define

$$Q_{j}^{avg}=\frac{Q_{j}^{T}}{K}$$

The relationship derived by summing over all investors can now be written,

$$P_{i}=\frac{1}{1+p}\left[E_{i}^{\$\,avg}-2\sum_{j}\left(\frac{C_{ij}^{\$}}{\lambda}\right)^{avg}Q_{j}^{avg}\right]$$

If there is complete agreement, every investor will hold the same (average) view. The formula derived in the earlier discussions of this section can thus be considered a special case of this more general result.

E.

PORTFOLIO ANALYSIS WITH SIMPLIFIED MODELS

PORTFOLIO ANALYSIS WITH INDEX MODELS

As indicated in Chap. 7, it is possible to take advantage of the special structure of an index model when performing a portfolio analysis. Substantial amounts of computer time can be saved. Moreover, problems involving many securities can be solved with a relatively small machine, since there is no need to store certain entries that are known to remain equal to zero throughout the calculations.

For complete generality, a procedure for handling a multiindex model with correlated indexes will be described. The method may also be employed for simpler cases (e.g., a multiindex model with uncorrelated indexes or a single-index model).

The assumed structure follows. For each of N securities,

$$R_i = a_i + (b_{i1}I_1 + b_{i2}I_2 + \cdots + b_{iM}I_M) + c_i$$

where $a_i, b_{i1}, b_{i2}, \ldots, b_{iM}$ are constants, and c_i is an uncertain variable with an expected value of zero, and a variance of $\sigma^2_{c_i}$. c_i is assumed to be uncorrelated with every other variable.

Given the assumed lack of correlation of each c_i term with every other term, portfolio variance will be

$$\sigma^2_p = \sum_{i=1}^{N} X_i^2 \sigma^2_{c_i} + \sum_{j=1}^{M} \sum_{k=1}^{M} b_{pj} b_{pk} C_{jk}$$

where X_i = proportion of portfolio invested in security i

C_{jk} = covariance between index j and index k

$$b_{pj} = \sum_{i=1}^{N} X_i b_{ij} \qquad \text{by definition}$$

As always, the expected return of a portfolio will be

$$E_p = \sum_{i=1}^{N} X_i E_i$$

where E_i = the expected return of security i.

The portfolio-analysis problem is thus:

Minimize $\sigma^2_p - \lambda E_p$

subject to $b_{p1} = \sum\limits_{i=1}^{N} X_i b_{i1}$

$$b_{p2} = \sum_{i=1}^{N} X_i b_{i2}$$

$$\vdots$$

$$b_{pM} = \sum_{i=1}^{N} X_i b_{iM}$$

$$\sum_{i=1}^{N} X_i = 1$$

There are $N + M$ decision variables: $X_1, X_2, \ldots, X_N$ and $b_{p1}, b_{p2}, \ldots, b_{pM}$.

As usual, the constraints are added to the objective function:

Minimize $Z' = \sigma^2_p - \lambda E_p + \lambda_1 \left(b_{p1} - \sum\limits_{i=1}^{N} X_i b_{i1} \right)$

$$+ \lambda_2 \left(b_{p2} - \sum_{i=1}^{N} X_i b_{i2} \right)$$

$$\vdots$$

$$+ \lambda_M \left(b_{pM} - \sum_{i=1}^{N} X_i b_{iM} \right)$$

$$+ \lambda_f \left(1 - \sum_{i=1}^{N} X_i \right)$$

The solution requires that the partial derivative of Z' with respect to each variable be zero.

For each i from 1 to N,

$$\frac{\partial Z'}{\partial X_i} = 2\sigma_{c_i}^2 X_i - E_i \lambda - \lambda_f - \lambda_1 b_{i1} - \cdots - \lambda_M b_{iM} = 0$$

For each j from 1 to M,

$$\frac{\partial Z'}{\partial b_{pj}} = 2b_{p1} C_{j1} + 2b_{p2} C_{j2} + \cdots + 2b_{pM} C_{jM} + \lambda_j = 0$$

For each j from 1 to M,

$$\frac{\partial Z'}{\partial \lambda_j} = b_{pj} - b_{1j} X_1 - b_{2j} X_2 - \cdots - b_{Nj} X_N = 0$$

For λ_f,

$$\frac{\partial Z'}{\partial \lambda f} = 1 - X_1 - X_2 - \cdots - X_N = 0$$

Figure E-1 shows the problem in tabular format. Positions in which

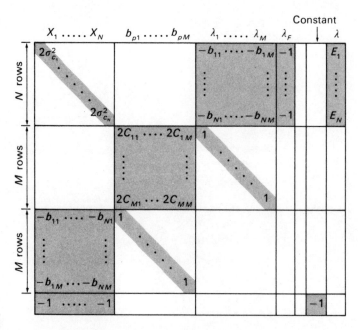

FIGURE E-1

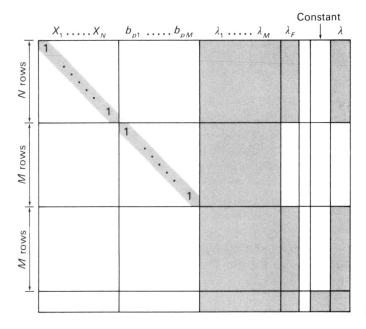

Constant

nonzero values may appear have been shaded for emphasis. Note the large number of zero-valued entries. This is the distinguishing characteristic of a portfolio-analysis problem based on an index model. The goal is to take advantage of it.

To begin, it is useful to revise the table rather extensively. The first step involves the initial N rows. It is a simple matter to obtain 1s along the diagonal. Every element of row i is divided by $\sigma_{c_i}^2$. The result will have the appearance indicated in the first N rows of Fig. E-2.

The second step involves the next M rows of the table. Using standard row operations, it is possible to obtain 1s along the diagonal and 0s above and below it, as shown in Fig. E-2. Note that the coefficients obtained for these rows do not depend in any way on those in the first N rows.

The last step requires the transformation of the remaining $M + 1$ rows to the form shown in Fig. E-2. The procedure involves the use of the first $N + M$ rows.

Figure E-3 illustrates the manner in which the jth row of the final set of M rows is transformed.

Figure E-3a shows the row in its original form. Figure E-3b shows

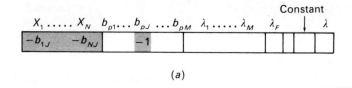

(a)

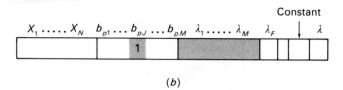

(b)

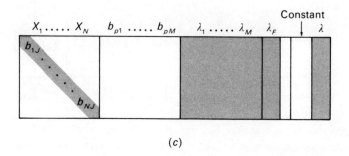

(c)

FIGURE E-3

(d)

the corresponding row from the middle set of M rows in the table shown in Fig. E-2.

Now consider the effect of multiplying every element in the first row of the table shown in Fig. E-2 by b_{1j}, then multiplying every element in the second row by b_{2j}, etc. The result would be N rows of the type shown in Fig. E-3c.

Finally, let all the rows shown in Fig. E-3a to c be added together. The result would have the form shown in Fig. E-3d, as desired.

In practice, the first N rows of the table do not have to be altered for this purpose. The coefficients can be added directly to the appropriate columns of the jth row as they are computed.

THE MATHEMATICAL FOUNDATION

The procedure illustrated in Fig. E-3 provides a simple method for modifying the set of M rows. The final row of the table can be altered even more easily. The first N rows are simply added to it, giving the desired result.

The solution can now be obtained by operating on the final $M + 1$ rows of Fig. E-2. The goal is to get 1s along the diagonal and 0s below it. Relatively little effort is required. Once the desired values have been obtained, the overall solution can be found by working back through the table in the usual manner. The large number of zero-valued elements also facilitates this task.

Thus far nothing has been said about upper and lower bounds. It is now time to deal with them. Expand the problem to include the following set of constraints:

$$L_1 \leqq X_1 \leqq U_1$$
$$L_2 \leqq X_2 \leqq U_2$$
$$\vdots$$
$$L_N \leqq X_N \leqq U_N$$

Assume that variable i is up. What changes are required? First, the relevant row of the initial table must be altered.

Thus, in Fig. E-1, row i becomes

$$X_1 \cdots X_i \cdots X_N \ b_p \cdots \cdots b_{pN} \ \lambda_1 \cdots \cdots \lambda_M \ \lambda_F = \text{constant } \lambda$$

	1					U_i	

No other changes must be made in the initial table.

What about the revised table shown in Fig. E-2? Row i will be exactly the same as in Fig. E-1. The other rows in the initial set of N rows will be unchanged. The first set of M rows will also be unchanged (recall that they were obtained directly from the corresponding set of rows in the initial table).

The final set of $M + 1$ rows in Fig. E-2 will be affected by any change in the first N rows. But the effect is simple enough to determine. Each of the $M + 1$ rows was computed by adding together a specific set of transformed rows (as shown in Fig. E-3). One of these transformed rows has now been changed. Obviously the contribution of the old version of the row should be subtracted out and that of the new one added in.

The entire procedure required to perform a portfolio analysis with upper and lower bounds can now be specified:

1. Find the first (max-E_p) portfolio in the usual manner.
2. Set up the initial table (in the form shown in Fig. E-1), selecting the appropriate form for each of the first N rows, depending on whether the security in question is *down*, *in*, or *up*.
3. Obtain a revised table (in the form shown in Fig. E-2).
4. Transform the final $M + 1$ rows in the revised table, then work back through the table to obtain the solution.
5. Check to see if all corner portfolios have been found (that is, $\lambda = 0$); if so, stop. If not, determine the next variable to change status. Alter the corresponding row in the revised table and the final $M + 1$ rows. Then return to step 4.

In practice, relatively little information need be stored explicitly, and actual alteration of some rows will not be required. A number of tricks may be employed to produce an efficient program for any particular computer.

The method may be simplified considerably if all indexes are assumed to be uncorrelated. Each of the rows in the middle set of M rows in Fig. E-1 would then contain only two values. The jth row in the set would have:

$2\sigma_{Ij}^2$ in the column corresponding to b_{pj} and 1 in the column corresponding to λ_j.

Dividing the two values by the first transforms the row to the desired form. Moreover, the revised version includes only two values, instead of $M + 1$, simplifying the remaining calculations and reducing the required storage. As shown in Chap. 7, it may not be unreasonable to restrict multiindex models to formulations in which indexes are defined in such a manner that they will, in fact, be uncorrelated.

PORTFOLIO ANALYSIS BASED ON RESPONSIVENESS

Chapter 7 described a graphical method for solving portfolio-analysis problems with responsiveness (b_p) used to measure risk. It is not difficult to program a computer to perform the analysis. The only part of the task that requires any substantial restatement involves finding the location at which the border line must be changed. This portion of the section provides the necessary formulation.

The equation of the line representing security i is

$$z_i = (1 - \lambda)E_i - \lambda b_i$$

Rewriting,

$$z_i = E_i - (E_i + b_i)\lambda$$

Obviously the slope of security i's line is $-(E_i + b_i)$.

Consider two lines, one with a slope of -1, the other with a slope

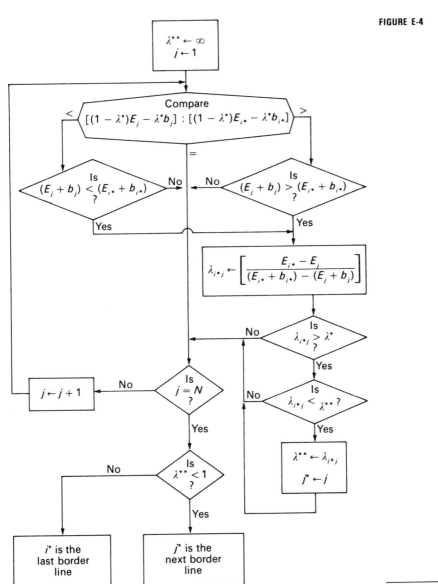

of -2. Obviously the latter is steeper. In general, security j's line is steeper than security i's line if:

$$(E_j + b_j) > (E_i + b_i)$$

At what value of λ will two lines cross? Consider securities i and j. The two cross when $z_i = z_j$; that is, when

$$(1 - \lambda)E_i - \lambda b_i = (1 - \lambda)E_j - \lambda b_j$$

Denote the corresponding value of λ as λ_{ij}. Then

$$\lambda_{ij} = \frac{E_i - E_j}{(E_i + b_i) - (E_j + b_j)}$$

Now let security i^* be associated with the current border line, and let λ^* be the current value of λ. The goal is to determine the first line intersecting the current border line to the right of λ^*. It may come from either of two groups:

1. Steeper lines that are above i^* at λ^*
2. Flatter lines that are below i^* at λ^*

As shown in Chap. 7, if the new line comes from group 1, only the border line changes; if it comes from group 2, both the border line and the efficient portfolio change.

Figure E-4 shows a procedure for finding the next border line. It begins with the assignment of a very large value to λ^{**} and continues until either (1) the new border line is found, or (2) it is determined that the current border line is the last one (i.e., the current portfolio is the minimum-risk portfolio).

To perform the entire portfolio analysis, this procedure is repeated until the minimum-risk portfolio is obtained, changing the border line each time and noting changes in the composition of the efficient portfolios.

BIBLIOGRAPHY

Angell, J. W.: Uncertainty Likelihoods and Investment Decisions, *Quart. J. Econ.*, February, 1960, pp. 1-28.

Arditti, Fred D.: Risk and the Required Return on Equity, *J. Finan.*, March, 1967, pp. 19—36.

Arrow, Kenneth J.: Alternative Approaches to the Theory of Choice in Risk-taking Situations, *Econometrica*, October, 1951, pp. 404—437.

Arrow, Kenneth J.: The Portfolio Approach: Comment, *Rev. Econ. and Stat.*, February, 1963, pp. 24—27.

Arrow, Kenneth J.: Uncertainty and the Welfare Economics of Medical Care, *Amer. Econ. Rev.*, December, 1963, pp. 941—973.

Arrow, Kenneth J.: The Role of Securities in the Optimal Allocation of Risk-bearing, *Rev. Econ. Studies*, April, 1964, pp. 91—96.

Ayres, Herbert F.: Risk Aversion in the Warrant Markets, *Ind. Manag. Rev.*, Fall, 1963, pp. 45–53.

Baumol, William J.: An Expected Gain—Confidence Limit Criterion for Portfolio Selection, *Manag. Sci.*, October, 1963, pp. 174–182.

Baumol, William J., and Burton G. Malkiel: The Firm's Optimal Debt-Equity Combination and the Cost of Capital, *Quart. J. Econ.*, November, 1967, pp. 547–578.

Beja, Avraham: "Capital Markets with Delayed Learning," EES Student Thesis Series, Institute in Engineering-Economic Systems, Stanford University, Stanford, Calif., February, 1967.

Bernoulli, D.: Exposition of a New Theory on the Measurement of Risk (translated from the 1730 version), *Econometrica*, January, 1954, pp. 23–36.

Bierman, Harold, Jr.: Using Investment Portfolios to Change Risk, *J. Finan. and Quant. Anal.*, June, 1968, pp. 151–156.

Bierman, Harold, Jr.: Risk and the Addition of Debt to the Capital Structure, *J. Finan. and Quant. Anal.*, December, 1968, pp. 415–426.

Bierwag, G. O., and M. A. Grove: Portfolio Selection and Taxation, *Oxford Econ. Papers,* July, 1957, pp. 215–221.

Bierwag, G. O., and M. A. Grove: On Capital Asset Prices: Comment, *J. Finan.*, March, 1965, pp. 89–95.

Blume, Marshall E., II: "The Assessment of Portfolio Performance: An Application of Portfolio Theory," doctoral dissertation, University of Chicago, Ill., March, 1968.

Borch, Karl: A Note on Utility and Attitudes to Risk, *Manag. Sci.*, July, 1964, pp. 697–700.

Borch, Karl: The Theory of Risk, *J. Roy. Stat. Soc.*, 1967, pp. 432–452.

Borch, Karl: The Economic Theory of Insurance, *Astin Bull.*, July, 1967, pp. 252–264.

Borch, Karl: The Economics of Uncertainty, in Martin Shubik (ed.), "Essays in Mathematical Economics in Honor of Oskar Morgenstern," Princeton University Press, Princeton, N.J., 1967.

Borch, Karl: Indifference Curves and Uncertainty, *Swed. J. Econ.*, 1968, pp. 19–24.

Borch, Karl: "The Economics of Uncertainty," Princeton University Press, Princeton, N.J., 1968.

Borch, Karl: General Equilibrium in the Economics of Uncertainty, in Karl Borch and Jan Mossin (eds.), "Risk and Uncertainty," St. Martin's Press, Inc., New York, 1968.

Bower, Richard S., J. Peter Williamson, and Ronald F. Wippern: Financial Research, Investment Analysis and the Computer: Work Done at the Amos Tuck School, *Tuck Bull. 31*, Amos Tuck School, Hanover, N.H., 1967.

Breen, William: Homogeneous Risk Measures and the Construction of Composite Assets, *J. Finan. and Quant. Anal.*, December, 1968, pp. 405–413.

Brownlee, O. H., and I. O. Scott: Utility, Liquidity and Debt Management, *Econometrica*, July, 1963, pp. 349–362.

Chase, Richard H., Jr., William C. Gifford, Jr., Richard S. Bower, and J. Peter Williamson: Computer Applications in Investment Analysis, *Tuck Bulletin 30*, Amos Tuck School, Hanover, N.H., September, 1966.

Cheng, Pao Lun: Optimum Bond Portfolio Selection, *Manag. Sci.*, July, 1962, pp. 490–499.

Clarkson, Geoffrey P.: "Portfolio Selection: A Simulation of Trust Investment," Prentice-Hall, Inc., Englewood Cliffs, N.J., 1962.

Clarkson, Geoffrey P., and Allan H. Meltzer: Portfolio Selection: A Heuristic Approach, *J. Finan.*, December, 1960, pp. 465–480.

Cohen, Kalman J., and Edwin J. Elton: Inter-Temporal Portfolio Analysis Based on Simulation of Joint Returns, *Manag. Sci.*, September, 1967, pp. 5–17.

Cohen, Kalman J., and Bruce P. Fitch: The Average Investment Performance Index, *Manag. Sci.*, February, 1966, pp. B195–B215.

Cohen, Kalman J., and Jerry A. Pogue: An Empirical Evaluation of Alternative Portfolio Selection Models, *J. Bus.*, April, 1967, pp. 166–193.

Commitee on Interstate and Foreign Commerce: "A Study of Mutual Funda Prepared for the Securities and Exchange Commission by the Wharton School of Finance and Commerce," House Report No. 2274, U.S. Government Printing Office, Washington, D.C., 1962.

Committee on Interstate and Foreign Commerce: "Report of the Securities and Exchange Commission on the Public Policy Implications of Investment Company Growth," House Report No. 2337, U.S. Government Printing Office, Washington, D.C., 1966.

Conrad, Gordon R., and Irving H. Plotkin: Risk/Return: U.S. Industry Pattern, *Harvard Bus. Rev.*, March-April, 1968, pp. 90–99.

Cord, Joel: A Method of Allocating Funds to Investment Projects When Returns Are Subject to Uncertainty, *Manag. Sci.*, January, 1964, pp. 335–341.

Debreu, Gerard: "Theory of Value: An Axiomatic Analysis of Economic Equilibrium," John Wiley & Sons, Inc., New York, 1959.

Diamond, Peter A.: The Role of a Stock Market in a General Equilibrium Model with Technological Uncertainty, *Amer. Econ. Rev.*, September, 1967, pp. 759–776.

Dyckman, T. R.: Allocating Funds to Investment Projects When

Returns Are Subject to Uncertainty: A Comment, *Manag. Sci.,* November, 1964, p. 348.

Edgerton, R. A. D.: Investment, Uncertainty and Expectations, *Rev. Econ. Studies,* 1955, pp. 143–150.

Edgerton, R. A. D.: The Holding of Assets: Gambler Preference or Safety First?, *Oxford Econ. Papers,* February, 1956, pp. 51–59.

Ellsberg, Daniel: Risk, Ambiguity and the Savage Axioms, *Quart. J. Econ.,* November, 1961, pp. 643–669.

Evans, John L.: "Diversification and the Reduction of Dispersion: An Empirical Analysis," doctoral dissertation, School of Business Administration, University of Washington, Seattle, Wash., 1968.

Evans, John L.: The Random Walk Hypothesis, Portfolio Analysis and the Buy-and-Hold Criterion, *J. Finan. and Quant. Anal.,* September, 1968, pp. 327–342.

Fama, Eugene F.: Mandelbrot and the Stable Paretian Hypothesis, *J. Bus.,* October, 1963, pp. 420–429.

Fama, Eugene F.: The Behavior of Stock-Market Prices, *J. Bus.,* January, 1965, pp. 34–105.

Fama, Eugene F.: Portfolio Analysis in a Stable Paretian Market, *Manag. Sci.,* January, 1965, pp. 404–419.

Fama, Eugene F.: Risk, Return and Equilibrium: Some Clarifying Comments, *J. Finan.,* March, 1968, pp. 29–40.

Fama, Eugene F.: Risk and the Evaluation of Pension Fund Performance, in "Measuring the Investment Performance of Pension Funds for the Purpose of Inter-Fund Comparison," Bank Administration Institute, Park Ridge, Ill., 1968, pp. 191–224.

Fama, Eugene F., and Marshall E. Blume: Filter Rules and Stock-Market Trading, *J. Bus.,* January, 1966, pp. 226–241.

Farrar, Donald E.: "The Investment Decision under Uncertainty," Prentice-Hall, Inc., Englewood Cliffs, N.J., 1962.

Feeney, George J., and Donald D. Hester: Stock Market Indices: A Principal Components Analysis, in Donald D. Hester and James Tobin (eds.), "Risk Aversion and Portfolio Choice," John Wiley & Sons, Inc., New York, 1967, pp. 110–138.

Fellner, William: Profit as the Risk-Taker's Surplus: A Probabilistic Theory, *Rev. Econ. and Stat.,* May, 1963, pp. 173–184.

Fisher, Lawrence: Some New Stock-Market Indexes, *J. Bus.,* January, 1966, pp. 191–225.

Fisher, Lawrence, and James H. Lorie: Rates of Return on Investments in Common Stock: The Year-by-Year Record, 1926–1965, *J. Bus.,* July, 1968, pp. 291–316.

Freimer, Marshall, and Myron J. Gordon: Investment Behavior with Utility a Concave Function of Wealth, in Karl Borch and Jan Mossin (eds.), "Risk and Uncertainty," St. Martin's Press, Inc., New York, 1968, pp. 94–109.

Friedman, M., and Leonard J. Savage: The Expected Utility Hypothesis and the Measurability of Utility, *J. Polit. Econ.*, December, 1952, pp. 463–475.

Friend, Irwin, and Douglas Vickers: Portfolio Selection and Investment Performance, *J. Finan.*, September, 1965, pp. 391–415.

Grossman, Herschel I.: Risk Aversion, Financial Intermediation, and the Term Structure of Interest Rates, *J. Finan.*, December, 1967, pp. 611–622.

Hammond, John S., III: Better Decisions with Preference Theory, *Harvard Bus. Rev.*, November-December, 1967, pp. 123–141.

Hanssman, Fred: Probability of Survival as an Investment Criterion, *Manag. Sci.*, September, 1968, pp. 33–48.

Hastie, K. Larry: The Determination of Optimal Investment Policy, *Manag. Sci.*, August, 1967, pp. B757–B774.

Hertz, David B.: Investment Policies that Pay Off, *Harvard Bus. Rev.*, January-February, 1968, pp. 96–108.

Hester, Donald D.: Efficient Portfolios with Short Sales and Margin Holdings, in Donald D. Hester and James Tobin (eds.), "Risk Aversion and Portfolio Choice," John Wiley & Sons, Inc., New York, 1967, pp. 41–50.

Hester, Donald D.: An Empirical Analysis of Risk-taking by Firms in the Savings and Loan Industry, in Karl Borch and Jan Mossin (eds.), "Risk and Uncertainty," St. Martin's Press, Inc., New York, 1968, pp. 33–61.

Hicks, J. R.: Liquidity, *Econ. J.*, December, 1962, pp. 787–802.

Hicks, J. R.: "Critical Essays in Monetary Theory," Oxford University Press, Fair Lawn, N.J., 1967, pp. 103–125.

Hillier, Frederick S.: Derivation of Probabilistic Information for the Evaluation of Risky Investment, *Manag. Sci.*, April, 1963, pp. 443–457.

Hirshleifer, Jack: On the Theory of Optimal Investment Decision, *J. Polit. Econ.*, August, 1958, pp. 329–352.

Hirshleifer, Jack: Risk, the Discount Rate, and Investment Decision, *Amer. Econ. Rev.*, May, 1961, pp. 112–120.

Hirshleifer, Jack: Efficient Allocation of Capital in an Uncertain World, *Amer. Econ. Rev.*, May, 1964, pp. 77–85.

Hirshleifer, Jack: Investment Decision under Uncertainty: Choice-Theoretic Approaches, *Quart. J. Econ.*, November, 1965, pp. 509–536.

Hirshleifer, Jack: Investment Decision under Uncertainty: Applications of the State-Preference Approach, *Quart. J. Econ.*, May, 1966, pp. 252–277.

Horowitz, Ira: The Reward-To-Variability Ratio and Mutual Fund Performance, *J. Bus.*, October, 1966, pp. 485–488.

International Business Machines, Inc.: "General Information Manual —Portfolio Selection: A New Mathematical Approach to

Investment Planning," International Business Machines, Inc., New York, 1962.

International Business Machines, Inc.: "IBM Portfolio Selection Program (IB PS 90)," International Business Machines, Inc., New York, 1962.

Jensen, Michael C.: The Performance of Mutual Funds in the Period 1945–1964, *J. Finan.*, May, 1968, pp. 389–416.

Jensen, Michael C.: "Risk, the Pricing of Capital Assets, and the Evaluation of Investment Portfolios" doctoral dissertation, University of Chicago, Ill., 1968.

Jensen, Michael C.: Risk, the Pricing of Capital Assets, and the Evaluation of Investment Portfolios, *J. Bus.*, April, 1969, pp. 167–247.

Kalymon, Basil A.: Estimation Risk in the Portfolio Selection Model, *Admin. Sci. Tech. Rep. No. 23*, Yale University, New Haven, Conn., May, 1968.

King, Benjamin F.: Market and Industry Factors in Stock Price Behavior, *J. Bus.*, January, 1966, pp. 139–190.

Latané, Henry A.: Criteria for Choice among Risky Ventures, *J. Polit. Econ.*, April, 1959, pp. 144–155.

Latané, Henry A.: Individual Risk Preference in Portfolio Selection, *J. Finan.*, March, 1960, pp. 45–52.

Latané, Henry A.: Investment Criteria—A Three-asset Portfolio Balance Model, *Rev. Econ. and Stat.*, November, 1963, pp. 427–430.

Latané, Henry A., and Donald L. Tuttle: Criteria for Portfolio Building, *J. Finan.*, September, 1967, pp. 359–373.

Lepper, Susan J.: Effects of Alternative Tax Structures on Individuals' Holdings of Financial Assets, in Donald D. Hester and James Tobin (eds.), "Risk Aversion and Portfolio Choice," John Wiley & Sons, Inc., New York, 1967, pp. 51–109.

Lintner, John: The Cost of Capital and Optimal Financing of Corporate Growth, *J. Finan.*, May, 1963, pp. 292–310.

Lintner, John: Optimal Dividends and Corporate Growth under Uncertainty, *Quart. J. Econ.*, February, 1964, pp. 49–95.

Lintner, John: The Valuation of Risk Assets and the Selection of Risky Investments in Stock Portfolios and Capital Budgets, *Rev. Econ. and Stat.*, February, 1965, pp. 13–37.

Lintner, John: Security Prices, Risk and Maximal Gains from Diversification, *J. Finan.*, December, 1965, pp. 587–615.

Lorie, James H.: Some Comments on Recent Quantitative and Formal Research on the Stock Market, *J. Bus.*, January, 1966, pp. 107–110.

Maccrimmon, Kenneth R.: Descriptive and Normative Implications of the Decision-Theory Postulates, in Karl Borch and Jan

Mossin (eds.), "Risk and Uncertainty," St. Martin's Press, Inc., New York, 1968, pp. 3–23.

Mandelbrot, Benoit: The Variation of Certain Speculative Prices, *J. Bus.*, October, 1963, pp. 394–419.

Mandelbrot, Benoit: Forecasts of Future Prices, Unbiased Markets, and Martingale Models, *J. Bus.*, January, 1966, pp. 242–255.

Mandelbrot, Benoit: The Variation of Some Other Speculative Prices, *J. Bus.*, October, 1967, pp. 393–413.

Mandelbrot, Benoit, and Howard M. Taylor: On the Distribution of Stock Price Differentials, *Operations Res.*, November-December, 1967, pp. 1057–1062.

Markowitz, Harry: The Utility of Wealth, *J. Polit. Econ.*, 1952, pp. 151–158.

Markowitz, Harry: Portfolio Selection, *J. Finan.*, March, 1952, pp. 77–91.

Markowitz, Harry: The Optimization of a Quadratic Function Subject to Linear Constraints, *Naval Res. Logistics Quart.*, March-June, 1956, pp. 111–133.

Markowitz, Harry: "Portfolio Selection: Efficient Diversification of Investments," John Wiley & Sons, Inc., New York, 1959.

Massé, Pierre: "Optimal Investment Decisions: Rules for Action and Criteria for Choice," Prentice-Hall, Inc., Englewood Cliffs, N.J., 1962.

Michaelsen, Jacob B.: The Term Structure of Interest Rates and Holding-Period Yields on Government Securities, *J. Finan.*, September, 1965, pp. 444–463.

Michaelsen, Jacob B., and Robert C. Goshay: Portfolio Selection in Financial Intermediaries: A New Approach, *J. Finan. and Quant. Anal.*, June, 1967, pp. 166–199.

Modigliani, Franco, and Merton H. Miller: The Cost of Capital, Corporation Finance and the Theory of Investment, *Amer. Econ. Rev.*, June, 1958, pp. 261–297.

Modigliani, Franco, and Merton H. Miller: Corporate Income Taxes and the Cost of Capital: A Correction, *Amer. Econ. Rev.*, June, 1963, pp. 433–443.

Moore, Basil J.: "An Introduction to the Theory of Finance: Assetholder Behavior under Uncertainty," The Free Press of Glencoe, New York, 1968.

Mossin, Jan: Equilibrium in a Capital Asset Market, *Econometrica*, October, 1966, pp. 768–783.

Mossin, Jan: Optimal Multiperiod Portfolio Policies, *J. Bus.*, April, 1968, pp. 215–229.

Myers, Stewart C.: "Procedures for Capital Budgeting Under Uncertainty," Alfred P. Sloan School of Management Paper 259–67, M.I.T., Cambridge, Mass., May, 1967.

Myers, Stewart C.: "A Time-State Preference Model of Security Valuation," Alfred P. Sloan School of Management Paper 265–67, M.I.T., Cambridge, Mass., June, 1967.

Naslund, Bertil: A Model of Capital Budgeting under Risk, *J. Bus.*, April, 1966, pp. 257–271.

Naslund, Bertil, and Andrew Whinston: A Model of Multi-period Investment under Uncertainty, *Manag. Sci.*, January, 1962, pp. 184–200.

Osborne, M. F. M.: Brownian Motion in the Stock Market, *Operations Res.*, March-April, 1959, pp. 145–173.

Phelps, Edmund S.: The Accumulation of Risky Capital: A Sequential Utility Analysis, in Donald D. Hester and James Tobin (eds.), "Risk Aversion and Portfolio Choice," John Wiley & Sons, Inc., New York, 1967, pp. 139–153.

Pogue, Jerry A.: "An Adaptive Model for Investment Management," doctoral dissertation, Carnegie Institute of Technology, Pittsburgh, Pa., July, 1967.

Pratt, John W.: Risk Aversion in the Small and in the Large, *Econometrica*, January-April, 1964, pp. 122–136.

Pratt, John W., Howard Raiffa, and Robert Schlaifer: The Foundations of Decisions under Uncertainty: An Elementary Exposition, *Amer. Stat. Assoc. J.*, June, 1964, pp. 353–375.

Pratt, Shannon P.: "Relationship Between Risk and Rate of Return for Common Stocks," doctoral dissertation, Dept. of Business Administration, Indiana University, Bloomington, Ind. 1966.

Pye, Gordon: Portfolio Selection and Security Prices, *Rev. Econ. and Stat.*, February, 1967, pp. 111–115.

Radner, Roy: Competitive Equilibrium under Uncertainty, *Econometrica*, January, 1968, pp. 821–824.

Raiffa, Howard: "Decision Analysis: Introductory Lectures on Choices under Uncertainty," Addison-Wesley Publishing Company, Inc., Reading, Mass., 1968.

Renshaw, Edward F.: Portfolio Balance Models in Perspective: Some Generalizations that Can Be Derived from the Two-asset Case, *J. Finan. and Quant. Anal.*, June, 1967, pp. 123–149.

Renshaw, Edward F.: The Random Walk Hypothesis, Performance Management, and Portfolio Theory, *Finan. Analysts' J.*, March-April, 1968, pp. 1–6.

Renwick, Fred B.: Theory of Investment Behavior and Empirical Analysis of Stock Market Price Relatives, *Manag. Sci.*, September, 1968, pp. 57–71.

Richter, M. K.: Cardinal Utility, Portfolio Selection and Taxation, *Rev. Econ. Studies*, June, 1960, pp. 152–166.

Robichek, Alexander A., and Stewart C. Meyers: "Optimal Financing

Decisions," Prentice-Hall, Inc., Englewood Cliffs, N.J., 1965.

Robichek, Alexander A., and Stewart C. Myers: Valuation of the Firm: Effects of Uncertainty in the Market Context, *J. Finan.*, May, 1966, pp. 215–227.

Rosett, Richard N.: Estimating the Utility of Wealth from Call Options Data, in Donald D. Hester and James Tobin (eds.), "Risk Aversion and Portfolio Choice," John Wiley & Sons, Inc., New York, 1967, pp. 154–169.

Rosett, Richard N.: Measuring the Perception of Risk, in Karl Borch and Jan Mossin (eds.), "Risk and Uncertainty," St. Martin's Press, Inc., New York, 1968, pp. 68–84.

Roy, A. D.: Safety First and the Holding of Assets, *Econometrica*, July, 1952, pp. 431–449.

Royama, Shoichi, and Koichi Hamada: Substitution and Complementarity in the Choice of Risky Assets, in Donald D. Hester and James Tobin (eds.), "Risk Aversion and Portfolio Choice," John Wiley & Sons, Inc., New York, 1967, pp. 27–40.

Samuelson, Paul A.: Proof that Properly Anticipated Prices Fluctuate Randomly, *Ind. Manag. Rev.*, Spring, 1965, pp. 41–49.

Samuelson, Paul A.: General Proof that Diversification Pays, *J. Finan. and Quant. Anal.*, March, 1967, pp. 1–13.

Samuelson, Paul A.: Efficient Portfolio Selection for Pareto-Levy Investments, *J. Finan. and Quant. Anal.*, June, 1967, pp. 107–122.

Schrock, Nicholas W.: Asset Choice under Uncertainty with Borrowing Introduced, *West. Econ. J.*, March, 1967, pp. 201–209.

Sharpe, William F.: A Simplified Model for Portfolio Analysis, *Manag. Sci.*, January, 1963, pp. 277–293.

Sharpe, William F.: Mathematical Investment Portfolio Selection: Some Early Results, *Univ. Washington Bus. Rev.*, April, 1963, pp. 14–27.

Sharpe, William F.: Capital Asset Prices: A Theory of Market Equilibrium under Conditions of Risk, *J. Finan.*, September, 1964, pp. 425–442.

Sharpe, William F.: Risk Aversion in the Stock Market: Some Empirical Evidence, *J. Finan.*, September, 1965, pp. 416–422.

Sharpe, William F.: Mutual Fund Performance, *J. Bus.*, January, 1966, pp. 119–138.

Sharpe, William F.: A Linear Programming Algorithm for Mutual Fund Portfolio. Selection, *Manag. Sci.*, March, 1967, pp. 499–510.

Sharpe, William F.: Portfolio Analysis, *J. Finan. and Quant. Anal.*, June, 1967, pp. 76–84.

Sharpe, William F.: Mutual Fund Performance and the Theory of Capital Asset Pricing: Reply, *J. Bus.*, April, 1968, pp. 235–236.

Shelton, John P.: The Value Line Contest: A Test of the Predictability of Stock Price Changes, *J. Bus.*, July, 1967, pp. 251–269.

Smith, Keith V.: Alternative Procedures for Revising Investment Portfolios, *J. Finan. and Quant. Anal.*, December, 1968, pp. 371–403.

Soldofsky, Robert M.: Yield-Risk Performance Measurements, *Finan. Analysts' J.*, September-October, 1968, pp. 130–139.

Stigler, George J.: The Development of Utility Theory, *J. Polit. Econ.*, August, 1950, pp. 307–327.

Stigler, George J.: The Development of Utility Theory, *J. Polit. Econ.*, October, 1950, pp. 373–396.

Tobin, James: Liquidity Preference as Behavior Towards Risk, *Rev. Econ. Studies*, February, 1958, pp. 65–86.

Treynor, Jack L.: How To Rate Management of Investment Funds, *Harvard Bus. Rev.*, January-February, 1965, pp. 63–75.

Treynor, Jack L., and Kay K. Mazuy: Can Mutual Funds Outguess the Market?, *Harvard Bus. Rev.*, July-August, 1966, pp. 131–136.

Treynor, Jack L., William W. Priest, Jr., Lawrence Fisher, and Catherine A. Higgins: Using Portfolio Composition to Estimate Risk, *Finan. Analysts' J.*, September-October, 1968, pp. 93–100.

Van Horne, James: Capital-Budgeting Decisions Involving Combinations of Risky Investments, *Manag. Sci.*, October, 1966, pp. B84–B92.

Wallingford, Buckner A., II: A Survey and Comparison of Portfolio Selection Models, *J. Finan. and Quant. Anal.*, June, 1967, pp. 85–106.

West, Richard R.: Mutual Fund Performance and the Theory of Capital Asset Pricing: Some Comments, *J. Bus.*, April, 1968, pp. 230–234.

Yaari, Menahem E.: Convexity in the Theory of Choice under Risk, *Quart. J. Econ.*, May, 1965, pp. 278–290.

INDEX

LETTERS ON SOUTH AMERICA (VOLUME 3); COMPRISING TRAVELS ON THE BANKS OF THE PARANÁ AND RIO DE LA PLATA. BY J.P. AND W.P. ROBERTSON

LETTERS ON SOUTH AMERICA (VOLUME 3); COMPRISING TRAVELS ON THE BANKS OF THE PARANÁ AND RIO DE LA PLATA. BY J.P. AND W.P. ROBERTSON

John Parish Robertson and William Parish Robertson

www.General-Books.net

Publication Data:

Title: Letters on South America
Subtitle: Comprising Travels on the Banks of the Paraná and Rio De La Plata. by J.p. and W.p. Robertson
Volume: 3
Author: John Parish Robertson and William Parish Robertson
General Books publication date: 2009
Original publication date: 1843

CONTENTS

SECTION 1

LETTERS ON SOUTH AMERICA.
LETTER XLIV.
J. P. R. toGeneralMiller.

A Leak sprung – Departure from Buenos Ay res for England – Hopes and Anticipations – Arrival at the Isle of Wight – My Impressions of an English Hotel – Departure from Cowes – Bath Society – Arrival in London – London Society.

London, 1842.

Everythingwas now prepared for my sailing for England. A fine large ship called the Friends was chartered for me, and laden with a rich cargo. A sumptuous dinner was partaken of (for John Bull can manage nothing without a dinner) by my Buenos Ayres acquaintance, English and South American; when, after dinner, at the moment of my health and a prosperous voyage being proposed, in, upon the company, with lugubrious countenance, walked the first officer of the good ship Friends, and whispered in the ear of the captain (Stephenson,) who was

VOL. III. B

2 DEPARTURE FOR ENGLAND.

sitting near me, that the ship had sprung a leak, and was making water very fast. Full of alarm, the captain arose from the table, went onboard, and found it really to be so, I was petrified. My luggage, provisions, servant, were all on board; and my own longing heart, palpitating with the anticipated joy of revisiting my native country, was stopped short in its heavings, as if congealed. I never thought how much better it was that the leak should have been discovered in port than in the midst of the Atlantic, where, had it been sprung, we must have furnished a meal for the monsters of the deep.

In litigation, discharging of the cargo, and unshipping of it to another vessel, three months elapsed; but at length, after one more parting dinner and not a few more last words, I embarked in a fine vessel called the Elizabeth, Captain Swinburne, laden with the fruits of Paraguay and Corrientes speculation.

This was in the year 1817- I had been absent fiom my own country nearly nine years; and I had grown up, during that time, from boyhood to man's estate. I had left. Scotland a stripling of fourteen, in pursuit, like most other people(*especially*Scotchmen), of that goddess Fortune, who receives the

DEPARTURE FOR ENGLAND., i

addresses of all men, dupes many, disappoints thousands, and ruins tens of thousands more, because, not content with what she has granted them, they aspire at favours which she is so far from granting, that to mark her disapprobation of the suit, she brings about the total overthrow of the suitor.

At the period of which I speak, she had been propitious to me; for, in spite of Francia and Arli- guenos, I had been so far successful in life as not only to have laid a good foundation for the future, but to attract the flattering attention and patronage of an old and rich relation, who never having discovered any particular merit in me while I was jogging along the common-place path of mediocrity, or climbing up the steeps of perilous adventure, found out, when I could return to England in comparative independence, that I was, as he styled it, " a chip of the old block." This relative – an old gentleman of large fortune, fond of fashionable society, and intimate with many of the titled members of it – invited me to come home, offered me his house, and promised to furnish me with first- rate introductions to many great personages, as well in business as out of it.

4 HOPES AND ANTICIPATIONS.

I was elated at the prospect of emerging from the back settlements of South America to spring forth into the enjoyment of polished society and of solid comfort in this country. I was overjoyed, too, at the anticipation of meeting parents, brothers, sisters, and the schoolboy companions of my earliest days. Many of these I had long made to stare at the wondrous tales, from time to time transmitted home, of my adventures by flood and field; but what was this to the meetings, and embraces, and fire-side conversations, which I now anticipated, as I tried to imagine how most of them would look under the transitions from the state of boys and girls to, now, that of men and women. It is nothing to witness this transition, as by slow degrees it takes place under our every day's observation; but to find all at once, – in a night, as it were, – the boy, your brother, grown to man's estate, or the little girl, your sister or cousin, become a mother, gives rise to very complicated feelings, bewilders your brain, and turns almost to scepticism the very evidence of your senses.

At length, after a ten weeks' passage, we were boarded, in the English Channel, during a thick fog, by a pilot, who told us we were not far from the
ARRIVAL AT THE ISLE OF WIGHT. D
Isle of Wight. The mist cleared away, and presently that beautiful spot came in view. As my eye wandered over its smooth and swardy downs covered with sheep, and as I contemplated the rural industry and cultivation of the valleys and plains – the neat cottages, the cheerful gardens, and sturdy swains in all directions pursuing their labours in the fields, upon the lawns, and in the shrubberies – I recognized at once what admirable handmaidens industry and cultivation are to Nature, when they dress and do not*overdress*her.

When we had sailed through that curious channel the Needles, – forts, harbours, men-of-war, noblemen's and gentlemen's yachts, boats, skiffs, hale-looking soldiers and sailors performing their respective duties under the unfurled standard of Old England, all strikingly contrasted with the scenes and objects to which I had been so long accustomed. We had lately been at war, but the wooden walls were still manned, the ramparts lined with red coats and glittering muskets; while the hammers of the arsenals, the din of cannon, the clanging of bugles, the beating of drums, and the music of shrill fifes, gave a stirring and animated effect to the whole.
O THE ISLE OF WIGHT.
Just as we came slowly up channel, the wind failed us; but having determined not to be a moment on board of ship when I could prosecute my journey by terra firma, I landed at Cowes. Strange as it may seem, I did so chiefly for this reason, that the Isle of Wight being called the garden of England, I thought I must not expect to see any such beautiful scenery thenceforward. In this respect, however, I soon found out my mistake; but for the time being I was confirmed in my belief that I was in fairy land.

No sooner had I got ashore than half a dozen active fellows wrangled in polite officiousness for the honour of carrying my luggage, while three smart-looking gentlemen, with damask napkins in their hands, contended for the pleasure of conducting me to their respective houses. I desired to be led to that which was pointed out to me as the largest and best. My first impression on entering it was that I had certainly mistaken some nobleman's mansion for a hostelry. The well-dressed males and females that were buzzing about the stairs covered with Brussels carpets; the splendid drawing-room into which I was introduced; the capacious hall from which I had come up, with its
MYIMPRESSIONSOFANENGLISHHOTEL.7
paraphernalia of lamps, pictures, mahogany tables, and livery servants, seated in waiting on their masters, – all surpassed any notion or remembrance I ever had of a hotel. What greatly added to keep up the delusion was, that I could not discriminate between the landlady and her servants, nor the landlord, his waiters, and other well-dressed personages coming and going to and fro. I took them all for ladies and gentlemen, even after the waiters had laid my table with plate and crystal over a damask table-cloth, and after a pretty, captivating, and genteel fair one, with rosy cheeks and auburn curls, a plated candlestick and a wax taper in her hand, had conducted me to a capacious room, which she told me was my bed-room. It was curtained, festooned, carpeted, and furnished with a bed of state. Everything was

richer and better than anything I had seen in the houses of the richest men in South America. How was I *possibly* to connect the few rude inns there, or the Pampa post-houses, with the notion of their being all, like the Cowes hotel, mere houses for the accommodation of travellers. This could not be; for the first three or four hours which I spent in the hotel at Cowes, I might as well have been in a magical or enchanted

8 AN ENGLISH HOTEL.

castle. I came bowing into the drawing-room, and kept calling the waiter " Sir," and the chambermaid " Ma'am," till a naval officer, who had been my only fellow-passenger home, by his continual remonstrances and ludicrous appeals to my judgment, brought objects down to me a little more in their real forms and dimensions. After all, however, as I travelled about, and came to many more splendid hotels than that at Cowes, I was for a few days like a man who has been blind and by the removal of a cataract begins gradually to distinguish one object from another.

I ordered a conveyance to Newport, and the landlord, with a bow, said, " Yes, Sir, a chaise and pair, I suppose.5' I could never reconcile it to myself, on my first arrival from the Pampas, to be driven by a pair of horses. I ordered four; and when the Cowes carriage was ready for my reception, the landlord and landlady, waiters, chambermaids, grooms, and a little crowd at the door, kept bowing and wondering who I could be. When two smart postillions, in buckskins, sky-blue jackets, and black caps, scampered off with me, how was it possible I should conceive that the persons around me constituted only the living machinery of hotels

DEPARTURE FROM COWES. 9

like those in Buenos Ayres, or that driving was like that of the tatterdemalion gauchos of the plains! I found everything at the hotels very cheap, considering the luxury with which it was provided, and everything on the road very reasonable, except driving post with four horses. I, therefore, soon reduced mine to a pair; and only took to four again by travelling in the mails or stages, after I had become a little more knowing in the ways of the road. From Portsmouth I drove to Bath, where I was received by the old gentleman, my relative, with all the cordiality, and even distinction, imaginable. I was located in two of the best rooms of his mansion, drove out with him in his barouche and four, had the command of an excellent cellar, the favour of the German butler and French cook, the attendance of grooms and footmen, an introduction to the best society in Bath, as well resident as merely drinkers of the waters, or passengers en route for other places. The old gentleman knew them all, but was especially delighted with those who would play whist at his house, read the private letters he received from his friends, frank those he wrote in reply, and subscribe to the Penitentiary. I had the honour of losing many a

10 BTH SOCIETY.

guinea to expert dowagers and to some of the other sex more uncommonly expert at "*sauter la coupe.*"This is a genteel designation of the game called, in ordinary parlance, " beggar my neighbour." The old gentleman was generally a winner; and I cannot but say that he seemed not less pleased than some of his titled associates to lay his hands upon the doubloons of the new arrival from South America. I found my living and society, though both agreeable, yet rather expensive; and as I had now spent a month in idleness and frivolous dissipation, gained thus a little knowledge of the genteel slaves and fashionable devotees of superficial society, I prepared to change my quarters for more stirring and varied scenes.

Furnished with letters of introduction for all parts of the country, and especially for London, I, after dinner, got into the Bath coach, and breakfasted next morning at Brunei's hotel, to which I had been directed by the old gentleman to go, as it was, lie said, " a place of resort for foreigners of distinction." I did not find it exactly such; but a very good Frenchified retreat for foreigners of*no*distinction, who occupied their own suite of apartments.

From hence, as from a central point, I sallied ARRIVAL IN LONDON. 11 forth to gaze upon the endless wonders of overgrown London. For days and nights I was lost, whenever I walked beyond the precincts of my own hotel in Leicester Square; and I consequently moved about to all great distances in a glass coach, with Mogg's map of London outspread upon my knee. It was also consulted for many a day in my chamber before I could master the topography of the huge metropolis, so as to proceed on foot with tolerable certainty from one place to another.

Meantime I was becoming, unconsciously, a citizen of London, – spending my mornings chiefly among the great men of the East, and my evenings among those of the West. Many a merchant and banker did I see making himself a slave, in an obscure counting-house, in the fore part of the day, that he might enjoy, in the evening, the substantial comforts or refined luxuries of a well-appointed establishment in the purlieus of Portland Place, Harley Street, or Wimpole Street, Cavendish, Berkeley, or even Grosvenor Square.

His sons had been educated at the universities; and his daughters were not only accomplished in manners and the fashionable agremens and attain12 LONDON SO-CIETY.

ments which render society gay and agreeable, but they possessed many of those attractive and perhaps more solid charms which, combining vivacity of imagination with a fund of useful knowledge and reflection, are called forth in society, at once to embellish and improve it. Then for the table, equipages, horses, servants, and general style of your Grosvenor Square and Piccadilly merchant or banker; they were all recherches, – assimilating, some of them, to those of the nobility, and many of them going beyond even these.

I found*grades*of society and exclusive circles among the merchants and bankers, as well as among the oligarchy; and the terms of admission of their city peers to the former were often more stringent and scrutinizing than those of the nobility in the case of gentlemen of every rank and denomination, so long as they*were*gentlemen. High and exclusive as in this country the nobility are, they are by no means the only class of society that as much as possible keep within their own sphere. The truth is, that we are as much a nation of castes as the Chinese, not subject, to be sure, to the same despotism which crushes them, but quite

ENGLISH SOCIETY. 13

as jealous as they are of losing caste in society. From the peer to the petty tradesman, how many social circles there are, all animated by one principle, – that of treading upon the heels of their betters, and of keeping their inferiors at a distance. The tradesman feels honoured by the company of the shopman; the shopman by that of the inferior merchant; and he by the society of a man of higher standing in the same vocation.

It is, however, a gratifying fact that great good sense and knowledge of the world distinguish the *generality* of our higher traders in England, and make them not only an intelligent but a well-bred and agreeable community. Yet Heaven defend us, on the other hand, from the company of your purse- proud man of business, and his more stately spouse. They have between them more airs to play off upon their humbler guests, more ostentatious display, and more tiresome egotism, all tending to mark their distinguished place in society, than any ten of the nobility put together. And yet nothing more frequent than to hear your City aristocrat of this class cry shame upon the pride and pomp and *exclu- siveness* of your peer, who is not in spirit one whit14 ENGLISH SOCIETY.

more of an aristocrat, though in a different *sphere* to be sure, and with the claims of respect due to *education* and manners, in addition to those of rank and fortune.

Always your's,

J. P. R.

2

SECTION 2

LETTER XLV.

J. P. R. toGeneralMiller.

The Difficulty in giving News about England and Scotland – Arrival at the Home of my Boyhood – A Scotch Postilion – A Family roused – Introduction to Strangers – The Recognition – New Relations – My Mother – A Scotch Breakfast – The Lion of the Morning – A Confession – Edinburgh Society – Auld Reekie not Athens – The Calton Hill – Leith Walk – Arthur's Seat – Salisbury Craigs – The Pentland Hills – Surrounding Scenery – Edinburgh Castle – Holyrood House or Palace – Neighbourhood of the Abbey – The New Town of Edinburgh – Inhabitants of the New Town – Their Society – A Bon-Mot

*London,*1842.

WhenI tell you that my preceding letter, this one, and another will contain all I have for the present to say on England and Scotland, you will not expect much to be said in detail of these countries. They are too well known, – they have been loo frequently traversed, to admit of my saying much of them, especially as South America is the country on which we have promised chiefly to write. In England, steam by sea and steam by land, newspapers, periodicals, reviews, novels, books of travel, steamboat companions, Macadamized roads, light coaches, fast mails, and flying Posts, together with reports

16 ARRIVAL AT THE HOME OF MY BOYHOOD.

of committees, debates in Parliament, public dinners, and public meetings to deliberate on every topic under the sun, all warn me that there is already almost enough said, much more written than is read, of England, its habits, society, and peculiarities.

After greatly multiplying acquaintance, friends, and correspondents in London, and laying there the foundation for my future operations in this country and South America, I started for Scotland.

At five o'clock in the mornincr I drove in a chaise

from the mail-coach office, in Edinburgh, to the residence, a little way in the country, of my parents. Less precipitation, – that is to say, my having lain down three hours to sleep, after travelling three successive nights in the mail, would have refreshed me, and spared the inmates of my paternal home the shock and confusion of being unexpectedly roused from bed at so unseemly an hour as five o'clock, A. m. All my loud knocks, and all my impatient rings, as my hand passed in rapid succession from the knocker to the bell, and back again from the bell to the knocker, brought no one to my relief. The postilion thought that a little delay in my visit would have answered all purposesA SCOTCH POSTILION. 17

better, for he said to*me*, "Od, sir, I'm thinkin' y'ere may be frae far awa, an diuna ken the customs o' Scotlan'. Its only y'ere puir labourin' bodies that's afit at this hour. As for yere gentry, aye an' even yere gentry's man-servants an' maids, they'll no be stirrin' till acht or nine o'clock Depend upon't, they'll tak' us for nae better than we ocht to be. Let me advise ye, sir, to gang awa back to the Black Bull an' tak' a nap, an' I'll bring ye here at ten. Ye may be sure ye'll be time enough, an' to spare, for them; an' maybe ye'll be welcomer than ye wad be the noo."

Neither the postilion's remonstrance and advice, nor his insinuation toward the close of his harangue, had much weight with me. They seemed to have as little with himself, after I told him that this was the house of my parents, and that I had been nine years absent from it; for instantly he redoubled the knock, and rang so effectually, that a little urchin of a foot-boy asked from the area, " Wha's there?" while, at the same moment, two female servants peeped forth from an attic with their hair in papers, nightcaps, and what in Scotland are appropriately termed short gowns, for they reach only to the waist. Like the foot-boy, they

18 A FAMILY ROUSED.

too called aloud, " Wha's there?" till perceiving the carriage at the door, and concluding that the expected stranger had arrived, they withdrew instantly, the one assuring the other, that " as shure's death, that was the young maister." They shut the window with great impetus; and presently all was stir, bustle, and trepidation within.

In the domestic attempts, upon such an emergency, to do everything at once, that which I thought should have been attended to first was thought of last: I mean the door. It was full five minutes before it was opened; and*when*opened, I thought I must have come to the wrong house after all, – for in the lobby there stood a group to receive me, of which I neither knew a single face nor recognized a single figure. The servants were strangers to me; a grown up youth of sixteen I thought I had never seen; one tall lady and one rather petite were alike unknown; and two females of about eighteen and twenty, who were hurrying down stairs, were perfect incognitas. An old gentleman in his dressing-gown, bent down with infirmity and a grievous cough, I recognized not at all; and a lady verging to corpulence, with locks turning grey, I fancied must be some Scotch dowager on a visit

THE RECOGNITION. 19

to the family. Yet I was in the very midst of my own nearest relations; and soon was I convinced of this, – not by the testimony of my eyes, for they kept deceiving me more and more, but by that of my hearing, which, when the rather corpulent lady took me in her arms, and with a flood of tears sobbed aloud, " My own dear boy," would have made me stake the life I had received from her against a pin that it was no dowager, but my own good mother. Then the old gentleman's voice announced him to be my father; and that of the youth, my youngest brother. Of the four young ladies I was sure that two were my sisters; but which two (for I had no more sisters) I could not tell: all the four were very much alike, and their voices identical. I eagerly inquired which was one and which another; and of the other two, which of my cousins I had the pleasure of seeing. By this time the group had reached the breakfast- parlour. A strange glow of novel sensations, and a never-ending repetition of mutual salutations and welcomes followed.

There were yet two to be added to the family party, – two little urchins of curly-haired cousins; and one of the servants, rather " pawky," as they

20 NEW RELATIONS.

say in Scotland, brought them down stairs, the one beating a fine brass-barreled drum, and the other blowing shrill discordance through a child's whistle. In they marched; but seeing a stranger, stopped their music; nor would they resume it, till I had made myself familiar with them by caressing and calling them by their names, Archy and Geordie. A happier little circle, especially at that time of the morning, it would not have been easy to find near us. Sleep was banished; and the process of familiarizing ourselves with each other proceeded with great rapidity. I was glad to see my sisters rather pretty, – my cousins charming; and most of all to find, that so far from *missing* any one whom I expected to see, I had made the acquaintance of two additional members of the family.

By degrees, the young ladies retired to make their toilets; and the old gentleman, rather fastidious at his, went to show that he had not forgotten his youthful days.

The old lady alone remained; and her anxiety was equally divided between getting all the news about her son that was still in South America, and seeing a proper breakfast laid out for the new-comer.

A SCOTCH BREAKFAST. 21

Every one knows what a Scotch breakfast is: tea piping hot, coffee redolent of the bean, rich cream, hot rolls, warm toast, oaten cakes as thin as a wafer, barley scons, kipper salmon, Finnin haddocks, cold game, cold ham, cold beef, brawn, eggs, honey, jellies, marmalade, sausages, with other et ceteras. The dram, it must be allowed, is mostly confined to the highlands; but in the present case, my mother insisted upon its being introduced, as she was sure I must be cold after my long ride.

At nine o'clock the family party assembled over many of the specified dainties. I was of course the lion of the morning; and experienced the usual fate of your travelling lions, – that is, everything I said that was really true I could see met with rather an incredulous reception, while the little embellishments I introduced, with a grave face, in the Mun- chausen style, were treasured up with avidity as exhibiting singular modes of life and manners.

This much shall suffice on family affairs. They constitute a topic too exclusively interesting to the parties immediately concerned, to admit a hope of their properly estimating the comparative coolness or weariness with which others constrain themselves, from pure good breeding, to listen to them with

Z2EDINBURGH SOCIETY.

their outward ears, while their inner man is passing sentence, " how tiresome! "

" How," asks an acute moralist, " can you expect others to be more interested in your affairs than you are in theirs?" I confess I see not how we should; and I therefore, at once, bid adieu to*my*father and*my*mother, to*my*pretty sisters and*my*charming cousins, confessing that there is nothing romantic enough in the modern survivors of the clan to serve as a foundation for fiction, and still less that would lend the aid of novelty or interest even to sober truth.

The first day of my arrival I gave up entirely to the enjoyments of home. The next I sallied forth to deliver the various credentials and introductions with which I had been furnished for several gentlemen of the faculties of law, medicine, and divinity. I had also letters introductory to some highland lairds, then sojourning in the metropolis, and to some of their peers the lowland landlords, who seemed, however, to have little in common with their northern brethren of the hills, except that they were both owners of land.

As I drove from door to door, leaving my card, and some friend's certificate that I was entitled

AULDREEKIENOTATHENS.23

to a dinner, I could not but admire the magnificent site, and many of the fine buildings of that Edina, which her too partial devotees have called " Modern Athens." The very ruins of Athens forbid us, however, to identify her, as a city, with the capital of the North; while the polished acuteness, the deep reasoning, the classical refinement, the famed exploits, the overwhelming oratory, the fascinating philosophy, the ennobling poetry, the marble chiseled into life by little short of the magical inspiration of the sculptor, with all the pomp and circumstance of triumphal processions and athletic contests, contrasts in every way advantageously for the capital of Greece.

There is one noble spot in Edinburgh, which, whether you consider its central and commanding position, or the beauty, diversity, and extent of the romantic country around, I fancy is unequalled in the world: that spot is the Calton Hill. As I wended my way in circular progression, from the base to the apex of this magnificent cone, there opened up to my view, at every step and turning, new and enchanting beauties, – diversified in kind, yet all blending into one harmonious whole. As the eye swept the horizon on one side, it beheld the

24 LEITH WALK.

sheeny Forth laving far and wide the fertile coast of Fife, rich in crops, and wood, and busy villages; while on the other, it floated into the harbours of Midlothian and the adjacent counties the ships and barks of the weather-beaten sons of Caledonia. Skiffs and yachts bounded over the ever-breaking waves; and the port of Leith, as ships left and entered, as furnaces blazed, as loud hammers rang on the anvil, and as glass-houses sent forth their vapour and smoke, presented a stirring spectacle. The slope between Edinburgh and Leith is richly cultivated on each side of what is called "*Leith Walk,*"and displays a succession of nursery grounds and gardens, alike celebrated for the beauty they display and for the science with which, from the sturdy oak to the tender exotics, all the trees and shrubs of the forest are reared. There are no gardeners, I believe, who surpass the Scotch, whether in the laying-out of grounds or in the successful treatment of the young plantations which are to adorn them.

Turning from my view of the Forth, my eye rested on that singular geological phenomenon, Salisbury Craig; I glanced from thence at Arthur's Seat, to the envied pinnacle of which I had so often

PENTLAND HILLS. 25

climbed in youthful sport. The Pentland Hills became the next remarkable object of contemplation, sweeping, in the form of an amphitheatre, nearly one-fourth of the whole splendid circle formed by Nature around the Calton Hill. From the base of the Pentlands to the suburbs of the metropolis there intervenes as rich a country, and as finely cultivated, as can well, in such a latitude and climate, be conceived. There is a deficiency of wood, except upon the noblemen's and gentlemen's estates which adorn this part of the land; while the rest of the country, laid out in fields, exhibiting exquisite specimens of husbandry, and yielding luxuriant crops, is studded with villages and village-spires, and enriched with streams, which now wend their secluded way through woods and parks and lawns, and anon emerge, for the more general gratification of those who admire them, into the open country; from thence frisking and basking and rolling down their waters, for a season, in the sun, they seek again their more favourite retreat – the shade. There were only wanting, in order to make the beauty of this part of the scene complete, the fine hedge-row trees and green fences, which in England everywhere take from the country not only all appear-

VOL. III. C

26 EDINBURGH CASTLE.

ance of nakedness, but invest it with a gorgeousness not the less in place that it is at once ornamental and useful. In Scotland, there are few hedge-row trees; and the fences are cold, unrural, clumsy- looking fences, called dykes, or bare stone walls.

Having thus, from my commanding position, surveyed all the*distant*objects within eye-range, I drew a smaller optical circle around me, which only enclosed the city itself and its immediate environs. First and most prominent of all, nodding, or rather tottering, on a stupendous and nearly perpendicular rock, stood the Castle, as if to show how soon, if subjected to the ordeal of modern projectiles, it would fall from its high estate. On our first glance we are arrested by its grandeur, – but on a second view we are struck by its weakness. Leaving the question of its military insignificance out of the case, I was sorry not to be able to admire even its architectural structure; for some not over-skilful patcher of edifices dilapidated or of insufficient dimensions, has stuck on the feudal building two modern tenements, to answer as barracks, and built them exactly in the *"flat*style," – that is, story above story till you get into the clouds.

From this incongruous, though nobly-situated

HOLYROOD HOUSE OR PALACE. 27

pile of stones, I traced, with my eye, the prodigiously high piles of houses which flanked the north side of the High Street upon which the Castle frowned, as if threatening destruction to the Tron Church and Tolbooth as the chief obstacles to its guns reaching Holyrood.

Holyrood House, – that dark and dreary abode of royalty, – and its once beautiful, but now ruined Abbey, lay under my feet. As I looked upon them from the Calton Hill, as I saw the wretched buildings and filthy inhabitants all around, and as I remembered that these had been the residences and purlieus of the highest nobility, I could not but think, that the removal of a king, – his court, his nobles, and retainers, – is a sore calamity to the nation deserted; of which, immediately and inevitably, the whole of the rack-rental passes through the hands of stewards into the pockets of the landlords, to be spent on a foreign soil.

Turning from the neighbourhood of the Abbey, I saw houses built upon precipices to the awful height of fourteen stories, and streets running under bridges, from which it bewildered the eye to look down upon the inhabitants, diminished to the size of Lilliputians below.

28 THE NEW TOWN OF EDINBURGH.

Yet some of the buildings of those streets rose high above one of the bridges; the communication between the subterranean inhabitants and those of the upper regions being effected by dark and interminable flights of stone stairs, conducting you all the way down into *"flats,"* or floors, which are the abodes of wretched females, who thus seek to hide their shame from the glare of day.

But the truly magnificent part of Edinburgh is the New Town, – a city of itself, which has been appropriately called the City of Palaces. Whether its situation or its fine buildings of free-stone be considered, the magnificent width of its streets, its ornamental gardens, its noble prospects, its contrast with the fantastic piles of the Old Town, from which the New is completely and distinctly separated by the " Mound," it is impossible not to be struck with admiration of it.

You expect, and you are not disappointed, to meet with a quite different class of inhabitants in the Old and the New Town. Those of the former are generally shopkeepers, tradesmen, handicraftsmen, and, in certain neighbourhoods, a noisy, chattering, and filthy rabble from the Highlands.

In the New Town you have the Lowland lairds,

INHABITANTS OF THE NEW TOWN. SW

with their ladies, equipages, and footmen. Unable to make a show in London, the laird is content for a season to be the leader of the ton in Edinburgh: and most agreeable people the better class of the Lowland lairds generally are. Good sense, plain unaffected manners, much hospitality, and often no mean attainments, are to be found among the Scotch, – especially among the Scotch gentry of the Lowlands.

Then you have, in the New Town, the Judges and other officers of the Courts, your clever advocate, your wealthy writer to the Signet, your celebrated physician and still more celebrated surgeon, with the different professors of the not yet finished University.*

These different parties made up a society at once polished, instructive, and agreeable; and the company of the men was so charmingly enlivened by the naivete, the beauty of the ladies, – their frankness, their laughing eye, and their never-failing facility of saying something, and something always to the point, – that I scarcely know anything more

* Long since this letter was written, the University has been finished, and many other stupendous improvements have been made which had no existence, – which were not even, I believe, *designed,* – when I wrote.

30 SOCIETY OF EDINBURGH.

to be envied than a well-bred Scotch dinner-party, especially if followed by a ball and supper.

What astonished me most, however, in the New Town was, to see that every other house, – especially every other good house, – belonged either to a lawyer or to a physician; while every third or fourth person you met in the streets, except on the fashionable lounge of Prince's Street, seemed to be a man belonging to the Courts or a disciple of Esculapius. For the success of the lawyers I could in some measure account, after I had been informed of their innumerable sources of gain, especially in their dealings with the lairds; but how such a healthy, brawny, muscular, hardy race as the Scotch *should* want so many surgeons and physicians, it entirely puzzled me to comprehend.

The divines of the Scotch church, with the exception of a very few, – and they quite at the head of their profession, – do not take a prominent station in what is commonly called good society.

The sons of men of family, from whatever cause, do not often take holy orders. The stipends are too small, and the prospects of eventual preferment to a living of some $500 a-year too remote and contingent, to tempt any but those of the most

A BON MOT. 31

humble and moderate expectations in life to be come candidates for orders. In the Scotch clergy you find, accordingly, excellent men; but not *refined* men, nor, with a few rare but brilliant exceptions, men of much acquirement beyond the mere technicalities of not a very elevated theology.

I will close this too long letter with a rather pungent remark, which I was told had been made about the clergy and lawyers, in reference to two public buildings, one belonging to each of the two bodies, and which buildings had been erected in George's Street, precisely in front of each other.

The church *projected* beyond the regular line of buildings, and the legal edifice *receded* from that line. The remark made upon which was this: " That the impudence of the clergy and the modesty of the lawyers had spoiled one of the finest streets in the world."

Your's, &c.,

J. P. R.

3

SECTION 3

LETTER XLVI.

J. P. R. toGeneralMiller.

Departure from Edinburgh – The Old Gentleman's Remonstrance –
The Comparison – Anticipations – Journey to Glasgow – Arrival
there – Wealth and Industry of Glasgow – Hospitality there –
Glasgow Punch – Other Manufacturing Towns – Liverpool – Its
Merchants – San Martin retakes Chile.

*London,*1842.

Havingspent two months in Edinburgh, as forgetful of business as if I had nothing
to do with it, and as much in the enjoyment of life as if there were no necessary
connexion between industry, which must cater for the good things of it, and luxury,
which loves to enjoy them at her ease, I was reminded by an epistle from the old
gentleman at Bath that I had not yet feathered my nest, and that it would be a long time
ere I found a golden egg in it the size of a plum, if, instead of being up with the sun,
and making hay while it shone, I gave myself up to dancing at the petticoat-tails of the
ladies, and to drinking champagne and claret and jabbering politics and philosophy
with the gentlemen. " Why," he continued, " I have not

THK REMONSTRANCE. 33

had a price-current of produce from you for six weeks, nor a word about the funds, nor what prospect there is for. your manufacturing friends in the markets of South America. How do you think they are likely to take it, when, instead of finding you among themselves in Glasgow, Manchester, and Yorkshire, pointing out to them the goods best suited for the trade, they find you loitering away your time in a place like Edinburgh, where a man of business can learn and see absolutely nothing. Away with your universities and stuff; be a good boy; take my advice, – stick to ships, colonies, and commerce; and my word for it, this is your best course. See what Blucher and Wellington have achieved with their swords; and look what many have done with their pens and mother wit: why, many of them have reached the "head of their profession."

I thought some might demur to this sly comparison; but for myself, I had no inclination to disturb it in its stronghold; so, pleading in extenuation of my idle sojourn of two months with my own family, my long nine years' absence in Pampa wilds and Paraguay seclusion, I packed up my wardrobe, and bade adieu to Edinburgh and its

34 ANTICIPATIONS.

many fascinations. Blucher, Wellington, and the retired merchant of Bath were buzzing in my head; new speculations to all parts of America fanned my spirit of ambition; while the contemplation of new and unheard-of adventures among the giants of Patagonia, the tribes of Arauca, the natives of Chile, and the Indians of Peru, aroused within me all the ardour of the traveller, who never feels so little at home as when he is long detained in one place.

Perhaps the facility with which my imagination so readily carried me from home was increased by the dull, monotonous drive on a drizzly day from Edinburgh to Glasgow. I thought we never should have done with moss-bogs, stunted firs, black dykes, filthy clachans, nor, as we trundled slowly along, half-naked children, unseemly middens, and comfortless inns. At length we reached that vast emporium of wealth and industry, the capital of the west of Scotland. But I will not detain you long over a description of what is so well known. The city of Glasgow is a very splendid one. Its inhabitants generally are plain money-making men, more conspicuous for their sagacity and unwearied application than for highly cultivated manners or very

ARRIVAL AT GLASGOW. 35

refined education. Yet are there among them men

of great general knowledge, practical skill, and scientific attainment in all the arts of life that minister to the comfort and luxury of man. Their merchants send their ships laden with the beautiful, ingenious, and useful handiwork of the loom to every quarter of the globe; and they return richly freighted with the gold and silver of Peru; with the spices, cotton, sugar, and indigo of India, East and West; with the coffee of Brazils; the ivory and gold-dust of Africa; with the timber, hemp, and tallow of the' Baltic; with all the fruits of the Mediterranean; and with all the wines of Portugal, France, and Spain.

Machinery has attained great perfection in Glasgow. The spinning factories are stupendous monuments of productive power; and the patent loom manufactories look, each of them, as if they could weave in a day under-vestments for a nation. The chemist has lent all the aid of his discoveries to give lustrous effect to the chaste and beautiful designs of the painter, till in silks, muslins, shawls, scarfs, dresses, and all the other useful and ornamental parts of ladies' parure, the Glasgow manufacturer stands almost unrivalled.

36 GLASGOW HOSPITALITY.

Then come your " Paisley bodies/' the hand- loom weavers, and their thrifty wives and pretty daughters, the tambourers, each giving forth from their hands specimens of work the most elaborate and rich.

Your Paisley weaver is somewhat of a Radical j and he may often be seen in his lowly crib adjusting, with spectacles on his nose, some of the threads of his web, while his little urchin of a son, nine years of age, is spelling by his father's side Cob- bett's Register, the Edinburgh Review, or Paine's Age of Reason.

I made a great many acquaintance, friends, and correspondents among the Glasgow merchants and manufacturers, all anxious for news from any quarter of the globe to which they might send their manufactures. Their reception of me was kind; their hospitality plain and unostentatious; and their cheer abundant and substantial, – it was always good, and sometimes recherche'. Their wives were patterns of domestic economy; and they seemed to have the rare and laudable quality of interfering very little with their husbands, who, on the other hand, gave them all the credit of being excellent cooks and good managers. It was evident that the best dishes,

GLASGOW PUNCH. 37

if they had not been actually under their manipulation, had been subjected to their close inspection; and it was the husband's pleasure, – perhaps even his pride, – knowing this, always to recommend such dishes, with the irresistible inducement to partake of them, " that his wife had a knack at made dishes."

But the Glasgow punch is what the Glasgow landlord most prides himself upon; and in the brewing and distribution of that, after the ladies are gone, he sits lord paramount of the festive board. *

On leaving Glasgow, I visited all our other great manufacturing towns – Manchester, Leeds, Halifax, Rochdale, Blackburn, as well as those in the West of England. In all I found sleepless industry ever at work, waking ingenuity constantly employed, and restless invention for ever engaged in the new arrangement of known designs, or in the giving of a form and fashion to the original conceptions of her own creative fancy. Millions upon millions of capital were engaged in upholding this wonderful

* This punch-drinking habit has been nearly superseded of late years, except among bachelors, by the better custom of introducing in lieu of it excellent Madeira and good Claret.

38 ENGLISH MANUFACTURERS.

traffic, and in making Great Britain to the whole world an incomparably richer spot of varied commerce than ever Tyre, in all her glory, was to the neighbouring nations with which she had her traffic. What most I wondered at, and most admired, was the surprising elasticity of the minds of our manufacturers, – the comprehensive views they entertained of everything connected with their vocation, and the facility with which they could be made to look from their warehouses or looms to the most distant regions of the earth. Regardless at once of space and time, they supply those regions at their own risk with their own goods. To such an extent is this done, that, as a speculator, the merchant is driven nearly out of the export trade of the country in manufactures. He is content to become the agent abroad of the manufacturer, who, in point of fact, is the real merchant. It is he who regulates sales, orders and controls remittances; and, while you would think all his eyes were too few to overlook his colossal factories and immense warehouses at home, you yet find that, Argus-like, he extends his watchfulness to Europe, Asia, Africa, and America. He knows the markets of those countries as well as his agents who reside

LIVERPOOL. 39

there; and he examines their accounts, compares the advices of one time with those of another, and with the information he gets from other houses, till the agents at 10,000 miles' distance sometimes fancy, in the letters they receive, that they have their constituent himself at their shoulders.

Having fortified myself by connexion with many such intelligent, wealthy, and really respectable men as these, I finally ended a six months' tour of England and Scotland, and sat down at last in a quiet but genteel establishment of my own in Liverpool. It had been determined that I should remain there for a season, with a view to the extending and consolidating the support we were getting in this country to our several establishments, still carried on through agencies in Paraguay, Corrieutes, Santa Fe, but principally at Buenos Ayres, where my brother and another partner had now fixed their abode, at the head of a house extensively connected with many parts of the world.

In Liverpool I found the merchants not only agreeable and well-informed, but some highly cultivated, and really gentlemen. In manners, establishments, style, and elegance, they rank decidedly

40 LIVERPOOL MERCHANTS.

above the Glasgow community, – many of them treading closely upon the heels of their London competitors. The well-informed Liverpool merchant is, I should say, the most intelligent man in the mercantile community of this realm. He is in the very centre of its most active and varied commerce and manufactures, – North America is at his door; and the large manufacturing towns, scarcely a step from it, pour into his warehouses all their goods for exportation. Liverpool is a mart for the sale, or a port of transit, for the produce of Ireland; it nearly engrosses the trade of South America; and its ships are the first to enter the harbours of every country newly opened to our commerce. Calcutta, Canton, and Africa send large portions of their treasure to Liverpool; and the West Indies, Havannah, Guiana, Honduras, are all tributary to that great reservoir of wealth. What docks! what warehouses! Whence came all the ships to fill the one, and whence all the produce to gorge the other? From every creek and corner in which ships are built; from every patch of land where produce is grown; and from every busy haunt of man where art turns to practical utility the liberal donations of Nature.

SAN MARTIN RETAKES CHILE. 41

In the midst of this community, and with the view of becoming an active member of it, – well, and most agreeably introduced, – I sat myself down for a season, to observe what might be observed, gain what might be gained, enjoy what might be enjoyed, and bask in the sunshine of comparative ease and tranquillity, till circumstances should call me back, as I knew they likely would, to play in Chili and Peru a more conspicuous, stirring, and even hazardous part than I had hitherto performed on the stage of South America.

I remained in Liverpool till 1820, when, San Martin having conquered Osorio, retaken and liberated Chile, was co-operating with Lord Cochrane for the capture of Lima. My object was to establish houses in both places; and I had made all the preliminary arrangements necessary to carry my views into effect.

Your's, &c.,

J. P. E.

SECTION 4

LETTER XLVII.

    J. P. R. toGeneralMiller.

    Trip to the Highlands – The late Marquis of Huntly – Prince Leopold – Features of Scotch Scenery – A Highland Cortege – The Bagpipes – A Butt and Ben – Arrival at Kinrara – The Sport.

    London, 1842.

    ThoughLiverpool was my stationary place of abode, I made frequent excursions, in the course of the year, to the various spots worth seeing (and how many they are!) in England, Scotland, Ireland, and Wales. I shall content myself, however, with an account of a visit which I undertook to the Highlands, in pursuit of my favourite amusement, shooting; but which presented some incidents to my observation that do not always come in the way of your mere slaughterer of grouse and black cock. On one of my trips to Bath, I happened to meet, at a sort of state dinner-party at the old gentleman's, the late Marquis of Huntly, then in the prime of life, and the life itself of every society into which he ever came. His wit, his fascinating manners, his bonhommie, his ruddy, joyous countenance, and his

    PRINCE LEOPOLD. 43

gaiete de coeur, showed himself to be, and made those about him, " o'er a' the ills o' life victorious."

I happened to sit by him at dinner; and having heard of some of my strange adventures in Paraguay, he made his merry remarks upon them, drew from me, as your authors say, a good deal of new matter; and the whole ended by his inviting me to pass the first fortnight of the ensuing August at Kinrara Cottage, his beautiful seat in Inverness- shire, on the banks of the Spey.

Nothing loth, I expressed myself highly honoured by the invitation; and not the less so, that his lordship told me Prince Leopold was to be his guest, invited for the purpose of his endeavouring to chase away, for a season, on the moors, the brooding melancholy that had been overshadowing him since the never-to-be-forgotten loss, in the spring of that same year, of the devotedly beloved of the English people, – the late Princess Charlotte.

To see how the party most immediately affected by the shock, which had spread over a whole (. empire consternation and woe, would bear himself amid the general gloom, and to observe of what amount of alleviation the deep-felt sympathy of millions would be productive for the loss of the

44FEATURESOFSCOTCHSCENERY.

wife of his bosom, and for the death, just as he had received life, of her first-born son, an infant prince, " atavis edite regibus;" to observe this, under the same roof, at the same table, and on the same hills with the sufferer, would be to study a theme from which Philosophy herself, I thought, might derive a beneficial, however mournful, lesson.

August soon came round; and two days before the 12th, having passed through Stirling, Perth, the Carse of Gourie, the magnificent scenery of Dunkeld, and the yet more gorgeous woods and glens, and deep ravines, and rolling floods, and rocky precipices tufted with shrubs, which abound near the Blair of Athol, I came upon the inlet to the famous Pass of Killicranky – celebrated not less for its rare loveliness, than for the bloody tragedy of which it was the memorable theatre.

I had been told at the last stage, that Prince Leopold, with his suite, and many private carriages, cabriolets, and horsemen, had passed on a little before me, and that they were to be met by the Marquis of Huntly, at the head of the clan Gordon, in native costume, at the pass already mentioned.

I urged the postilion to get on; but my horses, which I had brought from Edinburgh (for there

A HIGHLAND CORTEGE. 45

were no relays in those days on the Highland roads), were so jaded, as just to be able, and no more, to bring me up with the splendid and novel cortege, as it was deploying from the wood into those frowning mountain tracts, o'erlaid with mists and capped with clouds, where trees grow not, and flowers, except the heath, blossom not; but scowling blasts drive sleet and rain, and frightened sheep and benumbed shepherds before them, while the traveller, caught in the storm, gathers up his cloak and pulls his bonnet over his eyes, and hastens with might and main to a place of shelter for the night.

Before I joined the cavalcade, and while it was yet in the pass wending its way among the trees and ravines, I got some splendid views of it from my carriage, in the rear; and as I saw the burnished claymores, the flowing plaids, the loose kilts, the gorgeous bonnets laden with black plumes, and as the sound of the bagpipes came upon me, softened in its shrillness by the medium of echo, the scene was one of truly martial grandeur. It would have carried me back to the year forty-five, but that the gentlemen's carriages, with their sporting inmates, the dogs, gamekeepers, and fowling-pieces, all assured me the war was to be with the feathered

46 THE BAGPIPES.%

tribes and not with the human race. Anything more exhilirating than the whole scene I never beheld. I was sorry I could not move forward with the clan-Huntly: for when my horses got to the small inn, from which the rear guard of the main body was just marching, both the animals and the postilion refused to move one inch, till after rest and refreshment taken, from the spot. Borrowing the innkeeper's pony, I rode forward to where the most noble marquis was, told him of my plight, and received anew the invitation to be at Kinrara on the 12th. " But," continued he, " if you wish to have a couple of days' sport on the best grounds on my domain, you will stop on your way to me at Dalwhinnie Inn, which, even with your tired cattle, you will reach in the course of to-morrow."

I thought him a noble-looking chieftain, as with eagle plume stuck in his rich velvet bonnet, a star on his breast, and a dirk studded with jewels in his belt, he rode on to the head of his clan, which marched with the nimble alacrity of sturdy mountaineers to the war-piercing sound of half-a-dozen bagpipes, from the long tubes of which more than a hundred variegated fillets of silk streamed upon the breeze.

THE SPORT. 47

At length the marquis, at the head of a troop of light horse, rode *off* with the carriages-and-four, which were soon lost to the eye among the mountains. I trotted back to the inn on my stubborn beast of a pony; and there, in all the dreariness of a wretched smoky " but an' ben," with two garrets up-stairs, I laid my account with yawning away the dull hours till my postilion should think the horses and himself had had enough of food, drink, and rest.

Three days after this, I had the honour of being introduced to Prince Leopold, and of dwelling with him under the same roof. Sir Robert Peel and many other great personages were there too; one of whom remarked, that Mr. Peel (he was then not a baronet) " was now thundering at the grouse, and by-and-by would thunder in the House." Nobody bagged fewer than twenty brace a-day, The cheer in-doors was excellent; all the stage-coaches that passed southward were filled with game; and after a fortnight's exhilarating sport under one of the most hospitable of roofs, I bent my way home again, greatly delighted with what I had seen of the Highlands.

Your's, &c.

J. P. R.

5

SECTION 5

LETTER XLVIII.

W. P. R. toGeneralMiller.

eturn to Corrientes – Compagnons de Voyage – Travelling – Post of Olmos – Family of Olmos – The Ladies – Waltzing in the Forenoon – Fuentes' Impatience – Entertainment and Departure – Pass through Santa F6, and arrive at Goya – Pass on to Corrientes.

London, 1842.

WhenI took my departure from Goya in the San Jose, I had no idea of revisiting the province of Corrientes. Our plan was to establish a house in the capital of the River Plate; and while my brother went to combine elements in England, I was to lie on my oars in Buenos Ayres, and ready at a moment's notice to give effect there to his arrangements at home.

But he was unexpectedly detained in the loading of his vessel; and the devotion of a couple of months to pleasure, made me sick of an idle life. The anticipation of a whole year to be spent without having any definite object to pursue, or any

COMPAGNONS DE VOYAGE. 49

active operation to undertake, filled me with ennui; and as, on the other hand, I could profitably fill up my time on our old beat, till I should receive my brother's advices from England, it was agreed that I should forthwith return to Corrientes, and there await the issue of our European plans.

I set off accordingly, in January, 1816, for Santa Fe, with three compagnons de voyage, – El Señor de Fuentes, a gentleman settled at the Bajada; Don Ciriaco Lezica, a member of one of the most distinguished families of Buenos Ayres; and our old friend Philip Parkin, already introduced to you.

I never in my life made a pleasanter journey. Fuentes was a native of one of the Canary Islands, a married man, wearing spectacles, – sedate and judicious in his general bearing, – amiable in every relation of life, – and withal possessed of a quiet but observing humour, which made him at once an instructive and a pleasing companion. Lezica was a dashing, enterprising, and clever young Creole of one-and-twenty, – mercurial in his spirit, and overflowing with fun. As for Don Felipe, he was all that could be wished for as a travelling companion, when neither bodily danger nor fatigue came to disturb the placidity of his temper. He

Vol. Hi. D

50 TRAVELLING.

was full of *bonhommie,* and, with his good-humour and bad Spanish, greatly amused us during the journey, but more particularly when he was playing *l'aimable,* as he constantly did at those post-houses where there was a buxom landlady, and still more where there were some pretty daughters, – of whom a little more anon.

We bought a fine old roomy carriage, – laid in a capital stock, including an ample supply of claret for the warm weather; and, as Don Ciriaco was going to remain for some time at Santa Fe, he carried with him a favourite black from his father's house – a clever man of all work, and a great wag to boot.

We travelled along very leisurely; by which I do not mean to say that when our horses were yoked, we went along at a slow pace, – for being driven as usual by six spirited animals, we scampered over the plains at the accustomed rate of three to four leagues an hour: but we took our time at our halting-places; set not off very early in the mornings; slept our siesta after due time given to a good dinner; halted for the night at an early hour, and at the most comfortable lodgings we could pick out; and making all due provision

THE POST OF OLMOS. 51

for our supper, spent the evening in glee and conviviality.

On the whole, an Englishman accustomed to all the luxuries of locomotion at home would consider South American travelling somewhat rough; but it carries with it, notwithstanding, here an incident and there an excitement, which are not to be found in our own unvarying comforts in posting from one place to another, and still less now-a-days, in being rapidly wheeled along in the easy-chair of a first- class railway-carriage. Of the truth of this remark I shall content myself with giving one illustration in the journey of which I am speaking.

On the road from Buenos Ayres lies the post- house of Olmos. It is not a mere hovel, like the greater number of those resting-places, but the comfortable habitation of an estanciero. The house is built of brick; and as the owner himself, with his family, resided at the time of which I speak at his estate, the place gave every indication not only of much rough and substantial comfort, but of a certain refinement which we were not accustomed to look for beyond the precincts of the capital.

We had made an effort to arrive at the Posta de

52 FAMILY OF OLMOS.

Olmos on the evening of the third day; but that effort, with our indolent mode of travelling, being an unsuccessful one, we did not drive up to it till about ten o'clock the next morning. Our host, at once the estanciero and postmaster, was standing at his corral as we came up to the house, and immediately advanced to meet us: he was a fine, hale, yeoman-looking man, and received us with unaffected cordiality, being personally acquainted with us all. Although none of us, save Lezica, had met with his family at the estancia, on our former journeys, the fame of his daughters' beauty had spread far and near, so that by name, " las buenas mozas de la posta de Holmos," – the pretty girls at the post of Holmos, – were known to every one in the province at large.

When the postmaster, therefore, took us into his sala, a plain but neat drawing-room, we were not surprised by the*beauty*of his three daughters, but we certainly were not prepared for their*style.*They were fashionable-looking young ladies, who had been brought up in Buenos Ayres, and generally resided there, – nicely dressed, – - and*not*in the dishabille in which the females of South America too generally indulge (or used

THE LADIES.

*then,*at least, to indulge) in the forenoon. Two of them sat sewing beside their mother, a handsome woman of forty; and the third was at a very good piano, playing with no small musical skill! The attractions of the young ladies, both in form and feature, were undeniable; and they lacked none of that grace of motion and polished yet natural and affable manner for which the Portenas are so pre-eminently distinguished.

Such a sight in the heart of the Pampas was indeed a novel one, and held us for a moment in suspense; but the bland and courteous salutations of the mother and daughters, and the hearty welcome of the estanciero himself, soon re-assured us, so that in ten minutes we were all as intimate with each other as if our acquaintance had been of ten years. As for Don Felipe Parkin, he sat quite entranced by the Elysium on which he had suddenly alighted; and when Lezica slily shook his head, as much as to say, " You see what a fool you were not to come on here yesterday evening," Philip seemed to feel the whole force of the rebuke, and looked determined to make up for his mistake by being in no hurry to move on.

54 WALTZING IN THE FORENOON.

Instead of being an impatient stoppage, then, for a change of horses, our halt at the post of Olmos turned out to be a fashionable morning visit. We had mate handed round to all, – segars to those who liked to smoke, – much animated conversation on the haut ton of Buenos Ayres, – some tolerable music; and, – yes, at eleven in the morning, – not a little dancing. The custom,' in those pleasant days, was quite a usual one, – to waltz round the room, or to walk the graceful minuet in boots, at a morning call. Who could resist it on the present occasion, with such partners, such music, and in such a place? It was like suddenly and unexpectedly falling on some hidden retreat of the Graces. So we waltzed with " las buenas mozas de Olmos," – and, booted and spurred, we gravely led them through the stately movements of the double Spanish minuet and minuet a la cour.

In these agreeable pursuits time fled with a rapidity imperceptible to us all, except to Mr. Fuentes, who, after a considerable absence from home, was on his return to his " dear little wife," and his two " sweet little children." Accordingly he kept casting a melancholy glance every now and then at the coach, which stood at the door ready

horsed, with some of our postilions and outriders lounging about, and others admiring at the window the exquisite dancing of " las buenas mozas de Olmos;" – or he coughed significantly to us when a new minuet, another tune, a song with the guitar, or a fantasia on the piano, was proposed. But his hints were in vain. It drew towards mid-day, – the sun was hot; and at last Mr. Parkin, with great gallantry, proposed, that as the ladies saw but little company at their retreat, we should remain with them that day, and proceed next morning. The proposition was received with " loud cheers from all sides of the house:" Mr. Fuentes alone sighed, and observed, " he had seen from the beginning how it would all end;" the horses (no doubt both to their surprise and pleasure) were let loose into their green fields and pastures; the postilions went into the kitchen to amuse themselves after the same fashion as their " patrones" in the drawing-room; and Lezica's slave, Antonio, having succeeded in getting a couple of bottles of wine for the kitchen party to drink to the health of " las buenas mozas de Olmos," glee and good-humour reigned throughout the hospitable home of our bluff old friend the postmaster.

56

ENTERTAINMENTANDDEPARTURE.

At two o'clock we sat down to what I can scarcely call less than a sumptuous dinner, – and while we praised the dishes, the ladies paid equal compliments to the wines and other little luxuries super- added to the feast from our travelling stock. At four we retired to a siesta; and after the sun had run his fiery race, we all walked out and strolled about in the soft moonlight, which necessarily led to our saying many soft things. At a very late hour we brought our day's pleasure to a close with music and dancing; and next morning, with many tender adieus, we took leave of our fair hostess and her daughters. Of course the postmaster of Olmos would neither permit of our paying for horses nor for anything else. He accompanied us a short way himself on a stout and gallant horse; and after he also had left us, the three bachelors in the coach, beginning to compare notes, found that each had left his heart deposited, for the time being, with one of the " buenas mozas de Olmos."

When any travelling-party in England can show that, at a " genteel hotel," they could pass the day, based on the same disinterested hospitality, with the hotel-keeper and his family as we passedPASS THROUGH SAXTA Ffi. 57

ours at Olmos, then I may be inclined to give a preference to a jaunty chaise and pair, smartly driven by the " postboy" along an English turnpike road, to a lumbering coach rattled by six horses and as many postilions over the Pampas of Buenos Ayres.

We pursued our journey pleasantly from the post of Holmos to Santa Fe, where we arrived on the sixth day. I remained for a week there, renewing my acquaintance with old and kind friends; and then crossing over to the Bajada with Mr. Parkin, we started together on horseback for Goya and Corrientes. The country was again in a very unsettled state in Entre Rios; but we took with us a couple of trustworthy and brave servants well armed, – one of them the principal driver of the coach in which we had come to Santa Fe, – and we ourselves were equally formidable in our equipment. We met many suspicious stragglers and armed marauders, but we were so well appointed that we were not molested by any of them on our way; so that, after a four days' gallop, we safely reached the hospitable abode of Don Pedro Quesney.

Surprised as he was to see me on my quick

58 ARRIVE AT GOYA.

return, he received me with great cordiality and apparent pleasure; and though on this occasion I came upon him and Vangture unawares, they were both instantly employed in Don Felipe's service and my own. It quickly flew ahroad that I was in the port, with the additional*supposition,*which was soon converted into the*fact,*that I had brought with me one or two thousand ounces of gold to recommence grand operations in the province; so that I held a levee of the inhabitants of the place during the evening in Don Pedro's salon, – every one professing, I am sure some of them sincerely, great pleasure on seeing me among them again. Mr. Tuckerman I had left, in Buenos Ayres, and Don Pedro Campbell was in Corrientes enjoying what he rarely did, a little*otium,*even if not*cum dignitate.*

I had been only about four months absent from Goya; but I rejoiced to see, even in that brief space, an alteration in it for the better. – The commerce, and consequently the population and wealth of the port, were steadily advancing. I was really glad I had not come with the intention of disturbing the many small dealers who had arisen after our departure; for, although I impressed on them that

ARRIVE AT CORRIENTES. 59

competition increases business, – benefiting instead of hurting it, – I could see, while they assented to my political maxims, they were not displeased to know that I had come more for pleasure than for business; and that, at any rate, Corrientes would be my place of residence. I except Don Pedro, who seemed desirous that I should remain at Goya; as did also my friend the comandante, the curate, and the family of Rodriguez, including his happy son-in-law. I told them that, although I could not make the port my head-quarters, I should make them frequent visits during my stay in the province.

On, this my first return visit, I was too impatient to get to the end of my journey, where Mr. Postle- thwaite's family looked for my arrival every day, to remain long at Goya. Therefore, although we had still an establishment at the port, I staid but four- and-twenty hours, – and in less than four-and-twenty more, after many warm greetings on either side, I was duly installed, – not as the guest, but as an integral part of Mr. Postletwhaite's household.

I am, &c.,

W. P. R.

6

SECTION 6

LETTER XLIX.

W. P. R. toGeneralMiller.

Mr. and the Misses Postlethwaite – Englishmen's Estimate of Foreigners – Englishmen's*Exclusiveness* – Not applicable to the Postlethwaites – Arrival of the Inglesita, with Tuckerman and Supplies – Tuckerman's and Parkin's Opinions of each other – Tuckerman complimentary to the Ladies.

*London,*1842.

As I had not been able to visit Mr. Postlethwaite in Corrientes on his first bringing his family from Buenos Ayres, I was pleased now to see what a truly comfortable and*English*home they had established in so unknown and remote a quarter of the globe. Happily, Mrs. Postlethwaite and her daughters were of so accommodating and lively a disposition, that they adapted themselves with wonderful tact and facility to the habits, feelings, and customs of the people among whom they resided; and with whom, as a natural consequence, they soon became great favourites. They were never heard to draw comparisons – so justly odious to the party disparaged by them – between their own country and the one in which they

MRS. AND THE MISSES POSTLETHWAITE. 61

resided. They made no complaints of the loss of English comforts, and the substitution of South American hardships. They maintained that what was suitable to the one country would be out of place in the other; and they found no want of such comforts and luxuries in Corrientes as the climate rendered it well for them to enjoy. They not only accommodated themselves to circumstances, but made the best of them; and instead of being unable, like some of our amiable John Bullish folks when they go abroad, to *endure* the people of the country, – Mrs. and the Misses Postlethwaite went beyond merely enduring the Correntinas, for they met their advances of friendship with that readiness which a conviction of the sincerity of the proffer drew forth.

In judging of foreigners, we English are much disinclined to make any allowance for them on the score of difference of education, associations, habits, and customs. We set up a standard of our own, and woe betide the man or the woman who shall either impugn or venture to depart from it. We are sure that *we* are right and foreigners wrong. And in our assumed superiority, we stop at 10 intermediate point or position.62Englishmen'sExclusiveness.

We do not even try to get them over to our way of thinking, – much less will we be at the trouble to make ourselves acquainted with their manners or habits. If there were a mine of virtues lying under the surface (and so there generally is), we would not be at the trouble even to attempt to dig for it. We say virtually, " let foreigners adopt our manners, our customs, our opinions, and our principles, and then there will be some use in holding intercourse with them." This is to demand too much; and not being granted, what happens? why, if only two English families are residing in a foreign town (of course I speak generally), they will doggedly keep to themselves, and shun " the natives."

All this, I think, is not as it ought to be: we are, *in every way,* too exclusive, – in every way we forget a great deal too much that we belong to the one great family of humanity, and not to the narrow limited circle beyond which our pride and our prejudices will not allow us even to peep.

Nothing of what I have here said was applicable to Mrs. Postlethwaite's family. Quite the reverse. They set about making themselves acquainted with the Spanish language, and diligently studied Cor-

ARRIVAL OF THE INGLESITA. 63

rientes' manners, feelings, and peculiarities. They visited and were visited; and it was pleasant to see the lively *Mrs.* Postlethwaite, where she could not understand her neighbours, getting one of her daughters to interpret, and then with many kind nods and looks ratifying the answer, which she gave by means of a translation.

After the "riotous living" I had seen in Buenos Ayres, the domestic enjoyments of which I now partook, under Mr. Postlethwaite's roof, were truly grateful and refreshing. I can recall to mind few portions of my life that I have spent more happily than I did the eight months of 1817 during which I remained in Corrientes; and the charm consisted in having there, where I could least expect to find it, a realization of home. With the drawing-room door shut, and all of us gathered round the table *at tea,* it required an effort of the imagination to fancy, what after all was the truth, – that I was an inhabitant of a remote, inland, and all but unknown part of South America.

On the 18th of March, five-and-twenty years ago, our little vessel, the Inglesita, – built in Paraguay, – arrived at Corrientes. This was the same "Inglesita" that was captured and plundered by

64 ARRIVAL OF THE INGLESITA

the Artiguenos, with my brother on board, on his last voyage to Assumption, the disasters of which, as we have elsewhere detailed,* led to our expulsion from Paraguay by Doctor Francia.

Very different, on greeting our little clipper, on her arrival at Corrientes, were my feelings from those with which I had seen her come to her moorings in Assumption. Now her peaceful passage had been obstructed by no warlike attack of licensed robbers; all that we looked for was safely brought to port, including, to the great satisfaction of our family circle, the romantic lover of " Charlotte," – Don Jorge Washington Tucker- man.

Persons who have all their lives been accustomed to the every-day luxuries of England can scarcely form an adequate idea of the pleasure which, in such a place as Corrientes, an arrival, – particularly of one's own vessel, dispatched by one's own friends, – does necessarily cause. There is pleasure, no doubt, at Christmas-time here, when presents flow in upon you from all quarters, and when friends go down to spend their holidays with you; – there is pleasure in the country when you receive a boxWITH TUCKERMAN AND SUPPLIKS. 65

* In " Francia's Reign of Terror."

from a branch of your family in London, to which all the family there has contributed; – there is pleasure when a vessel from Canton arrives and brings as passenger a friend of your friend there, who is the bearer of many family letters, and good news and Chinese curiosities; – there is pleasure, too, on the return of part of your family from the continent, after they have travelled for three months and brought you back their persons, and their affections, and their home feelings, and Brussels lace, and Bohemian glass, and long accounts of wonderful sights and wonderful places. But all this was nothing to the pleasure of the Inglesita's arrival at Corrientes from Buenos Ayres, with Mr. Tuckerman on board.

Having been detained from day to day by contrary winds and other *contre-temps,* new packets were daily put on board, and every one contained some additional piece of pleasant information, – all our wants had been thought of and supplied, – here a cask of brandy, there ten or twelve cases of claret. A short letter announced a box of clothes; another some late periodicals and newspapers from England. " The detention of the In- glesita," says a later date, " enables me to send

66 ARRIVAL OF SUPPLIES.

you some family letters which the Egham has just brought from England;" and " P. S. The Egham has brought some capital potatoes and cheese, of which I have ordered some to the Inglesita, and some double stout." Then we had " files of gazettes/' and " a hat," and " a box of tea/' and " some finery for the ladies," and nice stationery, and split peas, and pearl barley, – to say nothing of a new carpet for the drawing-room. Lastly, for all "news and scandal," we were referred to the delectable Mr. Tuckerman himself; quite the man to supply this indispensable want. See him, then, standing on deck, as the little vessel drew near, – kissing his hand with all the elegance of studied etiquette, and waiving his lily-white handkerchief, in the triumphant knowledge that he was the lion of the day. See a boy at his side with a whole sack of correspondence: behold us all standing on the river bank, returning Don Jorge's salutation with joyful impatience to see him on shore; – see all this, and consider what must be the pleasure of such " an arrival at Corrientes."

Tuckerman, as I have before hinted, was his own traveller in business, so that we could seldom keep him long at a time in Corrientes. But when there,

TUCKERMAN AND PARKIN. 67

he was a great acquisition to our society. He contrasted admirably with Philip Parkin. The one was Yankee, – the other, John Bull to the core. Parkin was from the south of England, – anything but bright, yet extremely good-natured and gentleman-like, save and except in his John Bullism. He saw everything through English optics; and therefore he seldom saw anything abroad in its right dimensions. He understood not the people; and he thought it not worth while to take any pains about the matter. Everything was wrong, and it was not his province to set anything right. "They are great asses.," said Don Felipe, "but that's their business, and not mine." As for Tuckerman, Parkin thought him little short of *non compos.* "What a fool," he would say, "Tuckerman is, with his rhodomontade, and his fine words that nobody understands, and his fine feelings in which nobody believes. He looks to me for all the world like a play-actor. I wonder he ain't ashamed of being so ridiculous. And such a scarecrow into the bargain, and fancying himself handsome." On saying which, Don Felipe would comb his scanty hairs, admire himself in a pocket looking-glass, pull down his waistcoat, look at his boots; and strut68 TUCKERMAN COMPLIMENTARY TO THE LADIES.

across the room. Tuckerman, on the other hand, regarded Parkin with an ill-concealed contempt. " He is the most stultified animal" (so Don Jorge alleged) " I ever came across; and how he ever separated himself from his father's stables and clover-fields is a mystery never to be fathomed. He has not two ideas of his own to put together; and like all such unintellectual beings, he sneers at those who, having a soul to feel, have a tongue to give utterance to the dictates of their glowing hearts."

Tuckerman never spoke to the two older Miss Postlethwaites (the oldest eighteen) without turning a compliment, or throwing himself into an attitude, or tinging with sentimentality whatever topic he had in hand. But he could not dance, – which Parkin looked upon as disgraceful, holding, as he did, that the true appeal to a young lady's kind regard lay in the heel and not in the head.

Altogether, with our own circle, and with the intercourse we kept up with the best of the Cor- rientes families, our society was a pleasant one; and it was with no small reluctance I absented myself from it, on two or three occasions during my stay, when business called me to Goya.

DON PEDRO CAMPBELL. 69

Campbell was still in our employment, – for, in fact, he had been continued on by Mr. Postlethwaite, – and he was as anxious as ever to "cut the camp," and do a sweeping business. But times had altered. I held myself ready to move at a day's notice: the trade of the province had spread (and I was glad to find it so) into a great many channels; and in this state of affairs, although Campbell lingered on with me, it was clear that he was beginning to sigh for that active and restless enterprize, without which he could scarcely live, and engaged in which he was reckless, as far as himself was concerned, as to the result.

It is not my intention to detain you much longer over my second Corrientes trip: nevertheless, two or three matters passed, during my last residence there, which demand some notice, and which I shall make the subject of my next letters.

Your's, &c.

W. P. R.

7

SECTION 7

LETTER L.

W. P. R. toGeneralMiller.

Increase of Corrientes Revenue – Mendez wants Warlike Stores – Applies to me to procure them – The Clyde detained – Discovery of the Vessel – Tuckerman brings Supplies – The North Wind, and Scarcity of Provisions – Arrival at Goya – Mendez, with his Staff and Soldiers, receives the Arms – The Municipal Body of Corrientes – The European-Spaniards ordered to the Head Quarters of Artigas – The Cabildo interprets the Decree as including the English and other Foreigners – Campbell desires to interfere – Harangue to the English – One Law for the Rich, another for the Poor – Interview with the Mayor – Protest – Conditional Release proposed – Proposals rejected – The Mayor deserted by his Colleagues, and the English liberated scot-free.

London, 1842.

Inspite of bad management, and of many individual peccadilloes, the natural consequence of the extraordinary prosperity of Corrientes, was a rapid improvement in the public finances. Revenue flowed in upon the delighted governor with so strong a tide, that, two or three months after my return, he found himself – *mirabile dictu!*with a clear surplus of six thousand pounds in the coffersINCREASE OF REVENUE. 71

of the Treasury. Like a boy in the country, who, being accustomed to a penny or twopence a-week of pocket-money, unexpectedly receives a present from a rich uncle from town of half-a-crown, and whose hand thenceforward is never out of his pocket till he gets quit of his treasure, with which he is to buy a hundred and fifty different things he has long coveted, so Governor Mendez could dream of nothing but of his " excess of revenue." Great and many were his projects, – long and deep his consultations on the vital question as to *how* he was to dispose of the enormous sum accumulated, and still accumulating, under the management of the talented minister of finance. Six thousand pounds! He thought of a navy; he meditated a mighty blow against the Portuguese; he talked of paying off all Artigas's incumbrances, which meant the national debt; and, after all, the mighty sum was destined to be transferred from the public coffers of Corrientes to the iron chest of Fair and Robertson.

Artigas, at the time of which I write, viewed with great jealousy, and with so determined a spirit of opposition and hatred, the projects of Brazil on the Banda Oriental, that he was anxious to see

72 MENDEZ WANTS WARLIKE STORES.

his dominions placed on a war establishment. Mendez, being a soldier and an adherent of the Protector, seconded with all his heart the views of the latter; and he proposed, therefore, himself to take the field, and co-operate with his chief in the impending struggle.

He could get plenty of men, but as he wanted arms and ammunition, he determined to turn his surplus revenue to the purchase of the *materiel* of war. Artigas approved of his plan, and Mendez looked to me as the agent through whom he could best carry into effect his warlike resolution.

Recollecting the trouble which our having dabbled in munitions of war had led us into in Paraguay, I did not much like the business, although a lucrative one, with the tempting addition of my being paid for the supplies which I was required to introduce before even ordering them; for such was the confidence which an Artigueno chief placed in an English merchant, that he felt if the money was accepted, his wants, at the day appointed, would be punctually supplied.

I agreed, in the end, to enter into the contract, and mainly on this score, – that the arms were wanted for the legitimate purpose of repelling an

APPLIES TO ME. 73

aggressive invasion of the country by the Portuguese, who had no more right to it than had the Emperor of China. I stipulated with Mendez, however, that the arms should be shipped with the knowledge and free permission of the government of Buenos Ayres, as well as with the acquiescence, and, in case of need, under the protection of our own commander on the station. These conditions arranged, I wrote to my friends at Buenos Ayres to give effect, if they could, to the contract.

The Buenos Ayres government cheerfully acquiesced in the shipment of the arms, and accordingly a small vessel, – that same little schooner, Clyde, in which we were tempest-tost on our voyage from the Guassu, – was despatched to me, with muskets, sabres, carbines, officers' swords, powder, musical instruments, – in short, a selection to the heart's content of the Governor. He neither allowed a day of rest to himself nor to me from the time of my informing him that the Clyde bad sailed. His impatience for her arrival knew no bounds. He had taken the field with his auxiliary force, and fixed his head quarters near the village of Saladas; but he purposed to move *en masse* to Goya the moment he heard of the arrival of his

VOL. III. V

74 THE CLYDE DETAINED.

military stores there, – the Clyde being bound for that port.

She was on this occasion fated to make one of her usual unlucky passages. About the middle of July, hearing she was close to Goya, I went down there, and took up my quarters with Don Pedro Quesney. But days passed away, and the Clyde appeared not. Tuckerman, observing my growing impatience, and my increasing fear that something had gone wrong (himself, at the same time, having some gold on board), volunteered his services to go down the river in a canoe in search of the Clyde; an offer which I gladly accepted. But after he had been gone for many days, the evenings again began to close in, and still no word of the Clyde, – no appearance of Tuckerman. At the end of ten days he arrived. Before meeting the cutter he had descended to a port called the Esquina, as far as 50 leagues, and thence a fair wind lasted them up to within 11 leagues of Goya. But here it failed them; their provisions ran short; and the kind-hearted Don Jorge, himself half-starved, had come up in the boat, with the view of at once relieving my mental anxiety and the corporeal wants of the Clyde's little crew.

DISCOVERY OF THE VESSEL. 75

Determined no longer to *wait* for the tiresome cutter, I put four men and a quantity of provisions into the boat, and taking the helm into my own hands, off we set that same night in search of the Clyde.

We started late, and my men pulled lustily, but after many hours exertion no Clyde could we find. At three o'clock in the morning we brought up at an islet, and there rested for three hours. Again we pulled, but no Clyde: we went out of one channel into another – up and down the river; and it was not till we had had eight and twenty hours of fatiguing exertions that we discovered the cutter moored to the bank of the river, and all but shut out from view by the trees!

The wind was north, and blew stronger and stronger every day. The men put forward extraordinary exertions to tow the little vessel up, but after six days of incessant toil we had got only four leagues nearer to Goya! We had nothing to eat – our men were dispirited (a very general consequence of an empty stomach); I was sick and tired of the whole business; but leave the Clyde again I would not.

On the seventh day, while we were tugging as

76 SCARCITY OF PROVISIONS.

usual, against wind and tide, a boat hove in sight, and I really can scarcely express the pleasure I felt on perceiving Tuckerman once more. To the famished peons the sight of the bee. he brought was like manna in the wilderness. They shouted with a sort of fiendish joy, that led Tuckerman to believe that, spare as he was, if he had not brought beef, they would have made a meal of himself.

I thought my troubles were at last at an end, for the sky began to portend a storm, and so strong was the appearance of a change of wind in our favour, that the peons ate up all the beef which Tuckerman had brought us, and which was the more easily done that we now mustered in all sixteen strong. But unfortunately our anticipations were not quite correct. The following day the wind blew stronger than ever from the north, and poor Tuckerman and his men passed from relievers to fellow-sufferers in the long fast which for one day they had so generously interrupted.

The penance continued up to the tenth day from my leaving Goya; the wind then began to round, – the breeze freshened, – the sails were hoisted; Tuckerman and I jumped into the boat which he had brought, and gaily bounding by the side of the

ARRIVAL AT GOYA. 77

cutter, we scudded along at the rate of six knots an hour against the stream.

As, towards the evening, we neared the port, we descried the Governor and his staff standing on the quay, waving their hats and pocket-handkerchiefs to us as we drew near. They had been straining their eyes for hours to catch the first glimpse of our approach, and it would be difficult to say whether the Governor's impatience to see us land, or mine to be once more on terra firma, was the greatest.

I had not been in bed for ten long anxious and weary nights; so that, requesting Mendez to leave business till the morning, I hastened to bed in the hope of enjoying some rest after the anxiety and fatigue I had undergone.

But nature, when rudely forced out of her own regular channel, resents the outrage, by refusing at our call immediately to return to her accustomed course. I could neither sleep nor rest in my own comfortable bed: cutters, arms, rivers, towings, north winds, beef suppers, and boatings, filled my disturbed imagination; so that I was glad when the dawning light came to dissipate the whole, and to allow me to enjoy the fresh morning air.

78 MENDEZ RECEIVES THE ARMS.

Mendez and his motley staff were early astir, and his two ragged regiments were drawn up in front of my door. The discharging of the cutter was forthwith commenced, – boxes were landed and hastily broken open on the beach, and as muskets, pistols, swords, carbines, and belts were drawn forth and scattered about, the governor's joy was. extreme. Superintending the disorderly operation, he sat at my cottage-door, drinking his stout and smoking his segar; while he freely distributed bread and cheese, porter, and spirits to all his officers and men. Muskets and carbines were loaded with blank cartridge and fired off, – sabres were drawn from their scabbards, – belts and cartouche-boxes were buckled on; and all was confusion. The whole day passed in this military disorder and excitement; and it was with no small contentment that I bade adieu, in the evening, to my worthy friend the Governor, who now, putting himself at the head of his well-armed though heterogeneous force, commenced his march for Saladas, where he held his encampment.

When Mendez left Corrientes to take a purely military command, Artigas delegated the political power of the province to the municipality, the first

THE MUNICIPAL BODY OF CORRIENTES. 79

alcalde, or mayor, being president of the local government. He was an old man of the name of Cabral, of a good family; but being irritable in his temper, as well as of a narrow mind and illiberal principles, he was no favourite with his fellow- citizens.

Most of the members of the Cabildo were engaged in mercantile pursuits; and they were of that class which viewed foreign trade with extreme jealousy and dislike.

Cabral might be called the head of this party; and, as a matter of course, the English enjoyed no favour with him or his colleagues. They could do us no harm, however; for the real power was kept by Artigas in his own hands, and they did not dare to run counter to his general policy.

But a curious incident arose/ by which Cabral thought he would at once get quit of every foreigner, and in particular of every Englishman, in Corrientes.

The European Spaniards, from some cause or other, fell under the displeasure of Artigas; and, with an arbitrary cruelty which ever and anon displayed itself in his character, he issued a proclamation throughout all his wide dominions that

80 SPANIARDS ORDERED TO PURIFICACION.

all of them, without distinction or exception, should be sent to his head-quarters at the Purification, and that without delay. The edict, considering the extent and nature of the country, was a bar- barous one, – but issued by Artigas, it was only to be obeyed.

While Spain held her Transatlantic colonies, her subjects there were distinguished simply by the names of*Europeans*and*Creoles,* – not European*Spaniards,*but Euro-peans, – indicating that no*other*Europeans than Spaniards could tread the soil. A Spaniard, therefore, when asked what he was, proudly said, " Soy Europeo," – which did not exactly mean, " I am a European," but*"*I am a Spaniard."

After the revolution the thing itself was changed, but the*name*continued in general use. "Los Europeos," in general parlance, meant " the Spaniards."

In this way, Artigas's proclamation was issued against " los Europeos," – meaning, as everybody knew, the Spaniards; but Cabral, with what he considered no small tact and cunning, took the expression literally, and so he held that the English being "Europeos" were comprehended in the edict.

THEDECREEINCLUDESTHEENGLISH.81

Mr. Postlethwaite's house was situated on the Point of San Sebastian, fronting the river, and of which a fine view was commanded from the drawing-room windows. Here, as he and I sat one evening in conversation with the ladies, an approaching mob, and the sound of drums, called our attention to the public announcement of a*Bando,*or proclamation. Surrounded by his retinue and soldiers, the public crier, or notary, came to a stop just under our window, and beginning to read the*bando*with his " Whereas," &c., he proceeded to proclaim that all Europeans, of every nation, whether Spaniard, Englishman, Italian, Frenchman, or any other, should assemble next morning at nine o'clock at the door of the town- hall, to be thence sent forward, under escort, to his excellency the Protector, at his general encampment*of La Purification.*

You may conceive the dismay with which the female part of Mr. Postlethwaite's family heard the announcement of the decree; but we immediately made a joke of it, and assured them that old Cabral dared not for his life carry his intentions into effect.

While we debated this knotty and novel question,

82HARANGUETOTHEENGLISH.

in came the redoubtable Don Pedro Campbell, at this time resident in Corrientes, and still in our employment. He breathed war and deßance to Cabral, and talked of instantly putting himself at the head of the foreigners in the place, – taking the Cabildo by assault, and himself carrying Cabral off as prisoner to his chief, Don Pepe Artigas.

I told Campbell that I had determined myself to lead the English on this important occasion, and I requested him to collect every one of them at Mr. Postlethwaite's house by half-past eight next morning. At the appointed hour Campbell was with me, leading a tag-rag and bobtail company of *seventeen* of our countrymen who had contrived to find their way to this remote part of the globe. "Now, my friends," said I, "provided you will agree to one stipulation which I have to make, I am willing to put myself at your head and to do my best to get you honourably out of the difficulty which threatens you." They at once agreed to follow me and abide by my orders. "Well then," I added, " I have to request that I alone may be spokesman; and that whatever aspect you may see the affair take, you are to leave the business entirely to be managed by me." This being assented to.

RICH AND POOR. 83

we proceeded to the Cabildo, or town-house, – every Englishman in the town, save Mr. Postlethwaite, – for I would not hear of his submitting to the indignity of being called up-like a felon before the spiteful old Cabral.

When we got to the Cabildo, we found most of the poor European Spaniards busy getting ready for their long, harassing, and inauspicious journey. It went to my heart to see their resigned but melancholy bearing, – the quiet, unobtrusive way in which they prepared for an expedition, the end of which, for aught they knew, might be their indiscriminate public execution. And as I contemplated their abject condition, I could not but reflect with a feeling of national pride that while *they* might suffer captivity and death unheeded, the generality of my followers, as Englishmen, knew they could not be ill-treated without the powerful arm of theif government being raised either to defend or to revenge them.

I missed, in the large group of Spaniards assembled, many, indeed most of their *rich* countrymen established in the place. These were intimately connected, by marriage or by interest, with some one or other, or with several of the Cabildantes, or

84 RICH AND POOR.

aldermen; and they were consequently screened by them. Go where we will, alas! we find one law for the rich, another for the poor. We deny it theoretically in England, but what do we every day practically see? *One law for the rich, another for the poor.* An unwelcome fact to many, – disputed, a* a fact, by more, – and yet aFactwell worthy of being steadily kept in view by all. It is true, as I have just observed, that we protect the weakest of our subjects from *foreign* aggression; but is any one of my readers prepared to say that we should have protected the just rights of Mr. M'Leod in *England* with a strictness and vigour equal to those with which we jealously watched over them in North America?

At the head of my tatterdemalion corps, – Campbell's countenance brewing terrible mischief, and being strongly expressive of a desire for a melee, – I marched up to the " Capitulary Saloon," where, sitting in state, I found the provost Cabral, the other high municipal officers, their secretary, and a legal adviser.

I advanced to the bar. " The provisional government," said Cabral, " has orders from his Excellency immediately to send off you and your countrymen

INTERVIEW WITH THE MAYOR. 5

residing here to La Purificacion, and I presume you are now ready to march."

" Quite ready," I answered, with a respectful bow, " provided you adhere to the interpretation you have given to his Excellency's bando, which, however, I suggest, does not apply at all to Englishmen."

" What!" replied Cabral, " do you come here to beard us in this august hall of justice? If you say more, I shall not only send you to La Purificacion, but you shall all go in chains."

"For that also," said I, " we are ready; here are our bodies, – do as you please. But first we enter, in the name of the British government, our solemn protest against the violence you are about to offer to our rights as subjects of a neutral and friendly power. We protest against the municipality at large, and against you, Mr. Provost, in particular, for all damage, hurt, and loss we may sustain in our persons and property; and we announce our determination instantly to seek redress at the hands of his Excellency the Protector Artigas, through the British commander on this station, for the unwarrantable insult and injustice offered to British subjects by his delegated authorities in

86 CONDITIONAL RELEASE PROPOSED.

Corrientes. Lastly, I request that our protest may be recorded by your notary in the journals of the court."

This grandiloquent appeal had the desired effect. The Cabildantes got frightened, and Cabral himself began to perceive that, in meddling with British subjects, to use a very homely adage, he had taken the wrong sow by the ear. He still blustered, but the other members of the court rose in almost open rebellion against him; and in the midst of their squabble we were desired to retire from the hall.

In twenty minutes we were recalled. With a strong eulogium on the forbearance and magnanimity which were characteristic of the court, Cabral intimated that they had determined to consult the Protector on the subject of the bando, requiring us, in the meantime, to give good and sufficient security not to leave Corrientes till the Protector's answer was received.

" For my own part," said I to this demand, "I will not give the security of a single dollar; but" (I turned to my followers) " he who chooses to give it, may."

" No!" vociferated Campbell, in a voice that

REJECTED PROPOSALS. 87

made old Cabral jump from his seat," No security!" and " No security!" was re-echoed from all the English shoemakers, carpenters, and sailors there and then assembled.

Another storm arose among the counsellors, and again we were ordered to retire.

We returned. " You will enter," said Cabral, suffocated with rage, " into your own recognizances to await the result of our consultation with the Protector."

" I came to this court," I replied, " with my mind made up to one of two results: to return home as free as I came, or to go as your prisoner to La Purificacion. From that determination, nothing you can say will move me." I then turned to Campbell, who was now rubbing his hands in glee, – and "No recognizances" was unanimously agreed to.

Cabral was almost beside himself on being thus bearded and baffled. But his colleagues had now an action of damages, – a British frigate, – and the infuriated

Artigas, vividly before their eyes. Support their chief magistrate they would not. Nay, they began to lay the whole blame of the whole proceeding on his shoulders; and, in fine, we were

88 THE ENGLISH LIBERATED.

sent away as I had made certain we should be – just as we came, – the poor Spaniards marching off unaccompanied by the European English.

The whole measure being obnoxious to the kind- hearted Correntinos, and the Cabildantes being in very bad odour with the citizens at large, our release was celebrated as a public victory over the crestfallen municipality, and we were congratulated on all hands. To complete Cabral's discomfiture, when Artigas heard of what had passed, he wrote iivthe most contemptuous as well as angry terms to the Cabildantes, telling them that only such a*burro*(ass) as a Corrientes alcalde could be ignorant that " Europeo" meant a Spaniard and not an Englishman.

Your's, &c.

W. P. R.

8

SECTION 8

LETTER LT.

W. P. R. toGeneralMiller.

Don Ysidoro and his Capataz in the Country – Don Ysidoro likes to talk about Tigers – His Adventures with them – Camalotes – A Tiger from one of them pays a visit to Don Ysidoro in his Town House – The Capataz attacked – The Assaulter shot dead – Results – Ball and Supper in Corrientes – Stealing no robbery at a Ball – Effect of English dishes upon the Correntinas – Costume – Leave Corrientes for good, and arrive in Buenos Ayres.

London, 1842.

DonYsidoro Martinez y Cires passed some years of his life in an estancia which he possessed in the interior of the province; and being well wooded, it was a favourite haunt of the tigers. Our friend's capataz, an old and faithful servant, was born in San Paulo, a province of Brazil, lying contiguous to the Banda Oriental, and, like many other Paulistas, he was a capital tiger hunter.

In the course of his country life, Don Ysidoro had many tiger adventures in company with his Paulista capataz; and when he sold his estancia, bought his town house, and thenceforward resided

90 CAMALOTES.

in the city, he delighted in going over his hard fought fields, and in recounting many a strange adventure and hair-breadth 'scape, connected with his and his capataz's tiger hunts. By degrees Don Ysidoro's tiger tales gradually assumed the form of a hobby, an amusing and innocent one, which, when we knew him, he was fond' of riding; and of course everything relating to tigers possessed an interest for our friend far exceeding that which he took in the generality of subjects which came before him. Thus imbued with the romance of tigers, an incident occurred, during my second visit to Corrientes which reached the very climax of Don Ysidoro's adventures in this line.

In great swellings and risings of the Parana, as we have had occasion to remark,* masses of vegetable matter get detached from the islands, and come floating down the stream; while it sometimes happens on these masses, or *camalotes,* that tigers descend, confused and frightened on finding the *island* going down the river with them.

Such a camalote in June 1817 came down the Parana, and was thrown by the current upon the river side, close to the port of Corrientes. An imTHE CAPATAZ ATTACKED. 91

* Letters on Paraguay, vol. ii. p. 221.

mense tiger descended with the mass, aud on being brought up by the river bank, the frightened animal walked on shore, and directed its footsteps towards the town. Fortunately the occurrence took place just at the dawn of day, when no one was astir, otherwise the consequences might have been disastrous.

In the tiger's proceeding to the town there was nothing extraordinary; such a thing had happened before; but it was somewhat singular that the tiger passed many other houses, and advanced to the very heart of the city. The animal's course was interrupted by a low wall which ran round the garden at the back of Don Ysidoro's house; and accordingly, springing over the wall, the tiger made the premises of Don Ysidoro the termination of its journey!

Walking up the centre of the garden, towards the family mansion, the fearful visitor came to some small out-houses, of which the gables formed one side of a small inner court belonging to the house. In one of these out-houses slept the unfortunate Paulista capataz. His door was standing open; he had just got up, and was sitting on the side of his bed in

J2 THE ASSAULTER SHOT DEAD.

the act of dressing; the tiger looked in, glared, and in an instant sprung upon his victim.

In the meantime it luckily happened that a man had seen the tiger just as it was vaulting over the garden wall, and he instantly ran to the front of Don Ysidoro's house, and thundered at the door. The word " Tiger," vociferated by the informant, instantly caught Don Ysidoro's ear. He sprung from bed, heard of the fatal entrance, and now surrounded by his servants, hastened to the court which I have already mentioned. Through a crevice in the gable wall of the room where the capataz lay, his master distinctly saw the unfortunate man stretched on his bed, motionless and covered with blood, while the tiger, with glaring eyes, stood over him. To open the door into the out-houses, and to give the tiger an opportunity of rushing upon them would have been madness. Don Ysidoro, therefore, sent a messenger to the guard-house in the Plaza mayor to bring over instantly three or four soldiers with loaded muskets. In the

meantime he made an aperture in the wall as nearly as possible on a level with the tiger's head. It heard the noise, gazed on the spot, but moved not. Don Ysidoro gently
RESULTS.
called to the capataz, who just moved one finger to show that he was alive, and again lay with the stillness and stiffness of death. All was right; Don Ysidoro took one of the muskets, the best; assured himself that it was loaded; got the muzzle in at the aperture; and with his old and wonted precision he sent the ball right into the head of the animal, which instantly fell dead on the body of the Paulista tiger hunter.

The poor fellow was dreadfully lacerated; but his wounds being dressed, the doctor expressed Ids hope that they would not prove fatal.

The news soon spread through Corrientes that Don Ysidoro had killed a tiger, and at an early hour Mr. Postlethwaite and I hastened to the scene of action. There stood Don Ysidoro, in the centre of his front patio or court, surrounded by his friends, and the huge tiger lying stretched at his feet. Our friend glowed with excitement and animation, another Wellington with the laurels of Waterloo fresh about his brows.

The particulars which I have given we obtained from Don Ysidoro himself. Happily the Paulista recovered; and the tiger's skin, one of the most magnificent I ever saw, having been stuffed to the
94
BALLANDSUPPERATCORRIENTES.
life with yerba, thenceforth adorned the hall of Don Ysidoro, the last and best of his trophies as a tiger hunter.

Before taking leave of Corrientes, I cannot refrain from mentioning that Mr. Postlethwaite gave a grand ball and supper to the fashionables of the place on his *saint's day*(St. John the Baptist's), in June. All the respectable part of the population was included in the invitation, and all of them thronged to the fete. Some of the ladies, pure descendants of the Spaniards, with still a tinge of noble blood in their veins, came loaded with the antique but rich ornaments which had descended from mother to daughter, and which consisted of large pearls, single and in rows, and of brilliants as well as rose diamonds, set with equal and ponderous clumsiness. Large lockets and miniature pictures dangled in front of the old ladies, whose dresses were equally old fashioned with their jewellery, faded brocade and figured satins with deep lace ruffles and frills, and fans of a foot in diameter. Some of the young Correntinas were neatly attired, although thej wanted that fashionable air which no provincials, in any part of the world, are able to attain.

BALLANDSUPPERATCORRIENTES.95
Of the South American*balls*I shall have occasion to speak when I get to Buenos Ayres; here I wish to mention some particulars about a*supper*which I never observed in the capital.

Mrs. Postlethwaite, aided by the young ladies and by one or two Correntinas of the best taste, laid out the tables so beautifully that, to look at them, no one could have fancied there was any lack of " all the delicacies of the season" in Corrientes. With the exception of ice creams, which in that warm country are not to be had for " love nor money," I cannot recollect anything which is placed on the tables in the supper-rooms when a ball is given in London that was not to be found on Mrs. Portlethwaite's tables in Corrientes.

Hours being earlier there than in Belgrave- square, the company was *admitted* to supper at twelve o'clock. I say admitted, not led; for although I doubt not the Correntinas of the present day can say *"Nous avans change tout cela,"* in 1817 the admission to the supper-room presented a curious scene. The ladies and their slaves and servants squeezed in at the door, higgledy piggledy, pretty much as hungry expectants of a new play at

96 STEALING NO ROBBERY AT A BALL.

Covent-garden crowd in at the pit-door the moment it is thrown open. The ladies, as fast as they could, secured seats, and the servants squatted behind them on the floor. The demolition which then commenced of the good things was astounding and truly laughable. Not content with the slow progress which half a dozen of us were making in carving, some of the ladies literally laid hold with their hands of the ducks, chickens, fowls, partridges, and tore them limb from limb. Then we found that the servants were placed as receptacles for whatever their mistresses could conveniently throw to them. *"Coina!"* (in Guarani, *Take if*) cried one dame, and away flew the leg of a goose into the lap (in which was spread out a large towel) of the squatted Mulatta behind. *"Coina!"* said another, and off went in a different direction the drumstick of a turkey. *"Coina!"* issued from an opposite side, and the half-consumed breast of a capon went over the shoulder of the sitter and into the wallet of the squatter. As this kind of sharp- shooting advanced it increased in vivacity, so that in all directions, and with unceasing velocity, pastry, poultry, cakes, ham, game, and many

STEALING AT A BALL NO ROBBERY. 97

other dainties flew from the table to the floor till the "maids" retired heavily laden with the spoils so dexterously acquired by the mistresses.

Some of our English dishes puzzled the Cor- rentinas. There were placed here and there small plates with fresh butter made up into pretty little *prints;* and a poor girl sitting next to me, mistaking one for a sweetmeat, put her fork into the print and transferred it *whole* into her mouth. What was she to do? she could neither gulp it down nor cry *"Coma!"* this no longer being a transferable property. She cast a piteous side glance at me, to see that I was not looking; and then she disposed of the "print of butter" in a manner which I must leave to my readers themselves to divine.

In the centre of the table stood a beautiful and to all appearance most inviting dish. It was a tipsey cake – a trifle – whipt up into beautiful but deceitful " flummery." A Correntino thrusting a spoon into it, carried the contents to his mouth, where it so instantly vanished into "thin air," that the visitor looked for all the world as if he had swallowed a spectre.

From the gentlemen who had attended the ball

Vol. Hi. F

98 LEAVE CORRIENTES FOR GOOD,

we had many complimentary visits the' following day; and as it happened also to be the Dia de San Guillermo, Saint William's day, it was believed as a matter of course to be my birth-day, and the compliment was accordingly extended to myself. As a curious illustration of the unrestrained scope which the ladies of Corrientes allowed to the whim of the moment, I must mention that the governor's*wife*came to pay her respects in the character of the governor himself. She walked quietly through the streets and into Mr. Postle- thwaite's drawing-room, dressed in the governor's military cloak, wearing his cocked hat, and with his long gold-headed cane of office in her hand. Seating herself on the sofa, she threw open her cloak and discovered the gold epaulettes on her shoulders and the sword buckled on her waist, saying at the same time, with much gravity, that the*governor*had come to express his delight with the entertainment of the previous night.

While I was thus agreeably passing my time in Corrientes, I received a summons to return without delay to Buenos Ayres. All things having prospered with my brother in England, I was called on immediately to proceed to organize our mercantileAND ARRIVE AT BUENOS AYRES. 99 establishment in the capital of the Argentine republic.

I spent two days, therefore, in bidding adieu to all my kind Corrientes friends. I separated from Mr Postlethwaite and his family with the regret which the loss of such agreeable society could not fail to inspire. I set off on horseback with a solitary servant; stopped a day at Goya to take leave of my friends there; took the route by the Bajada and Santa Fe; visited my friends Messrs. Fuentes and Lezica and many others on my way; and in November, 1817, after a gallop of about nine hundred miles, I found myself once more in the streets of the city of Buenos Ayres.

Yours, &c,

W. P. R.

9

SECTION 9

LETTER LIT.

W. P. R. toGeneralMiller.

I am established at Buenos Ayres – Then in a palmy state – Don
Antonio de Escalada – His Wife and Family – The two young
Escaladas – San Martin's Marriage – Digression upon Old Age –
Escalada's Tertulia – Dona Ana Riglos – Dona Melchora Sar-
ratea – Dona Mariquita Thompson – Madame Riglos – Their
Characters, individually – Dona Mariquita espouses the French
Consul.

*London,*1842.

AlthoughI had now (December, 1817) been four years in the provinces of the River
Plate, I knew little of Buenos Ayres, or its society. I had resided almost entirely in the
interior, among a people that I knew were essentially different in many points from
the Portenos, or inhabitants of the capital.

But I had now come to a conclusion of my wanderings. I set myself down as a
denizen of Buenos Ayres, and I naturally began to scan more closely the society of
which I was about to constitute myself a fixed member.

I now classified myself for the first time as an English merchant in a foreign country. What

I AM ESTABLISHED AT BUENOS AYRES. 101

I had considered our large operations in the interior gradually assumed an insignificant appearance in my eyes, as I surveyed the larger stage and wider range of mercantile character which presented themselves to my view in the great port of the eastern continent of Spanish South America. I found myself, by the exertions of our own immediate friends at home, launched into mercantile correspondence and commercial operations with the Barings, the Gladstones, the Inglis & Ellices, the Willinks, the Parishes, and many of the other leading merchants of Europe; so that I was soon deeply engaged in details vastly more complicated and extensive than those which arose out of the sale of goods and purchase of yerba in Paraguay, or of the barter of manufactures and doubloons for hides and wool at Corrientes.

I was much taken up, after my arrival, with the onerous duties which fell to my share in establishing our house; but the very extent of business which we soon found ourselves doing naturally brought me into contact with most of the principal inhabitants, native as well as foreign, of Buenos Ayres; and ere six months had passed away, I was on as intimate a footing with all my polished neigh-

102 BUENOS AYRES IN A PALMY STATE.

hours and genteel acquaintance of the capital, as that on which I had been with the primitive people of Paraguay, or the equally uncontaminated community of Corrientes.

Buenos Ayres, for the first twenty years that the English knew it, – that is, from 1810 to 1830, – might really be called a delightful place. From political causes there has been a sad change for the worse, in the construction of its society, from 1830 down to the present day; and although it is not our province at this time to enter into an examination of those causes, nor into a detail of their effects, it must hereafter form an interesting, although a painful chapter, in the link of events which it is our present intention by degrees to record.

In 1817, Buenos Ayres was in its most palmy state: tranquillity and prosperity at home, success and renown abroad, kept the capital in high spirits; and all the agreeable qualities of the Portenos were at that time seen to the highest advantage.

The general custom with all the families of any distinction was to keep open house, and nightly to hold those agreeable*reunions,*so well known by the name of*tertulias.*They were equivalent to the French*soiree*and Italian*conversazione.*Although

DON ANTONIO DE ESCALADA. 103

to those tertulias every respectable person, on a slight introduction, was welcome, they yet shaded off into certain distinctive sets; and accordingly each great family had its own regular*tertulianos,*with the occasional admixture of those who chose now and then to frequent the house. In this way, while I kept up a general acquaintance with all, I became more particularly the*tertuliano*of the party whose heads were the Escaladas, the Oromis, and the Rigloses.

Perhaps there were no two men so well known, so much respected, and so well liked as the brothers Escalada – Don Antonio and Don Francisco, both born in Buenos Ay res, and decided patriots. The latter was a perfect impersonation of the grave, dignified, but urbane Spaniard. He took a prominent lead in the municipal affairs of his native city; but neither he nor his family mixed much in what may be called gay society; and his tertulias accordingly were of a sombre cast, little frequented by those fond of spending a lively evening.

Don Antonio was exactly the reverse. He did not trouble himself with the details of public business: he was a lively, jocose old gentleman, fond of seeing his house crowded by the young and the gay,

104 THE TWO YOUNG ESCALADAS.

both of his own countrymen and countrywomen, and by foreigners, particularly English. His wife (a second one) had been a celebrated beauty, and was still a fine woman. His two sons by her, both in the army, were brave, gallant, and handsome young men; and his daughters were youthful, pretty, and engaging. He had also several granddaughters, great belles, the children of his first wife's daughter, now a matron, and married to Don Jose de Maria, whom we have had occasion honourably to mention in our first work, as long our agent in Paraguay.

Don Antonio Escalada's house was the one most frequented by Viscount Beresford, and often have I heard him there spoken of in terms of the most affectionate respect.

The brothers Escalada bore the very highest character among their fellow citizens for unblemished honour, high integrity, and disinterested patriotism. The one in private life, and the other in public,. being often called to a high, sometimes the highest magisterial situation, commanded the respect and possessed the affections of the Buenos Ayreans at large. They never condescended to party feeling; they had too much noble pride, too nice a sense ofSanMartin'sMarrtaqe.105

honour, ever to lend themselves to a party cabal; and thus, in turbulent times, among many changes, in the midst of faction and intrigue, surrounded by men at once ambitious and unscrupulous, who were to-day everything, to-morrow nothing, the brothers Escalada held on the even tenour of their way; were never molested by any party, were courted by all; and at last, in the fulness of time, they peacefully descended to their graves, leaving the universal feeling behind them, that they had lived and died good and worthy men.

With Don Antonio Escalada, and all the agreeable members of his numerous family, I lived, as a bachelor, on terms of much intimacy. Here also I became acquainted with the hero of the River Plate provinces, General San Martin, who, in 1817, after the battle of Chacabuco, paid his addresses to Dofia Remedios, the amiable and fascinating daughter of Don Antonio. How time passes! San Martin unhappily lost his estimable wife at an early age, remaining with an only daughter; and a year or two ago I had a pressing invitation from*her*husband, Don Mariano Balcarce, a protege in his youth of my own, to go over to Paris, and spend a day or two with his wife and the general, his father-

106 OLD AGE.

in-law, grandfather of the new stock of rising Bal- carces! When we are inclined, as we constantly are, to forget that we are*getting old,*these are the circumstances, the springing up of a second and a third generation, which remind us that time flies, and that we are steadily advancing and constantly drawing nearer to the goal at which we finish our career. When I first visited South America, Mrs. San Martin was little more than a child, and now I am invited to go and see her grandchildren, several years old.

One would think that this were sufficient to teach any man that he was no chicken: but no: I shrink (as I suppose all my neighbours do) from the confession to myself that I am*getting old;*and whereas at twenty-one I looked on a man of eight and forty as an "old gentleman,"*now,*when any one asks me if such a one is old, my ready reply is, " I should say not;*about my own age.*"For the present I have extended my elastic view of old age to the broken numbers which lie between 60 and 70; and I sometimes wonder, should I ever come to be a sexagenarian, how far I may then modify my designation of an*old man. I*should not at all be surprised if I still continued my present answer of " not old – *about my own age."*

Escalada's Tertulia.107

Without apologizing for this little digression, which may not be without its use to readers of my own standing, if they will extract the moral which may. be drawn from it, I proceed to say that Don Antonio Escalada's tertulias were the best attended, because the most agreeable of Buenos Ayres. They contained a happy mixture of native and foreign society: no ceremony, no preparation for a party. It was a family meeting. The charm lay in the society itself; and to enhance its value, it needed not the fashionable addition of fine suppers or elaborate refreshments. Conversation, music, dancing, high spirits, good humour, were the happily combined ingredients which gave a relish to the whole. The house itself boasted of half a dozen of as nice partners for the country dance and the minuet as Buenos Ayres could produce. Dona Remedies and her sister Nieves; Dona Encarna- cion, Dona Trinidad, and Dona Mercedes de Maria, to say nothing of the mother of these latter young ladies; and Dona Tomasa, the lady of the house, wife of Don Antonio. Then the charming Oromis,*cum multis aliis,*made up a tertulia of the choicest kind. The old gentleman, sometimes assisted by his gallant son, the youthful Colonel Escalada, sometimes by his next, Mariano, or, in their

108 DONA ANA RIGLOS.

absence, by young Oromi, presided over the whole; and it was indeed a treat to see the sexagenarian, full of spirits and glee, catch up two or three of the prettiest girls in the room by turns, and gracefully lead them through the movements of the minuet. We entered and departed as we pleased,*sans cere- monie;*and in this way you might visit two or three tertulias in the course of the evening, always certain of a frank welcome wherever you went.*Paso quel tempo*; but assuredly it was one not easily to be rivalled in the best times of any country with which I am acquainted. Some of my readers may fancy I am here painting the society of Buenos Ayres*couleur de rose;*but those who have best known it at the time of which I speak, will readily recognize the truthl'ulness of my picture.

Beside Escalada's, we had many other highly agreeable*casas de tertulia*where foreigners were received with the most marked kindness and hospitality. Among these, the Rigloses, the Alvears, Barquins, Balcarces, Sarrateas; the Balbastros, Rondeaus, Thompsons, Rubios, and Casamayors, were great leaders in the fashionable circles.

There were, among my more intimate acquaintance, three remarkable ladies; and as I think they belong to the domestic history of Buenos Ayres, I

CHARACTER OF MADAME RIGLOS. 109

must not pass them over in silence. They were Dona Ana Riglos, Dona Melchora Sarratea, and Dona Mariquita Thompson. They were the heads of three distinct parties, which I can scarcely call political, but which I may designate as public. One heard all the news at their morning levees: learned all the movements of the great men of the state, in power and out of power: the best of these men you met at their houses. Public events were discussed good humouredly, almost philosophically; and as the three ladies in question were all favourable to European alliances, their houses were the constant resort of both English and French naval commanders, consuls-general and other foreign envoys and diplomatists. There they got much better acquainted with all the *on dits* of the day than at the government palace; and there they indirectly promulgated their own opinions and views, in the certainty that they would reach the proper quarter.

Dona Ana Riglos, a widow, was a nice and intelligent old lady; vivacious, well bred, with a tinge of aristocratic etiquette of the old school, she was yet at home with every body, and her parties were of the pleasantest I knew. Her son, Don Miguel, was educated in England, and returned to

110 CHARACTER OF DONA HELCHORA SARRATEA,

Buenos Ayres in the same convoy with myself, in 1813. He was then a handsome, fair young man of twenty-one, spoke English remarkably well, dressed a la Bond-street, and was one of not very many who really profited by an English education. 4 mighty favourite (and deservedly so) he was of his mother and sister, and still more of his aunt, Dona Eusebia de la Sala – perhaps the best natured, kindest, and frankest woman in Buenos Ayres. Although of a certain age, she was always the person most courted in the tertulia; and she was an especial favourite with the great mass of our naval officers, from the hearty good nature with which she corrected their tripping tongues in the Spanish, and their awkward hitches in the figures of the country dance.

The house of Mrs. Riglos, or, as she was often styled,*Madame Riglos,*was the chief resort of the ministerialists, and she might properly be designated the lady leader of the Tory section of the Buenos Ayreans.

On the other hand, Dona Melchora Sarratea was, with certain allowances in favour of Madame de Stael, the Stael of the place. Her family was of the first and most honourable of the city; her brother, Don Manuel, her pride and boast, (ofAND OF DONA MAEIQUITA THOMPSON. Ill

whom, both as a public man and an agreeable friend, I shall have to speak hereafter), was educated at Madrid, and belonged to the Court there; and though she was a staunch adherent to the new order of things, Dona Melchora by no means liked to see the relaxation in public morals which the revolution, as she affirmed, had brought with it. She was herself a decidedly clever woman; had been in her younger days a reigning beauty; had been too particular to marry; and now, a still handsome, chatty, and most agreeable person, she kept Don Manuel's house, a perfect bijou of its kind, both brother and sister having an exquisite taste in all that pertains to the exterior embellishments of life. Mr. and Miss Sarratea had an immense fund of agreeable anecdote, with a perfect knowledge of everybody about them, and of everything which was happening around them, which they communicated in the most piquant way; and as besides all this, one went with a sort of tacit privilege to " murmurar" against all the abuses of the day, no wonder that Dona Melchora had always her hands full of public and private

* Since writing this I have had the pleasure of seeing Don Manuel, who is now Minister Plenipotentiary from the United Provinces of the River Plate, to the Court of the Tuilleries.

112 SHE MARRIES THE FRENCH CONSUL,

business, nor that she was considered to be decidedly of Whiggish principles.

But what shall I say of my dear friend, – alas! I must now say, my dear*old*friend Dona Mariquita Thompson that*was?*Run not away with the idea that because she bore the name of Thompson, she was in any way connected with the gentleman who, under that name, makes so remarkable a figure on our stage. Dona Mariquita Sanchez de Thompson was a Buenos Ayrean by birth, and so was Mr. Thompson himself, he being a descendant only of the family whose patronymic stamps it so undeniably as belonging to the race of John Bull. Mr. Thompson I never knew, Dona Mariquita being a handsome, gay, and fascinating young widow when I had first the honour of making her acquaintance in 1817- She is now Dona Mariquita Sanchez de Mandeville, having married the*ci-dcvant*French consul-general*(not*the English minister) at Buenos Ayres, an accomplished officer who had served under Bonaparte.

From the very circumstance of Dona Mariquita having married a French consul-general, you may infer that her rule lay in the foreign department,·and sure I am that Lord Palmerston, with all his acknowledged tact, with all his splendid talent, and

AND PLAYS L AGREABLE.

113

with all his*s avoir fair e*>never swayed the affairs of Downing-street with more success and brilliancy than did Dona Mariquita exercise her female diplomacy in her splendid mansion of the Calle del Empedrado. She played the parts of the easy English countess, the vivacious and witty French marquise, the elegant, graceful Portena patrician, in such wise that each country might have claimed her for its own, so happy an art had she of identifying herself for the time being, with the nation to which her friends or visitors belonged. Dona Mariquita had three or four pretty daughters just beginning to bud at the time of which I speak; who have since (many years ago) got married, and who, for aught I know to the contrary, are themselves by this time grandmothers.

There were many other agreeable persons who formed heads of political parties in Buenos Ayres, and whose tertulias were all extremely pleasant; but I have given you sufficient details to show you the kind of society of which at the time I have mentioned Buenos Ayres boasted.

Your's, &c.,

W. P. R.

10

SECTION 10

LETTER LIII.

W. P. R. toGeneralMiller.

Rupture among the Domestic Circles – English Females in Buenos
Ayres – Bachelor Society – Don Antonio and his Umitas –
Marriages – Society of the Naval Officers.

London, 1842.

WhenI began to nlix as a member with Buenos Ayres Society, although it consisted
of native and foreign, it could scarcely be said to be divided into these distinctive parts.
They so amalgamated and run into one; they were so homogeneous in their character,
that they often seemed to form but one community, have but one language, and to be
animated by one general national feeling. The English formed in this case a complete
exception to their general rule of non-intercourse with natives in a foreign country,
when they have a sufficient society among themselves.

I am sorry to say that this happy family union was lost before I took my final
departure from Buenos Ayres. I attribute it to two causes. 1st. RUPTURE AMONG
THE DOMESTIC CIRCLES. 115

To the political convulsions which attended the establishment of the two parties of
Federales and Unitarios. Hatred and rancour commenced with leading politicians, but

gradually extended their baneful influence to all the principal native families, dividing them and breaking up the formerly united society; and above all, putting an end to the nightly tertulias, the bond of union, as it were, between the Buenos Ayreans and foreigners. 2ndly. To the great increase of English families, many of the female heads of which gradually withdrew from native society as they found increasing claims on the part of their own; while new arrivals, finding an ample sufficiency of English, looked for no other or farther society. I do not suppose, that the intercourse is entirely at an end; but I believe it has sunk into the same sluggish apathy, which restrains the English in other places from mixing with the people of the foreign country in which they may happen to reside.

In 1818, and for ten years afterwards, it was different in Buenos Ayres; and having given you a sketch of native society at that time, you would not have a just view of the*whole,*if I said nothing of the foreign.

116 ENGLISH FEMALES IN BUENOS AYRES.

But it is not quite so easy for me to enter into a detail of the English, as of the Porteno families which stood at the head of our society. Those who contributed most to stamp it with a frank and open character which formed its leading charm, are indeed scattered, but I am still on terms of personal intimacy with many who have survived to the present day, (some alas! the nearest and dearest to me, have disappeared), and I am not sure that I shall have their sanction in introducing them to the notice of my readers, even though that be in the way of praise. I may have a note of remonstrance, dated Regent's Park, from Mrs. Dickson, if I mention her as the leader of English*haut ton,*at the "Quinta;"* another from Mrs. Brittain despatched from Blackheath, complaining of my unparliamentary conduct in not having given previous notice of my intention here to record her pleasant parties and agreeable tertulias atWaterloo. f Mrs. Fair, the amiable partner of a gentlemen of whom we have already had occasion repeatedly to

* A pretty Villa, standing on the Barranca or Cliff at the north end of Buenos Ayres, which Mr. Dickson rented of Mrs. Riglos.

f The name which Mr. Brittain, (now no more,) gave to the country house which he built at the commencement of the Barraca Road.

ENGLISH FEMALES. 117

speak, might beg of me from Edinburgh to omit her name in the second edition. Mrs. Cartwright, to whom, under a different name, my readers have already been introduced in our first volume, might from Frankfort-on-the-Maine express her doubts as to the policy of my going over such tender ground as the relative claims of herself and her friends to pre-eminence in the walks of fashion; and even my own relative, Mrs. Mackinlay and my friend and connexion, Mrs. Barton, might protest from Buenos Ayres against my referring now to the happy bygone days when we formed a united family, and looked on " Mackinlay's Quinta," as almost our common home.

Having thus, however, incidentally mentioned the names of some of our principal British residents at the time of which I speak, I may go on to say that the very pretty villa, which Mr. and Mrs. Dick- son occupied, stood on the north side of Buenos Ayres, while the country residences of Mr. and Mrs. Mackinlay, and Mr. and Mrs. Brittaiu were at the southern extremity of the city. These three agreeable families were among the earliest to settle in the place; they were decidedly the leaders of

118 ENGLISH FEMALES.

English society, and they mingled more with the Buenos Ayreans than did any of their successors. Mr. Fair married a sister of Mrs. Brittain in 1818, and the following year Mr. Cartwright led Miss Postlethwaite to the altar, both which events brought to our society a happy and lasting addition. I myself followed these good examples, and by degrees we were reinforced by other new comers, of whom I may have to speak, should we advance to another series.

With all the families mentioned, and with many which succeeded them, I not only had the pleasure of living on terms of strict intimacy and friendship, but what I think says something for the materials of which our English society was constructed, the great proportion, if not all of them, now, at a distance of four or five and twenty years, I reckon among the most valued of my friends. 1 may add, however, that, from circumstances which I need not at present detail, Mr. Mackinlay's house at Buenos Ayres ere long became the one of my principal resort.

If the married English society of Buenos Ayres was agreeable, that of the bachelors was very littleBachelor'sSociety.119

less so. I belonged to it for three years, and the intercourse we kept up with each other was really as if we had all belonged to one family. If there was not a community of goods, there was a community of dinners and dwellings. It was an understood thing that we dined at what table we pleased, without the formality of an invitation: and in fact, our doors at all hours were as much open to our friends as to ourselves. The highly irregular living of unmarried Englishmen, during the first years of their settlement at Buenos Ayres gradually gave way to the softening and humanizing influence of female society; so that in 1818 or 1819 we had sobered down to a very well conducted community.* As one curious illustration of the social intercourse which was generally maintained, I must mention a pleasant fashion of Don Antonio Escalada which he kept up year by year, and which when I first witnessed it much amused me.

* The two leading members of our bachelor society (although they both left at an early period) were Mr. R. Ponsonby Staples and Mr. John Macneile; and among the agreeable members of it were our personal friends Messrs. J. Buchanan, Robert and William Orr, William Cochran, Dr. Campbell and his brother William, W. M'Cracken, A. Jamieson, John Watson, T. Eastman, and many others.

120 DON ANTONIO ESCALADA's UMITAS.

Standing one day in our patio, or front court, just at our dinner hour, (I was then residing with my partner, Mr. Fair, and his lady,) in walked Don Antonio with a black slave behind him, bearing an immense silver dish covered with a white cloth. " Ola!" said the old gentleman, " I have come to dine with you to-day, and I have brought a better dish with me than even Mrs. Fair can place upon her table." So saying, he marched into the dining room, with his negro, and removing the white napkin from his dish, discovered a mountain of *umitas,* a delicacy much relished by the South American gourmand.*

Don Antonio then sat down to dinner without farther ceremony, and mightily pleased he was to hear the praises and see the rapid demolition of his umitas at the dinner table. To all his particular friends he paid a visit of a similar kind during the season of the umitas.

* The umitas can only be had when the*choc/en,*or early and tender Indian corn, come in. The head of maize being boiled, it is stripped of the corn, which is minced up fine with meat, spices, &c. The mince is made warm, and in small quantities placed in the broad leaves of the stalk of maize, each leaf being folded up with its contents (something like a Maintenon cutlet), and tied with a*strip*of the leaf itself. Of these umitas thus made up, Don Antonio brought about four dozen.

SOCIETY ENLIVENED BY NAVAL OFFICERS. 121

At an early stage of the River Plate independence, there were very few, scarcely any foreign families of note, except English, resident in the capital. Yet we had for some time Monsieur Bonpland, the famous botanist, and Madame; and Mr. and Mrs. Zimmermann, remarkably nice and pleasant Germans. Two or three English residents were married to Portenas, – Dr. Colin Campbell who became son-in-law of Don Francisco Escalada; Mr. Miller, as already mentioned, who espoused the beautiful and amiable Miss Balbastro; Mr. Edward Lawson, the husband of Dona Encarnacion de Maria, (daughter of Don Jose de Maria); and one or two others, including a universal favourite among us, now, alas! no more, Mr. W. E. Stewart, married to a Montevidean young lady.

Our society was always enlivened, and very generally improved, by the British naval commanders and officers, who succeeded each other on the River Plate station. From 1817 to a period beyond the one (1820) to which our present details extend, we had first commodore (now admiral) Bowles, and then commodore Sir Thomas Hardy, the late governor of Greenwich Hospital, both much esteemed by all classes, native and foreign, and both

122 SOCIETY ENLIVENED.

possessing, from their tact, good management, and moderation, much influence as public men. We found, without almost any exception, the officers belonging to the frigates, as well as those (including the commanders) of smaller vessels of war, most gentlemanlike persons, and great accessions to our general society.

Such is a sketch of some of the component elements of social life as I found it on my settling at Buenos Ayres; and the specimens I have given you may be taken as a fair sample of the whole. Your's, &c.

W. P. R.

11

SECTION 11

LETTER LIV.

W. P. R. toGeneralMiller.

Amusements – Theatre – Public Entertainments – 25th of May –
National Hymn – High Mass – Religious Ceremonies – Carnival
– Ash Wednesday – San Ysidro – San Jos$ de Flores – Horse
Racing – Pedestrian Feat.

London, 1842.

Theamusements of the people of Buenos Ayres were not very various, but those they possessed they very heartily enjoyed. They were seldom or never interrupted by bad weather; and not being such a money-making people as we are, nor pressed with a redundant population, which makes constant, unremitting labour in the masses an imperious necessity instead of a free choice, the Buenos Ayreans at large appropriated to themselves, throughout the year, every one of the holidays which the Roman Catholic Calendar so liberally permits to the followers of that creed. Exclusive of Sundays, I think we used to have in the course of the year some five and thirty or forly days, on which business of every kind was suspended.

124 BUENOS AYRES THBATRE.

The city boasted of one theatre, of the architectural beauty of which I am not able to speak in terms of praise; neither can I say that the appointments, decorations, and *dramatis personce,* were much on a Covent-garden or Drury-lane scale; and to this may be attributed the fact, that it was little, if at all frequented by foreigners, especially the English. However, it pleased the people themselves; while the provincials pronounced the scenery superb, and the acting incomparable. They had their Keans and their Madame Vestris's of their own; the viceroy's box was converted into that of the governor or supreme director, who, surrounded by his great officers, attended on occasion of " grandes funciones," or jubilee nights. The rest of the boxes were then crowded by the rank and beauty of the place; the national hymn (a very fine composition both as to poetry and music) was sung by " all the strength of the company," and enthusiastically received. In short, all was done in the theatre at Buenos Ayres which we see done in our great theatres here; and the people there happily thought as well of their " Casa de Comedia," as the English think of the crack playhouses of their own metropolis. Truth obliges me

PUBLIC ENTERTAINMENTS. 125

to add that the Buenos Ayres theatre, not having been built on the Mackintosh principle, that of being waterproof, whenever it rained heavily at the door- opening hour, every body knew, without the necessity of a public announcement, that there would be no performance that evening.* Visiting the ladies in their boxes was an indispensable piece of etiquette on the part of the gentlemen; and as one knew everybody present, a polite person generally made the round of the boxes in the course of the evening's entertainment.

The Buenos Ayreans are very fond of music; so that in the better times of the place we not only had an excellent Philharmonic Society, but for two seasons we boasted of an Italian opera, sustained by some really first rate *artistes* who had crossed the Atlantic, and delighted the Portenos with their vocal and instrumental performances. We had also a celebrated Spanish singer, of the name of Rosquellas, who was a mighty favourite on the Buenos Ayres boards.

Public entertainments of every kind in South America go by the generic name of *"funciones. "* There were theatrical funciones, funciones de 126 TWENTY-FIFTH OF MAY.

* Heavy rains, I must observe, used generally to stop both business and pleasure in Buenos Ayres.

Iglesia, or church processions, government fun- ciones, or public processions, and, above all, *las funcwnes mayas,* the annual celebration, on the 25th of May, of the independence of the country.

On this latter occasion the square was tastefully fitted up with a moveable boarding which constituted a continuous archway on the four sides, leading into the centre. This boarding was painted and decorated so as to produce a scenic display as viewed from within, the arches being hung with festooned garlands, and the panels covered with emblematic designs, which formed an agreeable vista during the day, and which were illuminated during the night. The rejoicings continued generally for three days. They commenced on the eve of the 25th with music and an illumination of the town, dancing, and a general promenade in the great square; at sunrise the following morning, a salute was fired from the guns of the fort; and the children of the various schools, all neatly dressed, assembled in the*plaza,*where they were formed round the " Pyramid," a not very handsome obelisk, which, standing in the centre, had been erected in commemoration of the Revolution, and on which were inscribed the names of those heroes who had been the leaders in the emancipation of the country. Here

NATIONAL HYMN. 127

the children sung the national hymn, of which the first verse runs thus:

Oid, mortales, el grito Sagrado
Libertad! Libertad! Libertad!
Oid el ruido de rotas Cadenas
Ved entrono la noble igualdad!
Se levanta u la faz de la tierra
Unanueva gloriosa nacion!
Coronada su sien de laureles,
Y il sus plantas rendido un leon!
Chorus.
Sean eternos los laureles
Que supimos couseguir;
Coronados de gloria vivamos!
O juremos con gloria morir!

Which may be closely if not literally translated thus:

Hear mortals hear! the ever sacred cry,
Which through the air resounds, – 'tis liberty!
Behold the broken chains 'neath which we've groaned;
And see equality on high enthroned!
With all a mother's anxious throes, the arth
Gives to a young and glorious nation birth;
With laurel leaves its brow is circled round,
And at its feet a lion* bites the ground.
* An allusion to the conquered "Leon de Iberia," or Lion of Spain.

128 HIGH MASS.

Chonu.

Green may the laurels ever be
Which we have gathered from on high!
Oh let us live but to be ftee!
Or, crowned with glory, let us die!

The hymn having been sung, and the children having retired, the square gradually filled during the forenoon with well dressed people. The troops appeared in nev uniforms; and a grand procession of the public bodies, including the governor, his staff, the*corps diplomatique,*and all the field officers, proceeded from the fort or government house to the cathedral, where high mass, with Te Deum, was celebrated. In the afternoon and during the whole evening bands of military music played popular airs on the balcony of the cabildo or town hall; the inhabitants in gay attire crowded the streets, as well as the plaza mayor or great square, and here a grand display of fire-works took place at nine o'clock, when several thousands assembled to witness them; the night closing in with tertulias given by many of the principal families, and with patriotic assemblages in all the principal cafes of the city. It was for several years remarked, during the fervid

RELIGIOUS CEREMONIES. 129

course of the revolution, that the 25th of May always brought good news; and these creating an enthusiasm which animated all classes, and throwing down for the moment the dikes of *classism,* it was wonderful to see what general hilarity distinguished the " Fiestas mayas" throughout.

The "Funciones de Iglesia," or church gala days, were less remarkable in Buenos Ay res than in any other parts of South America I have visited. There was a practical good sense among the people, a. steady mercantile pursuit, a constant admixture with foreign society, and an imbibing thence of the active business occupations of life, which were all anti- monastic, and opposed to the recurrent ceremonial practised by the Church of Rome. Religious street ceremonies, accordingly, were viewed with much coldness in the capital; and in the great processions of the church, as Corpus Christi and others, the care of them was principally left to the old Spaniards, to *beatas,* (or religious old ladies,) and to the lower classes of the community.

If all parties, however, did not join in the *ceremonies* of mother church, none were found wanting in celebrating her *festivities.* Among these we

130

CARNIVAL.

may reckon *carnival,* the three days which preceded the commencement of Lent.

Most of our readers have heard of the masques and carousals which in Italy marked the season of carnival; but they may not be aware of the mode in which the Buenos Ayreans observed this short space of madness.

The great agent made use of was *water;* and it was brought into play in every possible and imaginable manner. The Sunday afternoon being among all Catholics devoted to amusement and recreation, on the one which preceded Ash Wednesday, the carnival commenced. It approached with insidious moderation. As you walked along the street, you found yourself suddenly besprinkled with *eau de Cologne,* by some fair lady sitting at her window; and presently you saw a dandy throwing rose water in at some other casement. If you made a call, some scented water was perhaps gently discharged at you from a small ivory syringe; or two or three of the inmates might bedew you at once from their lavender bottles. Nay, a plover's egg might be thrown at you, which, breaking on your head or body, you found it to be only the shell filled with

CARNIVAL. 131

eau de mtlle fleuvs, which immediately perfumed both yourself and the room.

This would have been very well had the diversion stopped here. But on going out on Monday morning the streets gave signs here and there of being unusually well watered. Suddenly you found yourself partially drenched, not by *eau de mille fleurs,* but by common well water. As you stopped somewhat angrily to dry yourself, behold a sudden discharge from the other side of the street, which fell upon you like a shower-bath. You found by degrees that you had to proceed with increased caution; for, not only from the houses, but from passengers in the street, you were liable at every turn to have a ducking. After siesta, about four o'clock in the afternoon, the skirmishing evidently increased. Jars full of water were thrown on all passers-by, and those who were on one azotea exchanged shots with their neighbours on the next: immense syringes were used in the streets for attacking the house-tops; and egg shells, which had been in process of collection for many previous weeks, and which were sold by the dozen for the occasion filled with water, and closed at the end, flew about like so many bombs, amid the screams of the fair damsels who occupied the

132 CARNIVAL.

ramparts of the besieged citadels; that is, the azoteas of the houses, consisting generally of only the ground floor.

But Sunday and Monday sunk into utter insignificance when compared with Tuesday, the real " Derby" of the carnival week. As if the two previous days had only been a sort of trial of strength, the terrible battle was waged on the third and concluding day. It was as if Buenos Ayres were a city of mad-houses, and all the inmates of them simultaneously let loose. The highest families and the most delicate females caught the infection. One would have thought that they had invoked the god of the River Plate to come forth with all his stores, in order to give effect to the saturnalia of the "people of his capital. Tubs, casks, slipper-baths, jars, jugs, and mugs were all arranged on the azoteas, filled with water. The streets were paraded by masked horsemen, and by pedestrians, daring the fair ones on the housetops to battle. Family fought with family, and streams of water flowed through the streets, washed the walls, and filled the interior of the houses. Sometimes carried away by an irresistible paroxysm, the ladies would rush from the azotea to the front

CARNIVAL. 133

gate, to make quite sure of deluging some individual picked out from the crowd. Now a door was attacked by a band of young men, carried by them, and then they were seen on the azotea, engaged at close quarters in a water combat with the inmates. All of course were drenched to the skin, the robes of the ladies clinging to their forms, and the water dripping from them as if they had just come out of their baths. The encounters in the street were often of the rudest, nay, almost savage kind. Horsemen ran up against horsemen; knives sometimes gleamed; missiles went through the air, particularly ostrich eggs, which, from their immense weight, were always dangerous, and in some cases proved fatal; and every soul being dripping wet, horses and all, the irresistible feeling on a quiet spectator's mind was that universal insanity pervaded the town. Many accidents, of course, every year occurred; and I believe not a few females of delicate constitution died from the effects of cold, caught during their eight and forty hours continuous immersion in water.

I must here give you two anecdotes, rather curiously illustrative of our own sea and land

134 CARNIVAL.

service, and of their respective love and hatred of water.

The first is of a gallant post captain, who at the time of which I speak commanded a frigate on our station. He witnessed and partook of the fun of carnival on the Monday, and was so smitten with its excitement and novelty, that he prepared to join the battle *in real earnest* on the Tuesday. Early on that morning, he hied him on board of his frigate, and having there a small fire engine, he brought it on shore, inviting several of his officers, and commanding some of his men, to join in the play. They all came – captain,, officers, and men, in jackets and duck trousers. The commander paid some people of the town with English liberality to supply him constantly and abundantly with water. He marched with the engine and the hose attached to it into a principal street. Here he was met with a deluge of waters from each side, and with shouts of admiration and laughter from all assembled indoors and out. But our brave mariners went to work with imperturbable gravity and diligence. The captain took the hose, and directed the operations. He advanced steadily, and, though his

CARNIVAL. 135

progress was opposed with undaunted bravery, by every fair water thrower from the house tops of the street, he rapidly cleared each in turn with his irresistible engine. In this extraordinary enterprize he and his followers spent the whole day with a perseverance which no waters could extinguish, and which was worthy of the occasion, seeing the high and noble foes with whom he had to contend.

The second anecdote is of one whom I have the pleasure of calling my friend, and who is at this moment a resident of London, being now, as he was then, a retired officer of our own army. He travelled over a great part of South America, which he scanned with an acute vision, and observed in a philosophic spirit,*when he pleased;*but being at heart an Englishman, he could never practically bring himself to submit to those things which he considered as abuses, and which no." custom of the country," as he held, could ever render tolerable to a civilized being.

This worthy gentleman dined with me on a carnival Monday, and having come to my house early in the forenoon, he escaped with a few wettings from ladies in their balconies. He proposed

136 CARNIVAL.

to retire before sunset, and I then told him that if he did he was likely to get a drenching, instead of gentle shower, on his way home.

" Why, as to the women," said Captain,

" they may drench me as much as they please; but if any*man*attempt to throw water on me, let him take the consequences of such an insult."

I pointed out to my friend, what he very well saw, that it was the custom of the country to allow of an indiscriminate licence on these two or three days in the way of water throwing, whether by men or by women; and I argued that either we ought to keep at home, or that if we went out we must do as others did, and not resent as an insult what was plainly intended as a joke.

My argument did not avail. Captain

said he had a right to go home quietly at any hour he chose, without being molested, and off he set.

At the corner of the street in which I lived stood the Cafe de la Victoria, a large house, and frequented by many respectable people. On this occasion, the azotea of the cafe was crowded with young men throwing water, and as my friend passed, they saluted him with a tolerable shower.

CARNIVAL. 137

Seeing whence it came, he coolly gathered together some brick bats, and with these began to pelt his assailants.

Their anger was in a moment kindled, and in a body they rushed to the street to chastise the audacious foreigner.

I had been watching the Captain's progress from a front window, and as soon as I saw him commence throwing I hastened out. The cafe'carnival players were about him before I could get up, and single-handed he was confronting some fifteen or twenty exasperated men. Some called out"Dele una punalada!" (put a dagger into him)! others proposed to throw him into the great tank of the Victoria cafe; all hustled and covered him with abusive names. When I got to the side of

,and warmly expressed my indignation at

the treatment my countryman was receiving, they turned with equal wrath upon me. Some one at last called out, " It is Mr. Robertson!" but another instantly replied, " Well, what care we for him? Does he think that he or any other foreigner shall come and dictate to us?"

All were excited save Captain himself;

and his coolness, together with my own remon-

138 ASH WEDNESDAY.

strances at length induced one or two of more weight and judgment than the rest to take our part. The result was that an opening was sulkily made for both of us to pursue our course, which we slowly did; although it would be difficult to say which of the belligerent parties was most strongly impressed with the unwarrantable conduct of its opponent.

I recollect on one occasion, when I was anxious to proceed on a carnival Tuesday from our own house in town to Mr. Mackinlay's Quinta, in the suburbs, being desirous at the same time of doing so without a continuous ducking, I accomplished my purpose in this way. I made up some papers in the form of a large official packet, and mounting my horse, I held the pretended despatches aloft in my right hand. I set off at full speed, giving the word of " despatches " to my next door neighbour. They caught the eyes of all as I advanced: operations were suspended, in the supposition that I was the bearer of news, and in this way I reached Mr. Mackinlay's house with a dry skin.

On Ash Wednesday, after the conclusion of the carnival, all was as still and quiet in the town as if nothing had happened; and the people were to be seen every where going to church, all recollection

SAN YSIDRO. 139

of the follies of the preceding days being apparently buried in their devotions.

The two seasons of rational festivity in the capital of the River Plate provinces were those of Easter and Christmas, the first falling in that country in autumn, and the latter in the heat of summer. On these occasions all the better classes went out of town, and were to be found at their country houses, or in the adjacent villages, particularly at San Ysidro, a favourite resort of the fashionables. This village is prettily situated on a barranca or cliff of slight elevation on the banks of the river, about thirteen miles to the north of the city; and in good weather the two roads leading to it, one by the river side, and the other through the chacara grounds, form pleasing rides. The country is here dotted with villas, and there are some few good residences in San Ysidro itself, or round about it. These villas are favourite places for pic nics, or for an evening's recreation, and in many pleasant parties of this kind I have joined. Proceeding outwards from San Ysidro you come to the Punta de San Fernando, another, but secondary perch for the citizens; and further still you get to Las Conchas, which, although romantic in its river140 SAN JOSE DE FLORES.

scenery, is, from lying low, and being consequently inundated with mosquitos, the least agreeable of the three. In great crecientes, or overflowings of the Parana, the*concheros*may be seen paddling about from house to house in their canoes. The houses are built on piles driven into the ground. The huts are mostly made of wood; while palm trees, being cut longitudinally, and the pith extracted, the hollow semicircular trunks are used as a tiling.

Another favourite ride of the Buenos Ayreans used to be to San Jose de Flores, lying about nine miles inland; but the road to it was generally bad, impassible in winter and spring, and dusty in summer and autumn. For an afternoon's ride the Barraca road, lying immediately out of town towards the south, and some of the by-ways and lanes leading from it, were much frequented; and here is to be seen such*horse racing*as Buenos Ayres can boast of. You look in vain for a fine breezy course, or a grand stand. No " Derby" nor " Oaks," keep the citizens on the*qvi vive;*neither is there a Tattersalls for the betting world. The races at Buenos Ayres are run on the Barraca road, a wide and open highway of sand; no ladies grace the sport; carriages there are none; booths or

HORSE RACING. 141

stands are unheard of. Instead of all this you may see two lines of horsemen, reaching about 300 yards in length, and forming a free course between them. The spectators are made up of sedate looking estancieros on sleek horses, of gauchos, stray Englishmen, some mounted citizens, and a few nondescripts. The betting goes forward among these parties, sometimes to a large amount, as they sit waiting for the race or two which are to entertain them. A little bustle shows that the racers are on the ground, ready for the business of the day. Two horses and no more invariably run, and the mighty course to be gone over is sometimes 150, oftener 300, and very rarely 600 yards. The two racehorses are mounted,*quite bare backed,*by expert gauchos; and behold them now side by side, ready for a start

One would think that for so short a distance, the business would pass like a flash of lightning. By no means. The great and principal jockeyship of the gaucho consists in his getting*the best start,*and unlimited in the number of these, the two jockies are left to agree between themselves, which is to be the real and positive*start.*

They try one first – that won't do; so back to

1452 PEDESTRIAN FEAT.

their point. Another, no: another, unsuccessful; and thus they will go on for an hour, two hours, before they can agree upon the start. Nay, they sometimes waste a whole afternoon in this fruitless work, on which the estancieros and gauchos look with phlegmatic patience, and then disperse when they find in slang phraseology, that it is " no go."

When they do at last start, the horses are of course at once urged to the height of their speed, and for the short distance make a fine run; but so much preparation for *one heat* of 150 yards; so great a length of time spent over it, so great a stake, – sometimes one or two thousand dollars, – and such betting, combined with such a paltry performance, is laughable enough; and I think stamps the Buenos Ayres races as a thing unique of the kind.

Some of the early English residents were fond of the turf, and some tolerable racing, in our own English style, was got up by them; they had well- trained and good horses, with gentlemen jockeys to ride them j and these races were relished in the highest degree by the gauchos, surrounding chacar- reros, and estancieros settled in town.

We exhibited also on one occasion to the astonished eyes of the " natives," a pedestrian feat which

PEDESTRIAN FEAT. 143

was long remembered, with admiration, by them. A friend having deplored at my own table, that we lost in South America much of the mental and physical energy which we brought from England, that proposition was warmly combated; and the argument ended in our backing Dr. Dick, who was present, and who offered to walk twenty-four miles in six hours. In England it was thought this might he an easy task, but in Buenos Ayres, and in the summer season, it was considered as impossible by the knowing ones, who in betting, all took the side of my friend that had argued for the enervating effects. of the climate.

The match against time, in sporting phrase, " came off" on a piece of level ground which we selected a few miles from town. But it got well mentioned about, and a great concourse of spectators assembled; all the English, and many of the people of the country. Dr. Dick was and still is of very active habits, and of a fine elastic frame for walking. He got to the ground in a carriage, and commenced his task about nine in the morning, – in beautiful spring weather, clear and warm. He immediately gave proof that he was by far the best pedestrian on the ground. Two of the strongest,

144 PEDESTRIAN FEAT.

most athletic, and best made men on the ground (Mr. R. P. Staples and Mr. R. Carlisle) could only keep pace with the doctor for three miles, when they gave in; and no other person could keep up with him for more than one full mile. The result was, that Dr. Dick accomplished twenty-four miles with the utmost ease to himself, in five hours and seventeen minutes, and then walked one mile more to make all sure as to distance, which he did in twelve minutes more; concluding amid the cheers of every one on the ground. He was so little distressed, that he joined our party in town, immediately after dinner, and spent the evening in hilarity with several of our friends who had dined with me.

Your's, &c.

W. P. R.

12

SECTION 12

LETTER LV.

W. P. R. toGeneralMiller.

A new Partnership – Reid's Quinta – The Azotea – A Conspiracy – The Robbers detected – A Marriage – Mercantile Establishment – Smuggling Linens – A Bed of Dollars – Charque – Its Prohibition – Bribery and Corruption – Attended with Success – Benefits of Free Trade.

*London,*1842.

InBuenos Ayres, and amid society of the kind which I have briefly sketched, I passed my time very agreeably from the end of 1817 till March, 1820; and although I have little to say of this intermediate space which can interest the general reader, I have yet one or two little matters upon which I may make a passing remark.

The same friend and coadjutor who had shared my brother's fortunes in all his mercantile operations in the interior, now became his partner and my own, in a more extended and general business with Europe. This was Mr. Fair, a gentleman of whom, in our first series, we have had occasion to speak in high terms, and of whom we may

Vol. Hi. H

146Reid'sQuinta.

safely aver that, as he was for twenty and more years one of the best known Englishmen in Buenos Ayres, so he was one of the most respected and most esteemed.

With my brother, then, in England, and Mr. Fair in Buenos Ayres, I sat down to resume my commercial career. For a few months, during which we were organizing our business, I took up my abode with Mr. Fair at a well-known country residence, which passed under the name of" Reid's Quinta." It lies on the *bajo* or low ground which skirts the river on the south side of the town, and is a tall and somewhat awkward-looking house, erected by a Scotchman of the name of Reid, who was a builder by profession, and who, having by his industry in his calling (for, like many others, he went out with no other capital) amassed a considerable sum, he laid out most of his profits on this large house.

Mr. Fair was Mrs. Reid's only tenant, and here on all the holidays throughout the year he entertained such bachelor friends as chose to partake of his hospitality. No invitation was either given or expected; it was truly Bachelor's Hall. The dining-room table was laid out for a large party,

THE AZOTEA. 147

and all comers were sure of a hearty welcome, a capital dinner, and excellent wine. The company began to collect early in the forenoon, to enjoy the fine look-out from the azotea, which commanded the river and much of the circumjacent country, and on which Mr. Fair had always at command two or three capital telescopes. Many an " arrival" and many a " departure " was witnessed from Reid's azotea. In the evening, when the sun was descending and the sea breeze beginning to cool the air, the azotea was again sought, and lively conversation, cool claret, and fragrant Havanas induced many of the guests to linger till the last shades of night warned them to retire.

Mr. Fair was, strictly speaking, a popular man, not only among his own countrymen, but among all classes of the people of the country; and yet on one occasion (it was during my residence in the interior) he narrowly escaped becoming a victim to the cupidity of a band of worthless wretches, who are to be found in all countries. I must relate the incident.

Mr. Fair invariably went on horseback from his place of business in town to Reid's Quinta. He kept two spirited animals, of which he was

148 A CONSPIRACY.

very fond, and on one or other of them *he* was to be seen on the bajo every evening wending his way home. He was reputed among the people to be a man of great wealth; and the absurd notion grew up among some of the lower classes, that all his riches were accumulated at Reid's Quinta.

Under this persuasion a gang of villains determined to attack the house. They laid their plan cautiously and leisurely; they made themselves well acquainted with the premises, and ascertained the number and class of inmates with whom they were likely to have to cope. Their resolution was to murder those within who offered resistance, and, after ascertaining where his treasure lay, to take the life of Mr. Fair himself. They were fifteen or sixteen in number, bold, daring, and unflinching men.

Happily, however, one of them, who owed some obligations to Mr. Fair, repenting of the part which he had agreed to take in the diabolical plot, went to him and disclosed the whole affair. Information was given to the police, and, under the express orders of the*Gefe,*or Chief of that force, the burglars were left to follow up their plan in ignorance of their designs having been re-

THE ROBBERS DETECTED. 149

vealed. During the day on which the conspirators had fixed for their purpose, the police Chief had several of his men, in plain clothes, but well armed, introduced at different times into the house. These were so disposed as to command the staircase from the upper part of it, and the inmates of the house were also armed and ready for the attack. The burglars did not make it on the evening they had proposed, but the Chief kept his men in the house, feeling certain that the visit would be paid.

And so it was; for next night, towards twelve o'clock, the gang cautiously approached the house from the back part. The access was purposely made easy for them. They soon obtained an entrance, ascended the staircase, and, while many of them were upon it, the order was given to the police, who had hitherto remained still,*to fire.*In a moment (it was all in the dark) a volley was poured in among the robbers. It was wonderful that none of them were killed on the spot; but still more so that, although some of them were wounded, they made such a precipitate retreat in different directions, as all to get clear off. They left behind them two or three tracks of blood, from the appearance of which it was supposed that one of the assailants,

150 A MARRIAGE.

at any rate, must have been carried away by his associates, and have died of his wounds. The police, considering, I suppose, that the gang was sufficiently punished, made no strict search after its members, and on their side they never again made any attempt on Reid's Quinta.

Four or five months after my arrival in the capital, Mr. Fair shut up Bachelor's Hall, and became a married man. He married Miss Harriet Kendall, sister of the two young ladies who have been mentioned as fellow-passengers of General San Martin's when he came to Buenos Ayres in the George Canning; and one of whom became Mrs. James Brittain, while the other was married to Mr. John Ludlam, both members of our River Plate community. Mrs. Fair, whose many virtues and amiable disposition have won her golden opinions wherever she has gone, and made her justly dear to all her immediate friends, became a great acquisition to Buenos Ayres society, which for many years she adorned.

Mr. Fair took up his residence in town, and his lady had soon a very serious charge on her hands. In South America, and in a great many other foreign places, business is not conducted as inMERCANTILE ESTABLISHMENT. 151

England. The whole establishment is under one roof, the heads of the house and all the clerks living together, having one common table, and the counting-house and warehouse being in the same building as the dwelling-house. The whole forms one family, and the arrangement is advantageous for the young gentlemen employed in the business, as keeping them in good society and in good order, which, were they, as here, in lodgings, could never be done. Heads of houses, however., who were married, chose often to retire to a country house, leaving a junior partner or a responsible head clerk to manage the town establishment. Mr. Fair at the commencement placing himself at the head of ours, I, as a matter of course, took up my residence with him.

As our mercantile establishments in Buenos Ayres differed in their arrangements from those of England, so business itself was often much more erratic in its course than we find it here in the "City;" of which I will satisfy myself with giving one or two examples, taken from our own affairs.

Soon after we commenced, a vessel with a valuable cargo of linens arrived from Hamburg to our consignment. We had then a ruinous tariff in

152 SMUGGLING LINENS.

action, with a venal government, and the consequence was an unbounded system of contraband carried on by native merchants and others.

We ourselves could have nothing to do with smuggling; but how to dispose of our cargo of linens on the honest principle of paying the duties, without a ruinous loss to our friends, was a problem not easily to be solved. While we debated our difficulty, a native merchant came in and offered, under unexceptionable guarantee, to land the whole cargo for us for one-half the duties. But this was smuggling, and we could not accede to the proposal. Our friend then offered to *purchase* the cargo on board, receiving it in lighters in the usual and legal way. This was all correct, so the bargain was immediately struck. The goods becoming his, we had of course no right to inquire what he did with them after he got them from on board. A few days afterwards this gentleman asked me to rid out with him next morning before breakfast, which I did; and then, when we were a league from town, he pointed out to me, to my no small surprise, a number of carts loaded apparently with grass, but under which lay a multitude of pieces of German platillas, creas, creguelas, sheetings, and

A BED OF DOLLARS. 153

other manufactures, part and parcel of our fine cargo by the Palmyra. I could scarcely look at them without a twinge of conscience, or without feeling that I had made myself *particeps criminis* in the affair.

Shortly after the above transaction, we received orders to provide large amounts of Spanish dollars for three Indiamen which were to call at Buenos Ayres, and proceed with the remittances thus obtained to Bombay and Calcutta. The aggregate amount to be provided was about six or seven hundred thousand hard dollars. Carts were accordingly to be seen daily unloading bags of dollars at our warehouse, and before the vessels arrived we had got nearly the whole sum collected. At this time we had a warehouse unconnected with our dwelling; and as the heap of bags piled on the ground rose higher, so did our alarm at having this enormous sum in so bulky and visible a shape, in a place not inhabited by ourselves. At last I got a large mattrass and bed-clothes, which were spread over the heap of coin, and there, with a trusty servant, barring and double-locking ourselves in, I slept for several nights waiting the arrival of the

154 CHARQUE.

vessels. They came ere long, and all the dollars were safely put on board of them.*

Nothing could be more capricious and wrong- headed than some of the fiscal and commercial regulations enacted from time to time by the Buenos Ayres government. One of the latter, in 1818, was a total prohibition of the exportation of cured beef, known by the name of *charque,* and consumed to a vast extent by the negro population of the Island of Cuba. The article forms now, in fact, a great trade between Buenos

Ayres, as well as Monte Video and the Havana, and the preparation of the beef in the two former places gives employment to a large industrial class as well as to a good deal of foreign capital in the country, producing altogether au income of magnitude to the respective provinces.

Now, how such a trade could ever come to be prohibited is as unintelligible as would be the forbidding in this country of the manufacture of cotton goods. But prohibited it was, and nobody seemed

* It is a curious fact, that although the paper dollar of Buenos Ayres long represented the full value of the silver one, it would*now*require upwards of*ten millions*of the former to purchase the six hundred and fifty thousand of the latter which we shipped.

ITS PROHIBITION. 155

to think that it was anything out of the way so to embargo the industry and capital of the country. Under this*hiatus*in the jerk-beef trade, a large vessel came out to us with orders to load her with the produce in question, and send her to the Havana. We petitioned the government for a licence, but in vain. We represented, in every way our ingenuity could suggest, the unqualified evil which sprung from prohibition; the unqualified advantages which must flow from a free trade. It was all to no purpose. " No ha lugar," – " It cannot be conceded," – was all the answer we got to one petition after another; and we began to despair altogether of opening the eyes of the executive to its own (and no doubt to our) interest "*in re*" jerk beef.

One day, however, as I returned from one of many fruitless journeys I made to the secretary of state's office, – it was about dinner hour, half-past two, very hot, and the streets nearly tenantless – 1 heard myself called from the opposite side of the way, and on looking round saw a young man beckoning me to enter a shop nearly closed, like all the others during the hours of dinner and rest, comprehended under the name of siesta. I crossed the street, and entered the shop. Lounging at his ease

156 BRIBERY AND CORRUPTION,

on the counter was a jolly, good-natured, but gentlemanlike person, in the undress which dinner calls for in a warm climate. He was apparently waiting for a summons to attend to what Dr. Johnson designates as the most important business of a man's life. I recognized in the personage before me the*primer oftcial,*or first clerk of the secretary of state for the home department.

" Now, Mr. Robertson," said he, with an easy nod, " I know whence you come, and what you have been about. You have been to the Fort,* and you want a special licence to load a cargo of beef. Well, send us in a dozen of your good old port here, and you shall have your licence." I nodded assent, withdrew, and, – led away by considering how little could be lost, and how much might be gained by the transaction, – I became an agent in " bribery and corruption," and " treated " the first clerk to*two*dozen of prime old port. Perhaps I was induced thereto by the conviction that there was no jealous guardian of the public morals in Buenos Ayres, like Mr. Roebuck here, standing behind the scenes, ready to pounce, with uncompromising severity, on*me,*as he does in his*ATTENDED WITH SUCCESS. 157

* Where Ine government offices were held.

place on all compromising delinquents who try to hide their " diminished heads" in a crowd of Chiltern Hundreds.

Whether my port-wine friend, the first clerk, knew that the higher powers had already granted our prayer, or whether he himself was the Board of trade, and determined the questions which were mooted by the commercial body of the country, I will not venture to decide; but *defacto* I know that three days after I was guilty of treating, our licence was put into my hands duly countersigned by the " Ministro del Interior."

The two dozen of port, like the wonderful goose, laid many golden eggs. The large vessel employed, earned a famous freight. We paid to the manufacturers of the beef, which was about to rot in their *galpones,* about fifty thousand hard dollars – all clear gain to the country. We made an excellent commission for ourselves; we paid a considerable amount of duty into the custom-house, augmenting *ad hoc* the revenue of the state; the Havana planters were enabled to give good food to their slaves; and our constituents, who ordered the cargo in question, made a clear gain by the speculation of at least eight thousand pounds sterling, and

158 BENEFITS OF FREE TRADE.

were thus encouraged to follow up an active intercourse with the Republic, and to employ an augmented capital in its trade.* Prom all which premises this deduction may safely be drawn: that if governors and legislators were not so wofully self-blinded as they everywhere are, to the beneficial workings of an *Unshackled* Commerce, the world at large would be in a more prosperous state than it now is.

Yours, &c.,

W. P. R.

* We were shortly after, by means of a second special licence, enabled to repeat the operation with a large vessel, belonging to Liverpool friends, and with equal, if not greater success, for all parties concerned.

13

SECTION 13

LETTER LVI.

W. P. R. toGeneralMiller.

Corrientes in trouble – Miss Postlethwaite's MS. – Andresito's Invasion – . Campbell Comandante – Privations of the Indians – Indian Mothers – Andresito's Politeness – His Balls – Non-attendance punished – The fancy Dresses – Mexias – Abstinence and Surfeit – Anecdotes of Andresito – A Toast – An Assassination – Death of Andresito – Campbell and the Captive – Her rescue.

*London,*1842.

Towardsthe middle of 1819, the state of public affairs in Corrientes was so alarming, on account of the occupation of that city by an Indian force belonging to Artigas, that Mr. Postlethwaite commenced making arrangements for leaving the interior; and, as a preliminary step, he determined to send his two oldest daughters down to Buenos Ayres. It was with no small pleasure I saw them safely arrive on the 25th of July, at Las Conchas, whither I had gone to meet them; and the account they gave me of the state of affairs at my old place of residence, only made me anxious to see the other members of the family safely out of the remote but troubled province which Artigas had placed under Indian rule.

160MissPostlethwaite'sMs.

There was, indeed, so much picturesque barbarity in the invasion, as it might be styled, of Corrientes, by*Andresito Artigas,*an Indian and adopted son of the great Artigas himself, that, since commencing the letters which we are now addressing to you, I have applied to my friend Mrs. Cartwright (formerly Miss Postlethwaite) and her unmarried sister for some account not. only of that transaction, but of the principal events which occurred during their stay: with that account they have kindly favoured me; and not doubting my readers will find it as interesting as I myself did, I propose here to transfer it,*verbatim et literatim,*to our pages. It is written by Miss Postlethwaite, and is entitled –

"

extractsFromRecollectionsOfCorrientes."" In consequence of Francisco Bedoya, who commanded the troops in Corrientes, declaring in favour of Buenos Ayres, in which he was joined by the Cabildantes, and many of the respectable inhabitants, General Andresito* (the adopted son of Artigas, and an Indian), received orders from the Protector to march upon the town, and take posses-

* Andresito is the diminutive of Andres, and means "*little Andrew.*"

ANDRESITO'S INVASION. 161

sion of it; which he did with about 700*Guay- curu*Indians,

" The news of his approach had thrown the inhabitants into a state of great alarm, and all who were able collected together their property, and, either carrying it with them, or hiding it, fled from the town. Two men died of fright, one of them being the little*Escribano*(notary) who lived opposite to us. Poor old Bedoya buried a large sum of money in his garden; but one of his servants having unfortunately observed him in the act of concealing it, gave information where it was hidden, and it was speedily dug up. The Escobars, and several other persons with whom you were acquainted, benefitted, it was alleged, by the discovery.

"Amid this confusion and alarm,*we*did not, as you may suppose, feel very comfortable, and the reports which hourly arrived were not calculated to allay our fears. It was said the Indians, as they came along, were putting men, women, and children to death. This however was quite untrue; but as Bedoya had cruelly massacred the inhabitants of a small Indian village a few weeks previously, for refusing to join him, and take up arms against

162CAMPBELL, COMANDANTEDEMARINO.

Artigas, the*Correutinos* naturally feared the Indians would retaliate upon them. The village had contained about 30 families, and three individuals only escaped death. One of them, a poor woman, who fled after seeing her husband and children slaughtered, was brought into Corrientes with one or two ball wounds and several sabre cuts.

" My father sent poor Lee (who was afterwards murdered in Corrientes), and another Englishman whose name I forget, with a letter to Andresito, requesting to know whether his (my father's) family and property would be protected in the event of his remaining. He received a very polite letter in reply, desiring him not to think of moving, as he should meet with no molestation; Andresito begging at the same time to be placed at the feet of the Senora and Senoritas, and assuring them there was not the least cause for alarm.

" I do not think with even this assurance we should have felt quite comfortable had we not been reassured by the presence of Don Pedro Campbell, now*Comandante de Marinas,*an especial favourite with Andres. Campbell advised my father to take us into the square to see the Indians enter, for he thought Andresito would look upon it as a compli-

PRIVATIONS OF THE INDIANS. 163

ment to himself, and feel pleased by the attention shown him. We went accordingly, though not without some slight apprehensions, for which, however, there was no cause. The Indian troops marched in very quietly and orderly; were, after being drawn up in the square, dismissed to their barracks; and the general and his officers then attended high mass at San Francisco church.

" There was really much merit due to the Indians for their good conduct; for they had been suffering great hardships from want of clothing and food. They had frequently been compelled to boil pieces of dried hides and live upon them, not being able to procure even horse-flesh; and their clothing was truly miserable, many having only*ckiripds*(or kilts), and those who had any farther clothing being still quite in tatters. Some were armed with muskets, some with spears, and others with bows and arrows; while bringing up the rear, and armed with the latter weapons of a small size, came about two hundred little Indian boys. It appeared they had been carried off at different times by the Correntinos, and treated as slaves. Wherever Andres found any of these children he liberated them, and seized upon a corresponding number of the children of the men

164 INDIAN MOTHERS.

in whose service he found them. The parents of the children thus taken away, not knowing what was to be their fate, were of course thrown into a state of great mental distress and alarm. After keeping the children prisoners for about a week, Andres sent for the mothers. He forcibly pointed out to them the cruelty and injustice of which they had been guilty towards the poor Indians, appealing to their own feelings of anguish as the best corroboration of his charge. 'Take back your children,' concluded Andres, ' and remember in future that*Indian mothers have hearts'*

"We had scarcely been at home an hour when we heard a band of music approaching, and which we found was followed by the general, his officers and secretary (the latter a terrible villain), accompanied by the governor and his attendants. The*sala*was filled in an instant. The general said he was anxious to lose no time in placing himself at the feet of the*Senora*and*Senoritas,*and to assure them of his desire to show them every respect. We were rather nervous, you may be sure; but we certainly were treated with marked respect and attention, not only by Andresito himself, but by his officers and men during the whole time they occupied Corrientes.

ANDRESITO'S POLITENESS. 165

His visit, I think, lasted about*three hours,*after which he went on board the '*Capitana,'*lying off the custom-house. About an hour and a half afterwards we saw him carried past on the shoulders of his men, the excitement and the wine he had taken having completely overpowered the poor little man. But he recovered in the course of the afternoon, and to our no small surprise made us a second visit in the evening, being accompanied by*Admiral*Peter Campbell, and the bad secretary already mentioned.

" Andresito fortunately took a great fancy to my father, who obtained a considerable control over him; so that whenever 'the general' became violent, which he sometimes did after having drunk too much, my father was always sent for, and he commonly succeeded in soothing the Indian chief.

" The night after he took the town, we heard all the poor*Cabildantes*marching past our house, as prisoners in chains, and we learned next day that they had been taken on board the ' Capitana.' They all expected to be shot. Old Cabral,*alcalde de primer voto,* *nearly lost his senses from the

* The same provost Cabral who did his best to get Mr. Postle- thwaite and myself, as well as the other English, marched off inchains to Artigas, 300 leagues distant. Admiral Campbell had

166 ANDRESITO'S BALLS.

fright. My father was besieged on all sides to make ' empeno' or interest with the general, and after some time, and with much difficulty, he obtained the release of all the prisoners. The fact is, the Correntinos (and particularly the ladies) could not so far conquer the habitual contempt with which they looked down upon the Indians, as to take any pains, although at the absolute mercy of Andresito, to conciliate him. He had fixed his head-quarters at Bedoya's house; and after he had levied a contribution to clothe his men, and had thus equipped them very respectably, he gave two or three entertainments, to which he invited all the respectable inhabitants. These entertainments consisted of a kind of religious plays or dramas,* performed by the Indians, and taught them by the Jesuits. One of them was the representation of the '*tentacion de San Ignacio?*in the course of which some of their dances represented words, such as " encarnacion,"f each figure forming a letter in

now the upper hand. – See page 80, of this volume. – W. P. R. * Known to our forefathers by the name of "*Myteries.*"t One of the many Catholic titles of the Virgin Mary, is

"*Nuettra senora de la Eacarnacion,*"whence a common Christian

name of females is "*Encarnacioa.*"

NON-ATTENDANCE PUNISHED. 167

the word. The general being surprised and mortified at the non-attendance of the Correntinos, he inquired into the reason of their absence, and it was ill-naturedly reported to him in reply that the Correntinos said – ' Who would be at the trouble to go and see a set of Indians dance?'

"Andresito had hitherto submitted to a great many overt acts of contempt from the town, and had really shown more forbearance than could have been expected from him; but now being completely roused, he took an extraordinary way of punishing his enemies.

" ' So they do not choose to come and see the Indians dance,' said he, – ' well, let us try.' So the following morning (a very hot day) the drums beat to arms, and every man of respectability of the place, excepting Don Isidore Martinez, old Duran, and my father, was marshalled into the*plaza*(or square), and there they were made to pluck up the grass and weeds, level and clean it from one corner to the other. They were kept at work the whole day, under the blaze of a scorching sun; and really, however sorry one might feel for the unfortunate labourers, there was something laughable in the Indian's whim. I suppose the square was never

168 THE FANCY DRESSES.

before, nor has ever been since, in such perfect order. While the men were thus employed, their wives and daughters were taken off to the barracks, and made to dance all day with the Indians, – a much more unpardonable affront than. the manual labour imposed on the males.

" I must not omit to mention that for*hisfunciones*or plays, Andresito begged as a great favour that we would provide dresses for two of the performers, to which we of course agreed. After the dresses (fancy ones) were finished, and which we made as gay as possible, the men were sent to us to be dressed, and Tuckerman and Lee acted as valets. The Indians were so delighted with their own appearance, that Tuckerman found it almost impossible to get them along the streets to the general's house. Each would walk behind the other, that he might have the pleasure of viewing his own dress, for they were both exactly alike. The general was equally delighted, and exclaimed on seeing them, '*Que ninas de Plata!*'(What*silver*young ladies!); and he forthwith begged us to equip two more. These four performed the parts of the guardian angels of San Ignacio, although the wings put on for their performance did not well

THE SECRETARY MEXIAS. 169

accord with the helmets with which they would not part. When Andresito left Corrienles the angels rode before him for about two leagues out of town, and then their dresses were laid aside.

" Andres was himself a kind-hearted man, and much better informed than could have been expected. I believe he was educated in Monte Video. He was unfortunate in having a very wicked man at his elbow in his secretary Mexias, who prompted him to whatever evil he did. He (Mexias) became very jealous of my father's influence with Andres, and never rested till he had succeeded in poisoning against the former the mind of his Indian chief. My father was in consequence laid under a heavy contribution, which he refused to pay, and on which refusal he was sent, for twenty-four hours, to the common prison. We were so much alarmed, not knowing to what extent Andresito in his actual state of feeling might be persuaded to go (the secretary had made him tipsy before he could induce him to sign the order, and kept him in that state to prevent him from retracting), that we persuaded my father to pay a part of the sum levied, on the remainder being annulled.

VOL. III. I

170 ABSTINENCE AND SURFEIT.

Andres afterwards entreated our pardon for having been compelled to have recourse to such severe measures.

" The province being now once more in anarchy, provisions became often very scarce in Corrientes, so that, on more than one occasion, persons passing the barracks on horseback were made to dismount, their horses were taken possession of, and killed for food. Indeed Campbell told us on one occasion, that for four days his men had only one biscuit each daily! Andres always said that he would not give a farthing for a man unless he could fast for three or four days without inconvenience. When they did get food, the quantity they ate was beyond belief. Mr. Tuckerman declared that four of these men killed a heifer on his chacra, and never stirred till they had finished it; – roasting, eating, and sleeping, and roasting again, till the whole had disappeared. They wore broad bands made of the skin of the capiguara*, and when obliged to fast, these belts were tightened a little every day. During the seven months they had possession of the town, there

* A river pig, an amphibious tenant of the ParanS, and which burrows under iu kinks.

ANECDOTES OF ANDRESITO. 171

was only one robbery committed. The man went into a shop and demanded a handkerchief for " la patria.' l The tendero (shopkeeper) complained to Andresito, who asked him if he could point the man out? On the shopkeeper replying in the affirmative, Andres commanded his orderly to go with the complainant to the different quarters, and the delinquent being discovered he was publicly flogged in the Plaza. Generally, if anything went wrong, Andres punished the officers, not the men, alleging that if the former did their duty, the latter must do theirs.

" Andresito wore no sword, having lost his own in an engagement with the Portuguese; and he determined never to wear another till he had honourably won it. But whenever he was roused to anger, his officers instantly drew theirs and presented them to him; or they stood ready to inflict any punishment he might command. We nearly in this way witnessed a terrible scene in our own house. My father gave a dinner to Andres and his "officers, about forty persons. Of course all our wine glasses were in request; and after two or three toasts had been drank, the secretary Mexias gave one, tossing, in defiance of Andresito's prohibition, his glass over

172 A TOAST A LA ESPANOLA.

his shoulder.* His example was immediately followed by about a dozen more gentlemen; and no doubt every glass on the table would have shared the same fate, had not the general sprung to his feet and commanded them at their peril to break another. The secretary, whose courage had risen with his wine, seemed disposed to rebel, on which high words ensued. The general however exclaimed, ' Si quiebras otra copa, yo te quebrare el Alma,' – 'If you break another glass, I will break your pate;' upon which the officers instantly drew their swords, and surrounded Andres. Mexias, I suppose, thought it high time to submit, for he sat down, and continued in a sulky mood for the rest of the day. Though not present, we were within hearing, and not a little alarmed at the uproar; but it subsided the moment Mexias sat down, and the rest of the evening passed off quietly enough. Andres expressed himself as much pleased with the entertainment, and particularly with the plom puddin Ingles, of which national dish we had five or six samples at the table, all of which disappeared. One of the officers, on some being placed before

* This was the Spanish mode of drinking a toast " with all the honours."

MEXIAS ASSASSINATED. 173

him, not knowing what it was, very generously divided it., in order to pass one half to his orderly, who stood behind him. But before the poor fellow had time to take it, the officer had put a piece into his own mouth, and finding it a much better thing than he had anticipated, he promptly drew back his hand, and finished the whole of it himself.

'* The secretary, having occasion to go down to Goya on business, invited while there all the respectable inhabitants, male and female, to a feast. When they were about to separate, he hoped they had been pleased with their entertainment, and had enjoyed their dinner. On being answered in the affirmative, he informed them they had dined off *horse-flesh,* most of the dishes, though variously dressed, having consisted of this meat. This Mexias who was feared and justly detested by everybody, received, some time after quitting Corrientes, a command to attend Artigas, and setting out in consequence, he was assassinated on the way, the letter from the Protector being generally believed to be a forgery.

" About a year afterwards Andresito and his Indians were defeated by the Portuguese, taken prisoners, and carried to Rio de Janeiro; and

174 DEATH OF ANDRESITO.

although they were liberated, without much detention, Andresito died not long after. By his defeat the tribe of the Guaranis was almost annihilated: they were a harmless, amiable, and kindly- disposed race. Most of them could read and write, and play on some instrument, many of them on two or three. One old man among them called *Shernisha* (the comic actor or *buffo* in their plays) was a great favourite with us, and by his queer tricks used to afford us much amusement: he would occasionally take an immense segar and smoke it for some time, without any appearance of smoke from it, and then preparing to tell some amusing story, as he commenced relating it, the smoke which he had swallowed would pour forth from his eyes, ears, nose, and mouth, in a most extraordinary manner.

" Nothing could exceed the respect, attention, and civility which we received from these men the whole time we were in Corrientes. On one occasion, however, after a bando (proclamation) had been issued, commanding the presence of all the Correntinos in the square at a certain hour on the following day, my father happened to be in Ygnacio's (your old servant's) pulperia, at the corner of the

GENERAL POLITENESS OF THE INDIANS. 175

square, and, while in the act of speaking to him, received a severe *sablazo* (blow with a sabre) from an Indian officer, who mistook my father for a Correntino. The moment the Indian perceived his error he dropped on his knees, and implored my father not to tell the general; but, as he was not alone at the time, it did reach the ears of Andresito, who immediately put his officer in irons, and kept him in confinement for many days, notwithstanding all the interest my father used to have him forgiven. I mention this to show how strictly he fulfilled his promise of protection to us. The troops never passed us without presenting arms; and at the performances before mentioned, we had always seats placed at the right hand of the general, while the governor and his family sat on the left; nor were the performances allowed to commence till we arrived. The band, too, was sent every day to play for an hour before our house. We were not a little amused at their always addressing us as *paysanitas* (countrywomen), or *Indias rubias* (fair Indians). 'Were not,' they said, ' the ancient Britons Indians before they were conquered by the Romans? and was not Campbell one of themselves, always at the side of the general 176 CAMPBELL AND THE CAPTIVE.

to counteract the evil advice and wicked instigations of Mexias?'* The poor Correntinos would have fared much worse than they did, had not Andresito, fortunately for them, been generally more disposed to listen to good than bad advice, except when he was not quite sober. His wife was an unassuming, amiable little woman, and rather pretty.

"Some time after the Indians had left Corrientes, Campbell, being still Comandante de Marina, returned from the Bajada, bringing with him a poor*Cordovesa,*whom he had liberated from the Abipon Indians, and whom he delivered to us, begging we would give her a home. It appeared that, in coming up the river, he observed an Indian*ToJderia*(collection of wigwams) between Goya and Chamorro. Wondering what they could have to do on that side the river, f and not quite liking their appearance, he landed with his first lieutenant J and a small party of his men. Finding the Indians belonged to the tribe of the Abipones,

* Mexias was a Peruvian Spaniard.

t The Gran Chaco, inhabited by the Indians, as our readers know, is on the*west*side of the Parana, Goya and all the province of Corrieutes on the east bank.

t His quondam page Edwardo, of whom honourable mention has heretofore been made.

THE CAPTIVE. 177

he inquired what had brought them there. Upon which the cacique informed him that their village, San Geronimo,* having been attacked by a tribe of Indians, the*Macabis,*they had fled and crossed the river. While Campbell was talking to the cacique, Don Edwardo observed a poor girl with no other clothing than a poncho, leaning, in evident distress, against a tree. He walked up to her and asked her if she were an Indian? She cast an alarmed glance towards the cacique, and, after some hesitation, replied, ' No.' Was she a captive? – 'Yes.' Detained against her will? – ' Yes.' After asking her a few more questions, he turned to some other women, and appeared to take no more notice of her; but when Campbell had finished speaking to the chief, Don Edwardo conversed with the former for a few minutes, and then returned on board the Capitana. After addressing some remarks to the Indian women, Campbell, in his turn, went up to the poor girl. ' So you are a captive, I understand,' said he. – ' Yes.' 'Do you wish to be liberated?' – ' Ojala!' (' Would to God I were!') ejaculated the girl.

* This is the same village, lying*opposite* to Goya, which is spoken of by Don Pedro Quesuey, vol. i. page 219.

178 THE CAPTIVE RESCUED

" At this moment Lieutenant Edwardo appeared with eight or ten more men, when Campbell immediately stalked up to the cacique, and said, ' I find this young woman is a captive, and that she is anxious to be restored to her friends; I shall therefore take her with me.' The cacique looked much enraged; but, seeing he had no chance of resisting the number of armed men who immediately surrounded the captive, he yielded with as good a grace as he could, and she was taken on board. At Chamorro, Campbell begged or bought some clothes for her (she was simply wrapped in a poncho), and then he brought her to us."

So far Miss Postlethwaite's narrative. The remainder of it you will find in my next letter, commencing with the account which the rescued captive gave of herself to Mr. Postlethwaite's family.

Yours, &c.,
W. P. R.

14

SECTION 14

LETTER LVII.

W. P. R. toGeneralMiller.

The Captive's Story – The Sisters separated – The Younger murdered – Fears of the Cacique – The Abipon Indians – Theii Tolderia – The Indian Galvan – New Troubles in Corrientes – Fate of the Escobars – Murder of Montufar – The Indians in Goya – The Flight – Parting Notice of old Friends – Miss Postlethwaite's Narrative concludes.

*London,*1842.

MissPostlethwaitethus proceeds to give the captive's story: –

" Her father was a small estanciero in the neighbourhood of Cordova,* and one day, having been on a visit, accompanied by her mother, sister (about fourteen), and little brother, not more than six years of age, as they were returning home on horseback towards evening, the weather being extremely sultry, the girls alighted to gather some wild fruit by the way. As they were thus employed they heard the yell of the Indians, which

* The province of Cordova lies adjacent to *Upper Peru,* and consequently a great distance from Goya. The Indians must have carried their captive across the Gran Chaco.

180 THE CAPTURE.

they render more wild by rapidly clapping their hands on their mouths while they shout; and although the sisters, had they mounted instantly, would have had plenty of time to escape, they were so paralyzed with terror that they had no power to move, and their mother and brother would not leave them. The Indians, perceiving the unhappy group, immediately rushed upon them. The little boy was placed on one of the horses, to which the Indians applied a few lashes, and drove it off at full gallop towards his home, setting up one of their yells after it. They made the females mount behind them, and fled with all speed. They never pulled up till long after dark; and, for the last hour or two, their road lay through a dense forest, so that the captives had not the most remote idea of the direction in which they were going. At length they stopped at a place where they found a number of the wives and children of the Indians waiting their arrival. *Ascencion* (the girl's name) found that the man behind whom she had been riding was the cacique, who passed her over to his wife as soon as they arrived, (she guessed it might be about midnight.)

" While they were regaling themselves, one of their scouts came up in all haste, and informed the

THE SISTERS SEPARATED. 181

cacique that the soldiers of Cordova were close upon them. In a few minutes they were all on their horses again; but when they were about to start, it was perceived that the captive mother was missing, and, although search was immediately made, she was nowhere to be found. The girls hoped she had seized an opportunity to escape, and might reach the Cordova troops. On the following day they arrived at an Indian village, the home of some of the flying party. Here the poor girls found they were to be separated, and deprived of the only hope and consolation which had hitherto supported them in their trial. The younger one remained with her master in the village, and Ascencion proceeded with her mistress to another. They had been quickly deprived of their clothes by first one Indian woman, then another, taking a fancy to the different articles they wore. They were employed as servants, though not treated with harshness or unkindness.

" But soon after they were taken, they were filled with horror on being obliged to witness the murder of a young man, who also had been captured and carried off. He was placed on the ground; where the Indians formed a circle round him, and 182 The Captive's Sister Murdered.

each shot an arrow into his body.* This will show you that, although the Abipones profess Christianity, they possess little of its spirit.

"At the season when the fruit or bean of the Algarroba is ripe, the Indians make from it a fermented and highly intoxicating liquor. On the first brewing, all the males drink of their favourite liquor till they are quite inebriated, and then the women follow the example of their lords. It was at this season, when the men were incapable of defending themselves, that they were attacked by the tribe of the Macabis, who have ever been at enmity with the other tribes. They came upon the Abipones unawares, committing dreadful slaughter; and Ascencion's unhappy little sister was one of the slain. The inhabitants of the village in which Ascencion herself lived had time to escape; and, having secured the images of the Virgin and some others of their saints, they fled with their families across the Parana, – to the place where they were first discovered by Campbell. When her master saw him landing, he took Ascencion aside, and told her if she gave them

* It is to be remarked, that an arrow which has missed its mark is never used again.

HER FEARS OF THE CACIQUE. 183

to understand by look or by sign that she was a captive, he would put her to death the moment they were gone.

"When Edwardo the lieutenant, therefore, asked her if she were a captive, she hesitated in fear and trembling, not knowing how to reply; but, after a moment's reflection, thinking it might be her last and only chance of escape, she determined to run all risks. Her master, who had been watching her, gave her, when she replied, such a fearful look that her knees shook with fear; and when Edwardo turned away withput making any further remark, she gave herself up as lost.

" Ascencion conducted herself with the greatest propriety during the time she was with us (about two years); accompanied us to Buenos Ayres, where she was married to a respectable man; and was afterwards wet-nurse in my sister's family. She learned that her little brother reached home in safety; but her poor mother was never heard of, so that she probably fell a prey to wild beasts in the forest.

" Campbell, as you know, was much feared by the people, a look from him being quite enough to fill them with terror. On one occasion a poor fellow

184 THE ABIPON INDIANS.

was brought before him for having committed some offence, which appeared to excite Campbell's anger to the highest pitch. He told the culprit he deserved to lose his head, and, suiting the action to the word, he drew out his sharp knife, seized the man by his fine long platted queue, and severed it from his head, commanding him thereupon to be off. The poor wretch had quite expected to have his head taken off, and was not a little rejoiced to make his escape, minus only his tail. On another occasion I recollect Campbell's knocking a poor Correntino down for calling my father Don Juan*Postilion,*which was the nearest he could come, I fancy, to Postlethwaite.

" But to return to the Abipon Indians. When we arrived in Goya in the San Jose, on our way to Buenos Ayres, they came flocking down to the side of the vessel, and we were much amused to witness their astonishment and delight on beholding Ascencion. We were rather anxious she should keep out of sight, fearing they might make some attempt to get possession of her again; but she had no fear for herself, and the women were as much pleased to see her as if she had been a sister, paying us a daily visit during our stay there. They pressed us

THE TOLDERIA. 185

very much to go and see them at their*Tolderia;*and as we had some curiosity to see their manner of living, we went. These*toldos*consisted of small huts, of sticks and straw, built in a triangular form, and coming to a peak. They measured about nine feet by six. They contained nothing but a few cups made from gourds, and their bows and arrows, which were of an immense size. The bow belonging to the Cacique Benavides was about six feet in length, and of such strength that we found it impossible to bend it in the slightest degree. Their huts appeared only to be used as sleeping places. In one of them lay a poor old woman on the bare ground, without any covering. The poor creature, who they told me was sick, was really a horrid-looking being, and appeared to be quite withered with old age. She raised her head when we looked into the hovel, but took no further notice of us.

" The Indians appeared much pleased with our visit, and answered all our questions very good- naturedly. Most of the men were absent, some of them at the time being employed in loading the San Jose. They seemed all to be miserably poor.

186 THE INDIAN GALVAN.

for, although we wanted to make some purchases from them, they had nothing of any kind to sell.

" They are, without exception, the finest race of people I ever beheld, – tall, athletic, and beautifully formed, with a carriage as dignified as if they had all been born to be princes. The women were also tall and graceful, with the sweetest voices I ever heard, their language being pleasing and musical in its sound.

"The day before we left, one of the Indians, called Torivio Galvan, who had been employed as peon on board the San Jose, went up to my father and said, ' I have never seen the world, and I am very anxious to do so; will you give me a passage to Buenos Ayres? I will work very hard in return.' He went with us, and was by far the most active person we had on board, seeming ever on the watch to make himself useful. He was a fine, handsome-looking young man of about twenty- four or twenty-five, and a good natured, amiable creature. Nothing appeared to afford him so much amusement as watching us while we ate our dinner. As soon as he perceived Ascencion preparing to lay the cloth, he came up to the com-

NEWTROUBLESINCORRIENTES.187

panion, over which he leaned, and from which he could see all that was going on in the cabin. There he remained till we had finished dinner and all was cleared away, occasionally making remarks to himself in his own language, which Ascencion told us were exclamations of surprise and admiration: this he did every day. At first it was a little annoying, but we were unwilling to prevent the gratification of his curiosity, and afterwards we got accustomed to it.

" We left Corrientes about the end of May, 1819, and arrived in Buenos Ayres the 25th of July; our voyage down the river, if you recollect, having been considerably lengthened by our getting on a sand-bank, where we were detained ten days, having been unable to get the vessel afloat until we had discharged all the*troxa*cargo.

" After the Indians retired from Corrientes things remained tolerably quiet, but only for a short time. Another insurrection broke out, in which the Escobars were deeply implicated. Jose Luis and Domingo were defeated in an engagement which took place not very far from Goya, whilst we were there, on our way to Buenos Ayres. They were both killed, and Domingo received twenty-seven

188THEFATEOFTHEESCOBARS.

bayonet wounds before he would give himself up. Their heads were afterwards exhibited in front of the cabildo in Corrientes. Don Angel and Miguel made their escape into Paraguay, expecting to receive protection from Francia; but, after a short time, they were both led out and shot. The mother's sins were, indeed, awfully visited upon the children in this family. Two men in Chamorro confessed having been hired by this wretched old woman to murder her cousin, who, you may remember, was shot just as he was entering his own house.

"After the total defeat of Artigas, the state of affairs in Corrientes became dreadful. The most shocking atrocities were committed. A friend of my father, for whom he had the sincerest regard, of the name of Montufar, a son of the viceroy of Guatemala, was to have dined with him, as he usually did, on the Sunday. He passed in the morning, and told my father, who happened to be standing at the door, that he had received a message from Monteverde, then comandante de ma- rinos, to go on board the Capitana, which was lying on the other side of the river: he knew not for what he was wanted, and therefore could

MURDER OF MONTUFAR. 189

not say how long he might be detained. If he returned in time, he would take his dinner with them, but they were not to wait for him. About an hour after, as my sisters Jane and Anne were walking on the azotea of the house, they observed a boat crossing the river with four or five persons in it; when about half-way across, they heard the report of fire-arms, and perceived smoke issuing from the boat; but concluding it was only some soldiers from the Capitana firing off their muskets, they thought nothing more of it. Montufar did not make his appearance, and they dined without him. In the evening Monteverde walked into Perichon's, with whom Montufar lived, and throwing two human ears into the lap of Dona Pastora, said, ' There, Senora, are the ears of your friend Montufar.' The only reason assigned for this barbarous act was that they *suspected* him of being a spy. Little did my sisters imagine, when they heard the report of the fire-arms in the boat, that they were witnessing the awful murder of their poor friend.

" Matters at length became so bad, that my father determined at all risks to leave Corrientes, feeling there was no longer the slightest security for either life or property there; and he was glad to escape

190 THE INDIANS IN QOYA.

with his family, leaving his house and furniture just as he occupied it.

" On their arrival at Goya, they were invited to stay with the family of Sobrido, your agent; where they also, after their arrival, were terribly alarmed.

"One night, having just retired to their rooms, they were startled by a dreadful outcry, with the report of fire-arms, and they were immediately after informed that the Indians having entered the town, they must not lose an instant in getting on board. They waited for a few moments till the space between the house and vessel was clear, and then hastened down, *just as they were, in their night-dresses.* Poor Anne had got about half-way when some one called to her to return. She had been observed by two of the Indians. On making a second attempt, she was met by Juan, our cook, who caught her up in his arms, carried her to the vessel, and placed her upon the plank. Considering she was safe, he hastened back to my mother and Jane; but poor Anne, from her fright, slipped and fell into the river. She was speedily got out, dripping wet, and was taken on board, where she was presently joined by the rest. They found every

THE FLIGHT. 191

corner of the vessel crowded, and the captain of the port quarrelling with the patron, because the latter positively refused to loose the hawser until my father and his family were on board. Finding that no threat or persuasion availed with the *patron,* the captain seized a hatchet and ordered Francisco to cut the cable. He was in the act of so doing when my father stepped on board. Had they been a minute later, the vessel would have been carried by the current beyond their reach. One of Mrs. Sobrido's brothers was killed close to the vessel, in the sight of his wife, who was hourly expecting her confinement, and had escaped on board the San Jose with her children. It was a terrible scene.

" On the following day the people of Goya who had taken refuge on board returned, and found all quiet; but several persons had been killed and %vounded. These were the very Indians from whom Campbell had liberated Ascencion when my sistei and I stopped at Goya on our way to Buenos Ayres. They had pitched their *toldos* close to the town and were living very peaceably; but most of the men had been unwisely induced to enter the army; they were consequently provided with fire-arms, and on the first affront received from the

192 PARTING NOTICE OF OLD FRIENDS.

inhabitants they rose upon them in the way I have mentioned, and put to death all the persons obnoxious to them, after which they fled to the Chaco once more.

" My father and mother, with my sisters Jane and Anne, left in December, 1820, and arrived in Buenos Ayres on the second day of the following year.

"Of Dona Florinda we know little or nothing, except that she died in great poverty. Campbell made his escape into Paraguay about the time that Artigas fled there; and though he (Campbell,) was informed he must consider himself a prisoner, he was allowed to follow his own business, that of a tanner, at Neembucu, where he was still living when we last heard of him, although occasionally getting into hot water with the inhabitants.*

" Tuckerman took a chacara upon the banks of the Parana – Perichon's, with which you are well acquainted – about three leagues from Corrientes,

* Campbell had an inveterate dislike to the long platted queues of the Paraguayans. On one occasion, when admiral of Artigas's flotilla, he took a Paraguay vcwul, and landing the crew at Goya, he brought them one and all to the *block,* where, instead of decapitating them, he caused an executioner, with a sharp hatchet, to deprive them all of their queues. Thus shorn of their glory he sent them to Paraguay.

NARRATIVE CONCLUDES. 193

one of the most beautiful situations I ever saw in South America; and this place he named Mount Vernon, after Washington's estate. He became quite a chacarero in habits, dress, and manners. I believe he married a Correntina, not quite so enchanting a person as Charlotte, and had a large family after we left Corrientes."

Here Miss Postlethwaite's narrative concludes. The disasters and misery which overtook the province of Corrientes towards the close of Artigas's reign, and during the anarchy which ensued after his abandonment of the Protectorate and flight into Paraguay, form a painful contrast indeed to the peace and prosperity which it was enjoying during the period of our stay there, and up to the time of my quitting it for good.

The province, however, shortly after Mr. Postlethwaite's departure, got quit of its anarchical despoilers, and entered on a long course of uninterrupted industry and enterprise, and of consequent prosperity and happiness, of which we shall probably have to take some more particular notice in a future series of our letters.

Yours, &c.

W. P. R.

VOL. III. K LETTER LVIII.

W. P. R. toGeneralMillkk.

Excitement of Revolutionary Times – San Martin in Chili – Good
News – Colonel Escalada – The English Ball – Civil Wars – A
Horse in a Bedroom – The Montonera – Proposed Trip to Eng-
land – *Affaire* * *du Caeur* – Generals Rolon and Soler – General
Rolon's Fears – Our Departure – Our Captives – Captain H
resolves to take them to England – A fortunate Rencontre – First rate Navigation.
Lyndon, 1842.

Revolutionarytimes are times of excitement, and among such a lively people as the Buenos Ayreans there was, during their war of independence, no lack of illustration of this fact. They felt their reverses and their victories with equal sensibility; but, ardent and ambitious, both the one and the other stimulated them to new exertions, and fixed them more steadily in their purpose of achieving their independence of Spain.

Of the invasion of Chili by General San Martin, we shall have to speak historically; but I may here observe, that the inhabitants of Buenos Ayres, after having been greatly elated by the issue of the famous battle of Chacabuco – which at once opened

SANMARTININCHILI.195

up the waj' to the possession of Santiago, the capital of Chili, – were no less depressed by the dispersion of San Martin's army at Cancharayada, which threatened the immediate loss of their recent and most important acquisition.

It was not without reason that the news of this dispersion threw the deepest gloom over Buenos Ayres. The " patria" itself, that is, the independence of the country, was in imminent danger. All had been ventured on the great stake of Chili, and if that country were again to fall under the domination of Spain, the River Plate provinces – the "head and front" of the revolution – might well tremble for their own existence as a free and independent nation.

Nothing could be done at home – all was to be trusted to the genius of San Martin in Chili; and day by day we waited with the most intense anxiety for intelligence which all hoped, but none dared to anticipate, would be of a favourable character. I saywewaited, because foreigners really seemed to take as deep an interest in the issue as the people themselves.

This was about the middle of April, 1818, the dispersion having taken place on the 19th of March.

196 GOOD NEWS.

One afternoon, then, as eight or nine of us were sitting over our wine at Mr. Dickson's house, where we had congregated to dinner with and without invitation, and as we were discussing the question of the day, " What is to become of the country, should Chili be lost?" Captain S. (I think it was), having previously left the table and gone to the front gate, returned, and quietly putting his head inside of the dining-room door, said, " Colonel Escalada has just arrived with the news of the total overthrow of the Spaniards in Chili."

Now the gallant caplain having a great tendency to *quiz,* we only laughed at his news, and all the more that he went on *assuring* us that he had stated a fact. He retired, leaving us to our incredulity, and we resumed our long faces. But we had not sat long when, crack! off went one of the fort guns; and before we could hear another, the bells began to ring a merry peal. Out we all sallied, and found, to our joy, that Captain S's news was perfectly correct. The battle of Maypu had secured the independence of Chili. The enthusiasm of the people knew no bounds: they ran from street to street, and from house to

COLONgL ESCALADA. 197

house, congratulating and hugging each other. Huzzas and vivas filled the air; the whole population was intoxicated with national pride and joy. Our party made for the fort, close to Mr. Dickson's house, and we were just in time to meet our friend, Manuel Escalada, issuing from the first gate amid the acclamations of the throng. He was waving a Spanish colour which he had brought with him from the field of battle, and directing his course to his father's house, where he had not yet been.

I went there, as usual, to the evening tertulia, and a more gay, animated, and joyous scene than it presented could not well be imagined. The house was thronged during the whole night by all the respectable population of the place. The young colonel, who was one of General San Martin's aides-de-camp, found as much work on his hands in his father's sala that evening as he had had on the day of battle – different in its kind, no doubt, but equally fatiguing; and, considering the innumerable glances and admiring looks he had to stand from the brightest eyes and prettiest faces of Buenos Ayres, almost as dangerous. Indeed, he escaped scatheless from the plains of Maypii, but I am not sure if he did not receive a wound this very

198 THE ENGLISH BALL.

night of his arrival, which soon afterwards compelled him to quit the free ranks of the bachelors and submit to the silken bonds of the Benedicts. He married Dona Indalesia Oromi, (the younger sister of Dona Mariquita, heretofore mentioned,) a lady in every way deserving of the gallant young soldier.

The victory of Maypu was celebrated by convivial parties, tertulias, and balls; and among the latter, one given by the British residents, immediately after San Martin's return from Chili, was on a grand scale. It was held in Sarratea's house, occupied by Mr. Brittain as his house of business, which was very handsomely fitted up for the occasion; and the hero of Maypu expressed himself as highly gratified with the splendid mark of respect paid to him by his English friends. The ball went off with the utmost eclat, and was kept up by a great proportion of the beauty and fashion of Buenos Ayres till seven o'clock next morning. We had no disorder, although the patios were filled all night with *tapadas.* The custom of the country is to admit, on occasions of great tertulias and balls, *muffled females,* accompanied by beaux, to view the dancing from the

CIVIL WARS. 199

patios or courts of the house. They are admitted to the windows, the doors, even the passages and inner doors, although they never, on any occasion, attempt to go into the rooms. Hundreds thus congregate to view the party and the dancing; and many prefer going as *tapadas* to being invited to the ball. Families in mourning, who cannot with propriety accept an invitation, are sure to go as *tapadas*.

San Martin returned to Chili, to follow up the great career he had commenced, and to attack royalty in its strong-holds in South America. In the meantime, the volatile Buenos Ayreans, left free from all fear of any further interference with them on the part of the mother country, gave a loose to the reins of political intrigue at home; and after the fall of Pueyrredon, in 1819, a state of extraordinary anarchy arose in the following year.

But although revolutions and counter-revolutions became the order of the day; – although armies engaged in civil war were fighting in the provinces, and gradually drawing nearer to Buenos Ayres; – nay, although at last we saw our own country houses surrounded by the armed forces, savage and ragged gauchos of the provinces, who at last

200 A HORSE IN A BED-ROOM.

lorded it over the poor capital; – we all seemed to live as much at our ease as if the country were in perfect tranquillity. Our ears got so accustomed to the word *revolution,* that all fear of it was completely lost. Our greatest anxiety was when an order came out to seize *horses.* Having all our favourite nags and chargers, we used to resort to every means to preserve them. I recollect that even Sir Thomas Hardy, our commodore, and the Hon. Captain Robert Spencer (both now, alas! no more), were obliged to hide their horses on one occasion; and the latter treated his to a *bed-room* in the hotel where he was lodging.

The undisciplined, heterogeneous, and half-wild armed forces which the chiefs of the interior, at war with the capital, from time to time raised and maintained, went by the general name of the *montonera,* or mob troops. They were a lawless set in their mode of carrying on warfare, and were held in no small terror by the Buenos Ayreans. Yet when these montonera troops finished at last a successful campaign by triumphantly entering the capital at the commencement of the year 1820, they conducted themselves with very great moderation. I was residing at the time at a pleasant but some-

THE MONTONERA. 201

what lonely English country house, well known by the name of the " Paddock/' helonging to Mr. Staples, and I used often to traverse the road on horseback late at night, without ever being molested. When the montonera entered the town, ihey bivouakced round Mr. Mackinlay's quinta; but though the ladies were of course somewhat uneasy at the vicinity of such neighbours, the latter did little or no damage to the premises, and offered no violence of any kind. Their principal leader was one of the celebrated brothers *Carrera,* who having great influence over his men, used it to preserve physical order in the midst of the moral disorganization which prevailed.

It is true matters got so far worse afterwards, as to induce several families to relinquish their villas, and seek shelter in the city. But there was, perhaps, more of alarm than of much real danger, for Mr. Mackinlay never removed his family, and he was not molested by the marauders.

In the midst of these political disturbances, circumstances arose which led me to the sudden determination of visiting my native country. In fact, my close intercourse with Mr. Mackinlay's family had shown me how much my felicity would be increased

202PROPOSEDTRIPTOENGLAND.

were I permitted to become a member of it. I had the happiness to be accepted by his oldest daughter, and her parents approved of the union; but before settling down as a married man, perhaps for many years in South America, a desire to see my friends and relatives at home, as well as a necessity to arrange various business matters, determined me to make a flying visit to England.

There lay in our roadstead a fine East Indiaman, called the Aberdeen, commanded by a Lieutenant

H of our navy, a warm-hearted, but also a

very warm-tempered, man. He wanted, before proceeding on his voyage, about a hundred and fifty tons of freight, which I agreed to give him without delay, and to sail with him as passenger to England. I made my bargain on the 6th, and on the 22nd we were ready to put to sea.

Were I inclined to be romantic, or could I reckon on all my readers being of a romantic turn of mind, I might say a great many pretty things on my parting scenes from Buenos Ayres, on this, to me, momentous occasion. But there are two classes of readers of such a work as this. One of them comprises a great many of our friends, who, being of a staid and sedate character, look for " information"

AFFAIRES DU COEUR. 203

in our pages, and repudiate those lighter affairs of which what they call "trashy novels" are made up. They want statistics, politics, national traits, history, geography, geology, zoology, and all the other ologies; and to such subjects they conceive us to be bound to confine ourselves. I confess I am pretty much of the same opinion, and therefore I must beg of all our other readers who consider that *affaires du cceur* form a legitimate portion of general information, to call in their own imaginations, and so happily to supply any deficiency they may find in me. They can picture to themselves romantic strolls through fine grounds, and they can bring in the gentle moon, throwing a soft light into avenues of orange trees; they can fancy it now intercepted, and now shining forth in silvery and unclouded radiance. Then the flying hours and

the mutual vows in short, they can wander into

any region of romance they please.

At the time of which I speak, political dissensions and intestine convulsions were nearly at their height. The head of one party upset another, – triumphed for a day, – and by flight the following day, made room for a third. General Soler having taken a prominent part in this sort of civil war,

204 GENERALS ROLON AND SOLER.

and having been ousted in an attempt to overthrow one of the ephemeral governments of the day, sought for safety on board of an English vessel lying in the outer roads. Soon after, another convulsion upset Colonel, afterwards General Rolon, the bitter enemy of Soler. This was only a day or two before my embarking for England,

and on Rolon's application to me, I gave him an order to go on board of the Aberdeen. He wanted to get to Monte Video, and so did another friend, though a very opposite character to my military one, – the Reverend James Thomson, an amiable, zealous, and accomplished missionary, as well as an active labourer in the field for the Missionary Society, whose agent he was in South America. Captain

H, at my request, agreed to stand in to Monte

Video on our way down, and to put these two gentlemen, Rolon and Thomson, on shore in his boat.

We embarked in stormy weather on the 23rd of March. A strong head-wind prevented us from moving the next day, and in the forenoon, as we lay at anchor, we saw the government felucca, full of men and bearing a broad pendant, making for our vessel. Poor Colonel Rolon was in a fever. He made sure that an armed force was coming toGENERALROLON'sFEARS.205

drag him on shore, or to shoot him where he was;

and although H indignantly repelled the idea

of a foreign force daring to touch any one on board of his, a British vessel, – although he assured Colonel Rolon that he was as safe there as he could be in the King of England's palace, – Rolon's fears were superior to all such assertion, and he begged me to put him where he would be safe in case of any search being made. Much against

H 's will, therefore, the Colonel was stowed

away. The boat came alongside, but the commanding officer informed us that he was in search of*another*vessel, on board which General Soler, as already mentioned, had taken refuge from Rolon and his party. They had been sent to carry Soler back in triumph, and finding him in a brig close by, which he was nothing loth to quit, he came on board the Aberdeen to see me, in order to learn the news more particularly. Again Rolon, who had come on deck, was hidden, and he had to listen, from where he lay, to Soler in the cabin, denouncing vengeance against him whenever and wherever he could be caught. However, Soler proceeded to his triumph in Buenos Ayres, and my friend Rolon breathed freely once more.

206 OUR DEPARTURE.

The wind increased to a gale, and we lay three days in the outer roads unable to stir. We could not communicate with the shore, but we heard heavy firing and cannonading, which told me that the discord on shore was busily vying with the angry elements of the heavens on the water.

When we at last weighed anchor, we could make no way against the strong head wind which opposed our progress; and such was its obstinacy, that it kept us for the almost unprecedented term

of thirteen days in the river. Captain H, a

man of impetuous temper, was beside himself by being thus thwarted by the elements, and he unfortunately took up the idea that his ill-fortune was owing to his having on board my poor friends, Mr. Thomson and Colonel Rolon, the two Jonases who raised the tempest which tossed us to and fro on the River Plate.

At length, on the thirteenth day, the foul wind died away, and a beautiful breeze sprung up; it got stronger and stronger, and ere long we were scudding along at the rate of nine knots an hour. But here a new difficulty arose; we were so situated that if we stood over to Monte Video, which lay not in our track, we should find it

'I

GENERALROLONANDMR. THOMSON.207

difficult, if not impossibile, to avail ourselves of the fine breeze which was wafting us along. Such

a thing was not to be thought of by Captain H-,

so he resolved to take his*captive.?*(for such they might now consider themselves) to Maldonado, and put them on board of the guard-ship lying off that port. Accordingly, as we neared this vessel, the long boat was manned, and my two friends, with no small fear and trembling, – for the sea was running very high and the wind increasing to a gale, – took leave of us and descended to the boat. Off they set, * the impatient captain watching their movements with intense anxiety; not that he was disturbed about the personal safety of the party (as I was), but that he had a misgiving as to the boat getting to*windward*of the guard-ship, which was indispensable towards landing our passengers.

We were about a mile off when the boat began to mount one wave, sink into an abyss, and remount another; now it appeared stoutly to buffet with the storm, – now as if to be engulphed in the mighty deep. Captain H watched their every movement with nervous anxiety; he never withdrew from his eye the spy-glass with which he scanned every turn of the boat; but as it went nearer to or departed from the mark, his body, by a

208 CAPTAIN H RESOLVES

sympathetic influence, twisted from one side to another. He held earnest colloquy with himself, after this fashion – "They'll do! they're all right.

No! no! where the are they going to? Hold

up! There! No, – they're off again, by.

Now, they're right enough if They'll miss

her! by heaven, they'll miss her! No, they won't! Yes, they will! Oh! – Ah! – Oh, the lubberly

scoundrels! Hold up! holdup! They'll

never make her! There they go! there they go! Oh the villains! (Here the captain's feet went quickly in nervous agitation.) There! There! They've missed her! They're away to leeward! By! they'll never reach her!"

Here, in a paroxysm of rage, the captain paced the deck, and gave orders to back our sails and wait for the boat. It was too true that neither she nor our own vessel could possibly make the guard- ship. "They shall go to England!" cried H.

" By, they shall go to England! I would

not lose this breeze for the King of Great Britain! They shall go to England, and find their way back the best way they can."

Drenched and half drowned, Mr. Thomson and the Colonel approached the vessel, well knowing that a storm was raging on deck quite equal to that

TO TAKE THEM TO ENGLAND. 209

which agitated the sea; but they both looked utterly

confounded when Captain H walked up to

them and said they must make up their minds to go to England. Ere they could recover from their surprise, our sails were trimmed, and we were scudding on from all trace or view of the River Plate, at a speed of ten knots an hour.

Mr. Thomson, – the mildest and gentlest of men, and a truly practical follower of the precepts and example of his Great Master, – heard with perfect resignation of the unexpected and extraordinary interruption to all his plans and engagements. It was, of course, a grievous disappointment to him; but no murmur escaped his lips, no gloom, even momentary, overspread his placid countenance.

H added to his announcement, that if he fell

in with any vessel bound to the Plate (it was about a hundred chances to one that we should not), he would put his passengers on board; but he could by no means put into any port himself, which would complete the ruin of his already much damaged passage. Mr. Thomson said that ifHewho presided over all things saw meet, He would send a vessel to carry him back to the vineyard in which it had been his happiness to labour.

210AFORTUNATERENCONTRE.

As for Colonel Rolon, being nothing better than a banished man from his own country, he began to relish, a great deal more than I did, the prospect of his visiting England under*my*wing. " You know Don Guillermo," said he; "I am not acquainted with a single soul in England, and therefore be assured I shall never lose sight of*you*.Then you are to return quickly to Buenos Ayres, and I shall return with you, – just in time, I make no doubt, to find my own party once more at the helm of public affairs."

Behold us, then, all sailing away very contentedly for England, with a wind which promised to atone for our long detention. On the fifth day from our. adventure at Maldonado we were in the latitude of Rio de Janeiro. But here, to keep up its proverbial character for inconstancy, the wind failed us, and a light but adverse breeze prevented us from making further progress. While we thus lay, almost becalmed, a fine French brig, bound in a contrary direction, hove in sight. She steered towards us, when we hailed her and found she was bound for Monte Video! As vessels take quite different routes going and coming across the Atlantic, the rencontre was most unexpected; but our two friends were

FIRST RATE NAVIGATION. 211

quickly transferred to the Frenchman, and they arrived at Monte Video about six weeks after they left Buenos Ayres, where all hopes of their safety had been abandoned. They had been seen in the boat, which was supposed to have swamped in their endeavour to reach the guard ship.

We had no farther incident during our passage. As we approached England the weather was very boisterous, and we could make no observations for

two or three days. When, according to H 's

reckoning, we were nearing St. George's Channel, the wind was fair, but blowing a gale with a thick drizzling rain. We made norland, yet kept running on; and such was the precision of our commander's navigation, that within half an hour of his calculation we at midnight made the light he expected in the Channel, the first land or landmark we had seen, if I recollect well, from the time of our leaving the Plate.

Your's, &c.

W. P. R.

15

SECTION 15

LETTER LIX.

    W. P. R. toGeneralMiller.

    Arrival in Liverpool – The Surprise – Past Reviews and future Plans – What may be done in England – Contrasts – National Feelings – The Musselburgh Lass – Arrived at Home – Boyhood Scenes – Departure from Lasswade – The late Royal Tour – Loyalty of the Scotch – Beauties of the Tay – Six Weeks' Work – Leaving the River Mersey – The River cleared – Arrived at Mal- donado – Montevideo – Arrival at Buenos Ayres.

    *London,*1842.

    Mydetermination to visit England was so closely followed up by my departure from Buenos Ayres, that no intermediate opportunity offered by which I could advise my brother of my intended trip. I was, therefore, the bearer of my own news; and when I arrived in Liverpool my friends at home not only thought I was still at the River Plate, but they had not the remotest idea of seeing me for some years to come.

    On landing from the Aberdeen, I drove to my brother's house in George's Square, then, though now no longer, a fashionable quarter of Liverpool. It was about six in the evening of a very hot day, in the middle of June. On knocking at the door,

    THE SURPRISE. 213

it was opened by a man servant, who on seeing me started as if he had looked on an apparition, and on my speaking, his confusion evidently increased. The fact is, my brother and I were, at that stage of our career, constantly mistaken for each other, – first, from a similarity of personal appearance, confirmed, secondly, by an absolute identity of voice. So honest John, the man-servant, having just seen his master fast asleep on a sofa in his library, was greatly inclined to take me for his ghost, in which belief he was much confirmed by seeing me unceremoniously glide past him and walk up stairs. He stood transfixed at the bottom of them.

When I ran into the library and began to shake my brother out of his siesta, the bewilderment of the master was even greater than that of the man. He could not persuade himself that it was not a continuation of his dreams. In fact, there lay on his writing table finished packets, as well as a half- finished letter, addressed to myself, all intended for a vessel to sail the following day for Buenos Ayres; and " Don Juan" seemed sorely puzzled for a moment in his endeavour to find out whether he had been transported to the River Plate, or Buenos Ayres had come across the Atlantic to give him the meeting in England. It was really a pleasant

214 PAST REVIEWS AND FUTURE PLANS.

meeting, and I don't know that I ever enjoyed anything more than the amazement and excitement caused in my brother's household by my sudden and unlocked for appearance.

We spent the whole of that night on a review of our mutual proceedings since we had parted in Buenos Ayres in 1816, – in arrangements for the present, and in projects for the future. It was determined that I should immediately proceed to "drum"* for a handsome cargo of goods in Manchester, and ship myself with them for my old headquarters, Buenos Ayres. Resolving also to extend our sphere of action to the shores of the Pacific, in South America, we further covenanted that my brother should break up his establishment in Liverpool, and proceed, as soon as possible, to establish a house in Santiago, the capital of Chili.

After seven years' absence from home, and with a prospect of returning for twice that number of years to a distant foreign land, it may be supposed that I might have given a few months, at least, to my family and friends in my native place. But business in England is all imperative, and an, what

*Drumming, among commission merchants and manufacturers, i3 a well-known term. For the benefit of the uninitiated, I may explain that it means soliciting consignments of goods for foreign establishments on commission.

WHAT MAY BE DONE IN ENGLAND. 215

still more powerful agent than even business impelled me onwards to a quick return to Buenos Ayres. On getting back there I was to change my status from a useless and insignificant bachelor to that of the dignified and important married man; and, of course, I was all anxiety to return and enter on my new estate.

I propose just to sketch, as rapidly as I can, I saw and what I did during my stay in England and Scotland, and then my readers shall judge if there be another country on the face of the earth where so much can be accomplished in so short a space of time as in our own country.

I rested for a couple of days in Liverpool, where I got introduced to many of the merchant princes of that emporium, and then proceeded to make the acquaintance of the more substantial, though less dashing. capitalists and manufacturers of Manchester. Here I was so well received that my drumming became easy work, and many looms were soon set at work to produce the exact sort of goods which I recommended. After some days spent in the necessary process of canvassing friends, and leaving at last all quite arranged for my forthcoming cargo, my brother and 1 took mail for Bath, where

216 CONTRASTS.

I spent some days,*en prince,*with our old patron and relative, of Pultney-street. We visited Bristol and the surrounding country, and then posted off to London, where we landed at the Bedford Coffeehouse, under Covent Garden piazzas, then, as I believe now, a comfortable and somewhat fashionable and dear hotel.

When I went abroad next morning, I contrasted, in my mind's eye, the streets and the people of the mighty metropolis with those of Assumption and Corrientes, and I was amazed and bewildered on contemplating*man* – the same*genus* – under such widely differing aspects. I hurried through the sights and the public resorts, drove about the parks, admired the novel invention of cabs, – for even*then*there were no omnibuses, and a steamer was scarcely to be seen, – and stared at the gas lamps. In short, I whirled about, and at the end of a short time, with my brain half reeling under all that it had been obliged to take in, I started once more in the mail, in a northerly direction, leaving my brother to return to Liverpool to accelerate our mercantile movements there.

I proceeded to Leeds and was kindly received by the Messrs. Gotts, the great chiefs of our woollen

NATIONAL FEELINGS. 217

manufactures in Yorkshire. I went to York, just to have a peep at the Minster, and then hied me on to my native land. My imagination had been at work, during seven years of absence, in heightening all its natural beauties and all its moral and intellectual worth, while, as always happens, in such cases, I had gone on gradually throwing into the shade its less agreeable features, till they had become altogether invisible to my mental eye. When I came, therefore, to an actual view of Scotland, after travelling over some of the finest parts of England, my national feelings had, at first, to sustain many rude shocks. Comparisons are odious, and I therefore will not here draw them; but content myself with saying that since 1820, although my feelings have continued as national as ever they were, I think I have been able to take a more correct view of my native country, as compared with others, than I had done before that period. I am greatly mistaken if we Scotch would not have much more justice done to our native land could we temper, with some impartiality and judgment, that love of country, or rather enormous national vanity, which prompts us to de-

VOL. III. L

218 THE MUSSLEBURGH LASS.

mand such large concessions on every point in favour of Scotland.

I was bound for Glenesk, already I think mentioned by my brother in this work. The nearest point to which the mail could take me was Mussleburgh, a small fishing town six miles from the capital. Here I arrived at twelve o'clock at night, and the mail put me down at the door of the principal*inn,*the fashionable name of hotel not having as yet penetrated to the unsophisticated Mussleburgh. After thundering for nearly a quarter of an hour at the door, it was opened by a " barefit lass," who, half asleep, rubbed her eyes, and was anything but tidy in her person, or winning in her looks. We got my luggage into the house, and the " lass" looked very impatient to get to sleep again. But I, feeling more hungry than sleepy, wanted to coax her to get me a little supper. " Come," said I, " you surely wo'nt turn me off to bed without either meat or drink; pray let me have something to eat." The lass looked at me with angry surprise. " Lord hae a care o' us!" said she, " Wha d'ye think's gaun to get ye a sapper at this oor o' the nicht? It'sARRIVAL AT HOME. 219

twal o'clock." " Hoot! woman," I responded in my vernacular, " 'am sure ye wu'd nae send a Scotchman awa to his bed withoot his supper, whan he's come sceven thoosand mile to look for yin." This appeal had the desired effect. The " lass's" face was immediately lit up with a good humoured smile. " Od," said she, " I thocht ye were an Englisher, an ye ken theyre unco fashious sort o' folk; but sit doon," (she showed me into a parlour) " an al get ye some ham and some cheese and breed, and ony think to drink that ye like."

I got a comfortable supper, thanks to my Scotch dialect, and next morning at eight I was in a post- chaise, urging the post-boy to get quickly to Lass- wade. There I stopped at a pretty little cottage on the banks of the Esk, and in a moment after I was first in the arms of the old lady, my mother; and then embracing the young ones, my sisters. Those who have travelled, and returned after years of absence to their happy home, know all the joy of the first meeting; and those who have not so travelled, and returned, I advise to do so, for by this means alone can they know some of the most

220 BOYHOOD SCENES.

delightful sensations which are permitted to our nature.

The ground I was now on has lately been sketched, described, dwelt upon by those who have recorded the movements of the august party which a month ago visited Scotland. I will be bound to say that Majesty has viewed no more lovely scenery than that which lies between Dalkeith, Lasswade, and Roslin. They were all the scenes of my own early youth – every inch of the ground was familiar to me; and as I strolled along the romantic banks of the Esk, or wandered through the woods of Hawthornden; as I again revisited Roslin Chapel, one of the most beautiful of our Gothic ruins; as I retraced the scenes of my boyhood, visited Dalkeith school, where for five years I had occupied a place on*its forms*(as we term the*benches*in Scotland); as I thus occupied myself for three days, accompanied by those who had shared my early affections, now only strengthened by time as they had been hallowed by absence; I was amply repaid for every toil I might have undergone, every peril I might have encountered, every privation I might have endured: they were three of the happiest days of my life.

DEPARTUREFROMLASSWADE.221

" Oh friendly to the best pursuits of man,

Friendly to thought, to virtue, and to peace,

Domestic life in rural pleasure passed!

Few know thy value, and few taste thy sweets,

Though many boast thy favours, and affect

To understand and choose thee for their own.
But foolish man forgets his proper bliss,
E'en as his first progenitor, and quits,
Though placed in Paradise (for earth has still
Some traces of her youthful beauty left),
Substantial happiness for transient joy.
Scenes formed for contemplation, and to nurse
The growing seeds of wisdom, that suggest,
By every pleasing image they present,
Reflection such as meliorate the heart,
Compose the passions and exalt the mind."

At the end of seven short days, which flew quickly by, I found myself constrained to depart from Lasswade and Edinburgh; but as business called me farther north, and unwilling so soon to part with my sisters, I resolved to carry them with me on my little northern tour.

Taste and circumstances led me to make the very same tour which was lately the universal theme, as that of the Queen; and having made the vicinity of Edinburgh my head quarters, before I set off, I think I am fairly entitled to say, that few could have traced the progress of the royal cortege with more interest than myself. In the adjuncts of

222THELATEROYALTOUR.

the tour we doubtless could not cope with Her Majesty. What those of that august and most deservedly popular lady were, everybody knows. So everybody knows the enthusiastic feeling with which she was everywhere greeted by the people; the regal state with which she was welcomed by our gallant Scottish chiefs. It was a splendid affair – a heartstirring succession of very noble scenes.

Well,*we*travelled over the same ground in somewhat humbler guise. A post-chaise and pair was all we boasted of. We had no sleepy baillies to amuse us, no processions, turning out of clans, or public demonstrations to enhance the pleasure of the tour. But while public applause is a source of pleasure and just pride to a sovereign who rules in the affections of her people, every one who has made the same tour will agree that the scene itself is fraught with delights equally to be enjoyed by prince and people. It absorbs the mind and the attention so completely, that no want is felt, no desire arises for any additional pleasure than the contemplation of the scene before us. Had the Queen made her tour with Prince Albert only as her companion, and unknown in her public character, she must still have

LOYALTY OF THE SCOTCH. 223

derived great pleasure from an observation of all the various features of the country, as displayed both by nature and by art. Great indeed is the triumph of Scotland in this point of view, but I may, before leaving the royal progress, be permitted, as a Scotchman, to remark, that the display of her moral feeling, in connection with the Queen, was a still greater victory achieved by my native country. The people arose as one man, and in a burst of loyalty which resounded through the land, greeted the Queen as the fairest and the best impersonation of that monarchical principle which they reverence and cherish with the affection of the olden times. The Queen had " borne her faculties so meekly" in carrying out the principle; while she had maintained it entire, she had so scrupulously minded the rights of her people, that the judgment of her Scottish subjects ratified and strengthened that personal devotion to the royal person, which manifested itself so beautifully and so universally on whichever side Her Majesty turned, as she traversed the various parts of her northern domains.

To return to the tour itself. It undoubtedly embraces a considerable portion of our finest scenery, as all the world has seen in the late descriptions

224 BEAUTIES OF THE TAY.

and " illustrated news" of the Queen's royal progress. The views from Perth to Dunkeld, and along the banks of the Tay to Taymouth and the loch are matchless; and there is great, though gloomy grandeur, in the less traversed district of Crieff. I was particularly struck by the wildness of the scene there, and the primitive character of the people, owing no doubt to its being out of the highway of tourists and sight seers.

By the way of Crieff we went to Stirling, and here an old friend met us to conduct my sisters back to Edinburgh, leaving me free to pursue my journey by way of Glasgow to Liverpool. We had spent six delightful days in our journey, and it may easily be imagined that the parting was a formidable affair.

I travelled to Glasgow so sadly, after the recent loss of my companions, that I saw nothing of sufficient interest to rouse my attention till I got to that great emporium of our cotton and other manufactures in the north. There I was immersed for a short time in business during the day, and called on to drink double deep potations of punch during the night. But this not suiting my head, unaccustomed to the fumes of Jamaica rum, even thoughsixWeeks'Work.225

qualified with the finest West India limes, I set*off*after a couple of days for Liverpool, where my brother was anxiously expecting me to join my loaded barque, now ready for sea, and having a cargo of goods, two-thirds of which had been manufactured for me since my arrival from Buenos Ayres,

From the day that I landed in Liverpool till that of returning to it to take my departure for the river Plate, just forty-two days elapsed, and I often look back with surprise on the amount of business and pleasure, and travelling which I was able to cram into these six weeks. I went over upwards of 1500 miles of ground, spent twenty days with my friends in different cities and towns, and half as many between Liverpool and Manchester in attending to general business, as well as in ordering and selecting from thirty to forty thousand pounds worth of goods, to be taken abroad on account of thirty or forty persons, on consignment. I transacted business besides in London, Halifax, Leeds, Perth, Paisley, and Glasgow, and I saw much of the finest scenery of the country, extending from Somersetshire in England, to Perthshire in the highlands of Scotland. All this was compressed into six weeks, and I feel assured that in Great

226 LEAVING THE RIVER MERSE1T.

Britain alone could such an aggregate of affairs be got through within an equal space of time. And, be it remembered that in those days we had neither steam boats nor railways, the great agency by which I effected my locomotion when on business, having been*night travelling by the mail.*

I was as anxious to keep up the " go ahead" system by sea as by land; and therefore we chartered a beautiful schooner called the Antelope, for my return voyage – her sailing qualities being of the very first order. We were all ready for sea by the 1st of August, but westerly winds which had for some time prevailed, detained me for six days longer in Liverpool.

There is not a more animated nor yet a more curious sight to be seen than the disgorging of the mighty docks of Liverpool, after a long succession of westerly winds. When we got out, I think there must have been from one hundred and fifty to two hundred sail of merchant vessels tacking backwards and forwards at once on the river Mersey, each more anxious than his neighbour to get out to the open sea. In those days there were few, if any, tug boats to assist the operation; but only here and there the newly introduced steamers, employed as

THE RIVER CLEARED. 227

ferry boats, were seen provokingly to shoot ahead, in defiance of the wind, while we were fain to propitiate its scanty favours by making what is technically called a long leg and a short one, zigzagging, " 'bout ship," from one side to another, and coming tardily and obliquely to the point we had in view. But so many vessels with their sails set and glittering in the sun, thus passing and repass- ing one another, closely wedged in, almost scraping each other's sides yet never coming in contact, – and then the lively banks of the river, – the succession of towns, fields, villages, gardens, villas, lawns; the whole formed a very animated and singular scene.

We sailed in the forenoon, and made much better way than most of our competitors; so that as we descended the Mersey the surrounding naval ranks thinned at every tack; and towards evening we had cleared the mass, the sea being only dotted here and there with some other clippers which had made as good speed as ourselves.

We had a very boisterous passage, and what was a great deal worse, we had an ignorant and incompetent skipper. We were twice in the utmost peril of being totally lost, and when we got to the latitude

228 ARRIVAL AT MALDONADO.

of Buenos Ayres, instead of being off the Plate we found ourselves on the ground of the sperm whale fishers! From one of the whalers we learned we were many degrees out of our longitude. Ere we could get into the Plate, we were overtaken by a furious gale (a pampero) which first obliged us to lie to for nearly three days, and then, after much buffeting, we were forced to take shelter in Mal- donado, the scene of General Rolon's and Mr. Thomson's mishap. But here I fared a great deal better. Our commodore, Sir Thomas Hardy's flag ship, the Superb, one of our seventy-fours, was lying in the harbour, and I experienced the utmost kindness from all the officers on board. The honourable Frederick Spencer, then a lieutenant in his brother's frigate, the Owen Glendower, happened to be on a visit to the Superb, and to him, as an old acquaintance, I was indebted for many civilities. I spent two days agreeably in Maldo- nado, mostly on board of the man of war, and I had an opportunity of seeing the whole construction and working of one of our line of battle ships. It is a world, a perfect, curious world in miniature, within itself, and quite distinct from the *general* world in which we live.

MONTE VIDEO. 229

My little schooner, the Antelope, which lay like a cock-boat beside the gigantic man of war, yet which was much admired for its symmetrical beauty, had come in battered and weather beaten from our rough voyage: but a few expert hands from the Superb soon made her look as spruce as ever; and the weather moderating, I took leave of my kind friends, and proceeded on to Monte Video, where I had directed letters from Buenos Ayres to be waiting for me. The place was in possession of the Brazilians, a people devotedly attached to the system of *passports;* and as I had left free England unprovided with one, I paid for my temerity in landing without so essential a document, by spending a whole day in and out of the police office, apprehended and released by turns. One officer was more perplexed than another what to do with me; and it was not till I obtained an interview with General Lecor, the governor, that I was allowed to depart in peace.

Notwithstanding all our bad weather, and wretched navigation, we arrived in the outer roads of Buenos Ayres, after a passage of sixty-five days, which a clever skipper would undoubtedly have made in five and forty. My friend Captain Falcon,

230 ARRIVAL AT BUENOS AYRES.

commanding one of our vessels of war, landed me, as our own boat could scarcely " live" in such a sea as was then running; and after an absence of *less than* seven months, I again found myself, surrounded by many friends, in " old Buenos Ayres."

And there I leave myself for the present. It is high time to pause and observe how you and our other readers, view our letters so far on South America. If they are found tedious, dull, insipid, or profitless, we are content to withdraw to a corner, and sin no more: but if the story, so far told, should happily lead to a desire to hear the sequel, why then, – we can talk of that hereafter.

Meantime you know with what pleasure I record myself once more as your affectionate friend

W. P. R.

16

SECTION 16

LETTER LX.

J. P. R. toGeneralMiller.

My Brother's Departure for Buenos Ayres – I follow in the Cossack – Prospect of crossing the Andes – Departure from Buenos Ayres for Chile and Peru.

London, 1842.

Mybrother having sailed with a valuable cargo, as mentioned in his last letter, was speedily followed by me in a ship three times the size, chartered to go round Cape Horn. The vessel in which he sailed, gliding through the deep with the rapidity of a dolphin, soon reached its port of destination, – Buenos Ayres.

On breaking up my household establishment in Liverpool, I took with me all my domestic goods and chattels, my English servants, and several young gentlemen, in quality of mercantile attaches. Knowing so much of South America as I did, I was resolved to carry with me as many of the elements of English comfort as I could, especially as I was bound for more distant parts (Chile and232 MY THIRD DEPARTURE FROM ENGLAND.

Peru) than any in which I had yet been. The mercantile affairs of the house in Liverpool I left in the hands of two brothers, Messrs. John and Richard Hancock; and we had agencies also in London and Glasgow.

Every possible measure was taken to lay the foundation of prosperous and extensive establishments in Santiago, the capital of Chile, and in Lima (when it should fall to San Martin), the capital of Peru. Our affairs in Buenos Ayres were prospering in the hands of my brother; and so our connexion stretched, we may say, from Paraguay to Corrientes, from Corrientes to Santa Fe, from Santa Fe to Buenos Ayres; and it was now intended to complete the chain, round Cape Horn and across the Andes, by the formation, under my own eye, of the contemplated establishments in Chile and Peru.

My imagination was buoyant with the prospect of visiting the countries in which the Yncas had flourished. Pizarro fought, and Ercilla sung his magnificent Araucana. Then to cross the Andes, – those stupendous monuments of Almighty power; – to see the wild guanaco bounding from mountain to mountain, or skirting its almost perpendicular

PROSPECT OF CROSSING THE ANDES. 233

midway height; – to see dark lakes in the silent seclusion of Nature, shut up in basins formed by vast pyramidal piles of earth, thousands of feet above the level of the sea; – to behold here the arid ascent, – a day's journey to its cloud-capt and snow-covered apex; – to see, far, far beneath, the foaming cataract, and hear the thunder of its roar; – to descend anon from the Cumbre into the romantic and wooded passes which conduct to the fruitful and umbrageous valleys of Chile: the anticipation of all this both charmed and warmed my imagination, till I began to think every day of our voyage in the Cossack a week, every week a month, and every month a year.

At length we reached the River Plate, and I was landed at Buenos Ayres, where I once more met my brother, and from whence I proposed again to cross the Pampas; not now in the direction of Paraguay but in that of Mendoza, *en route* for Chile.

I only stayed a few days, for refreshment, at my brother's country-house, making occasional visits to the counting-house. They were short, but sufficient to show me that all was going on prosperously.

The Cossack then sailed, with all my establishment, for Valparaiso; and taking, after an absence

234

DEPARTUREFROMBUENOSAYRESFORCHILE.

of now four years from South America, to my old Pampa habits, I started *off*, under the halloo of the postilions, in my old hide-and-thong-bound carriage, accompanied by a large *posse comitatus* of Spanish and English friends to the first post- house. Foremost, as principal outrider, on his cavallo bianco, went Don Felipe, scampering, capering, and making frequent appeals to the *chifle*, or silver-tipped horn, which dangled at his saddle- peak. We all parted, half merry, after dinner: my friends on their return to Buenos Ayres, and I to make another post or two in advance toward Mendoza.

Here, for the present, I bid farewell to you and my readers, faithfully promising, if they give me encouragement, to prosecute, in another Series, my adventures and observations on the most interesting of all the countries I have yet visited, – Chile and Peru.

Your's, &c.

J. P. R.

LETTER LXI.

TheAuthorsToGeneralMiller.

HistoricalReviewResumedAndConcluded. Pueyrredon's Government – Its Despotic Nature – The National Congress subservient to the Executive – Arrests and Banishments – Brazil and the Banda Oriental – General Lecor – General San Martin – His Crossing the Andes – His Operations – Prepares for Attacking – His Despatch – Battle of Chacabuco – Its Results – Its Heroes – O'Higgins Director – San Martin refuses Promotion – The War in Upper Peru – Miscellaneous.

*London,*1842.

Theinstallation of a National Congress and the election of a Supreme Director of the State, in the person of Don Juan Martin de Pueyrredon, gave the united provinces of the River Plate, for the first time, the character of an independent nation under a settled form of government.

That form was democratic, theoretically speaking; but the temper and education of the new director were essentially calculated, in point of fact, to place the institutions of the country under the dominion of an oligarchy, if not to make them those of an absolute monarchy. Pueyrredon had chosen the career of a soldier, and as such he had attained a fair reputation. But he was proud, haughty, and aristocratic in his feelings. He236Pueyrredon'sGovernment.

carried his respect for military discipline into the cabinet; and, however willing he might be to allow the people to talk of liberty and free institutions, he was not even remotely inclined to allow these principles to interfere with his supreme command.

Had Pueyrredon, with this tendency to exercise something like a military despotism, possessed high principles of honour, and unsullied political integrity, perhaps his policy would have been the best adapted to the actual circumstances of the country; for party spirit ran high, and the recent transition from a state approaching to slavery to one of unlimited freedom, had engendered a spirit of licence, not unlikely to degenerate into anarchy, which could only be controuled and corrected by a strong and determined executive.

But there was little of Roman virtue in Don Juan Martin de Pueyrredon; and, without wishing to attack him personally, truth compels us to say that his government was corrupt and venal to a melancholy and too notorious extent. Its military power and influence were used, not to preserve order and uphold good institutions at home, – not to consolidate the independence of the country, or resist the encroachment of insidious enemies abroad, – but to put down, openly and tyrannically, all those

THE NATIONAL CONGRESS. 237

citizens who dared to murmur at the dilapidations of the public treasury, or the inglorious apathy which marked the public career of the Directory.

The Congress in no way tended to ameliorate this state of affairs. It had been convoked in Tucuman, and there it absurdly met and continued to sit, eight or nine hundred miles distant from the seat of the national executive! It may well be conceived, therefore, that the*Tucuman*Congress was a nullity. This became so evident at last that the profusion of doctors and other individuals who composed the " august" body, were brought at the public expense, for it was a*paid*legislature, to Buenos Ayres, where it opened its sessions in great state on the 12th of May, 1817.

By whatever means it was brought about, the Congress, when translated to Buenos Ayres, became entirely subservient to the executive. It sunk into the mere creature of Pueyrredon and his government; and sanctioned with its authority, such as it was, whatever measures the executive chose to submit to its approval.

But the system which the executive established for the Congress was, that it should interfere as little as possible with the active measures of the govern-

238

SUBSERVIENTTOTHEEXECUTIVE.

ment; tlie doctors were left to discuss the articles of the constitution – to decide whether it should be a*permanent*constitution, or a provisional regulation; and to amuse themselves with all and every matter*of form*on which any honourable member chose to make a motion, and the Congress should resolve to make a subject of discussion.*

As the constitution was still in suspense, no*laws*were passed; and the matters of any practical moment which were " resolved " and agreed to, were only such as the executive suggested for its own use, or demanded for its additional authority, as sanctioned by the Congress.

The supineness of the Government during the invasion of the Banda Oriental by the Brazilians, (to be presently spoken of), and its laxity of morals at home, having called forth the indignant and spirited remonstrances of a paper, called the Cronica Argentina, no fewer than nine respectable individuals, supposed to be most inimical to the Government, were arrested at one and the same

* In the session held on the 1st of September, 1816, we find that " the Sovereign Congress, named by acclamation as patroness of the National Independence, the Glorious American Virgin,*Santa Row of Lima,*with the reserve of opportunely applying to the Supreme Pontiff for a concession of the corresponding favours and privileges."

ARRESTS AND BANISHMENTS 239

hour on the 12th of February. They were hurried, without process or trial, nay, without being allowed to communicate with their families, on board of an English merchant vessel, the captain of which illegally and shamefully agreed, for a sum of eight hundred pounds, to carry these exiles to the United States. Among them was one whose abilities and known public probity rendered him a thorn in the side of the Government – our friend Don Manuel Moreno, now minister at our Court, and of whom we have had occasion so often to speak in terms of praise.

The violation of personal freedom in this case, and the outrage on law and public rights in a country catling itself free, was bad enough; but what was worse, Pueyrredon had the temerity to publish a manifesto, justifying his proceedings, – as if his*dictum*were the law of the land, and his hired and secret emissaries the proper administrators of that law.

Many other arrests, confinements, and banishments took place; among the rest, General Cor- nelio Saavedra, he who acted so prominent a part on the deposition of the Spanish authorities, was kept for some time under arrest at Ensenada, though

240 BRAZIL AND THE BANDA ORIENTAL.

on being released, he had the satisfaction of a public note from the Secretary of State, saying he was a prudent and circumspect person, and that " his confinement had originated in principles which in no way tarnished his name!"

While the government of Pueyrredon was busy suffocating public opinion at home; while, founded on a system of proscription, it was establishing an absolute and irresponsible power, which paralyzed the country during the whole of the Directory; we must see what progress the affairs of the republic were making abroad.

The Brazilians had ever kept a watchful eye on the Banda Oriental. They never for a moment lost sight of the advantages which the incorporation of that rich and admirably situated province would yield to the Brazilian empire; and many furtive attempts accordingly, they made to possess themselves of it.

The open war at last which Artigas, the Oriental chief, waged on the central Government of the united provinces of the River Plate, and his public assertion of the independence of the Banda Oriental, offered to the Brazilians an occasion to take possession of it, too tempting to be easilyBRAZIL AND THE BANDA ORIENTAL. 241

resisted. General Lecor, an able and crafty politician, as well as an accredited military leader, was placed at the head of a respectable force, and ordered to advance, cautiously and quietly, on the Banda Oriental. He gave out that his object was to repress any disorder which might spring from the anarchical sway of Artigas. Lecor affected to consider the country as separated from and independent of the government of Buenos Ayres. He deprecated the allegation that he was infringing any former compact made with the united provinces, and he cajoled Pueyrredon with smooth words and a subdued style in his communications. Indeed the remonstrances of the Buenos Ayres Government were so very polite, that, according to general opinion, Pueyrredon looked on the Brazilians as more legitimate occupants of the Banda Oriental, than was his hated enemy, the Protector Artigas.

Taking it for granted, however, that there was no*collusion*between the Directorate of Buenos Ayres and General Lecor, for the free occupation by the latter of Monte Video, nothing could be more pusillanimous, nay, more criminal, than the conduct of Pueyrredon and his advisers. Without

Vol. in. M

242 GENERAL LECOR.

obstacle, almost without a remonstrance, General Lecor advanced steadily and slowly on the eastern capital of the River Plate; entered it on the 6th of February, 1817; and then quietly told the Montevideans and inhabitants of the province at large, that they were under the mild and beneficent sway of the Emperor of Brazil.

The Buenos Ayres Government Gazette made a few philosophical observations on the new order of things in the Banda Oriental; and then, equally no doubt to Lecor's surprise and satisfaction, the country was left quietly in his possession. For reprobating such cruel apathy on the part of the Buenos Ayres executive, many of her patriotic citizens were proscribed and banished.

While this most inglorious transaction was passing on the eastern bank of the Plate, a very different course of events was going forward on the other side of the Andes, – the invasion of Chile by General San Martin, and the final establishment of the independence of that country through his indefatigable exertions, and splendid military achievements. The glory of his deeds was reflected on the whole union of the River Plate; but the severity of historical truth demands of us

GENERAL SAN MARTIN. 243

to say that to San Martin, and to San Martin alone, must be ascribed the praise of first conceiving and then executing the plan, of giving emancipation to Chile by the force of his country's arms.

We have already seen that, after the accession of Pueyrredon to supreme power, San Martin was thrown on his own resources, or on such as he could call into life in the poor and distant provinces of Cuyo. Nay, a jealousy was entertained of his growing renown; and it is a fact, that a sorry intrigue was set on foot to deprive him of the governorship of Mendoza, and so to cripple his action in the great project which he had undertaken. San Martin's own sagacity and prudence, aided by the enthusiasm of those around him. who were closely linked in his undertaking, caused the intrigue to fail; but enough transpired to show the*animus*of those who would have thrown intd the shade, but could not eclipse his fame.

At the close of our historical matter in the preceding volume, we left San Martin at Mendoza, concluding his preparations for his passage of the Andes. In vain the royalists had endeavoured to divert him from his purpose, by a threatened244SanMartin'sCrossing

descent of their army in Upper Peru, on the River Plate provinces. San Martin, on his part, made a feint of proceeding to the relief of General Bel- grano, but on the 20th of January he was ready to move with all his forces on Chili. On the 28th he arrived with his army in the best order at "*los Manantiales,*on the road of*el Pato*;" and from this point he determined so to direct and combine his movements, as to secure the passage of the four*cordilleras,*or roads which lead from the eastern to the western base of the mighty Andes.

To those who, like ourselves, know what the crossing of the Andes is, this great and preliminary movement of General San Martin cannot fail to stand boldly out, as one of the grandest military operations which was ever undertaken in any age or nation. "The transit alone of the mountains," says San Martin most justly, in one of his despatches, " is of itself a triumph. Figure to yourself the aggregate of an army moving with the embarrassing bulk of provisions and provender requisite for nearly a month's consumption, arms, ammunition, and other appurtenances, on a march of three hundred miles, the road traversed by rugged

OF THE ANDES. 245

heights, defiles, deep glens, and intersected by four chains of mountains; a march, in short, where the asperity of the ground is disputed by the rigidity of the climate. Such is the road of*Los Patos,*which we had to traverse."

Let us here add to San Martin's hasty military sketch of the passage of the Andes, that the chains or*Cordilleras*he had to pass were abrupt in their ascents and descents; the valleys or*caxones,*narrow and difficult for the passage of an army; that the passes, properly speaking, were, in some instances, excavations on the face of rocks, which rose nearly in a perpendicular form above, and in like manner descended to a mountain torrent below; and that the extreme heights to which they had to climb were eleven, twelve, or thirteen thousand feet above the level of the sea.

The valleys of the Andes are called*caxones,*or*boxes,*as being quite of that figure; a narrow bottom or ravine, hemmed in by a mass of rock, rising perpendicularly on either side. San Martin, therefore, resolved to secure the four passes of the Cordillera, and break through the obstacles that might be opposed to him in the defiles, by which he proposed to penetrate into Chile. For this246SanMartin'sCrossing

purpose he formed his army into two divisions: the first, which was to march as the vanguard, was commanded by Brigadier Don Estanislao Soler, and consisted of the grenadiers and light companies of the 7th and 8th regiments, the Commander's escort, the 3rd and 4th squadrons of the grenadier cavalry, and five pieces of flying artillery: the second, of the 7th and 8th battalions, commanded by Brigadier Don Bernardo O'Higgins, and the 1st and 2nd squadrons under Colonel Zapiola; while the commander of the artillery with his men, and the miners and sappers, followed immediately after. At the same time San Martin ordered that the chief of the engineers, with two hundred men, advancing on the left, and penetrating by the*boquete*or gorge of Vallehermoso, should fall upon the Cienego, where there was an enemy's guard; and finally, that re-ascending the heights of Cuzco, and having on his rearguard the mountains (or cor- dilleras) of Piuqucnes, he should open up these passes, then inarch on the Achupallas, – take this point, which is the neck of the valley, and put it in a state of defence, in order to re-unite the army with security, and enable it to disgorge (desembocar) in Putaendo. Colonel Don Juan Gregorio de las

OF THE ANDES. 247

Heras took the road of Uspallata, with the view of occupying Santa Rosa, the village which terminates that entrance into Chile.

The enemy offered resistance in all the different routes, but in every direction they were forced to retire before the dexterous manoeuvres and gallant attacks of the various chiefs who led the army across the different cordilleras. Those officers already named distinguished themselves in the highest degree; and a gallant attack of the cavalry commanded by Colonel Necochea, finally enabled the great body of the army to enter the town of San Felipe, capital of the province of Aconcagua. The advance was no less picturesque than heroic; and various despatches written by the intrepid leaders from the frowning heights or the deep valleys of the Andes, are full of life and spirit, as they depict their own irresistible progress, and the unwilling retreat of the royalists from their various strongholds in the mountains.

"At length," says General San Martin, from San Felipe de Aconcagua, on the 8th of February, " the enemy has entirely abandoned the province, falling back upon Santiago, (the capital). Sorry I am that I must, before I can follow him, allow a lapse of six days, which will be necessary towards

248 GENERAL SAN MARTIN'S OPERATIONS.

collecting horses, to enable us to move and to act. Without this help, we can do nothing on a large scale. The army has come over on foot. Twelve hundred horses which we brought with us were, in spite of every precaution, rendered useless on the road, – so rugged is the passage of the Andes. But Chile will soon be free. The co-operation of its gallant sons is every moment more decisive. To-morrow I leave this place to cover the hills of Chacabuco, and other approaches to Santiago."

It will be seen, from the sketch we have here given, that in eleven days, San Martin, with an army and all its*materiel,*sweeping before him every obstacle which came in his way, passed from the eastern base of the Andes into a principal town of one of the fertile provinces of Chile. He had four distinct passes of the mountains to penetrate, each guarded in a narrow gorge by a watchful enemy; and when we speak of a pass, we are not to imagine a glen or a ravine of so many hundred yards in length, but a series of huge mountains and deep valleys, embracing four great ridges, and stretching from the plains of La Plata on one side, to the low lands of Chile on the other, to a total length ofThreeHundredMiles. Such, accordingly, as is the Andes, so was San Martin's

HE PREPARES FOR ATTACKING. 249

enterprize – gigantic, in no exaggerated sense of the word.

Although General San Martin, on the 8th of February, writes to his Government that he would require six days to place his army on such a footing as would enable him to follow up his successes, his indefatigable and energetic spirit would not allow him to rest even so long, after his first great move into the heart of his enemy's territory; for he thus takes up the thread of his story.

"At daybreak on the*ninth,*I replaced the bridge across the river Aconcagua, and ordered the Commandant Millan to march with his squadron on the hill of Chacabuco, there to observe the enemy; the army, now completed by the division of Colonel Las Heras,* who had orders to join at this point, followed and encamped at the opening of the valley.

It was on the heights of Chacabuco that the royalists made their stand, determined there to oppose the farther progress of the daring invaders.250 GENERAL SAN MARTIN'S DISPATCH.

* Las Heras had crossed the Andes by*tixJJspallata*road, which terminates at Santa Rosa, a village of Chile. He gallantly carried *"La Guardia,"*which defends this entrance into the country.

The advanced guard of San Martin took up a position within musket range of the enemy, and on the 10th and lllh all necessary surveys were made towards entering on a decisive engagement at the dan of the 12th.

The detail of the engagement which ensued we cannot give half so well as in General San Martin's own dispatch. It can scarcely be considered otherwise than well worthy of insertion here, since it led to results of the utmost magnitude in the history of the emancipation of South America.

" I gave," says our gallant friend, for as such it is our boast to speak of him,"I gave to Brigadier Soler the command of the right wing, consisting of the rifle regiment, No. 1, grenadier, and light companies of the 7th and 8th, under Lieutenant-Colonel Anacleto Martinez; seven pieces of artillery, No. 11; my escort, and the 4th squadron of mounted grenadiers. This force was to flank and surround them, while Brigadier O'Higgins, who had the command of the left, was to attack them in front with the battalions No. 7 and 8, the squadrons 1,2, and 3, and two pieces of artillery. The result of our first movement was, as it ought to be, the abandonment of our enemy's position on the heights. The rapidity of our movements did not

THE DISPATCH. 251

give them time to bring up their forces from the farm-houses of Chacabuco to dispute our ascent. We had necessarily contemplated this first success; the enemy's infantry, in their retreat, had to cross a plain of four leagues, and although their infantry was sustained by a good column of cavalry, experience had taught us that one squadron of ours was sufficient to carry the whole of the other before it, and to cut it to pieces. Our position was most advantageous. General O'Higgins could continue his attack in front, while General Soler was in a position to flank the enemy if he attempted to maintain his ground before retiring to the plain. To insure my plan, I made Colonel Zapiola march forward with the 1st, 2nd, and 3rd squadrons, either to charge or to keep the enemy in play till the 7th and 8th battalions arrived. This movement succeeded, and the enemy was obliged to take a retrograde position. On the right, General Soler continued his movement, which he directed with such combination and skill that, although he had to climb the most rugged and impracticable heights, he approached the enemy unnoticed, till he was commanding their own position and threatening their flank.

252 BATTLE OF CHACABUCO.

" The resistance which was here opposed to us was vigorous and stubborn. A destructive fire was opened upon us, and for upwards of an hour our victory was disputed with the utmost ardour. The fact is, that there was at this point fifteen hundred of the flower of the enemy's infantry sustained by a considerable corps of cavalry. The decisive moment, notwithstanding, approached. The brave Brigadier O'Higgins unites the 7th and 8th battalions under their respective chiefs, Cromer and Conde, – he forms close columns of attack, and at the head of the 7th charges the left of the enemy with the bayonet. Colonel Zapiola, at the front of the 1st, 2nd, and 3rd squadrons, with their commanders, Melian and Molina, breaks in on the right. It was an instantaneous effort. General Soler, at the same time, fell on the height which upheld his position. This formed his support on his extreme; the enemy had detached two hundred men to defend it, but the Commandant Alvarado arrives with his rifles, detaches two companies, and attacks the height; and to turn the enemy, and destroy them at the point of the bayonet, was the work of an instant. Lieutenant Zorria distinguished himself in this action.

RESULTSOFTHEBATTLE.253

" In the meantime the squadrons, commanded by their intrepid leaders and officers, charged in the bravest manner; all the enemy's infantry was broken and destroyed, the slaughter was terrible, the victory complete and decisive."

The routed enemy was closely followed up by San Martin. The whole of the infantry was taken, dispersed, or destroyed, the prisoners being six hundred men and thirty-two officers; an equal number was killed, while all the *materiel* of the royalist army, together with the colours of the regiment of Chiloe, fell into the hands of the victors.

Among the great results of the battle of Chaca- buco, perhaps the most immediately important was the capture of the President of Chile himself – Don Francisco Marcd del Pont, a Spaniard of distinguished family, and field-marshal in the Spanish army. In the midst of the confusion which prevailed in the capital on the rout of the army being known, he abandoned it with such troops as he could muster, and retired to Valparaiso. But afraid, apparently, of trusting himself there, or wrongly informed that the port was already in the hands of the enemy, he turned off towards San Antonio, lying on the coast south of Valparaiso;

254THEHEROESOFCHACABUCO.

and having been betrayed by some countryman, the President and his escort were surprised in a cottage and taken prisoners by one Captain Aldado. Great were the difficulties which the President Marco had all along had to contend against, for it might almost be said, from the amount of disaffection towards the rule of Old Spain, which- it had been impossible to smother in the breasts of the people at large, that he had for some time been ruling in an enemy's country.

Among the officers who most distinguished themselves were all the leaders already mentioned, Colonels Baruti and Hilarion de la Quintana, as well as General San Martin's aides-de-camp Don Joze Antonio Alvarez, Don Antonio Arcos, Don Manuel Escalada, and Captain O'Brien; the latter a brave Irishman.* In a subsequent and distinct despatch, too, General San Martin speaks in terms of the highest praise of another countryman of our own, Mr. Parroissien, then at the head of the medical staff', with the grade of lieutenant-colonel.

The victorious army, within a day or two after

* When Mr. W. P. R. visited Chile, in 1827, his old friend Colonel, now General, O'Brien, went from Santiago de Chile to Santa Rosa to meet Mr. R., who had the pleasure of going over the field of Chacabuco with the gallant Colonel.

GENERAL O'HIGGINS DIRECTOR. 255

the battle, entered Santiago, the capital, in triumph. On the 15th General O'Higgins was, by acclamation, proclaimed Supreme Director of the state. In the rest of the country the new order of things was promptly established. " In a word," says San Martin, "the echo of patriotism resounds in every quarter, and with the army of the Andes rests for ever the glory of saying, 'In twenty-four days we have finished the campaign, we have passed the highest mountains in the globe, we have extinguished tyranny, and we have given liberty to Chile.'"

It is pleasant to find credit given to those who really most deserved it, for the extraordinary efforts made to recover the independence of Chile. It was mainly achieved, as we have already had occasion to show, by the genius of San Martin, and by the generous and devoted co-operation of the poor inhabitants of the province of Cuyo, of which Men- doza (where the army of the Andes was formed) is the chief town.

" The sacrifices of the province of Cuyo," says General O'Higgins, the Supreme Director of Chile, in a public despatch, " are inconceivable. We have there seen, in the midst of absolute poverty, an256 SAN MARTIN REFUSES PROMOTION.

army of four thousand men formed, clothed, maintained, paid, and equipped for a lengthened campaign, by the exertions of a rural population, badly remunerated, through foreign competition, for the products of their labour. There, an armoury (maestranza), a manufacture of saltpetre and of powder, another of clothes were established j in short, from nothing everything has sprung, in spite of poverty and without a murmur being heard. An enterprizing genius found in the Cuyanos that generosity of soul which meets all demands with alacrity, making them take the character of free offerings."

General San Martin, himself, was offered the rank of brigadier, but he resolutely refused this honour, and remained with his colonel's commission.

Although the defeat of the royalists on the plains of Chacabuco was complete, they still maintained a footing in the country. They retired on the southern province of Conception, where they re-organized their scattered and diminished forces. They became again so far formidable as to induce the Director himself, General O'Higgins, to take the field; and, although we find many successes re-

THE WAR IN UPPER PERU. 257

corded, he was not able to drive the enemy out of the country. He, however, shut them up in Tal- cahuano, the port of Conception, his head quarters being established at the latter city, only six miles from Talcahuano. He made on the 6th of December a brave but ineffectual attack, when he lost many gallant officers; and, on the 14th of the same month, the Government announced to the people the approach of another expedition from Lima to re-conquer Chile.

The operations of the army in Upper Peru were, on the whole, this year of an unimportant character. We ought to have mentioned in the historical matter of our second volume, that, in lieu of General Rondeau, General Belgrano was, in 1816, named commander-in-chief of the Peruvian army. He fixed his head quarters at Tucuman, where he remained during the year; but the governor of Salta, commandant-general of the vanguard, Martin Giiemes, kept up a desultory and guerilla warfare with General La Serna, who commanded the royalist army.

It is somewhat curious, indeed, to read the many bulletins in which the successes of the patriots are detailed, while, in point of fact, they were always

258THEWARINUPPERPERU.

obliged to retire before La Serna when he chose to make a decided movement upon them. He made Jujui for some time his head quarters, and then he descended to Salta, the capital of Guemes's own province. This town La Serna kept possession of for twenty days, committing many excesses; hence he made a somewhat disastrous retreat to Jujui, Giiemes hanging on his rear and worrying him with his guerilla attacks. Then the gallant Colonel La Madrid took Tarija in April, and it was recaptured in July by the royalists. Again La Serna retired from Jujui towards Upper Peru, and being called to Lima by the increasing difficulties of the Spanish cause, General Olaneta was left in command. At the end of the year this commander was at Tilcara, and the patriots had possession of Jujui. No general action was risked by either party during the year; although a gallant attack by a Commandant Roxas on a squadron of Estremadura cavalry, at a place called San Pedrito, in which he had the glory, as he says, of " pasando a degiiello," that is, of cutting the throats of the whole party of one hundred and forty men, was magnified by the patriots, in the dearth of other events, into a great victory. The truth is, that

MISCELLANEOUS. 259

General Belgrano was not supported energetically nor, in fact, at all by his Government; so that, as a necessary consequence, the campaign languished under his hands.

One or two domestic matters call for a passing notice. Doctor Funes, the amiable and learned Dean of Cordova, published this year his Political Essay on Paraguay, the first historical work which belongs to the Revolution, and one of considerable merit. The extension of the frontier towards the south, – that is, an acquisition of the territory of Patagonia, inhabited by the Indians, was decreed. Although Pueyrredon and Lecor seemed to be on good terms, Spain protested against the occupation of the Banda Oriental by Portugal. The privateers fitted out under the letters of marque granted by the Government, sent many valuable vessels and crews into Buenos Ayres, which were all sold as good prizes. Finally, the official organ of the Government, instead of claiming triumphs for it, was obliged constantly to stand on the defensive, – now denying that a league between Pueyrredon and Lecor existed – now that the former granted special licences for the supply of the latter with flour and other provisions; – anon it rebutted

260 MISCELLANEOUS.

the charge that the Director had any thing to do with the contraband which,*even through the customhouse itself,*was notoriously carried on; and it parried other blows aimed at his reputation of an equally heavy and stunning kind.

Yours, &c.

TheAuthors.

17

SECTION 17

LETTER LXII.

TheAuthorstoGeneralMiller.

Operations in Chile and Lower Peru – Pezuela and Ordonez – General Osorio – Rout of Cancha Rayada – Approaching Struggle – General Guido's Letter – Preparations for Battle – Battle of Maypo – Its Results – Honours to the Victors – San Martin's entry into Buenos Ayres – His Letter to Pezuela – The Spanish Expedition – The Deserters – Rise of a Chilean Fleet – Its first Achievements – Admiral Blanco – The Army of Upper Peru- War in Peru and Banda Oriental – A Venal Government – North American Commissioners – Dear Provisions.

*London,*1842.

Thegreat political events of 1818, like those of its predecessor, were in connexion with Chile and Lower Peru; and with these, therefore, we shall commence our sketch of the year.

When the battle of Chacabuco placed the capital of Chile and the northern provinces in the hands of the patriots, the royalists had retired, as we have seen, upon their strongholds in the south. The country was yet theirs from the river Maule to Conception; and, going still southward, from the Bio-Bio to Valdiviaand the Island of Chiloe. The king's cause was headed by Ordonez, a brave and expert officer, and he determined at all hazards to

262 PEZUELA AND ORDONEZ.

hold his footing in Chile till he should receive those new and extensive succours which his declining cause, under the energy, ability, and enthusiasm of the patriots, made every day more and more necessary, and which he energetically demanded from the Viceroy of Peru, General Pezuela.

General O'Higgins had taken the field against his still formidable enemy; and although he reduced them to their fortress of Talcahuano, which commanded the beautiful bay of the same name, he was not able to drive them from that position. The Spaniards are proverbial for the tenacity and courage with which they hold a fortified place.

Pezuela hastened not only to relieve Ordonez, but to make a bold attempt to recover at once all that had been lost to the king's cause by the battle of Chacabuco. He accordingly fitted out an expedition of from two to three thousand men, and placing it under the command of General Osorio, an experienced chief, despatched it to Talcahuano. Here the new commander found one thousand five hundred men more; and thus, with a well organized army, upwards of five thousand strong, he marched in February towards the river Maule, and passed it without opposition.

In the meantime General San Martin had been

GENERAL OSORIO. 263

busy organizing his own army, and having brought it up to something like the numbers of his enemy, he put himself in motion as soon as the former had abandoned Curico, a village on the road leading to Talca, which again is on the high way to Santiago.

San Martin reckoned with certainty on obtaining a victory, and all his movements had for their object the making of that victory complete and decisive: as he himself says, he contrived constantly to flank Osorio, and to threaten an attack front and rear. "In this position both armies," again says General San Martin, " fell at the same time on Talca, whence it was impossible for the enemy either to retreat or to repass the Maule."

But here, by a decisive*coup de main,*General Osorio evaded even the proverbial vigilance of San Martin; and but for the energy for which he was equally remarkable, all the fruits of his former exertions might suddenly have been snatched from his hand.

The fact is, that General San Martin's army did not get up to its position in front of Talca till night-fall; and he was still forming his provisional lines, towards nine o'clock, without the remotest idea of any interruption, both forces being completely jaded by the day's operations, when

264ROUTOFCANCHARAYADA.

Osorio fell suddenly upon the patriots and attacked them with the utmost fury. Instantaneous confusion pervaded the whole of the Chilean army. A rout – a total dispersion of the left wing – took place, after a short and ineffectual resistance; and although the right wing and cavalry made a retreat in tolerable order, all the*materiel*of San Martin's army was lost, and the greater number of his troops were flying hither and thither. Such was the memorable dispersion of Cancha Rayada on the 19th of March. The patriot army, it might be said, was disbanded.

Well may it be supposed the consternation into which the country was thrown by a reverse like this, at the very moment of a universally anticipated victory. San Martin happily stood undismayed. Luckily for him, too, Osorio did not follow up his extraordinary advantage with all the quickness which one might have expected from his daring and impetuous attack. Every moment which he lost San Martin turned to advantage with the most surprising industry and energy. He was ably seconded by his officers. " The deep interest," says the gallant soldier, " the energy and firmness with which the chiefs and all the officers of the army co-operated for the re-establishment of order and

APPROACHINGSTRUGGLE,265

discipline, does them the greatest honour. The truth is, our forces were very inferior to those of the enemy: many of our corps had been reduced to skeletons, and we had battalions that did not form two hundred men."

San Martin was necessarily forced, in his embarrassing position, to retreat rapidly upon Santiago, where alone he could replace the*materiel*he had lost; and in the incredibly short space of three days his army was reorganized in 1he immediate vicinity of the capital.

Accordingly, before the country at large had time to recover from the shock which the dispersion of Cancha Rayada produced, San Martin was again prepared to meet the enemy. He reassured his men, and encouraged them to regain their honour only momentarily lost; and he so filled them with a renewed ardor in the cause, that after a retreat of eighty leagues, under the most dispiriting circumstances, the patriots felt as secure as ever of victory in the forthcoming struggle, which was fated shortly to decide the question on the plains of Maypo.

General Don Tomas Guide, whose talents both in the camp and the cabinet have rendered him a conspicuous public character throughout the revolution, and whose winning address and social quali-

VOL. III. N

266 GENERAL GUIDo's LETTER.

ties have always made him a favourite with all parties, was at this time envoy from the United Provinces to the Republic of Chile; and having- proceeded to head quarters, he writes, on the 29th of March, to his Government thus: –

" At five this afternoon the encampment of Maypu, distant a league from this city, was entered by the division of the combined army, consisting of three thousand five hundred infantry, commanded by Brigadier General Balcarce, who placed himself at its head at Rancagua, to which point the division had been conducted by Colonel de las Heras. The commander-in-chief, General San Martin, had arrived two days previously with the battalions of the fourth regiment of the line, that of the infantry 'de la patria,' and the piquets to a considerable number of all the corps which were dispersed on the night of the 19th.

" The re-union of the troops was announced by a grand salute of artillery and the ringing of all the church bells of the capital. The rear-guard of cavalry were left at

Rancagua, whither five hundred more proceed to-morrow, as fully equipped as before the action of the 19th. The enemy has not moved from his position at Talca.

" The enthusiasm of the troops has been mani-

PREPARATION FOR BATTLE. 267

fested in the order and subordination which they have observed up to the time of their encampment- and the energetic measures of the Government as well as the talents of the commanders of the army, give promise of a happy result should the enemy approach this province."

Approach the province they certainly did, for on the 1st of April they crossed the river Maypo, about seven leagues distant from Santiago. On the 2nd San Martin took up his position on the*Asequias de Espejo;**and on that and the two succeeding days he was engaged in guerilla skirmishes with the enemy's forces.

At length, on the 5th, Osorio marched onwards. He appeared desirous of doubling San Martin's right, in the distance, – of threatening the capital, cutting off a communication with Aconcagua, and securing for himself the road of Valparaiso. When San Martin saw all this, he thought the moment for attacking Osorio had arrived, and making a change of direction on his own right, accordingly, he placed himself in front of his enemy.

General Balcarce had the command of all the infantry; the right under Colonel Las Heras, the268

**Astquias*are small canals with which all the country is intei- sected for the purpose of irrigating the land.

BATTLE OF MAYPO.

left led by Colonel Alvarado, while the reserve was headed by Colonel Quintana. The cavalry on ihe right was commanded by Colonel Zapiola, and the left by Colonel Freyre.

General Osorio took up a strong position on a rising ground, detaching a battalion of light cavalry to a small height near him, to sustain four pieces of artillery, placed on the face of the hill. " This was a good movement," says San Martin, " for it completely secured his (Osorio's) left, and his fire flanked and swept all the front of the position."

San Martin's line, formed in close and parallel columns, inclined towards the right of the enemy, presenting an oblique attack on this flank, which in truth was left uncovered. It was exposed also to San Martin's reserve in the rear, which was in a position to turn that flank and to support his right. Eight pieces of artillery, commanded by General Blanco Ciceron, were situated on one point, and four more, under the Commandant Plaza, on another.

Thus disposed, the patriot columns descended the slight eminence which formed their position, and advanced to charge the enemy's line, at the point of the bayonet. A terrible fire was opened upon them, – the artillery placed on the hill, as already

BATTLE OF MAYPO. 269

mentioned, doing great execution, without, however, preventing the advance. At the same instant a large body of the royalist cavalry fell, sword in hand, on the mounted grenadiers of the patriot army, which, formed in columns, kept advancing in front. The head squadron was commanded by Colonel Esca- lada, who no sooner saw himself threatened by his enemy, than he rushed upon him. He was followed by Commandant

Medina, and, turning the royalists, they were hotly pressed back on the rising ground, till in turn Escalada was forced to give way to the galling fire of the infantry and cannon. They defiled off to the right, whence they again attacked the enemy's cavalry; and, after various charges and movements, succeeded in scattering the whole body of the latter.

In the meantime, the heat of the battle was kept up between the royalist right and patriot left wing, coming, after a heavy fire, to close quarters. Victory and defeat hung equipoised in the balance; the patriot line vacillated; the infantry " de la Patria " gave way; but Colonel Quintana coming up with his reserve, charged in the most brilliant manner, being well seconded by his commandants, Ribera, Lopez, and Conde. This charge, and another of

270 BATTLE OF MAYPO.

Commandant Tonson, at the head of the first Coquimbo regiment, gave a new impulse to the patriot line, so that it returned to the attack with more decision than before.

Meantime Colonel Freyre's cavalry charged, and was attacked successively by an opposite force. " It is not possible," says San Martin, " to give an idea of the brilliant and distinguished actions of the day, both by entire bodies, by their chiefs, and by individual officers; but I may say, that it would be difficult to see a braver, more rapid, and better sustaiued attack; while it may also be affirmed that a more vigorous, firm, and tenacious resistance could not be offered. The constancy of our soldiers and their heroic efforts at last prevailed; the position they fought for was taken, irrigating it with blood, and driving the enemy from it at the point of the bayonet."

This first success seemed to ensure the victory, but the enemy's centre columns marching in mass, could not so easily be disordered. Though cut up in the flank and rearguard, they advanced to the Callejones de Espejo (San Martin's ground), and took possession of a height there. A new combat commenced, which lasted for an hour; but the

.–IRESULTSOFTHEBATTLE.271

whole force of the patriots being brought by degrees to bear upon this last hope of the royalists, they were beaten and dispersed, San Martin remaining undisputed master of the field.

General Osorio himself, with two hundred cavalry, escaped, though pursued in all directions; his other generals, one hundred and ninety officers, and three thousand men were made prisoners; the field of battle was strewn with two thousand dead and wounded; all the royalist artillery, their*materiel,*their hospital and medical staff, their military chest, every component part of the royal army, fell, dead or alive, into the patriots' power. San Martin estimated his own loss at a thousand men; probably, it was considerably more; and if we take the aggregate loss of the opposing forces at three thousand five hundred men, it may be affirmed that there is scarcely on record a general engagement, where, in proportion to the numbers engaged, the loss was so great, that is, one-third of the whole.

San Martin pays a just tribute to all who shared the glory of the day; and besides those whose names have already appeared, he mentions the engineer Dable, the surgeon Major Parroissien,

272RESULTSOFTHEBATTLE.

Majors O'Brien and Guzman, the war secretary Zenteno, and his own secretary Marzan. General O'Higgins, who was suffering from a severe wound, when he heard of the approaching battle, left his sick couch, and joined the army, though he was unable to arrive before the conquest was ensured. General Guido was also mentioned in terms of much deserved praise.

It will at once be perceived, that although the battle of Chacabuco caused the power of the Peninsula to reel in Chile, the fatal blow to the king's cause was struck on the plains of Maypo. It was there that the independence of the country was sealed.

But the victory of Maypo not only secured Chile to the patriots; it opened up the way to the last great stronghold of Spanish power in South America, the land of the Incas. And we shall find accordingly, that the Viceroy of Peru, no longer inclined to play the desperate game of regaining Chile, was thenceforward intent only on making such cautious moves as would avert a check-mate at home from his bold and vigorous antagonist.

The news of the victory of Maypo were received

HONOURS TO THE VICTORS. 273

in Buenos Ayres with such transports of joy as baffle all description. We have already alluded to it in another part of our work. " The public rejoicings," says the Government Gazette, "have been beyond the power of exaggeration.' *Ya tenemos Patria,'* – we have now a mother country, said the citizens, throwing themselves into the arms of each other without distinction, and of whoever was nearest to receive this demonstration of tenderness. '*Ya tenemos Patria,*'that is, our freedom is consolidated: our sacrifices are at an end; the good which we believed was only reserved for our children is our own, and we can enjoy it without being agitated by the melancholy fear that we may be robbed of the fruit of so many labours, and so much blood."

Many honours and premiums were decreed to General San Martin and his brave companions in arms, but we are not sure that they were carried into effect. The Congress ordered " that an engraving should be struck*off,*representing San Martin in the centre, with Liberty on the left, and Victory on the right, holding a crown of laurel over the head of the victor. Military trophies, below were to be surmounted by the flags of the'274SanMartin'sEntryIntoBuenosAyres.

Republics of Chile and the River Plate, and the inscription around of ' National gratitude to the conquering General-in-chief and army of Chaca- buco and Maypo.'" In the distance, a view of these battles was to fill up the engraving; one, however, which we have never yet seen. A copy of this engraving was to be placed in the town halls of all the principal cities of the River Plate provinces. A pyramid on the plains of Maypo, was about the same time, and with a like object, decreed by the Chile Executive; but we are not sure that it was ever erected.

Something like the severe economy of republican virtue was displayed in the amount of the pensions granted to the families of General San Martin and Antonio Balcarce, viz., $120 per annum to each. The grade of brigadier, before refused, was again offered to San Martin, and now accepted; and all the principal officers engaged in the two battles were promoted a step in the army.

On the 11th of May, San Martin returned to Buenos Ayres: but entering*incognito,*he evaded a public demonstration, which was prepared for his reception. He was, however, conducted in state*to*the great Hall of Congress, then sitting, on the

HIS LETTERS TO PEZUELA. 275

17th of May, and there received from that body the public thanks of the nation for his eminent services. He went through the ceremony with that modesty, which on all occasions characterized him.

It must here be mentioned to the honour of General Antonio Balcarce, that he peremptorily refused to accept of the pay of three thousand dollars annually, ($600), which was proffered to him by Chile.

Before leaving that state, San Martin wrote two admirable letters to General Pezuela, the viceroy of Lima; the first, calling on him to make an exchange of prisoners; the second, inviting him to an amicable arrangement, in regard to the emancipation of Peru. The first proposition led to an ineffectual negotiation; and the second, in an evil hour for Spain, was, we believe, silently and scornfully spurned.

The remainder of this year presented a succession of disasters to the royalist cause on the west coast of South America.

The patriots generally had been kept in a state of considerable anxiety for upwards of two years, by reports (held, indeed, to be exaggerated), of a great armament fitting out at Cadiz, for some

276 THE SPANISH EXPEDITION.

unknown point of the ex-colonies of Spain. The real extent of this vaunted expedition came to light in an unexpected and extraordinary manner. On the 26th of August, a transport, called the Trinidad, with two hundred infantry of the Spanish line, entered the port of Ensenada, a few leagues below Buenos Ayres, when a formal surrender of the vessel and troops was made to the River Plate authorities. Some of the non-commissioned officers had, before leaving Cadiz, conspired to rise upon their superiors, and take the vessel into Buenos Ayres; they communicated their design by degrees to the men, who readily entered into it. The expedition consisted of transports, carrying two thousand men, protected by one fine frigate. The Trinidad parted company in five degrees north latitude, and having passed the line without falling in with any of the convoy, the leaders of the revolt determined to strike their blow on the 25th of July. They met with the most determined resistance from most of their officers, fourteen in number, aided only by one Serjeant and two corporals; and nine of these brave fellows, including the three non-commissioned officers, perished in defence of the rights of their country. The captain

THE DESERTERS, 277

of the vessel was then ordered to steer for Buenos Ayres, and arriving safely, it may not be doubted the guilty rebels were received with open arms by the Government of Buenos Ayres. It could not reasonably be expected that it should do otherwise. Mr. W. P. R. recollects well seeing these men marched into the*Plaxa Mayor*of Buenos Ayres; and although they were harangued and applauded by the chief of the staff, General Rondeau, which was only politic under the circumstances of the case, Mr. R. could not help fancying he saw the scowl of a murderer in each of these renegade deserters from their own colours. The high- spirited*Portenos*seemed to view them pretty much in the same light. The Government wisely allowed these men freely to choose their own career, and the result, which is curious, was as follows. – Two captains returned to Spain; one captain, one lieutenant, two ensigns, one drum-major, one assistant, six drummers, two corporals, and ten rank and file remained in the Buenos Ayres army; two lieutenants, two Serjeants, one drummer, nine corporals, and eight rank and file joined the army of the Andes; and nine Serjeants, eighteen corporals, and one hundred and eleven rank and file were dis-

278 RI8E OF A CHILEAN FLEET.

banded in the country. The chaplain, a friar of the order of Mercedes, also preferred remaining in the country.

Nearly the whole of the ill-fated Spanish expedition fell into the hands of the patriots, and the body of it in a more satisfactory way than the transport ship Trinidad. For by this time the republic of Chile being able to boast of a fleet, it was fitted out and sent off to intercept the expedition in question. The Chilean maritime force consisted of the *San Martin,* formerly the Wyndham, a large English merchantman, bought and fitted out as a sixty gun ship; the frigate *Lautaro* of forty-six guns; the corvette *Chacabuco* of twenty; and the brig *Arau- cano* of sixteen. With this squadron Admiral Blanco Encalada sailed from Valparaiso on the 10th of November, and made for Talcahuano. The *Chacabuco* parted company on the voyage, and Blanco detached the Araucano; but learning at the island of Santa Maria that the fine Spanish frigate *Reyna Maria Isabel,* and her convoy, were an-. chored in the bay of Talcahuano, he hesitated not a moment to go and attack them with the crazy old Wyndham, now dignified into a ship of the line, and the Lautaro. " Ambitious," as he says in his

.

ITS FIRST ACHIEVEMENTS. 279

despatch, " that the marine of Chile should mark the day of its birth as that of its glory; and resolute to sacrifice myself for it on this occasion, or to place it, at one blow, on such a point of elevation as might render it distinct to the eyes of Europe."

Admiral Blanco found the Maria Isabel *alone* in Talcahuano Bay, and when he went in to attack her, she fired a broadside, hoisted her sails, and ran ashore. She struck her colours on being fired into, and the patriots took possession of her. But how to get her away? that was the difficulty; for she was stranded, and the royalists had a large land force at Conception close by. Blanco sent a force on shore to defend his prize; but ere his men could gain the heights, the enemy approached and attacked them. The San Martin and Lautaro could not, wiihout imminent danger to their own forces on shore, fire on the royalists, but the former made good their retreat to their boats, and thence on board. Night coming on, put an end to the contest of that day.

At three o'clock next morning the royalists endeavoured to board the Maria Isabel, but were driven back by the force which Blanco had placed on board. At five a warm contest ensued, the

280 ADMIRAL BLANCO.

enemy attacking with both musketry and artillery from the immediate heights of Talcahuano: but the patriots were not to be shaken from their determination to get the valuable prize afloat, and into their own power. They continued the work indefatigably and bravely, and to the dismay and surprise of the royalists, they saw at eleven o'clock the Maria Isabel majestically floating once more on the waters. Their fire ceased; and in silent wonder they looked on the frigate receding from their shore amidst shouts of Viva la Patria from the San Martin and Lautaro.

Admiral Blanco bestows unqualified praise on all his officers, among whom were many Englishmen. He mentions their names individually; and among the bravest of the brave appears *General William Miller,* then major of artillery in the Chilean service.

Blanco hastened to intercept the convoy, of which he took three, which had left with thirty-six officers and six hundred and sixteen men, " of whom," he says, " two hundred and thirteen had died on the passage; two hundred and sixty-seven were sick, and only the small remnant in health, although ready to perish from want." Shortly afterwards the Chacabuco took two more, the remainder of

THEARMYOFUPPERPERU.281

the convoy, – one or two of the transports only having got into Valdivia.

Such was the conclusion, glorious to the patriots, miserable to the royalists, of the Spanish auxiliary expedition.

From the battle of Maypo, Osorio fled to Tal- cahuano, and thence he himself embarked for Lima. Colonel Zapiola taking the command of a force which marched to the south, in pursuit of the enemy, he entered on the 13th of November the strong town of Chilian, which the royalist chief Lantano, evacuated with seven hundred men; and it was clear that the royalists would be able to make no effectual stand till they reached Valdivia, one of the strongest forts in South America, and situated on the extreme south of the Chilean territory.

The army of Upper Peru, commanded by General Belgrano, remained in almost total inaction during the whole of this year. He himself never moved from Tucuman, and what little was done was under the orders of the Gaucho chief of the vanguard, Giiemes, governor of Salta. There were now no active spirits at the head of affairs in Buenos Ayres to second the commander in Peru. Destitute

282 WAR IN PEKU AND BANDA ORIENTAL.

of resources, he was compelled to lie in a state of repose. In January the royalists took possession of Jujui, which they evacuated in four days. It remained during the rest of the year in Guemes's hands; indeed he was elected governor of the province. He kept up his guerillas, but they are not of sufficient interest to merit any detail. It may be observed, however, that Guemes was reduced to a necessity so pressing for means, that he permitted the coinage, and then enforced the receipt, of a false coin which went by the name of Guemes's money. This illegal act was then converted into a public robbery by Pueyrredon's denouncing the money in question, and ordering all parties holding it to give it up, under pain of being prosecuted as " utterers, receivers, and fabricators of false coin." Monte Video was now in quiet possession of the Portuguese; but great confusion prevailed in the Banda Oriental, Entrerios, Corrientes, and Santa Fe, where a desultory but desolating warfare was kept up between the protector Artigas and the director Pueyrredon. The poor provincials scarcely knew who or what they were fighting for: all they did know was, that they were sacrificed to the ambition, hatred, and wretched policy of those who led

A VENAL GOVERNMENT. 283

them against each other. Artigas's power was on the wane; but the distrust and jealousy entertained by the provinces of the capital seemed only to gather strength with the weakness of its arch enemy, the protector of the Banda Oriental. General Lecor, the Portuguese governor of Monte Video saw with pleasure the two contending parties destroying each other instead of attacking *him*.

The domestic affairs of Buenos Ayres during this year are soon recapitulated. Public spirit was at its lowest point, venality and contraband in their zenith. So unblushingly, so shamelessly was the latter carried on by the friends of the Government, particularly by one great native merchant who was said to have *all* the colonels in his pay, that the smuggled goods, manufactures, wines, brandies, every article of value of great bulk or of small, passed through the very custom-house at mid-day, and *without* paying duties, went into the warehouses and vaults of the great smugglers. The Government praised the high tariff, denounced publicly the open contraband which was carried on, and connived privately at all its ramifications. To such a low ebb did public morals sink!

It is just, at the same time, and pleasing to

284 NORTH AMERICAN COMMISSIONERS.

record one redeeming good act in the midst of so much political profligacy. On the 16th of July a new university, called *El Colegio de la Union del Sud,* was founded and opened with great pomp, by the director and his officers of state, the different corporations of the city, and the heads of the church. Its object was of course to provide a complete classical school for the higher youth of the republic, and the measure constituted, as the Government justly says, " the greatest work of the actual administration." In truth it was the only one on which praise can be bestowed. Every public office in Buenos Ayres, the army, the church, all contributed towards the endowment of the college.

On the 28th of February three individuals of rank, Messrs. Rodney, Grahame, and Bland, arrived in the capital, invested with a sort of diplomatic character, from the United States, charged with the commission of reporting on the actual political and commercial state of the River Plate provinces. They remained for some few months – their report was published; and it led speedily to a friendly intercourse between the two republics.

Much agitation prevailed in the public mind during one portion of the year, on a " provisions"

DEAR PROVISIONS. 285

question, viz. the dearness of beef. Decrees were issued, and warm discussions were kept up. The best beef had risen to three half-pence per pound; and the public clamour only ceased when it was reduced to its usual price of a penny.

Yours, &c.,
The Authors.

18

SECTION 18

LETTER LXIII.

The Authors to General Miller.

Evils of the Directorate – War with the provinces – Military law – Dupuy's butchery – Murder of Colonel Morgado, and of twenty- six other officers – Dupuy's despatch – Reflections – Pueyrredon resigns in favour of Rondeau – Spanish expedition – Frustrated – The civil war – Don Manuel de Sarratea, Governor – Lord Coch- rane – General Antonio Balcarce – The retreat of Sanchez – Bal- carce's death – Vicente Benavides – Sir William Scott's decision – Earthquake at Copiap6 – The brothers Carrera – Their execution – Reflectiora – Conclusion.

London, 1842.

The Directorate of Pueyrredon, aided and assisted by the National Congress, un- doubtedly laid the foundation of incalculable evils for Buenos Ayres. It was a military despotism, sanctioned by law. It was a government of proscriptions and of profligate venality. Bribery and corruption were the means chiefly depended upon for the sup- port of the executive, and under its patronage a system of contraband was organized on so large a scale as to dilapidate and ruin the public exchequer, while it filled the pockets of all connected with the revenue, from the first mandatory of the state down to its meanest official.

WAR WITH THE PROVINCES. 287

But as the proscriptions increased, so did the enemies of the Pueyrredonistas; and as the financial difficulties of the country augmented, public indignation grew stronger, presaging the downfall of the corruptionists.

Most of the provinces having been treated with haughty disdain, it was among them that the enemies of Pueyrredon found the readiest means of compassing his ruin. Federalism was the favourite object of most of the provinces; and while it was found easy to lead some of them on to establish it by force of arms, none of them would actively help the capital in repelling this inroad on her own individual power and influence.

Santa Fe, Entrerios, and Corrientes, in concert with the great enemy of Buenos Ayres, Artigas, took the lead in the civil war, and they were, at the commencement of this year, in open campaign against the " national" forces. General Juan Ramon Balcarce, afterwards substituted by General Viamont, was placed at the head of an army called that of "Observation on Santa Fe," but neither of them could put down the refractory and rebellious provincials.

With a view of accommodating matters, General
288 CONGRESS AND THE DIRECTOR.

Belgrano left the auxiliary army of Peru near Cordova, and, proceeding to Viamont's head-quarters at Rosario, he immediately had an interview with Lopez, Governor of Santa Fe, who commanded the federal forces. The latter, a wily and astute Gaucho, saw the difficulty of having enemies both in rear and in front, and he therefore concluded an armistice with Belgrano in April, agreeing that commissioners, fully empowered by the contending parties, should meet and conclude a treaty of peace. But Lopez was only amusing the Buenos Ayres Government, as we shall presently see.

In the mean time, on the 25th of February, Pueyrredon opened the sessions of Congress; and his own account of the state of affairs shows what sort of a government his must have been. He speaks thus: –

" The means adopted by our enemies" (he alludcH to the inhabitants of Buenos Ayres) " to destroy our peace and our liberty are public and notorious. Seductions, deceits, conspiracies against the lives of the first authorities, libels to render their reputation infamous, pasquins of the lowest kind, – these are the arms which are daily employed to disturb the harmony in which the United

MILITARY LAW. 289

Provinces repose. It is bitter even to the hardest heart to have to employ proscription and banishment with the frequency which *crimes of perturbation* demand. It is against the credit of the state to see authority *always armed* and always chastising the turbulent. So violent a position either tires out the people who look on, or disheartens the authority which executes."

And in this conclusion Pueyrredon was right; for as he did not get disheartened in his armed system of proscription and banishment, *the people* got tired of witnessing it, and proscribed him and his in the end, as he and his agents had proscribed so many others.

The address of the Director on opening Congress was very significant; for on the 4th of March, the first week of the sittings of the Doctors, he was authorized to establish a military tribunal – or, in other words, to establish military law – for the trial of all cases of sedition or crimes of perturbation. This tribunal commenced by trying two Frenchmen for sedition, and sentenced them to be shot. Their friends, on the 25th of May, the anniversary of the independence of the country, appealed to Congress, – Congress sent them to Pueyrredon, – Pueyrredon

Vol. in. o

200 DUPUY's BUTCHERY.

to the tribunal, – and *Robert* and *Lagressc* were executed.

Pueyrredon's pretended *panacea* for all the evils of the state was the publication by Congress of a paper constitution, which had long engaged their abstruse sittings and meditations. It was printed, published, and proclaimed, and, we need scarcely add, it had no perceptible effect on the proscrip-> lions and pasquins.

The Spanish prisoners of war taken in Chile, as well as at Monte Video in an early part of the revolution, were sent to San Luis, – a wretched village, though dignified with the name of the *city* of San Luis. It lies about eighty leagues from Mendoza, on the high way between that place and Buenos Ayres.

The Governor of San Luis was one Colonel Vicente Dupuy, – a ferocious coward, if we may so speak, – a creature of Pueyrredon, and gaoler of the Spanish officers, prisoners of war.

A horrible massacre of these prisoners took place on the 8th of February; and before making any remarks upon it, we shall give, as clearly as we can, Dupuy's own account of the affair.

At eleven o'clock on the morning of tho 8th he

DUPUY'S BUTCHERY. 291

informs Luzuriaga, the governor of the province of Cuyo, that, two hours before, he had received a complimentary visit from the Spanish Brigadier Ordonez, Colonel Rivera, Colonel Morgado, Lieutenant-Colonel Morla, Captain Carretero, and Lieutenant Barguillo. *After the compliments of the day,* Carretero, rising up, said, " Scoundrel! these are the moments in which you are to expire! All America is lost, and *you* will not now escape."

At the same instant, Carretero, Barguillo, and Rivera fell upon the Governor Dupuy *with poniards,* the others preparing to do the same. Dupuy got to the farther end of the room, and there with his fist knocked Morgado down. The others rushing upon him, he could not help coming to the ground, where he received *some contusions on the face* before he was able to get again, as he did, upon his feet. At this point firing from without was heard: it was the town resisting the other prisoners. " I must observe to you " – such is the incomprehensible paragraph of Dupuy's despatch at this point of the narrative – " I must observe to you that the very circumstance from which they promised themselves a triumph, viz., a simultaneous action, has overturned their plans.

292 MURDER OF COLONEL MORG. VDO,

For having attacked the barracks at the same moment at which they besieged my house, the troops were alarmed, and the town, *as if by an electric explosion,* took up arms, and observing my door shut, they tried to open it, which showed to those who were with me that their plan had failed."

Full of terror, the officers supplicated the safety of their lives from Dupuv, who, under the pretext of quieting the people at the door, went out. Those outside then rushed in and charged the prisoners, who made such resistance as they could, mortally wounding Dupuy's secretary, Captain Riveros.

" This was the instant," continues Dupuy, " in which my authority and the indignation of the people went hand in hand. I ordered all the throats of the prisoners immediately to be cut; and they expiated their crime in *my* presence, and before an innocent and generous people *Colonel*

Morgado died by my hands. "

After eulogizing the moderation of the people and his own excellent general regulations, Dupuy goes on thus: –

" Those who were prisoners in the barracks, combined with the others on parole, experienced the same fate [had their throats cut], although *In The*

AND OF TWENTY-SIX OTHER OFFICERS. 293

FirstMomentOfSurprise they took up arms; but they soon lost them, or died with them in their hands. Among these the paymaster of the army, Barroeta, and Lieutenant-Colonel *A rras,* distinguished themselves; for the one with sword in hand, and the other with a musket, eacli defended himself till he expired."

Besides Captain Riveros, Dupuy says he had only *two soldiers* wounded.

Such is the substance of Dupuy's horrible despatch, and it winds up with the ominous list of the poor Spanish officers who were butchered, viz., –

1 Brigadier-general (the brave Ordonez).

3 Colonels.

2 Lieutenant-colonels.

6 Captains.

6 Lieutenants.

7 Ensigns.

1 Paymaster of the army.'

1 Assistant of the paymaster.

In all 27 officers.

On the llth of February, Dupuy sends a copy of the despatch just analysed to Pueyrredon, adding that there was no doubt the Spanish conspirators intended to unite with Generals Alvear and Car-

294 DUPUV'S DESPATCH.

rera; but this part of Dupuy's despatch has an air so truly apocryphal – indeed so extravagant – that we have no doubt it is an interpolation of the editor of the ministerial Gazette, who, *per fas et per nefas,* wished to turn everything to account of the machinations of Pueyrredon's personal enemies.

On the 21st of February, Dupuy sends to the Director of the State his *despatch proper,* in which we find one or two important discrepancies with his *original* despatch to Luzuriaga. Dupuy now states that only three, Morgado, Morla, and Carretero, of the six officers originally mentioned, entered his room at first; and then he says that Carretero, after the most refined expressions of friendship, drew a poniard from his breast and directed a blow against him (Dupuy), which he warded off with his left arm. Then came in the others; and then follows the astounding assertion that, after having been on the ground, attacked with daggers – six men against one, that one unarmed, – he got up with some bruises on the face!

In this*second*despatch, too, Dupuy says that the royalist Colonel Rivera, shot himself with his own carbine. With his own carbine! Prisoners of war, making a visit of etiquette to the governor, andDupuy'sDespatch.295

one of them a colonel in the service – a prisoner of war – with a carbine in his hand! And poniards and carbines, and six brave officers against one man, seeking to assassinate him; and he on the ground, and then getting up with some*contusions*on his face!

If anything were wanting to stamp the despatches of Dupuy, from beginning to end, with the indelible brand of*falsehood,*it is to be found in the exculpatory*notes*of the editor of the ministerial Gazette. Here are extracts from three of these damnatory notes: –

" The enemies of America [he means of Pueyrre- don] will try to persuade the world that the affair of San Luis has been the effect of*sinister workings*on the part of the Lieutenant-Governor Dupuy, and perhaps the suspicion may extend*to a higher authority.*"

"The despatch does not well explain how what ought to have been*wounds*were only*contusions.*"

"Our enemies, – and even those who do not appear to be such, – see little lenity in the execution of men who had surrendered themselves to the mercy of their assailants. Blood ought to be spared, – that is our principle. Is it believed that this principle

296 REFLECTIONS.

has not been maintained in San Luis? That is according*to the mew which one takes of the case.*"

On referring to our notes, after reading Dupuy's despatches, three in number, we find them stated thus: –

" Feb. 8. – Massacre of the Spanish officers, prisoners of war.

" Feb. 11. – More of Dupuy's butchery.

" Feb. '21. – The butcher Dupuy."

Perhaps, after a careful reading of his despatches, our readers will be inclined to sum up as we did.

We have omitted to mention that, after the first massacre, Dupuy ordered six more officers and two soldiers to be shot, – and shot they were accordingly.

We must not close the details of this massacre – for such no doubt it was – without a passing remark. The War of Independence in the River Plate, Chile, and Peru was not, like the same war in Ca- raccas, one of slaughter and extermination. There the fierce, murderous, and relentless cruelty of the royalist General Morillo, traced in characters of blood every step which was taken in advance for the establishment of liberty. In the countries first mentioned there was a humanizing principle at work on both sides, which greatly alleviated the horrors

PUEYHREDON RESIGNS. 297

of war. No doubt ihere were occasional cruelties mutually committed; but we firmly believe the fewest were by the South Americans.

The act of Dupuy, therefore, though we cannot consider it other than a foul and murderous stain which mars a page of South American history, is not to be taken as indicative of the character of the people, but rather as an exception to the general rule of humanity and forbearance which they habitually exercised towards their enemies.

The difficulties of Pueyrredon's position began this year to be palpable to every one, and he himself, fully persuaded of their progress, resolved on the wise step of retiring into the shade, while he yet lent his influence to the system which he had established. According to the custom of the River Plate rulers, he thrice made a formal renunciation of the Directory before it was accepted by the Congress. At length, on the 9th of June, his wish to retire was complied with. In his stt-ad General Rondeau was elected to serve till the " meeting of the Chambers" created by the new constitution; and after one modest renunciation, Bondeau accordingly became Director.

General Pueyrrcdon was a fine, handsome-look

SPANISH EXPEDITION

ing man, of an aristocratic bearing, and of polished manners and exterior. He was not possessed of any high talents, although not destitute of good natural abilities. During the time of his Directorate he was entirely guided and governed by one man, Doctor Tagle, his principal Secretary of State, a most unscrupulous minister, and a very bad, though a clever man. Most of the evils of Pueyrredon's reign were ascribed to the sinister influence of this

South American Machiavel, and he was hated accordingly by the country at large.

One of the first public acts of the new Director Rondeau was to announce to the people, by proclamation, the equipment of an expedition from Spain, destined to invade the River Plate. " Everything," he says, "announces a vast plan – a great project for a hostile invasion. The last accounts assure us that, in all this month [June] at latest, the fleet so often announced will sail from Cadiz."

Vast indeed were the exertions made by Spain to strike a decisive blow for the recovery of her Transatlantic possessions, and resolutely did the South Americans prepare to resist it. The expedition was to consist of no fewer than thirty vessels of war, as many gun-boats, and one hundred and

FRUSTRATED. 299

twenty transports conveying twenty thousand men The stout-hearted Buenos Ayreans looked at the danger, and were quite undismayed.

Yet the great expedition was fated never to leave Cadiz. The extraordinary events which turned the course of the enterprise, paralysed it, and ultimately dissipated all its formidable elements, belong to the history of Spain. It is sufficient here to say that the disaffection of the troops – the wavering of the commanders – the *yellow fever* – the rise and progress and ultimate victory of the Constitutionalists over the Absolutists – struck successive blows at the expedition, and finally turned it altogether from its original destination.

So that before the end of 1819, San Martin was again able to turn all his attention to the invasion of Peru, and the Buenos Ayreans were left to renew with ardour their own intestine divisions.

Lopez, the Governor of Santa Fe, having, as mentioned p. 288, concluded an armistice, in order to gain time, he continued to amuse the Buenos Ayres Commissioners till October, when, without ceremony, he recommenced hostilities against the capital. On the 1st of November the Director Rondeau took the field in person, finding

300 THE CIVIL WAR.

that the allied federals, under Lopez, Ramirez and Carrera were making rapid strides towards the metropolis. The inhabitants were distracted and split into parties, – the federals were united, and accordingly they steadily gained ground. Inexpressible confusion reigned in the city, while the provincial forces were advancing upon it, after an action gained on the 1st of February, 1820. On that same day, Don Juan Pedro Aguirre was elected Director Substitute, – the first public act influenced by the federal party in town. Then on the 4th, Congress ordered the city to be placed in a state of defence; it was all in vain. On the 7th Buenos Ayres resolved to treat. The cabildo, or municipality, was the busy body in the bustle. Several of its members were the commissioners named on the 9th to treat with the general of the federal army, Don Francisco Ramirez. On the 11th Congress was tu- multuously dissolved, Rondeau ordered to resign; and these two events gave the*coup de grace*to the Pueyrredonista party and the central power of the capital. The citizens may be said to have surrendered at discretion to the Gauchos; and Buenos Ayres was made to feel, for a time, that imperious law from her rebellious children of the provinces,

DON MANUEL DE SARRATEA GOVERNOR. 301

which she for ten years had so liberally dealt out to them.

The municipality itself, which had been so busy in all the confusion of parties, was, in a*cabildo abierto,*or public meeting, dissolved on the 16th, a certain number of influential citizens being authorized to name a governor of Buenos Ayres. On the 17th they elected Don Manuel de Sarratea, a gentleman of talent and high character, but strenuously opposed to Pueyrredon. Another cabildo, favourable to the new order of things, was created; and the Federalists were now in the zenith of their power.

We must observe that General Pueyrredon, finding his person in jeopardy, escaped on the 31st, furtively and in disguise, on board of an English vessel, in the outer roads, having been assisted by one of the influential British merchants of the place.

While these affairs were transacting at the capital of the River Plate, public events wore a more prosperous and satisfactory aspect in Chile and Peru.

At the commencement of the year (1819) Lord Cochrane, who had joined the South American

302 LORD COCHRAXE.

cause, took the command of admiral of the squadron of Chile with universal applause. He hoisted his flag on board of the frigate O'Higgins, the squadron consisting of that vessel, the San Martin, Lautaro, Chacabuco, Pueyrredon, and Galvarino. He proceeded to blockade Callao, with part of his force, and to keep the coast in alarm with the remainder. He made a gallant attack on the vessels in Callao on the 28th of February, which caused the rovalists thenceforward to keep close under the guns of their batteries. He made various successful descents on the coast, and took some valuable prizes. In short, with so active a spirit as that of Cochrane to deal with, Pezuela was kept on the constant*qui vive.*The admiral made a prize of a United States brig, as it was entering Callao, with a large supply of arms and ammunition: he took out of a French vessel, sixty thousand dollars Spanish property; and attacking and obtaining possession of Pay ta, he seized all the public property he found there. Every where he used the*patriots*well, and circulated many proclamations and other documents calling on them to throw off the yoke of Spain. Lord Cochrane's attempts to throw Con- greve rockets and bombs into the castles of Callao

GENERAL ANTONIO BALCARCE. 303

were not very successful, although well deserved praise is bestowed on Colonel Charles and Major Miller for their great exertions; and particularly on the latter for the skill with which the bombs were directed by him. These were the principal naval events of the year.

The royalist land forces, after the victory of Maypo, were unable to make any stand against the patriots. General Antonio Balcarce followed Lan- tano from Chilian across the Bio-Bio; and thence the latter, retiring on the fortress of Valdivia, was still hotly pursued by Balcarce, so that nearly a total dispersion of the royalists took place in the rugged mountains and impenetrable forests of the far South. General San Martin calls their retreat, under such circumstances, " the conclusion of the war in all the extent of the state of Chile;" and this happy result he attributes to " the intelligence and celerity of the military measures which were adopted in this campaign by General Balcarce;" adding, that they would redound in all time to his glory. " We are not," concludes San Martin, " because the campaign has not been a bloody one, the less to applaud the valour and energy of those who have conducted it to its end."

304 THE RETREAT OF SANCHEZ.

This was the conclusion of the royalist force under Lantano, nd a like fate overtook that which was commanded by the royalist Colonel Sanchez. " He was," says General Balcarce, " most tena- rious and efficient in holding the province of Conception; but now driven from it he will not again involve it in the horrors and misery in which for the long space of eight years it has been sunk hy him."

When Sanchez knew of Balcarce having passed the Bio-Bio, he went into the Indian territory, to a place called Argol. Thence he hastily retired by the painful route of the Cordillera, from which lie had at last to descend to the coast to seek Valdivia. Destitute of every resource, Balcarce considered Sanchez's retreat as likely to be accompanied by immense disaster. " His men have only the dress they wear; they have only the ammunition which is in their cartridge-boxes: the greater part march on foot, without shoes. Their provisions dirt not exceed twenty bullocks on leaving Argol. The enemy is followed by a great number of women, including the nuns of Conception, all on foot and unshod, and watering with their tears every step they take. So lamentable a picture induced me to

GENERAL BALCARCE's DEATH. 305

offer Sanchez a generous capitulation, but as yet I have had no reply from him. His crimes are so deep that nothing will persuade him he can be pardoned."

All who turned back Balcarce left in peace to go their way. The force which finally followed Sanchez amounted to four or five hundred men, the sad remains of the Cadiz expedition which had come out under convoy of the Maria Isabel.

Such was indeed the miserable termination of the Spanish dominion over Chile! a dominion then lost, destined never to be regained.

Balcarce was seconded in his campaign in a noble manner by his officers, all of whom he mentions in terms of unqualified praise: among them we find our friend Colonel Manuel Escalada, and many of the other brave officers already mentioned in former campaigns. General Balcarce himself, alas! sunk under the fatigues which he had undergone, and he died about the middle of this year. He was one of the best men, as well as bravest officers, which the revolution produced, and all parties wept his loss. Public funereal honours were decreed to him in Buenos Ayres, at the expense of the state.

306 VICENTE BENAVIDES.

We have yet to mention Vicente Benavides as a royalist leader, who was obliged also to take shelter in the south. He was pursued by Colonel Freyre, a distinguished Chilean officer, who relates atrocities of the man which makes the blood run cold. He escaped with a few followers, but his crimes met, at a subsequent period, the condign punishment which they deserved. It is to be observed, that, though proclaiming the royalist cause as his, he was more a leader of lawless banditti, than a recognized officer of the king's forces.

With respect to the war in Upper Peru, nothing whatever was done in the early part of 1819, and, towards May, the royalist General La Serna commenced his retreat towards Potosi, where he arrived on the 10th of May. This put an end to the war in that quarter altogether, – the field of operations being removed to Lower Peru.

In this year a celebrated cause having immediate reference to the new order of things in the River Plate provinces was decided by Sir William Scott in the Court of Admiralty.

The ship Hercules having been presented by the Buenos Ayres Government to Admiral William Brown, already honourably mentioned in theseSirWilliamScott'sDecision.307 volumes, he fitted her out as a privateer, and made many prizes in the Pacific.* He was at a subsequent period, and after quitting the west coast, forced, by the want of provisions, bad state of his ship, and mutinous conduct of the crew, into Barbadoes. Here he took in refreshments with the concurrence of the authorities, and proceeding to sea, he was soon after boarded and taken possession of by Captain Stirling of H. M. S. Brazen, by whom Brown was carried as a prize into Antigua, where his vessel and valuable cargo were condemned, on the plea of his having violated our revenue laws. Brown appealed to the High Court of Admiralty; and there Sir William Scott pronounced a most elaborate judgment, annulling the whole proceedings at Antigua, and restoring the vessel and cargo to Brown. The Spanish minister applied to the Court for the cargo, as being Spanish property; but Sir William refused to interfere, alleging that his Court had no jurisdiction.

On the 9th of May, Don Tomas Guido informs his government of a terrible earthquake which took place at Copiapo in Chile. It destroyed the church

* See Vol. II. p. 253.

308 EARTHQUAKE AT COPIAPO.

of La Merced and half of the houses of the town, the terror-stricken inhabitants flying to the woods. Messrs. Good and Stewart, two English gentlemen, travelling from Ballenar to Copiapo were thrown from their horses, while the earth trembled for several minutes in ihe most frightful manner. " The earth," says Mr. Guido, in another despatch, " yawned in various parts, leaving profound cavities betwixt, the sea rushed beyond the boundary of high-water mark, to the distance of five*quadras*(seven hundred yards); and more than three thousand persons were to be seen flying from the devastation of the earthquake."

The last matter which must painfully engage our attention in this year is the fate of the three brothers Carrera.

They have already been mentioned incidentally in the course of these volumes. They belonged to a first rate family in Chile, and they were the earliest, the steadiest, and the most gallant as- serters of their country's independence. This part of their history pertains to Chile, and will come properly under observation should we be led hereafter into that country. But though decided patriots, THEBROTHP. RSCABRERA.

309

the Carreras were proud, ambitious, and headstrong men. Not only the Spaniards but many of the Chileans were afraid of them and their designs.

They were unsuccessful in their attempts to liberate Chile (about 1813 and 1814), and they were obliged to fly to Buenos Ayres, the father, the three sons, and a daughter. Meantime San Martin took up the cause of Chile, as we have seen, and succeeded in wresting it from Old Spain. It is supposed that the Carreras (whose turbulent character did not suit the quiet but austere tone of San Martin), saw with great disgust the emancipation of Chile committed to the hands of a stranger; and it is alleged (for no proofs are publicly brought forward), that they intrigued incessantly through their partisans in Chile, to upset the actual authors of the revolution, – San Martin and O'Higgins.

Be that as it may, it was considered that a*political necessity*had arisen for getting quit of these gallant men, and Pueyrredon was a willing accessary and instrument for the completion of a fatal determination like this. Two of the brothers accordingly, while believing that they enjoyed the

310 THEIR EXECUTION.

protection of a friendly power, were arrested in Buenos Ayres at night, and sent off to Mendoza. There a mock trial was held; the details of it were too wretched ever to be permitted to see the light of day; and the result, as previously arranged, was the judicial assassination of the two brothers. They were taken out together and shot. The third brother, stung to madness, and thirsting for revenge, took up arms, and joined the*Montonera*troops. Defeated in his hopes of vengeance through their means, he joined a horde of Indians; committed some excesses; was taken, and also shot. The sister, during these events, was kept a close prisoner in a cloister.

The darkest scene of the tragedy remains to be shown. The father of the Carreras fell ill from grief and anxiety on seeing his two sons arrested and taken to Mendoza. While labouring under his mental and bodily afflictions, and confined to bed, the Buenos Ayres Government, with a refinement of cruelty which is perhaps without a parallel, allowed its officers to send to the old man an account of*the expenses incurred in executing his two sons,*demanding payment of the same. He

REFLECTIONS. 311

looked at the account; then thrust it under his pillow; refused all further consolation, and died two or three days afterwards.

Such facts as these, when we believe them to be undeniably authenticated, we do not consider ourselves at liberty to withhold from our historical register. But we again warn our readers against considering them otherwise than as exceptions, at least at the time of which we write, from the general rule of action in the revolution. The feeling of the people at large was to spare, not to sacrifice; and with such men as San Martin and O'Higgins it was only the strongest apprehension of danger to the cause, an exaggerated fear of the effects of intrigue, that could so offuscate their mental vision as to lead them into either the commission or permission of such a dark political crime as that of the judicial murder of the Carreras.

There is a recognized distinction among mankind between public and private delinquency which is anything but favourable to the advancement of pure patriotism. Political expediency is the wretched excuse set up for a shameless dereliction from the broadest and plainest principles of public justice and morality; and thousands who, in their

312 REFLECTIONS.

private capacity, would shudder at the commission of great crimes, do not hesitate, as public men. to sanction them with their names, and to involve themselves in actions, the perpetration of which very often constitutes a guilt of the deepest dye.

But in these cases the nation at large must be carefully distinguished from the public delinquents in particular. There is seldom or never a sympathy between the one and the other; but, on the contrary, public opinion almost always indelibly stamps with opprobrium those acts of violence, outrage, or bloodshed, for which no better defence can be set up than that they were the result of political expediency, or public necessity. The inhabitants of the River Plate were a brave and therefore a humane people taken as a whole: and accordingly, although they were often placed in a position which precluded them from controlling their governments, they were ever ready to do justice to all that was good in their rulers, and to stigmatize among themselves those public acts which were of too flagrant a nature to bear open investigation, or to challenge a public scrutiny.

The fall of the Directorate, and the dissolution of the National Congress, concluded the first great

CONCLUSION.

epoch of the revolution in the River Plate provinces;and with these events accordingly we have thought we could most naturally terminate this series of our Letters on South America.

Yours, &c.,

TheAuthors.

VOL. III.

19

SECTION 19

APPENDIX.

AppendixI. (Vol. i., p. 11.)

Thefollowing letter was received after we had gone to press. It is inserted here verbatim, with the suppression only of name, which, in the still unsettled state of circumstances, it might be injurious to the writer, his friends and relations, to give. For the authenticity, however, and correctness of it we can vouch; the writer having been much engaged in the management for many years of our affairs.

Gentlemen,*Montevideo, 8th October,*1841.

Onthe llth of August I left the Republic,* and arrived at this port on the 19th of last month. Your friend, Don Andres Gomez, was long kept in a dungeon, without access to him of any of his friends, and strongly ironed. On the 13th of May, 1835, he underwent the las) penalty of the law, without any form of process being instituted against him. On the 2nd of September, 1840, the dictator died, and on the 20th of October, I, with a hundred * Paraguay.

APPENDIX. 315

and twenty-two other individuals of the capital* was set at liberty, from the dungeons, in which the greater part had been immured since the 18th of December, 1827.

The present Government, although slowly, follows a directly counter course to that of Francia. Neither would you, nor any other person who once knew Paraguay, recognize in it, now, the same country. It has been desolated, and made a waste by twenty years of tranquillity.

I am now at the head of a new business concern, and shall feel much obliged by hearing from you, in regard to some of the concerns committed to your management.

I shortly intend returning to Paraguay, with a view of forming a house, and of establishing myself there. I have good support offered me from Buenos Ayres, and full powers from some friends there, to make contracts with the new Government.

I flatter myself I shall not be disappointed in my hopes of success; and I venture to solicit your influence and support in favour of my undertaking.

Yours, &c. (Signed)

* Assumption.

316 Al'PENDIX.

The interesting documents in this Appendix, signed with the initials M. M., have been furnished by our amiable and intelligent friend, his Excellency Don Manuel de Moreno. He is brother of the late lamented Doctor Mariano de Moreno, the originator, we may say, of the South American revolution, and, as all acknowledge, the most eloquent advocate of its principles. The surviving brother ia at present minister plenipotentiary at the English Court; and we are the better pleased to insert bis remarks and historical notes, that he has been throughout a principal actor in the busy scenes for the emancipation of his countrymen, and an acute, impartial observer of the whole course of the revolution. No one's testimony, therefore, could be higher than his of the veracity and accuracy of our historical details, which, before going to press, were submitted in manuscript to his perusal.

TheAuthors.

APPENDIX. 317

AppendixII. (Vol. ii., p. 81.)

Theconstruction put by Mr. Robertson on the exclamation*of*Moreno is the correct one. The war of the revolution, or of independence, was necessary, was to be looked for, and in fact*was*looked for and adopted, in the enthusiasm of the 25th of May.

But what has deceived the patriots of that day is the civil war and discord among the Americans themselves, which even now, after the lapse of thirty- three years, is waged as rancorously as ever. Such is the melancholy lot which has fallen, almost without an exception, to the generous men who hailed with so much confidence the aurora of the liberty of their country; and this civil war has been the cause of the retardation, or rather privation, of that liberty, so ardently invoked at first. The generation which sent abroad the shout for revolution and*reform*has passed away under the pressure and persecution of parties. Those who have followed it, and who are now managing the affairs of those countries, are yet far from enjoying all the liberty and bless-

318 APPENDIX.

ings which they had invoked on the 25th of May, 1810, albeit the possession of them seemed so easy and secure. Hence the illusions, which I cannot but with pain record, and to which, as an individual who participated in them on that memorable day, I would pay the tribute of my regret, which is not repentance, but a kind of protest against the failures and faults of the revolution.

M. M.

APPENDIX. 319

AppendixIII. (Vol. ii., p. 83.)

Liniers.

Likierswas a Frenchman, not only by origin, but by birth, as was also his brother, the Count of Liniers, who died in Buenos Ayres in the time of his brother's government. Both were in the service of Spain, and had been for many years, even from their youth.

The Count held the rank of colonel of infantry, while his brother was captain of a line of battle ship in the royal navy. It is not known how they emigrated to Spain, but it is supposed that it would be after the example of many Irishmen of good family but small fortune, who were, and still are, in the service of Spain. It is not strange that the fact of Liniers being a Frenchman, should have led, during his government, to suspicion, and made him obnoxious; for the real question related to France.

Liniers spoke very bad Spanish, much worse than Napoleon French, an accident which tended to keep

320 APPENDIX.

liis origin for ever before the people. The Count spoke still less of the language of the country; so that in the government circle scarcely anything was spoken but French, the language of a nation at that time decidedly opposed to Spain.

At the court of some of the kings of England, this circumstance has led to political results registered by the historian, – as for instance to the monarch's surrounding himself by foreign friends, and submitting to French adulation, as in the case of Liniers.

Although the character given of him is strictly correct and true, his frank and generous spirit redeemed not a few of his foibles; and it is not easy to withhold from him compassion for his fate, although it was brought upon himself by his errors and imprudence.

M. M.

20

SECTION 20

APPENDIX. 321
. appendixIV. (Vol. ii., p. 103.)

Picking of Teeth.

Itis natural that in Europe the foregoing charge in an official document should appear strange, and even puerile. But it is necessary to consider that the habits of thought and the customs of the elevated classes of Spanish America qualify this breach of good breeding on the part of the Attorney-general, as an unpardonable insult, nor could they ever consider it otherwise than as a premeditated one to the Junta.

Till lately, if a respectable person was walking through the streets of Buenos Ayres, and saw that another passed him without a salutation, or the taking off of his hat, he considered himself to be mortally affronted. This excess of courtesy and. urbanity has been almost entirely suppressed, by the commerce and intercourse of foreigners: but in 1810 it existed, and there are still some lingering symptoms of it observable. Greetings to persons unknown are continued in the country; and a

322 APPENDIX.

Gaucho is capable not only of hating one who thus neglects him by passing him without saying good morning, but to begin by picking a quarrel with him, and to end by stabbing him.

Thus it was not only held to be improper in Buenos Ayres to pick one's teeth, but, on the contrary, to be a grievous offence, and proving clearly the hauteur and insolence of the Attorney-general towards the Government. In every country, things are embodied into being and importance, from received ideas or adopted customs. In 1830, Senor Anchorena, minister of the Government, sent to prison a French engineer named *Ponce,* for not having taken off his hat to him in the street, with an order that he should not be liberated without making *three bows to the hangman.*

Ponce acceded to this, bowing profoundly, as he was ordered to do, to this distinguished officer of justice; after which the Frenchman was liberated. Fortunately *Monsieur Ponce* was a man of pacific and placable disposition, and so the thing ended. At another time such a case would have produced a quarrel with the French consul, and probably a

blockade.

M. M.

APPENDIX. 323

Appendix V. (Vol. ii., p. 118.)

The Twenty-two Members of the Executive.

This *exotic,* and, not to say the worst of it, this ignorant resolution, which transformed into executive ministers and administrators of the revolution those who had been assembled to be its legislators, had, as it was natural to expect it should, the most fatal results. The edifice appeared from that moment to be weakened, and tottering on its ill laid foundations. The ship of the state might be represented, not only under the motto of other *United Provinces,* more prudent, *incerta quo fata ferant,* but actually as having sprung a leak, and making so much water, as could scarcely fail to strand and sink her.

The said deputies having declined to constitute the congress, which they *could,* and which they *might* to have established, the anarchy and confusion which took hold of men's minds, subsequently hindered the formation and stability of such a body; and though, on different occasions, future legislators endeavoured to form a regular deliberative assembly,

324 APPENDIX.

the state is still without any defined. convention., and without the division of powers, and legislative bodies, which the civilization of the present day require.-, and which other states, even of South America, enjoy. This is the explanation of the strange anomaly which we behold; and the defect is truly to be deplored in the actual constitution, or organization, of the Government of Buenos Ayres.

The great error of the deputies of 1810, and the revolution (or *emeute*) of Saavedra of the 5th and 6th of April, 1811, which was its corollary, are the two deeds which adulterated, and truly corrupted reform in its birth, aye, in its very cradle.

Of this *emeitte* of the 5th and 6th of April, directed and led on by Saavedra, against a solemn covenant of the Government, and against the principal patriots, it will be necessary to speak hereafter.

The Junta was not content with having turned everything upside down in the capital, but was desirous of doing the same thing in the provinces; and so it ordered that juntas should be established in every one of them. It is next to a miracle that this series of blunders and disasters should not have been the ruin of the revolution.

M. M.

APPENDIX. 325

Appendix VI. (Vol. ii., p. 130.;

Those who commence revolutions are mistaken if they think that they will always be able to direct and control them. *So far shalt l/iou come and no farther.* Revolutions generally leave their authors in the shade: these are supplanted, and promptly succeeded by others, who make themselves masters of the stage, men *du lendemain,* as they are designated by the French. Revolutions may be likened to certain pieces on the stage, in which there is always some one *deceived, qnelque tin de dupe,* unless when the drama is a real tragedy, which calls for the death of the principal actor.

M. M.

326 APPENDIX.

Appendix VII. (Vol. ii., p. 133.)

The limits of our work have not permitted us to go into the details of all the various intrigues which brought about the infinite varieties of change of Government, with which the history of the United Provinces of the River Plate is fraught; but the following history of the *emeute* of the 5th and 6th of April, as given by Mr. Moreno, is a good specimen of such intrigues, and will give our readers some idea of the movements generally by which one Government was superseded by another.

Tumult or *Emeute* of the 5th and Cth April, 1811.

The tumult or revolution of Saavedra, as it has been appropriately styled, is a secret perhaps more remarkable in the eyes of every observer than any other which can be gleaned from the series of commotions and of changes which we then began to see with frequent recurrence.

The most striking part of this revolution was its being organized for the purpose of giving a *coup*

APPENDIX. 327

d'etat to those who had originated that of the 25th of May of the preceding year. The authors of the present revolution (that I mean of the 5th and 6th of April, 1811), for the purpose of making sure of their blow, organized a seditious popular assembly, aided, encouraged, and abetted it.

Under this double aspect it is at once curious and important to relate it in some detail, seeing it was the first rupture, or *split,* among that class of Americans who were working out the revolution of the 25th of May, 1810, and that it also had its origin, like many subsequent movements, in profound personal resentments.

The authors of that revolution – those who had staked their all upon a die, friends, every one of them, of Doctor Don Mariano de Moreno – had seen with astonishment the deputies take their seats with the executive body, as well as the high bearing which Saavedra assumed in the legislature. The incapacity of this mixed Government – or rather this huge chaos of a Government – was more clearly discovered, and became more obvious day after day. Besides its nullity, the ambiguous measures it adopted, together with the suspicion that hung over it of an intention to coalesce with

328 APPENDIX.

Spain or the Infanta Dona Carlota, gave rise to question its loyalty even in the short period which had elapsed since its installation.

As there was neither a rostrum nor a press, by means of which public feeling might have vent, nor any oilier safety-valve by which discontent could be discharged, the citizens expressed their disapproval in the only manner in which it was possible for them to do so, first in private conversation, and then in murmurings more or less loud and determined. But they were all oral, *unaccompanied by any one deed* which could give offence; so that all which passed could not be said to go beyond a simple *agitation.*

At length they determined to establish a meeting under the title of *The Patriotic Society,* or rather Tertulia, which opened its session in the saloon of Marco's coffee-house; and there they established a *cathedra,* which before such an epoch, would have been in the hands of the scholastics of the college. The rostrum was free to any one, to the first comer, to the most animated and *detjaye* member, who felt disposed to harangue. The speeches which from time to time were made, had more in them of what was speculative than practical: they treated, in

APPENDIX. 329

abstract, of the love of liberty, and of the dangers by which the cause was surrounded. The only occasion on which this society interfered with the measures of Government was by a respectful petition, soliciting the revocation of its decree, published (but with little intention of giving it effect) for the expulsion, in three days, of all the unmarried Spaniards in the city. This petition was strengthened by another from the Cabildo (municipal body) to the same effect, and was immediately received by the Government with entire approbation – nay, with extravagant demonstrations of joy – it being thus made obvious that on its part, there never had been the least intention of carrying its own measure into effect.

The formula by which the decree against the Spaniards was annulled, in answer to the petition, is so characteristic that we think it worth transcribing here verbatim: –

"*Buenos Ayres, 23rd March,* 1811.

" The Government being animated by the same noble sentiments which inspire the people of Buenos Ayres, how could it refuse to lend itself, with the greatest satisfaction, to so generous a request?

(Signed) "Saavedha,"&c.

.330 APPENDIX.

Notwithstanding the apparent harmony of sentiments which we have just witnessed, Saavedra could not endure the opposition which was evidently directed against his person; and in those very days he worked assiduously with the Junta in order to induce this body to fulminate measures of severity against the discontented. He denounced these as agents and promoters of a conspiracy which would very soon break out, if not immediately arrested. According to advices which he professed to have received, the conspirators, or members of the Patriotic Society, were hatching plans against his life and that of four members of the Junta – Doctor Funes, Don Felipe Molina, Don Manuel Ignacio Molina, and Don Juan Garcia de Cosio. He could not, however, persuade the Junta of the reality of such machinations, nor from the majority draw the decrees of rigour for which lie contended against the disaffected. Taking counsel, then, of his own rancour, and giving himself up to the impetuosity of his passions, he determined to act for himself. His plan of attack rested, in part, upon the calling together of the military force, and partly upon the concurrence of the people, who were to be stimulated to the execution of his plans

APPENDIX.

331

by being harangued and led on by some of his confidential agents.

On the night of the 5th to the 6th of April, while the inhabitants of the city were enjoying their usual repose, the Great Square became the resort of bodies, on horseback, of armed Gauchos, whom Saavedra had caused secretly to approach from the neighbourhood of the Magdalena.

Those who, under the shades of night, saw these trdopers unsaddle their horses in the square, and prepare to bivouac there for the night, could find no solution of the object of such strange and mysterious conduct. All became apparent, however, and explained a little before break of day.

It was then known that the groups in the square had been ordered by Government to assemble there; that the veteran troops were in their barracks, and that the inhabitants of the suburbs, under the command of the Alcaldes de Barrio (local justices of the peace) and a certain *Grigera,* most devoted to Saavedra, were marching to the square for the purpose of exercising their sovereign rights, seeing they were not properly administered by the Cabildo. These country people brought a long-written paper with them, containing the con-

332 APPENDIX

ditions drawn up for them by their factious leaders, iind which were to be instantly complied with at t he peril of their supposed enemies.

The conditions contained eighteen articles, to which the Government, with much docility, and with only one or two slight alterations, assented. It forthwith caused the document to be officially published under the title of Petition of the People.* In substance, the following were the demands: –

" The banishment of all the European Spaniards in the city, of whatever class or rank, as irreconcile- able enemies of the American system." – Thus explained by the Government: That this banishment of the European Spaniards was to be understood of such of them as had not accredited their adhesion to the new cause, the classification being referred to a committee of the Cabildo.

"That all the civil and military employes should also be expelled." – Explained and qualified as above.

" That all salaries and emoluments allowed to the above classes should be with-drawn, seeing it was not consistent with justice that the public treasure should go to the maintenance of its enemies,

* See Gazette Extraordinary of 15th April, 1811.

APPENDIX. 333

in preference to that of good citizens, *of whom many were wit/tout employment.*

"That upon the goods and chattels of the Spaniards to be banished there should be raised a contribution for the state." – Agreed to entirely.

" That the members of Government, Don Nicolas Pena and Don Hypolito de Vieytes, as illegally elected, should be expelled from the Government, and ordered immediately to quit the territory."

The Junta explains that in their opinion these nominations had been made according to existing forms and regulations; but that seeing, in this condition, *the general. will of the people,* the elections should thenceforward be made with their intervention.

'.' That the members of the Junta, Don Miguel de Ascuenaga, and Don Juan Larrea should be also expelled, and sent out of the country." Agreed to entirely.

" That the vacant places in the Junta should be occupied by certain individuals, to be named by the petitioners." Entirely conceded.

" That the authors of the sedition which had just occurred,* Colonel French, Lieutenant-colonel

* There was no sedition but their own, and this was only in process of being enacted.

334 APPENDIX.

Beruti, Don Agustin Donado, Don Genrasio Posadas, and the Presbiter Vieytes should be deprived of their offices and banished." Conceded in full.

Finally, and by way of appendix, the petitioners directed that *a tribunal of public safety* should be established for the purpose of watching over the welfare of the citizens; and they designated, by name, four judges, with a notary, who should constitute the tribunal. "They required, moreover, that mass should be celebrated by the reverend bishop, as a testimony of thanks for the happiness which had been diffused by the overthrow, without commission of the least violence, of factious men."

The Government did not linger over that part of the duty which it had to perform. According to the circular which it addressed to the provinces, communicating these events, it appears that its four colleagues, having been proscribed, were that day *en route,* under an escort, for their place of banishment. A like unseemly haste was observable in regard to the other men banished by the decree of the supreme people. To none of them was allowed even the time necessary to make slight provision for their journey; nor was any sympathy evinced, but insults were heaped upon them.

APPENDIX. 335

The deposed members of the Government were actually taken from their seats, in the sala of their official deliberations; and as to Senor Pena,* he was pushed from his chair, and collared by the Comandante Rodriguez. Meantime the Junta of Vigilance began on the same day to fill the prisons with persons of all classes, – many of them highly respectable, – civilians, military men, and even physicians and divines, in such numbers, that the city appeared terror-stricken, and deserted. It looked as if it had been invaded by an enemy, or as if the people had betaken themselves to the suburbs, from whence had flashed upon them the lightning of this *sovereignty.*

Processes were got up against those arrested, ami against the Patriotic Society, calculated to fix upon them the crime of glaring and perverse sedition, which would have burst (as they said), if it had not been *judiciously* extinguished by the Government in power. But all the investigations of this noisy experiment tended particularly to prove that Doctor Moreno, or Doctor Moreno's spirit, was the author of the imaginary conspiracy, which was now the

* This is the same Pena who assisted Lord Beresford in his escape.

336 APPENDIX.

object of prosecution. To the confusion of these casuists, and for the misfortune of the country, Doctor Moreno had died at sea upwards of a montii before.

Notwithstanding this, the great process was followed up, for several months; it gave rise to many vexatious acts toward the prisoners; till at length it was abandoned, without any decision being come to upon it by its authors.

The saying of Brennus, "*Vce J'ictis,*" had in this instance its complete fulfilment.

Government issued a proclamation explanatory of the movement of the 5th and 6th of April, acrimoniously insulting those banished, as well as those imprisoned, and defaming them with all sorts of accusations and invectives.

We have already said that this proto-tumult was called in the country, *the Revolution of Saavedra;* and the people in the suburbs were long designated as the *people of Grigera.*

The triumph, which appeared so complete, was very ephemeral for Saavedra and his deputies. A few months only had elapsed since the *emeute* of April, when we find the deputies endeavouring to get rid of their president, and to evade the

APPENDIX. 337

responsibility, which the overbearing and irascible spirit of the latter had brought upon them all. We then find Saavedra accepting, from his associates, a diplomatic mission to the interior provinces, – leaving his *patricians* and citizens, and departing. He had not got half way on his journey. when his commission is not only revoked, but converted into an order for his banishment; and Saavedra falls under a cloud of obscurity, from which he is destined never to emerge. After residing for some time in San Luis, he withdrew for a season to Chili. He died suddenly in Buenos Ayres, in 1829, as a private individual, without fortune, with little credit, and with fewer friends.

Great crimes may be sometimes forgotten; but contumelies and personal offences are seldom forgiven. The tumult of April, in addition to being the most fertile in producing individual violence, the most memorable, from being the *first* of the kind, and from the number of persons outraged, cannot be extenuated on the score even of its not having given rise to bloodshed.

Too much blood was shed on the 8th of the following December, in consequence of the mutiny of the regiment of Patricios, which was truly con-

VOL. III. Q

338 APPENDIX.

sidered to be a consequence of the events of April, and the last dying words and confession of the party of the Ex-president Saavedra.

In regard to other more general disasters and dissensions, suffice it to observe, that from that time the cruel path of civil re-action was laid wide open to all aspirants.

M. M.

21

SECTION 21

APPENDIX. 339

Appendix VIII. (Vol. ii., p. 229.)

Don Carlos de Alvear.

It may appear that too much importance is attached to the administration of General Alvear, and that too much is said of himself, as he was scarcely three months at the head of affairs. The article relating to him might perhaps be considerably curtailed and condensed. Nevertheless, detailed as it is, it does not contain the half of what might be recorded of this active, but ambitious genius.

It is necessary to record that Alvear endeavoured to appropriate to himself all the glories of his day; although it is far from being incontestable that his titles to them were without a flaw. He superseded Rondeau in the siege of Monte Video only some eight days before it capitulated, and when every one knew that it *must* surrender.

Monte Video being thus taken, without any trouble or great merit on the part of Alvear, as the shadow follows the body, so Alvear followed Rondeau a second time to supersede him, in the

340 APPENDIX.

command of the army in Peru; but when with this design he arrived at Cordova, he got notice that the army refused to receive him as their commander, He therefore retraced his steps to Buenos Ayres; where, no sooner had he arrived, than he relieved his relative, Senor Posadas, from the burthen of the presidency. *Si licet in parvis exemplis gran- dibus uti;* there is in all this a certain something that appears like the movements and journeys of Napoleon.

Notwithstanding Alvear's talent and military knowledge, which are admitted, and although he was about to enter the city on the 15th of April, with all the veteran troops, assembled for that purpose, he was arrested in his designs by a civilian, the alcalde de primer voto (or lord mayor), Don Francisco Antonio de Escalada. The saloon of the Cabildo, or Guildhall, if you like, was the head quarters of the oppositionists to Alvear. In the various despatches received every hour there, during the most exciting time of the movements, there arrived a messenger saying that General Alvear was approaching the city (Buenos Ayres) with his whole army, and that his vanguard was already entering.

APPENDIX. 341

" Let them erect a gallows," said the intrepid Escalada, *"for him,* if we gain the day; and for *ourselves* if we lose it." El Senor Escalada was a sexagenarian.

M. M.

P. S. We knew Don Francisco Escalada well, and our readers will find some further account of him at p. 103, of Vol. iii. A more decided, venerable, and impartial citizen never did greater honour to a civic gown. To see him with his old- fashioned cocked hat and his black wand; to scrutinize his bland, yet uncompromising features, his erect gait, his courtly demeanour, yet thorough independence, reminded one of a gentleman of the old school, in its best of times. He belonged to one of the highest families of the place, and his public conduct was irreproachable. So much as a small tribute of praise to one of the late most dignified citizens of Buenos Ayres.

The Authors.

342 APPENDIX.

Appendix IX. (Vol. ii., p. 254.)

Artigas.

It is also true, that Artigas laid himself open to the accusation of having committed a capital crime against the patriotic cause, which crime, according to all laws of discipline, must be considered as desertion and treason. For while the siege of Monte Video was still pending, Artigas deserted from the army of Rondeau, and taking up a position in his rear, not only cut off his supplies, and deprived him of all moans of communication, but, in prosecution of his own views, broke out in hostilities against his own general, as if this latter had been an ally of Vigodet the governor of the besieged fortress. Seeing that this was the case, the Government of Uucnos Ayres, as far as the inimical proceeding against Artigas is concerned, cannot be considered unjust, although, perhaps, the proscription of the rebel, and especially his restoration to favour, may be censured as hasty and versatile. Both the one and the other measure was wrong, and did no credit to the authors of them.

M. M.

APPENDIX. 343

Appendix X. (Vol. ii., p. 262.)

Despatch of the Captain-General of the Province (Mendoza) and Commander-in-Chief of the Army of Andes, Colonel Don Jos6 <le San Martin, to his Excellency the Director of the State.

Thedesire to pay a well-merited homage to the noble patriotism of the inhabitants of the province, impels me to lay a sketch of their services before your Excellency, even though I may trespass on your already well occupied time.

For two years, during which Chili has been occupied by the Spaniards, the commerce of Mendoza has been paralyzed, and her industry and funds have proportionally decreased. But as if the paucity of resources had lent her new courage and firmness in drawing them forth to the uttermost, no effort has been spared in doing so, – the common sphere of action has in every direction been enlarged.

It is, in fact, truly surprising that the inhabitants of a thinly populated country, without a public treasury, without commerce or great capitalists, –

344 APPENDIX.

destitute of timber, leather, (or hides,) wool, cattle, (in a great measure,) and of an infinite number of other primary materials and important articles; – should yet have been able to raise, in the midst of themselves, an army of three thousand men, giving up even their slaves, the only hands employed in agriculture; to pay and feed not only the troops, but emigrants (from Chili), to the number of a thousand; to encourage the establishment for furnishing warlike stores and equipments; to create a manufactory of gunpowder; procure arms, artillery, quarters, encampments; to provide upwards of three thousand horses, seven thousand mules, and an immense number of horned cattle; in short, saying all in a word, to furnish all imaginable requisites, without assistance drawn from the capital for the creation, progress, and support of the army of the Andes.

I will say nothing of the continual and unwearied service of the militia, in detachments among the Andes, garrison duty, and other fatigues; neither of the indefatigable although unpaid industry of the artisans in the public works. In truth, the fortunes of individuals are here public property; the great majority of the neighbourhood only think of laying

APPENDIX. 345

their worldly possessions on the altar of their country.

America is free. Her oppressors must tremble on the contemplation of a display of solid virtue like this. Hence, they may calculate the united power of the whole nation. For myself, I am content to represent in terms, which, if feeble, are at least most sincere, those virtues which adorn the province of Cuyo; assured that the Supreme Government will extend to its inhabitants the high appreciation to which in justice it is entitled. God preserve your Excellency many years.

(Signed)JoseDeSanMartin.

*Head Quarters, Mendoza, 2lst October,*1816.

Finis.

London: l'rinte. l byWilliamClowiiandSons, Stamford Street.